COO

BALTIC
SEA

HEYDEKRUG, VI

EAST PRUSSIA

Danzig

Bialystok

THORN, XXA

SCHUBIN
XXB

Vistula

POSEN, XXC

Warsaw

REICHSKOMMISSARIAT

UKRAINE

GENERAL

GOVERNMENT

OF POLAND

Lemberg

MORAVIA

SLOVAKIA
Tri Duby

Vienna

RUMANIA

KAISERSTEIN BEI
BRUCH, XVII A

Budapest

H U N G A R Y

⊙ AIRMENS' CAMPS (STALAG LUFT)
◆ OFFICERS' CAMPS (OFLAG)
□ OTHER RANKS' CAMPS (STALAG)
✕ CONCENTRATION CAMPS
▬·▬·▬ BOUNDARY OF GERMANY, 1937
—·—·— OTHER 1937 BOUNDARIES
▬▬▬ BOUNDARY OF "GREATER GERMANY", 1942
– – – OTHER 1942 BOUNDARIES

0   MILES   200

CROATIA

KILOMETRES   300

COLDITZ

COLDITZ

The Untold Story of
World War II's Great Escapes

Henry Chancellor

wm

WILLIAM MORROW
An Imprint of HarperCollins*Publishers*

FIRST U.S. EDITION

Printed on acid-free paper

Library of Congress Cataloging-in-Publication Data
has been applied for.

ISBN 0-06-001252-8

02   03   04   05   06   RRD   10   9   8   7   6   5   4   3   2   1

This book is dedicated to all those who 'didn't like being locked up' and dared to do something about it.

Contents

List of Illustrations

Illustrations within the text

Plate sections

Section One

1. Colditz castle by daylight, and searchlight
2. The Laufen Six
   The Polish contingent
3. The first men out: Alain Le Ray and Pierre Mairesse Lebrun
   The Toilet Escapers in their home-made civvies
4. Testing the boundaries: Peter Allan posing in costume at his point of exit
   The canteen tunnel emerges
   Part of the 120 foot rope descent
5. Home-made impersonations

Picture Acknowledgements
The publisher and author thank the following individuals
and collections for their kind permission to reproduce the
photographs, drawings and maps: Lady Barry, Colditz
Museum, Brigadier Gris Davies-Scourfield, Major Mike
Edwards, Kenneth Lockwood, M19 Archives, Jean-Claude
Tiné, © Estate of John Watton and Private Collections.

Endpapers
Adapted from an original map in *M19: Escape and Evasion
1939–1945* by M. R. D. Foot and J. M. Langley (copyright
© M. R. D. Foot and J. M. Langley 1979) by permission of
PFD on behalf of Professor M. R. D. Foot and the Estate of
J. M. Langley.

Preface

Many people's first reaction on picking up yet another book about Colditz will invariably be – not another one. Surely more than enough has been said about the camp already; the bones of the castle have been sucked clean by successive generations of enthusiasts, to the embarrassment of those men who were actually there. Whenever the word escape is mentioned, people invariably think of Colditz. They do not think of Warburg, Spangenberg, Heydekrug, Rawa Ruska in the Ukraine, and many other camps that were the scenes of equally daring and often more successful escapes. The truth is, not many officers escaped from Colditz; over 310 attempts were made, thirty-two of which were successful, but only fifteen of these took place from inside the castle walls. The Germans succeeded in keeping the majority of the unruly captives inside. Also, the small number of officers who escaped is a fraction of the four thousand other-ranks escapers who successfully reached Switzerland during the Second World War. Of course, Colditz was much harder to get out of than other camps, but the difficult border crossings – where many were recaptured, often only yards from freedom – were the same for all.

The idea of this book is to tell the story of the experience of being at Colditz, from the point of view of escapers, non-escapers, guards and orderlies from all the different nationalities in the camp. It is not a blow-by-blow account of every escape attempt – though there are a good many here – nor is it a diary, though there is a good deal of everyday life in it. The book is based on a collection of seventy-six interviews conducted over fourteen years, in addition to diaries, privately published memoirs and almost forty books that have been written about the camp in five different languages. But first, a disclaimer: no book about Colditz can ever be truly 'definitive', for the simple reason that all the sources, whether written or verbal, have their shortcomings. Even among the seventy-six interviewees there are disagreements as to when escapes happened, who took part and where they took place; which is the inevitable result of recalling events of over fifty years ago. There are similar discrepancies among the written sources: Pat Reid, the British officer who successfully escaped from Colditz in 1942, did much to propagate the legend of Colditz. After the war he wrote *The Colditz Story*, *The Latter Days*, and finally *Colditz the Full Story*, all of which vary in their degrees of accuracy, particularly in covering events after he left the camp. Another major source, the Reverend Ellison Platt's exhaustive day-by-day account of over four years of life inside the camp, edited by Margaret Duggan into *Padre in Colditz*, was regularly read by the German censors, and for that reason he deliberately obscures dates, events and even the identities of those whom he is writing about. Platt also suffered from being over-diligent; he spent so much time writing his diary and so little time among his comrades that he relied heavily on them to tell him what was going on, which resulted in the padre copying down some fantastic stories, much to his companions' amusement. Reinhold Eggers – the Security Officer – whose book *Colditz: the German Story* offers the other side of the coin, but of course he did not know half of what was happening inside the castle. Every other written source, from unpublished diaries to autobiographies, also tells only a part of the story – after all, that is their intention. And there is another, more fundamental reason why nothing 'definitive' can ever be written about Colditz: the castle was full of secrets; its warren of rooms and staircases concealed all manner of nefarious activities that were kept from all but those who witnessed them. This element of security was so effective that new stories about Colditz are still being unearthed sixty years after the event, and now many will never be known. Every officer had his own particular experience of Colditz; some knew more than others, but no one knew everything.

Aside from the written sources, the material for this book began to be collected back in 1986, when the project first began. I am much indebted to the cast-iron research of Dominic Flessati, who with Sonja Leadlay spent over a year meeting veterans, all over Europe, listening to their stories, transcribing and analysing them. It is through their diligence that I am able to reproduce conversations with men who have long since died. In addition, I am profoundly grateful to the Colditz Association, whose members have all given their time and energy to the project; those who have contributed are listed at the end. It is difficult to single any one out, but I would like to thank Kenneth Lockwood in particular, whose encouragement, help and unrivalled knowledge have made this book possible. I would also like to thank Gris Davies-Scourfield, Tommy Catlow, Jim Rogers, Bernard Cazaumayou, Jack Pringle, Michael Alexander and the Earl of Harewood for allowing me to reproduce parts of their books, and Pierre Mairesse Lebrun, Alain Le Ray, Tony Luteyn and Francis Steinmetz, whose stories of their successful home runs are integral to this book. I am also indebted to Mike Edwards, Tony Rolt and Pete Tunstall for their impromptu interviews and help, Jock Hamilton-Baillie for allowing me to borrow and photograph his objects, Bill 'Tiger' Watson for allowing the reproduction of his poster, Desirée Roderick for lending me her letter to her brother Joe Houghton and John C. Watton for allowing the reproduction of his father's work. I thank Jimmy Yule for *Ballet Nonsense*, Lady Barry for kind permission to use her husband's recollections and his photo album, Jean Claude Tiné for his own, and the Colditz museum for their collection of photographs. I must also thank Colin Burgess for allowing me to reproduce parts of *Diggers of Colditz*, and Bill Goldfinch and Jack Best, whose enthusiasm and help enabled the replica of the original Colditz glider 'Spirit of Colditz' to be built. I would like to acknowledge Robert Hale, William Kimber, Hodder and Stoughton, the Imperial War Museum Sound Archive, and also David Ray for his assistance and his contributions to the Appendix. David Dugan, Ian Duncan and Oliver Morse at Windfall Films persisted with this project for a tortuous ten years as the Second World War came in and out and then back into fashion again; it would not have been possible without them, nor without Chris Durlacher, Adam English and Melissa Parker, my co-producer/directors of the television series, and the work of Jeremy Llewellyn-Jones and the research of Gerald Lorenz, David Coward and Joe West. I would like to thank Roland Philipps at Hodder for his useful advice, Juliet Brightmore, Roseanne Boyle and Lizzie Dipple. Thanks in no small part to Edward Platt, Alain de Botton for his realism, and Charlotte Stewart for her comments. Finally I would like to thank Chloe for more than I can say.

In the Bag . . .

The story of Colditz, Oflag 4C, is not about the war: it is about prisoners in a castle. Far away from the battlegrounds of Europe, the Allied officers who were sent to Colditz had one thing in common; they had escaped, or proven themselves to be *Deutschfeindlich*, anti-German. They were 'bad boys', and Colditz was to become the bad boys' camp. The Germans referred to it as a 'Sonderlager', a high-security, special camp, the only one of its kind in Germany. Within the ancient walls the prisoners' fortunes were often diametrically opposed to those of others in the world around them; indeed, the camp was at its most dynamic when the Allies were at their lowest ebb. The prisoners at Colditz were fighting their own private battle against a scrupulous and correct enemy, which had little to do with the events in Europe, and as the war went on, less and less to do with

Nazi Germany. So, before embarking on the unique story of Colditz, it is worth recording the last time many of its prisoners had any connection with that war. Notable parties of soldiers, sailors, and airmen continued to step through its gates right up until the final months of 1945, but the majority of the prisoners at Colditz were captured during the early summer of 1940. Within the space of a few desperate weeks these young officers would gain their first and last experience of the conflict that would change their lives irrevocably.

On 10 May 1940 Germany's Blitzkrieg invasion of France began, and so overwhelmed the British Expeditionary Force and the French Army with its speed and violence that many thousands of soldiers found themselves 'in the bag', cut off from their lines of supply and the coast, enveloped by the mass of German divisions that poured towards them. On 26 May – barely two weeks after the German invasion of France had begun – the Navy began its rescue operations at Dunkirk. For the next nine days these continued, while across northern France units fought desperate rearguard actions, holding strongpoints until they either ran out of ammunition, were outflanked or overrun. The armada of 'little ships' that evacuated 338,226 soldiers from the beach was made possible only by the actions of these men, defending the ever-shrinking perimeter around Dunkirk. And there were others, including the King's Royal Rifles Corps and the Rifle Brigade, landing at Calais at the last minute in the forlorn hope of defending the town and holding up the crushing advance of the 1st and 10th Panzer divisions.

By 3 June the last man had been taken off the beach, and the 'miracle' of Dunkirk was complete. 'Wars are not won by evacuations,' remarked Churchill ruefully, well aware that, in addition to sacrificing vast numbers of tanks, motorcycles, field guns and 7,000 tons of ammunition, there were still 34,000 British troops left in the fields of northern France; and they too were abandoned to become prisoners of war. Over the next few weeks others would join them as 46,000 French and British troops surrendered to Rommel at St Valery, including 8,000 men of the 51st Highland Division. They were exhausted, confused and many were wounded. By the end of the month German troops had reached the Spanish frontier, and the battle for France was over. In addition to the BEF well over a million Frenchmen and Belgians were taken prisoner. All of these men were now the charges of the German Army.

Over the next few weeks the captured troops began an odyssey which varied in its details but was generally similar. Men of all ranks and nationalities were herded together to form long columns, and then marched for hours on end across the French and Belgian countryside. If they were lucky they spent their nights in makeshift billets; if not, they lay down in the fields beside the road. Food and water were scarce. Once the German front-line troops handed them over to the support units, callous and brutal treatment was not uncommon. These soldiers were flushed with their victory and relished every opportunity to belittle their prisoners. 'Für Sie der Krieg ist vorbei,' rang the old cliché; for you the war is over. Those who answered back were beaten; others who fell by the wayside were shot. During these weeks there were many opportunities for escape, which the captives came to look back on with regret. But the confusion of the moment was overwhelming. Escape; where to? France had capitulated so there was no guarantee of safe haven among the people. All along the endless roads to the east they passed convoys of field guns, ordinance and collapsible boats moving in the opposite direction. It was clear that on the north-west coast of France a German invasion force was gathering. The footsore prisoners could only look on and wonder.

Long marches across France brought the POWs to concentration points from where they continued their journeys deeper into Germany by other means. Some were herded on to cattle trucks, others were loaded on to barges or lorries, and conditions remained squalid. After several days' travel they arrived in western Germany, where a first great sorting was carried out. Nationalities were separated, and officers split from the ranks. From now on their fates were to follow totally different paths, as ordained by the Geneva Convention, the international agreement drawn up in 1929 which set out how prisoners of war were to be treated. Its central tenet states that officers cannot be forced to work for their captors. They were sent to Oflags, while their men – who were permitted to work for the Germans – were sent to Stalags, or Arbeitskommando (labour camps). Paradoxically, this enforced idleness laid a psychological burden on officers, many of whom initially struggled to employ their time usefully. Labour would have come as a relief. As it was, routine and self-discipline were required to fill the long hours of captivity, and for that reason some Oflags became more like schools or colleges than prisoner-of-war camps, with organised sports, language classes and lectures. In these camps officers were allowed to grow vegetables, even keep rabbits in return for good behaviour. For a small number of others, who are the subject of this book, these restless hours of inactivity contributed significantly to their desire to escape.

By the late summer of 1940 most of the 2,000-odd officers captured with the BEF found themselves in one of the cluster of Oflags in central or southern Germany. Hundreds were crammed into Spangenberg Castle, which had served as a Napoleonic jail. More were at Tittmoning, a squat medieval castle overlooking the Salzach river which had once separated Germany from Austria, now subsumed into Hitler's expanding empire. Laufen held the largest contingent; 1,500 British prisoners of war were crammed into this sprawling edifice that was once the grand country residence of the Archbishop of Salzburg. Many of them possessed nothing more than the clothes they stood up in.

Here in their cramped and insanitary jail they came to terms with the shock of their new condition. The British Expeditionary Force was formed from regular divisions and front-line territorials, at the time the cream of the British Army. Many officers were from military academies or were university men, career soldiers following in their fathers' footsteps. Others were keen Territorials or young recruits fresh from public school who had joined up when they believed their country was in danger. Yesterday they had dreamed of glory on the battlefield; they had anticipated medals – even death – but not capture. When they arrived at the camp they were searched and deloused, were given a number and photographed. Then their heads were shaved, and they began a struggle for the petty necessities of life. They had all become prisoners of war . . .

CHAPTER ONE

The Road to Colditz

It was an unremarkable beginning. On 7 November 1940, in the afternoon, a small train pulled into Colditz station. On board were six British officers, a squad of guards and a half-empty barrel of potatoes. They had never heard of Colditz, and judging from what they could see from the train windows there was no reason why they should. The district line had chugged along beside the Mulde river as it wound through the fields of central Saxony, stopping at one indistinguishable village after another; Göritzhain Wechselberg, Rochlitz, Colditz. There was no camp, no people, no visible signs that this would be their journey's end. The guards stood up and motioned to them to get out, and with a certain amount of trepidation the six men stepped down on to the platform. Kenneth Lockwood, then a twenty-nine-year-old captain in the Queen's Royal Regiment, remembers it well. 'We had not the slightest idea where we were being taken. One of the guards mentioned that here was a Sonderlager, a special camp. I half thought that we were going to be shot.'

In the fading light they marched up the wet cobbled streets, crossing a bridge towards the main square, and here for the first time they saw what they presumed to be their destination. High above the rooftops stood a castle, looming against the dark sky. Picturesque and brutal, its dun-coloured walls suggested a mental institution – or a prison. After a steep climb they arrived at the gatehouse; the sign read Oflag 4C. Their names were taken and identities checked, then they were marched on across the bridge spanning a dry moat, underneath a large painted coat of arms and through an archway into a cobbled courtyard. There was a grey truck parked in the corner, and a sentry stood beside a tunnel gateway on the far side. It was quiet. The six men and their escort then continued on, through another deep arch and up a cobbled alley. This final windy stretch ended in the guardhouse; to its right was a massive wooden door. Inside, they found themselves in a small dark court-yard, surrounded on all sides by towering buildings. This was evidently the end of their journey. As Kenneth Lockwood became accustomed to the half-light, he saw thin white faces staring out at him from the windows. '*Anglitsi, Anglitsi*, they shouted. Poles. It cheered us up no end because our arrival was so gloomy and depressing. It meant that there was life here, there were people here and that made all the difference.'

Kenneth Lockwood, Peter Allan, Pat Reid, Rupert Barry, Dick Howe and Harry Elliott were the first British officers to be sent to Colditz. They became known as the 'Laufen Six', after the camp from where they had made the first

British escape of the war. For four of them, this small courtyard would be their home until April 1945.

They were led to a staircase, hustled up to the top floor
and then locked in an attic. Three Canadian airmen were
there to greet them: Hank Wardle, Keith Milne and Donald
Middleton, who had arrived the night before. They had
escaped from Spangenberg camp, and the guards had told
them they had been sent to Colditz to be shot. At dawn
that day they had been marched down to the park below
the castle and lined up in front of a wall. 'Strange thoughts
passed through my mind and in my imagination I heard the
NCO giving his final instruction to the guard,' wrote Flight
Lieutenant Keith Milne. 'He turned to the guards. "It seemed
a pity," he said, "that the first British officers in Colditz were
leaving so soon."' The line up turned out to be an elaborate
joke, and as the guards began to laugh the Canadians realised
this was their half an hour's exercise. The three airmen were
then returned to their attic. They had no idea what the
purpose of Colditz castle was; neither had they met the
mysterious Poles on the other side of the courtyard. As darkness fell the officers settled down for the night.

'We'd been asleep for about twenty minutes when there
was a scratching sound at the door,' remembers Lockwood.
'The handle turned and, to our absolute astonishment, four
Poles walked into the room. They were all smiles and
delighted to see us. A slight language problem, of course, but
we managed with a mixture of French, German and English.
It was fun – they brought some beer with them.' There were
140 Poles in the castle, many of whom had been prisoners
of war for over a year. They were well aware that their captors
regarded them as *untermenschen*, subhumans, and soldiers of a
country that since its invasion in 1939 technically no longer
existed. Nevertheless, in defeat they had remained defiant,

escaping from other camps and causing trouble, for which they had been sent to Colditz a week before, under their commanding officer, General Piskor. They were told that this castle, formerly used as a transit camp for Poles and Belgians, was now a Sonderlager, a special camp for officer prisoners who were, or had shown themselves to be, a high security risk. The guards bragged that the castle had served as an 'escape-proof' camp during the First World War, and now it would revert to that role. 'From here there will be no escape.'

As the Poles sat drinking with their new companions, the sounds of boots echoed up the spiral staircase. 'The Poles didn't seem to be at all concerned,' recalls Kenneth Lockwood. 'They simply dived under our beds and kept absolutely still. The Germans came in, looked round, counted us, went out again and right away the party went on. The Poles left us some beer, and off they went. And I remember Pat Reid saying, "I wonder how they got here, because when we arrived we'd gone up one staircase, whereas the Poles, they were on the other side." It did concentrate our minds away from the unpleasant situation we had found ourselves in. If they could get from one place to the other through locked doors, well, so could we. We went to sleep.'

Colditz Castle seemed the perfect site for a high-security prison. A fortress had stood on this rocky outcrop above the Mulde river since 1014, and in the fifteenth century it was ceded to the Electors of Saxony, who converted the castle into a hunting lodge. Successive generations continued to embellish it, and in 1694 it began its greatest transformation under Augustus 'the Strong', whom Thomas Carlyle described as 'The Saxon Man of Sin', whose 'lifelong pursuit of debauchery' had resulted in 354 offspring. Augustus enlarged the schloss considerably to house his progeny, adding a second courtyard adjacent to the original castle. The 700-room edifice he created was not to his successors' taste, however, and by 1800 the castle's cavernous size was no longer comfortable or practical for the Saxon nobility. It became a poorhouse, and then in 1829 it was converted into an asylum. It retained this use for much of the next century, during which time a Dr Voppel and his extended family lived in the castle with the inmates, the last domestic residents in its long history. When Hitler came to power in 1933 the castle was transformed into a labour camp in which to house his communist enemies, and by the outbreak of war Colditz Castle had shed much of its former opulence and was now divided by its two grey courtyards. The larger outer courtyard, known to the prisoners as the Kommandantur, housed the 200-strong German garrison, and contained the only two exits from the castle, one leading out across the moat to the town, the other towards the woods that fell away to the east. The prisoners lived next door, in the older, smaller courtyard. Here the ninety-foot-high buildings huddled around a stretch of cobbles not much bigger than a tennis court. Sunlight rarely penetrated this place, and whatever the season it was invariably dark, draughty and cold. On the north side stood the chapel and the clock tower; to the south was the delousing shed and prisoners' kitchen. All around the edifice the ground fell away in terraces, patrolled by sentries and encircled with barbed wire. The castle remained floodlit throughout the night, so to many new arrivals it appeared 'like a fairytale castle floating high above the town'. From the outside Colditz certainly looked remote and impregnable. 'It probably was,' wrote Reinhold Eggers, one of Colditz's security officers. 'But apart from putting bars on the windows it had never really been built for the purpose of keeping people *in*. A more unsuitable place to hold prisoners will probably never again be chosen.'

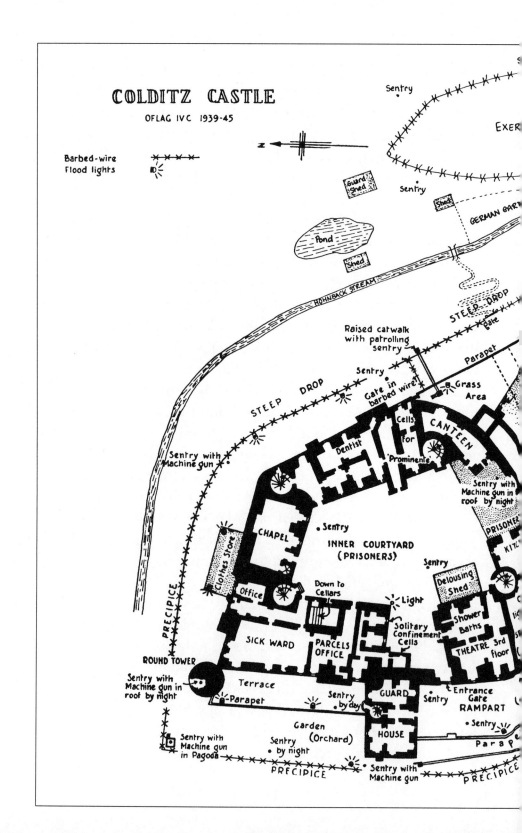

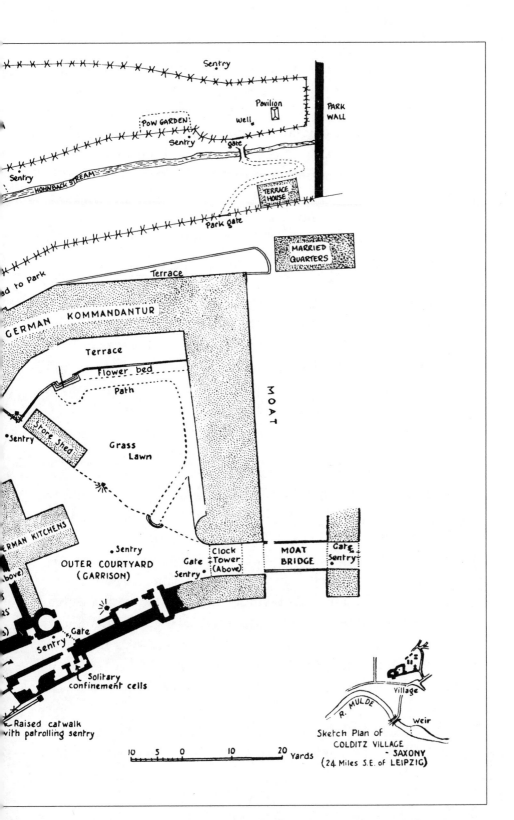

Sentry

Pavilion

PARK WALL

POW GARDEN

well

Sentry   gate

Sentry

HOHNBACK STREAM

TERRACE HOUSE

Park gate

Road to Park

Terrace

MARRIED QUARTERS

GERMAN KOMMANDANTUR

Terrace

Flower bed

Path

M O A T

Store Shed

Sentry

Grass Lawn

GERMAN KITCHENS

Sentry

OUTER COURTYARD (GARRISON)

Clock Tower (Above)

Gate

Sentry

MOAT BRIDGE

Gate Sentry

Gate

Sentry

Solitary confinement cells

Raised catwalk with patrolling sentry

R. MULDE

Village

weir

Sketch Plan of
COLDITZ VILLAGE
– SAXONY
(24 Miles S.E. of LEIPZIG)

10   5   0   10   20 Yards

As the Poles had demonstrated to their new British comrades that very first night, Colditz Castle was vulnerable from within. It was a warren of passageways, doors with simple locks, attics that connected one building with another, sewers that had not been used for centuries. Though Colditz could never be regarded as easy to escape from, the castle possessed all the idiosyncrasies of a building that had been adapted down the centuries, and in the next four years, every element of its ancient fabric would be examined to find a potential way out.

After a week or so, the British were given permanent quarters in the Fürstenhaus – the so-called Princes' House – the east wing of the courtyard. At first sight their new home seemed civilised – comfortable even. Each man slept in a bunk on a 'palliasse', a mattress stuffed with straw and covered in regulation blue-and-white checks. There were a few cupboards for clothes, and a stove by which to keep warm. There were bathrooms and sometimes hot water, though this regularly 'disappeared' as a collective punishment for individual misdemeanours. And there was even a separate mess-room in which to eat, which the Laufen Six considered a great luxury; in that camp they had dined on their bunks. On the whole German food consisted of ersatz coffee (made from acorns) and watery soups, with the occasional piece of black bread and ersatz jam thrown in for good measure. This insubstantial diet was so tedious that food soon became an obsession; there was great excitement on the rare occasions when a carcass or a horse's head was brought into the yard. With the exception of a few root vegetables, nothing fresh ever legally entered the prisoners' diet.

To supplement this meagre fare the prisoners relied heavily upon their Red Cross parcels, which began to reach Colditz at Christmas 1940. Sanctioned by the Geneva Convention, these boxes contained an exotic array of tinned foods, bully beef, Canadian creamery butter, curry powder, pickled eggs, chocolate, and another essential – cigarettes. Each POW was allowed one parcel a week, and any officer displaying the slightest interest in culinary matters became a best friend. Later in the war the British looked forward to their invitations to the French quarters for dinner, and an Indian doctor, Biren Mazumdar, became famous for his curries. Had it not been for the Red Cross parcels, most prisoners believe they would have died of starvation within two years. As it was, they ensured that the British POWs at Colditz and other Oflags across Germany became steadily better nourished than their captors. Only during the last exceptionally cold winter of 1944 did the supply of parcels dwindle to nothing as the German infrastructure broke down, and the immediate, near-famine conditions this shortage created demonstrated just how important these parcels had become.

The Germans distributed their meagre rations from the kitchen in the yard, next to the prisoners' canteen. Here POWs could buy a few creature comforts such as razors, German cigarettes, stationery and blankets, which they paid for in *Lagergeld*, camp money. As serving members of the armed forces the officers were still entitled to a wage, and as this 'joke money' was invalid anywhere else in Germany the canteen became the only place to spend it. It was not long before art materials, theatre make-up and even musical instruments arrived. Real German Reichsmarks never legally entered the prisoners' courtyard, though Kenneth Lockwood, the first canteen officer, quickly found a ready supply through the cigarette trade. 'The Germans allowed us three cigarettes per day,' he recalls. 'And as we were the lowest of the low in Germany these were the worst cigarettes you could buy. They were so awful no one would smoke them. As it happened I had become friendly with the elderly guard who used to drive the horse and cart that delivered the revolting food. I told him about all these cigarettes we'd got and his eyes lit up; he said he'd buy them for a pfennig each. Well, as I had eighty thousand of the wretched things that amounted to eight hundred Reichsmarks hard cash; and this was my supply.' Petty cash would be an essential part of any escaper's kit.

Despite the luxuries of a mess-room, Red Cross parcels, hot water and electric light, Colditz did have one significant disadvantage: lack of space for exercise. Most of the time the POWs were confined to their inner courtyard, and this was the focus of their world. Throughout the year this small cobbled square was filled with prisoners, endlessly walking up and down or idling about on the benches. In fine weather the yard hosted a jumble of activities – volleyball, sunbathing, cricket – often all happening at the same time; it was a common sight to see two officers knocking a tennis ball back and forth over the heads of those milling about. And here in the yard – at all hours of the day and night – the prisoners were summoned to be counted at roll-call.

As inmates of a Sonderlager, Colditz prisoners were closely watched, and the Germans introduced various measures designed to make their lives more difficult. In other Oflags, there were two *Appells* (roll-calls) a day; at Colditz there were first three, and then four. At 7.30 in the morning they were roused by German NCOs stamping through the dormitories. At 8 a.m. orderlies and officers carried cauldrons of ersatz coffee from the camp kitchen to the mess-rooms; here prisoners made their own breakfast from whatever they had in their Red Cross parcels, and half an hour later was the first *Appell*. All ranks lined up in the courtyard, each nationality forming up together. The place closest to the guards was reserved for the most troublesome nation, and as this was a bad boys' camp the spot was fiercely contested. The German NCOs would then move up and down each line counting their charges, rank by rank. Numbers would be tallied and presented to the senior German officer. This simple task often took hours as numbers were confused, officers moving around and generally disrupting the proceedings. After the counts had been completed, any announcements would be made, and the parade dismissed – until the next *Appell*. The final *Appell* was held at 9 p.m. and 'lights out' would occur soon after, whereupon the staircases were locked and the yard closed. 'Snap' *Appells* were called if the Germans suspected some mischief was afoot or if an escape was discovered. Reinhold Eggers calculated that on average there was one escape attempt every ten days throughout the four years he was a security officer at Colditz; snap *Appells* were a regular feature of Colditz life.

Appells provided the main opportunity for both the prisoners and their gaolers to square up to each other, and unsurprisingly it was the characters within the German guard company who had most bearing upon their daily life. The first Kommandant of the camp, Oberstleutnant Schmidt, was a veteran of the First World War, who lived peacefully in the Kommandantur with his wife. He rarely, if ever, ventured into the prisoners' courtyard. This job was left to the security and camp officers, who, with the assistance of a few NCOs, kept a careful watch over their charges. Captain Lange, a former merchant in peacetime, was in charge of overall security. The post of senior camp officer was initially held by Hauptmann Priem, an epicurean ex-schoolmaster with a fondness for the bottle. The prisoners liked him – 'he was the only German with a sense of humour' – but his inebriation would occasionally reveal a vicious malevolence towards them. He was assisted by Reinhold Eggers, another schoolmaster, who preferred a game of skat to alcohol, and whose experience with schoolboys, he believed, stood him in good stead in dealing with the troublesome POWs. He was a man who was apt to answer every provocation with a smile, and many chose to be wary of his methods. 'He was a thorn in our side because he was very good at his job,' recalls Kenneth Lockwood. 'Furthermore he'd done a swap with an English school in Cheltenham before the war so he could speak good English. He thought he understood how the British mentality worked, and was rather slimy in that regard.' Eggers would come and talk to the prisoners in their quarters in the evening, ostensibly to find out what they thought about the war and events in the camp. If any of them inadvertently revealed a misdemeanour, it was noted, and the following day he would punish them.

Priem and Eggers were ably assisted by a small number of NCOs who were in constant contact with the prisoners. Sergeant-Major Gephard, known as 'Mussolini', was the senior, and had his own office inside the prisoners' courtyard beside the sick bay. He was 'straight' and widely regarded as unbribable. His deputy was the infamous Corporal Schädlich, known to the French as 'La Fouine', and to the British as 'Dixon Hawke'. Schädlich was one of several 'ferrets' who moved noiselessly around the prisoners' quarters in special rubber-soled shoes hoping to find the prisoners engaged in some nefarious activity. They were often successful.

However devious the methods of Eggers and the ferrets may have seemed, the Wehrmacht garrison at Colditz attempted to operate exclusively by the book; which in this case happened to be the Geneva Convention. Drawn up in 1929 and signed by forty-seven nations (though significantly not Russia or Japan), it laid out, in a generalised military code, how prisoners of war should be housed, fed, punished and disciplined. Every aspect of their life and their relations with their captors was regulated by this agreement, which placed responsibility for the welfare of the captives in the hands of their neutral protecting power, the Swiss government. Germany, then under the libertarian Weimar government, had been a signatory of the document; but on the outbreak of war in 1939 there were signs that Hitler wished to reverse this aspect of Weimar policy, along with so many others. By the time the six British officers arrived at Colditz in November 1940, they were well aware of the protecting power of the Geneva Convention and the harsh uncertainties of life beyond its perimeter.

Five months earlier they had been marched from Northern France to Germany and, like so many British officers caught 'in the bag' during the Blitzkrieg summer of 1940, now found themselves interred at Laufen castle; now Oflag 7C. At first sight Laufen looked promising; this vast castle stood on the banks of the fast-flowing Salzach river, and from its windows there were magnificent views towards the steeples of Salzburg and the Austrian Alps beyond. The prisoners fancied that here Mozart had once played for the Archbishop of Salzburg, but this was little comfort to them now; Laufen Castle had been turned into a slum. 'We do not recognise the Geneva Convention,' the guards scolded. 'You are being treated like prisoners of war through the generosity of the Führer.' The 1,500 prisoners were packed into dormitories on two- or three-tier bunks, there was little sanitation or washing facilities, and they were all very hungry. Many of them lacked even the simplest of equipment such as a mess tin. The Geneva Convention laid down that prisoners of war were entitled to the same rations as their captors' base troops; at Laufen they received nothing like that. One loaf of bread a week and a few rotten potatoes were the standard fare, supplemented by eight cigarettes. 'We starved. And that's how the Germans wanted it,' recalls Jim Rogers, a South African ex-mining engineer and eventual Colditz prisoner. 'One day I was walking up the stairs to the first floor, and I got to my bed and heard a pump, pump, pump in the distance and thought, that's not my heart, is it? I took my watch and timed my pulse and I was doing thirty-nine. I said to the chap in the next bed, "What's your pulse going at?" He sat up in bed and said forty-two. So we went to see the doctor. He took our pulses and said, "We are getting half the rations that a patient will get in hospital. If we go on like this we shall all die."'

Prisoners took to eating dandelions and grass; even a maimed crow was not allowed to escape through the wire. They began to smoke their own bedstraw, and at night tied their weekly loaf of bread to their legs to prevent it from being stolen. The Germans could claim surprise as some excuse for these conditions – after all, they had never expected to capture so many prisoners so quickly. Besides the 40,000 British they had 1.2 million French and 600,000 Poles to look after. But the squalor at Laufen camp was exacerbated by an edge of sadism that was inexcusable. 'I got a parcel, one of the first in the camp,' recalls Jim Rogers. 'It made me more popular than I've ever been in my life, I think. I got cigarettes, meat and two vegetables, butter and chocolate. The guards would not give us containers, so they just poured everything from my parcel into a bowl, including the cigarettes, stirred it up into a brown mess, then handed it to me with a grin. I grinned back and said, "You bloody bastard," and I smiled while I said it, to give my ego some satisfaction. Their object in life was to make us suffer. I think they thought they'd won the war.'

Many believed that this arrogance was at the root of the bullying German behaviour. 'They were winning and they didn't give a rip about anyone else,' remembered one officer, and it was an attitude that would lead to tragedy. A young Durham Light Infantry Officer, Lieutenant Deedes, was leaning out of an upstairs window to sketch the distant Austrian landscape. Leaning out of windows at Laufen was forbidden, and the sentry immediately shouted at Deedes to stand back. Deedes remained oblivious, wrapped up in his work, so the sentry knelt, took careful aim and, in full view of the prisoners, shot him. Laufen was hell.

The long summer of 1940 dragged on, England uninvaded. The only contact the prisoners had with the outside world was the German newspapers, now full of the boasts of the Luftwaffe. 'London burns', 'A quarter of London's shipping sunk at anchor', 'Docklands on fire', ran the headlines accompanying aerial photographs of the destruction. The prisoners had little idea of the heroic drama unfolding in the skies above England, but it would soon have an effect on their lives. Since July 1940 a small but growing number of Luftwaffe airmen had been shot down and captured, and this led to an upturn in their fortunes. Prisoners of war were valuable counters in the game of propaganda; Churchill was well aware of this, as was Goebbels: he attempted to film fights between British and Polish POWs, and even produced a forged British POW diary, describing 'pornographic experiences in Paris', that was dropped over France in the hope of turning the British and French against each other. But both sides realised that the mistreatment of prisoners — especially those whose countries had signed the Geneva

Convention – was internationally embarrassing, and with the fear of reprisals it also proved unpopular at home.

In August the first letters began to arrive from England, bringing clothes and small comforts that made life more tolerable. A trickle of Red Cross parcels followed, and for the first time in the three months since their capture, officers became less preoccupied with their precarious day-to-day existence. Sports and other activities were organised, books were passed around. And some minds began to turn towards escape.

If captured, it is the duty of every officer to escape and try to rejoin their country's fighting forces. The code of all Western armies allows for it, and so does the Geneva Convention. In particular Article 54 of the Convention states that, once a POW has been caught escaping, the maximum punishment he should receive is one month in solitary confinement. Those were the stakes, but no one knew whether Germany would honour them, nor was it clear what would happen if officers were caught escaping in civilian clothing. Once out of military uniform, an escaper threw away his protection under the Convention and ran the risk of being executed as a spy. Escaping was dangerous – but then so was staying inside the camp. Laufen was overcrowded, filthy and, as a result of the rotten potatoes, gastroenteritis – 'the squits' – had reached epidemic proportions. Several officers were convinced that if they didn't succumb to the inevitable diseases they would go mad, and it was this fear of indefinite captivity which motivated Pat Reid. Reid was a captain in the Royal Army Service Corps who had been captured at Cassel outside Dunkirk. A stocky, single-minded man, he claimed he had once climbed up the goalposts before an England–Ireland Rugby international at Twickenham and placed a bunch of shamrocks on top. To add to this flagrant disregard for heights, Reid had trained as a civil engineer before the war, and he knew how buildings were constructed. It was a skill that would stand him in good stead as an escaper. Reid shared a room with Rupert Barry, a tall, moustachioed captain in the Oxford and Buckinghamshire Light Infantry with a penchant for cricket sweaters. He too was beginning to feel the strain of captivity at Laufen, and while prospecting the castle for a suitable way out he had found an underground storeroom in the north block adjacent to the exterior wall. Together the two officers decided to drive a tunnel out of the storeroom, under a lane next to the castle, and up into a woodshed on the other side. Their equipment consisted of two six-inch nails and a stone. Undeterred, they set to work and, with the help of four others, three weeks later they found themselves just beneath the surface of the woodshed. Gingerly Pat Reid broke the surface of the earth, and by luck found himself under a wooden platform on the floor. He couldn't have chosen a better exit point if he had tried. Kenneth Lockwood, Peter Allan, a boyish, kilted Scotsman who spoke fluent German, Harry Elliott and Dick Howe had all assisted in the digging of the tunnel, and therefore they qualified to go on the escape. Once out, they intended to split into two parties, and make their separate ways across Austria to the Yugoslav border. They wore crudely made civilian clothes, they had no papers and no idea what would happen to them if they were caught.

Timing was going to be critical. In the small lane beside the woodshed stood a sentry, who was relieved at 6 a.m. By 6.30 a German woman who worked in the camp was always busy in the woodshed on household chores. Their escape had to take place within that half an hour. At 4 a.m. on 5 September 1940 the six escapers crept to a lavatory near the storeroom in their roughly made civilian clothes. There they waited. At six o'clock the sentry was still on his beat. With every minute that passed their chances of escape diminished. At 6.15 the all-clear sounded. The six men scrambled into the tunnel in the order in which they intended to exit from the woodshed. They split into two families of three, Reid and Lockwood playing the 'mothers'. 'I was wearing a skirt and I had a bra to pad me out in the right places,' recalls Kenneth Lockwood. 'But I made the great mistake of filling it with biscuits, in an attempt not to waste space. Unfortunately by the time I had crawled through the tunnel the biscuits had turned to crumbs and everything was sagging.' Pat Reid's disguise had also suffered, but now he was more concerned with a final unseen obstacle; the door to the shed was padlocked on the outside. Reid attempted to pick the lock with a wire, without success. In the end he unscrewed the hasp, wasting more precious minutes. By now it was 6.35; the German woman could appear at any moment. Then the six men made a snap decision. Only Reid's party would go; Lockwood, Elliott and Howe would try again the following morning. The tunnel exit was hastily sealed, and the disappointed escapers returned the way they had come. For the rest, it was time to leave the woodshed. Pat Reid brushed himself down, straightened his skirt, and walked out into the sunlight. Allan and Barry waited for a moment; they knew the sentry was standing at the end of the lane, but there was no shot. Then they too left the woodshed, dressed as a father and son. 'One could almost feel the sentry's eyes boring into one's back,' recalls Barry. 'One had to fight an overwhelming desire to run.'

They walked thirty yards, then turned a corner and descended into the town, following Pat Reid at a discreet distance. 'The villagers were up and there were many women in the street. They took no notice of Peter and myself but found Pat Reid fascinating as he passed between them. They turned around to stare as he went by; it was a somewhat hair-raising experience.' Pat Reid waddled on, now convinced that the heavy boots behind him were a patrol. He paused on the bridge, assuming he was about to be arrested, and the boots marched by. He looked up to see Rupert Barry and Peter Allan, hiking off into the forest. Half a mile up the road the three escapers rendezvoused, and Reid discarded his disguise. They climbed a hill and there they gazed down at the towers of Laufen Castle, already far enough away to be indistinct. Rupert Barry noticed that his hands were shaking. 'I could light a cigarette only with the greatest of difficulty.' To the south stretched the misty September landscape they would cross on their 150-mile walk to Yugoslavia. They hoped to make it in ten days, using the time-honoured method of 'boy-scouting' described in all classic escape stories of the First World War. Boy-scouting involved sleeping in woods by day and walking by night, avoiding roads and having minimum contact with the population. It was ambitious but not impossible. Rupert Barry had a map and a British compass that he had carefully preserved through many searches, and they had some rations – a small bag of Quaker oats and a couple of Oxo cubes.

Walking by night was an uncertain business, and when they entered the hills on the second day every wrong turn was punished by extra miles and blistered feet. On their third morning they decided to abandon night navigation, and continued on through the empty woods towards the mountain ranges south-east of Salzburg. The weather was still warm and their confidence was high, but as the forests grew steeper they were forced out on to the roads, and here, inevitably, they met their first Germans. Some of these civilians were not content with a perfunctory 'Heil Hitler', and in every village young Peter Allan politely fended off the questions in his best Tirolean accent. The greatest hazards came from inquisitive girls, eager to talk to any young man they found. Walking through one village, the three escapers were alarmed to see three girls following them; they quickened their pace, the girls quickened theirs, and the chase lasted until a convenient bend in the road, when the three grown men bolted for the woods.

Four days out, and by now the escapers were very hungry. Apart from some stolen potatoes, they had eaten nothing but a few spoonfuls of porridge. Dishevelled and footsore, they tramped on up the mountain road, Rupert Barry with a blanket slung over his shoulder, Pat Reid wearing his scarf as a hat. They looked less and less like the hearty young hikers that had set out from Laufen. Locals began to stare as these outlandish strangers went by. At 11.30 p.m. they passed through the small village of Lungotz, high in the mountains and halfway to Yugoslavia. Suddenly an electric torch shone out of a window, and after a few seconds it went out. The escapers hurriedly took the left fork of a road out of the village, and to their relief they found themselves in deep woods. There was no sound but their boots on the tarmac. Then torches appeared out of the darkness ahead and the glint of rifles. '*Hande hoch, Hande hoch!*' A gang of suspicious villagers had tracked them from the road, and before they knew it they were arrested. Interrogated by the local police, they were described as 'dangerous enemies of the Reich' and put on a truck back to Laufen. Here they were greeted by Sergeant-Major Herman, 'a real four-letter man', recalled Rupert Barry. 'He had obviously had his tail twisted over us and was going to get his own back. He rushed at us, roaring his head off, punched us, tweaked our ears, spat at us and stuffed his filthy face within a centimetre of each of our noses in turn.' All three men were punished with up to twenty-eight days' solitary confinement in the town jail, on bread-and-water rations. A week into their sentence there was a loud banging down the corridor – Howe, Elliott and Lockwood had returned. They had successfully used the tunnel the following night, and were caught in the Tirol after eight days of freedom. All six were threatened with execution – for 'stealing bicycles', the property of the Reich, being in possession of a compass, and the 'destruction of a German blanket' that Rupert Barry had cut up and turned into a coat. The threats were not carried out, and a month later they were returned to Oflag 7C.

The six men had made one of the first escape attempts from Germany, and had given themselves and their comrades at Laufen much to think about. They had disguised themselves as civilians, but they had not been shot, and their punishment suggested that the Germans intended to honour the Geneva Convention. Also, they realised that without food and a good map, boy-scouting across Nazi Germany was a daunting prospect, and their experience encouraged many future escapers to travel around the country in the same manner as everyone else did; they would take the train.

A week later the Laufen Six were given an hour's notice to pack their bags. They were not told where they were going, but they knew they would not be coming back. Under heavy escort the six men were marched out of the main gate carrying their kit-bags and their travel rations, a five-gallon drum of cooked potatoes. A squad of guards accompanied them to the train station, and three days later they arrived at the bad boys' camp – Oflag 4C, Colditz. It would not be long before many of the friends they had left behind would join them.

CHAPTER TWO

Leaps and Bounds

By Christmas 1941 there were seventeen British prisoners in Colditz. The Poles entertained them well on Christmas Day, putting on a puppet show and once again managing to produce beer, brandy and cigarettes to make the party. All seventeen had been caught escaping, or proved themselves *Deutschfeindlich* – anti-German. This created a bond of trust between them. 'Arriving at Colditz was rather like joining a club,' recalls John Davies, who at twenty was the youngest man in the castle. 'We all knew the entry exam. The question was "How the hell are we going to get out of this?"'

Colditz Castle stood at the centre of a series of concentric rings of security. At its heart was the prisoners' courtyard, a tight circle of ninety-foot buildings built on thick medieval foundations. All of its doors were locked, its outside windows barred, and there was one exit, a large wooden gate, which was guarded day and night. Beyond the prisoners' courtyard lay the second ring of security. The castle was built on a high spur of rock, and beneath the grey walls were floodlit terraces, ringed with barbed wire. Beyond the wire the ground fell away precipitously on three sides. To the north and east the slope descended sharply down to the park, a relic of the castle's happier days as the pleasure gardens of the Electors of Saxony. At the bottom of this grassy valley ran a stream, and some fine trees covered the hillside beyond; all along its margin ran an eight-foot wall. The south side of the yard adjoined the German half of the castle; to escape from here involved passing through the German garrison courtyard undetected. Most tempting of all was the western aspect, where the prisoners looked out across the roofs to Colditz town and the forest beyond. They could see the bridge, the railway station, the town square – free civilian life. But directly beneath them were two floodlit terraces, separated by a thirty-foot drop. Beyond the parapet the cliff plummeted a further hundred feet down to the river below.

Once beyond these first two rings of security the obstacles to a successful escape were formidable. The moment an escape was detected the code word 'mousetrap' was transmitted to all police and train stations within a twenty-five-mile radius of the castle. Extra guards were mounted on platforms and photographs of escapers were distributed; civilians were encouraged to be vigilant. If an escaper managed to slip through this net he then faced the daunting task of crossing Germany. Colditz Castle stood in the heart of Saxony, four hundred miles from the nearest neutral frontier, and in 1941 the boundaries of Hitler's Greater Germany were still expanding. Once 'out' the greatest threat often came from the eager and inquisitive Hitler Youth. 'We couldn't give a damn about old men and women,' recalls the French escaper Pierre Mairesse Lebrun. 'But these Hitler Youth characters had only one thing on their minds. They were twelve, fourteen years old, and they all wanted to become heroes by catching an escaped prisoner. They reported anyone acting suspiciously and they were given money if they found someone. You needed a lot of luck to avoid them.'

Mairesse Lebrun was one of the early French arrivals, soon to be joined by two hundred Frenchmen under General Le Bleu in February 1941. Sixty of these men were not escapers but Jewish political prisoners, including a party of doctors and the banker Eli de Rothschild. The French contingent were given their own quarters on the west side of the court-yard, and they had barely settled in before a number of Frenchmen, including their senior officer, turned upon their Jewish companions-in-misfortune and asked for them to be segregated. The Kommandant was only too happy to oblige, and the Jews were removed to the attics. The British believed that this act was instigated by the Germans. 'For days the subject was heatedly discussed by every nation,' wrote the young Airey Neave, another recent British arrival. 'The camp was divided as to the wisdom and fairness of this anti-Semitism, for many of the French officers were suspected of sharing the defeatist sentiments of Vichy. Nevertheless, it was difficult to understand why they should respond to racial discrimination, and I never quite fathomed the psychology of this incident . . . Few of them [the Jews] were keen escapers, but the behaviour of their fellow officers in a fascist prison camp seemed to me outrageous.' Airey Neave was one of the few British officers who went to offer his support to the French Jews. The handful of other British officers chose to remain outside 'internal French affairs', though they did invite several Jewish officers to dinner in their mess. Word spread around the French quarters, 'the British are entertaining the Jews', and this became a very public statement of where their sympathies lay. The Germans' attitude towards Jews in Colditz was more ambiguous: from time to time Anthony Karpf, one of several Jewish Polish officers, was sent to the solitary cells 'because you're Jewish', yet Solly Goldman, the cockney orderly charged with running the German kitchen, was universally popular among guards and prisoners alike. As more British Jewish prisoners arrived, the Germans made no attempt to separate them from their compatriots, nor did they single them out for insults. Perhaps they realised that in contrast to the French contingent, there were no ready divisions here to exploit.

During these early months there was a particular mistrust between the British and the French, which took root long before 'the Great Jewish Row'. On their marches across northern France in 1940 the British prisoners noticed that several Frenchmen were carrying ready-packed suitcases, anticipating captivity, and they wanted to be sure that their new companions in Colditz were 'the right sort'. 'You had to be very wary of the French,' recalls John Davies, 'because only half of them wanted to carry on fighting. You always wondered that if the Vichyites didn't want to escape they might curry favour with the Germans.' Events outside the castle had only exacerbated the tensions: on 3 July 1940 the French fleet at Mers-el-Kebir refused to join the Allied forces, and after several ultimatums, the blockading British warships began their bombardment. In a mere five minutes 1,250 French lives were lost, and the action provoked the Vichy government to break off diplomatic relations with Churchill. Mers-el-Kebir echoed around the prisoners' courtyard, and it was only after the arrival of the forceful

General Le Brigant as the new Senior French Officer, and a Major Bergé captured in Crete, that the mistrust began to disperse. Bergé brought fresh reports of the Free French revival in the Middle East, and his stories steeled the nerves of any '*attentiste*' doubters among the French contingent.

Within the confines of the castle rumours flourished as nationalities took the measure of each other. They lived in separate quarters, on different sides of the courtyard, and would rarely visit each other uninvited. According to one officer, 'It was a Europe in miniature. The French were jealous of the Poles because they seemed to get on better with the British than they did. The Poles on the other hand despised the French because they reckoned they had put up a better defence of their country and lasted out longer against the Hun with inferior equipment. The Belgians just chattered away to everyone like magpies; and the two wretched Yugoslavs couldn't say a word to anyone except Jim Rogers, who happened to speak Serbo-Croat.' All the prisoners had been sent to Colditz because they were troublemakers; they had demonstrated to the Germans that they were *Deutsch-feindlich*. Now it became clear that there was another prize at stake, which they would fight for among themselves; the first to break out of the international escape academy that the German had unwittingly created. With ample time to kill, there were soon a dozen or more escape schemes under way in various parts of the castle. The German boast that Colditz was escape-proof was about to be tested.

As the castle's original inhabitants, it was the Poles who held the initiative. They discovered that most of the doors in the castle were secured with old-fashioned lever locks that were easily picked. During these first months the Poles even found doors with keys left in them, from which they filed the teeth away to make '*passepartout*' keys that opened most doors in the castle. Colditz had over seven hundred rooms, and it was not long before the Poles and their willing understudies, the British, were off exploring, looking for exits. Many of the officers had escaped from their previous camps via tunnels, and it occurred to them that this medieval schloss might very well contain passages and drains beneath ground level. Inside the clock tower adjacent to the French quarters, a small group of Frenchmen were trying to dig down into the cellars. Across the yard the Poles had begun a tunnel that they hoped would connect with the ancient sewer system. Pat Reid, the former civil engineer, also set to work exploring the drainage system; his route in would be via the canteen. As spring turned to summer 1941, all three tunnels were under way, each being constructed in secret.

One of the men hauling sacks of spoil out of the French tunnel was Alain Le Ray. A dark-haired lieutenant of the Chasseurs Alpins, he was both a career officer and a patriotic Frenchman who believed his occupied country still had a role to play in the war. 'Night after night I did my shift with the tunnel team,' he recalls. 'And I was happy to do it, to keep solidarity with my mates, but it was very hard work, and frustrating because progress was so slow. Who knows if it could survive without being discovered. I knew that tunnelling did not suit me, I was getting too impatient. What I wanted was something quick that I could execute alone.' In Colditz parlance, Alain Le Ray was looking for a 'snap escape'.

Two or three times a week, parties of officers were allowed out of their yard to take more vigorous exercise. This was known as 'the park walk', and led the prisoners out of their courtyard, through the German Kommandantur and down into the valley below the eastern side of the castle. Here the Germans erected two wire enclosures: a larger oval-shaped space used for walking or running, and adjacent to it a smaller rectangular area used for football. Beyond the six-foot wire fences the park ran out into woods which extended up the hillside opposite the castle. From the very beginning the camp authorities were worried about the security of the park. The Geneva Convention states that 'Fresh air must be available' to prisoners, though it does not stipulate how much. The Kommandant felt the park was a luxury and not a right, and frequently cancelled the park walk as a collective punishment for bad behaviour. This prompted the British to take the matter up with the Swiss government, their protecting power as prisoners of war, which in turn argued the case with the Oberkommando der Wehrmacht, the OKW, in Berlin. Reluctantly the Germans were forced to reinstitute the walk. 'The march down resembled on occasions a crowd going on an excursion down to the Black Forest,' wrote Reinhold Eggers, the security officer, who was under no illusions as to the prisoners' real intentions. 'They dribbled out of the yard one by one, then went back to call a comrade to join them. There was always a last-minute rush before the gate was closed. The babble and Babel of tongues reminded one of a parrot house. The variety of uniforms was certainly distracting – some would go down in shorts to play football, some to run, some to sleep . . . During the count no one was ever in a hurry, someone moved, someone shuffled, someone dropped his football, someone began to read aloud out of his book. Perhaps a recount was necessary, and then another one, and finally the total was written down in a book and off we went, in broken time, crocodiling around corners, concertinaing on the straight bits, jostling in the gateway, pointing, calling back, calling forward, dropping things, the whole time causing a diversion. And all the same again on the way back.'

It was during one of these walks down to the park that Alain Le Ray saw an opportunity for a snap escape. Descending the zigzag path down to the park, the route passed by a disused building known as the Terrace House. Some time in March 1941 Le Ray noticed that it was under repair, and the builders were storing their materials in a small room on the ground floor. The door was unlocked. His plan of escape was blindingly simple: taking his place in the column, he would march back up the hill on the flank nearest the Terrace House, and as he passed it he would break ranks and leap up the mound of earth to the door and hide inside. The nearest guard would be ten yards behind him, but as the path turned a corner Le Ray gambled he would not be seen. Whatever happened next would be a matter of luck.

Le Ray quietly went about his preparations. He made himself a suit of civilian clothes and a friend lent him a small quantity of German money. Then Peter Allan, one of the Laufen Six, helped him compile a map of the German railway system as far as the Swiss border, which he intended to cross at the Engadine, an area he knew from peacetime holidays. His intention was to ski across the frontier at Easter, when he hoped the trains would be crowded with holidaymakers and the guards would be fewer. If challenged, he was confident that his German was good enough for him to pass as a tourist.

On Good Friday 1941 Le Ray put his civilian clothes on under his uniform, threw his greatcoat over the top, and marched down to the park. Only two other officers knew his intentions, including André Tournon, the friend with whom he had escaped before Colditz. There was the usual game of football, then the prisoners were lined up, counted and marched back up the hill. Le Ray noticed that the guards were as attentive as ever, and decided not to try that day. Then, as they approached the corner of the Terrace House, he saw that the nearest guard was ten yards behind: he would have at least five seconds. 'This is it,' he said to Tournon, who was marching behind him. Without turning around, Tournon warned his comrades, 'Stay calm. Keep looking ahead.' He pulled off Le Ray's greatcoat. Le Ray leaped up on to the bank, and slipped – he was on all fours. 'I was sure they would see me scrabbling up the bank,' he remembers. 'But I went on. I got up, climbed to the top of the bank, and slid through the small door. No shouts, no chase, no dogs.' From the dark interior Le Ray heard the column tramp on up the hill, its clatter dying away.

He pulled off the rest of his uniform, rolled up his civilian trousers into plus-fours, and prepared to leave at once. Peeping through a chink in the door, he saw that some guards had entered the wire cage down below and were playing football. He had to wait, and trust that Tournon and the other comrade who knew of his escape, Pierre Mairesse Lebrun, could fudge the count back at the guardhouse. The minutes passed, then an hour. All must have gone well at the guardhouse. But then he began to worry about the evening *Appell* – would his absence be noted? The Germans played on till six, and then finally they left. Le Ray could not wait any longer. He slipped out of his hiding place and ran down the path. 'I felt the whole park was like a great eye watching me as I went along the barbed-wire fence,' he recalls. Running through the trees to the park wall, he clambered over and was away.

Le Ray never intended to boy-scout the four hundred miles to the Swiss border; walking to the small village of Rochlitz five miles from Colditz, he caught a local train to Penig, then another to Zwickau. It was here that he made the unfortunate discovery that most of his German money was invalid. For the next two stages of his journey he hid in the guard's van, eventually reaching Nuremberg. As evening fell he knocked down a man in a street and stole his wallet and overcoat – a crime that would certainly earn him the death penalty if he were recaptured. But the stolen money bought him a ticket to Anspach, which he reached on Easter Sunday, and then on to Stuttgart. Fatigue was catching up with him. 'I hadn't slept for three days and by now I felt I'd never make it over the Engadine mountains,' he recalls. 'So I decided to head for a nearer and flatter part of Switzerland – Schaffhausen.'

Late in the afternoon Le Ray stepped off the train at Singen, a few miles from the frontier. He elected to walk the last few miles to freedom. Not long after setting out, he somehow found himself in an empty factory yard; unnerved, he swung south into some thick forest, and here he had the misfortune to run into a border patrol. After a short chase through the woods he climbed up a tree and eluded them, but the incident persuaded him that he was safer back on the train. That night he crept back to Gottmadingen station, where he knew there would be a half past eleven train to Schaffhausen. Buying a ticket would be too dangerous, so he climbed over the station fence and hid in some bushes at the end of the platform. The train steamed in from Singen, on time. The guard came out on to the platform, and the engine pulled to a halt directly in front of his hiding place. Precious moments passed as Le Ray decided where to board the train. The guard looked up and down the empty plat-form, and as he blew his whistle Le Ray dashed from his bushes and stretched out on the buffers in front of the engine. He hoped to be invisible in the darkness behind the dazzling headlamps. The wheels turned – and they were off. As they crossed the border Le Ray sat up, his legs dangling between the buffers. 'I felt wild with hope and pride.' He was the first man to escape from Colditz to neutral soil, achieving a 'home run'. The French had opened the account.

At Colditz the evening *Appell* uncovered Le Ray's absence. It caused consternation, and Hauptmann Priem received a severe reprimand from Kommandant Schmidt. How could this escape-proof camp, with all its extra men and resources, fail in its purpose? A thorough search was conducted, but to no avail – there was nothing for the dogs to find. The Germans tentatively concluded that Le Ray had escaped over the roofs of the courtyard and climbed down the lightning conductor, a drop of nearly ninety feet. Barbed wire was installed around the chimneys and extra searchlights were set up.

Throughout April of that year more POWs trickled in. Six more British arrived, including Frank 'Errol' Flinn and a Canadian gymnast, Don Thom. Both had been caught trying to start a Heinkel in a Luftwaffe hangar with the intention of flying it back to Britain. Alain Le Ray's success gave the new boys heart – the Frenchman had been inside the Sonderlager for only forty-six days, demonstrating that even Colditz had its exits. The French home run certainly inspired Pat Reid. Among the growing band of British officers, the dominant personalities were beginning to emerge, and Reid's was one of them. 'The great game of escaping' soon became his main preoccupation. As far as he was concerned, 'Nothing was too difficult'.

While Le Ray had been looking for a snap escape, Reid's efforts concentrated on the drains that led away from the prisoners' canteen. During business hours an old German sergeant sat opposite the counter, watching the officers come and go. In the centre of the floor was a manhole cover, which, using a diversion, Reid had managed to open. Glancing down into the drain below, he saw that it was wide and ran away in the direction of the eastern terrace. To explore whether it continued under the exterior wall, Pat Reid needed to gain access when the room was empty; in other words when the canteen was closed up for the night. Kenneth Lockwood, who managed the canteen stores, came up with a plan to help his friend. 'After the sergeant came in he always put the keys in the top drawer of his desk,' he recalls. 'I asked a couple of the boys to come in and ask for something really complicated, like a double bass, that had to be ordered from Leipzig. While the sergeant was at the counter sorting this out, I nipped around the back of the desk and took the keys out. I had a piece of soap in my pocket, took imprints of the key in the soap and returned the key to its drawer.' The duplicate key was made by slicing up an iron bedpost, and a week later Reid was locked inside the canteen and able to inspect the drain at his leisure. Dropping down through the manhole, he followed the drain's course out under the castle wall; but a few yards on he came to a dead end. The only way out would be to tunnel up vertically and devise a way of breaking the surface of grass terrace without being noticed.

While Pat Reid and his accomplices began work on the canteen tunnel, another opportunity suddenly presented itself. On 10 May a German truck drove into the prisoners' yard and parked outside the British and Dutch quarters. A gang of French orderlies jumped off, and began to bring down palliasses stored on the top floor. There was a hurried consultation in the British quarters – this was a golden opportunity for a snap escape. All eyes fell on Peter Allan, the boyish Scotsman. He was small, light, and he spoke German; he could be sewn into one of the mattresses. Pat

Reid ran up to negotiate with the French orderlies as Allan was changed into some makeshift civilian clothes. 'It was all very quick,' recalls Allan. 'I found some white socks, shorts and a sort of jacket. I looked very young, and, I hoped, I was rather like a Hitler Youth.'

Allan had no time to get maps or papers. At the last minute Kenneth Lockwood gave him a fifty-Reichsmark note from his cigarette supply, and Allan was then bundled up the stairs to where the orderlies were working. With some difficulty Pat Reid had persuaded the Frenchmen to carry the small Scotsman down the stairs. 'I was just pushed inside the straw mattress,' he recalls. 'And they loaded me on to the cart and then of course another mattress came on the top, which didn't matter because it wasn't heavy. The hardest thing of the whole escape was trying not to sneeze.'

Within minutes the orderlies' job was done and the truck was on its way out of the yard. A few British officers wandered nonchalantly about, watching it go. 'I was thinking I hope to goodness he makes it,' recalls Lockwood. 'We didn't know how he was going to do it. He might have had a bayonet in his belly in the German courtyard for all we knew. He'd have to take his chances.' When Peter Allan's absence was discovered the alarms were raised and the castle searched. Once again the Germans emerged empty-handed. The days passed with no news and they began to hope that Peter Allan had matched the feat of Alain Le Ray. It was mid-May, and Colditz Castle had been operating as a Sonder-lager for barely six months; already the escaping season was in full swing.

Two days after Peter Allan left the camp it was the Poles' turn. Miki Surmanowicz, a 'weedy-looking daredevil', was one of the Polish officers to introduce himself to the British on their first night in captivity, and he had kept up the good relations ever since. A formidable lock-picker, whom Pat Reid claimed 'taught me everything I know', Surmanowicz told Reid he was planning an escape from the solitary cells, and mysteriously asked Kenneth Lockwood for a pair of rubber-soled shoes. These were duly provided, then he engineered a misdemeanour to place himself and another Pole, Mietek Chmiel, in the solitary confinement cells adjacent to the main gate in the prisoners' courtyard. Surmanowicz and Chmiel were about to embark on the most dangerous attempt yet to escape from Colditz. Once it was dark Surmanowicz managed to dismantle the bed and stool in his cell, and turn both into a lever. His plan was to slide the lever under the heavy wooden door, which was secured by a padlock and two iron bars at one end, and hinged at the other.

'I forced the end of the home-made lever with my legs,' he recalls. 'And very slowly, one millimetre at a time, the cell door began to lift. After two hours the door lifted off its hinges and I let it down very quietly on to the doorstep of the cell. There was now enough room between the door frame and the door for me to squeeze into the passage. It took me only a short time to pick the lock of Lieutenant Chmiel's cell, and the operation was done so quietly that I had to wake him up. The door to Chmiel's cell was relocked, then we reassembled the bed and stool in my cell and replaced the door on its hinges. I passed the guardroom like a ghost and Mietek followed like a shadow. The last door, leading into the courtyard, was no problem. One turn with my lock-pick and we were breathing the night air.'

How Surmanowicz managed to 'disappear' from his barred cell without picking the lock baffled Reinhold Eggers for the rest of the war; and more was to follow. Once out in the yard, Surmanowicz and Chmiel slipped through the shadows to the edge of the Kellerhaus. Silently a sheet rope was dropped to them from a window two storeys above; at its end were two rucksacks carrying their escape kit. Donning the rucksacks, the escapers shinned up the rope to a ledge that ran alongside the side of the building towards the roof of the German guardhouse. The ledge was a mere four inches wide – forty feet above the ground. Collecting the long length of rope, they held their nerve and crept along the ledge for ten yards till they could jump across to the guardhouse. Once on the relative safety of the roof, the two Poles found an open attic window, and from there a window that overlooked the town. Securing the rope to the window, they proceeded to shin down 120 feet to the ground. They were almost at the bottom when their luck – or bravado – ran out. Miki Surmanowicz in his rubber-soled boots travelled noiselessly down the face of the building, but Mietek Chmiel scraped and knocked against the guardhouse wall. Attracted by the thudding, a guard flung open the window and saw the bed rope ascending into the sky. Directly beneath him was Chmiel. 'Hands up, hands up!' The two daredevils were caught in midair and the alarm sounded. A snap *Appell* was called, at 5.30 a.m., and they returned to their empty cells. The British marvelled at Surmanowicz and Chmiel's daring but cursed the outcome, as the Germans now stationed a guard in the courtyard throughout the night, whose presence would compromise many later attempts.

Meanwhile the British canteen tunnel continued apace. Lead by Rupert Barry and Pat Reid, the officers dug a vertical shaft which ended just below the surface of the grass on the terrace. Underneath, Pat Reid constructed a wooden box which supported the grass above. At the moment of exit, he would simply raise the box, lifting up the square of turf above, and climb out. Maps, civilian clothes, compasses and false passes were prepared and concealed in a false buttress built behind the counter in the canteen. It had taken three months of work, and the escape was set for 29 May, after the evening *Appell*. The escape party consisted of eight British and four Poles, the latter earning their places through the close bonds that had developed between the two nations since the British arrival. The Polish inclusion was also a matter of expediency. By April 1941 there were 873,000 Poles working in Germany, providing escaping Polish officers with a ready disguise, and giving them an excuse to be travelling north to the Baltic ports with their 'mute' British friends in tow. There was only one small matter to deal with. Out on the terrace, precisely where the canteen tunnel was destined to surface, stood a guard. This man had already proved himself to be bribable, swapping eggs in return for Red Cross chocolate and cigarettes. The British decided to offer him 700 Reichsmarks if he looked the other way on the night of 29 May. This sum represented several weeks' wages, but unfortunately it was not large enough. The guard alerted Priem, who immediately held a security meeting, at which no one was able to offer an explanation as to where the money came from, except that it had been smuggled in. The Germans could only guess why the bribe had been offered, so they decided to let their victims lead them to their quarry. The guard was ordered to accept the money and say nothing.

On the night of the escape a well-laid plan swung into action. Using the skeleton key, Pat Reid and eleven others entered the canteen, kitted themselves out in escape gear, and descended into the tunnel. Outside the castle, the Germans waited. 'The tension among us was terrific,' recalls Eggers. 'It was at moments like these that the hotheads could make trouble.' Eggers was hiding with a party of guards farther down the terrace waiting to pounce. 'Suddenly came a movement on the grass. A square of turf appeared straight out of the ground, held in a wooden frame. A man's hands and arms followed, pushing up the turf and frame by the legs. Then the frame stood aside, and up came the British Captain Reid! *Heraus*!'

The Germans scrambled. Pat Reid crawled out to find a reception party of 'goons with their guns in the rabbiting position'. Kenneth Lockwood was right behind him. 'Pat quickly turned around and shouted to all of us in the tunnel "Get back!", so we all shot out the other end and found that the Germans had run round into the courtyard and opened the canteen. We were just sandwiched between the two of them. So we came out and just roared with laughter, and that defeated the Germans completely. They couldn't understand it at all. Well, what else could you do?'

The captured escapers included Guy German, the Senior British Officer, and a haul of escape equipment. Priem and Eggers were feeling very pleased with themselves. The guard who double-crossed the prisoners kept 100 marks of his bribe as a reward; and he was awarded extra leave, a promotion and a War Service Cross. The Kommandant, Oberstleutnant Schmidt, could afford to be generous – this was their first big success.

Since the British arrival in November 1940, there had been seventeen escape attempts in six months. Most had scarcely broken through the first and second rings of security around the castle, but the British still had one man out there, and it was to him that their thoughts now turned. Peter Allan was last seen hidden inside a palliasse on the back of a lorry that drove out of the courtyard; he had not been heard of for three weeks. The truck had carried the palliasses out of the castle down to a barn in Colditz town, where the French orderlies deposited its cargo. Once they had driven away, Peter Allan emerged. 'I brushed myself down and walked directly towards Colditz railway station,' he recalls. 'The great thing we had learned on our first escape from Laufen was that you must get out of the surrounding neighbourhood as soon as you can. So I went to the ticket office and said in German, because I spoke good German: "Chemnitz, please." And the chap said to me: "Single or return?" And keeping a straight face I said: "Single, please."'

Dressed in his shorts and white socks, and looking very much like a member of the Hitler Youth, Peter Allan took his seat. Only now, as Colditz station receded into the distance, was he able to collect his thoughts. 'Where was I going to go? What should I do? Because it was a snap escape I was very unprepared; it was no use going to Switzerland; I had no papers and no maps and no idea of the routes to get over there. There were only two possibilities. One I really didn't think of, which was going up to the Baltic and getting on a ship to Sweden. That didn't strike me at the time. I thought I'd have more luck if I went to see the Americans, who were not in the war, and I thought they might help me. I knew that they had a consulate in Vienna. So I took a train down as far as Regensberg, where I spent the night in the station lavatory and almost lost all my money, and then I started walking.'

Allan was no stranger to boy-scouting; he had tried it on his initial escape from Laufen. The challenge he now faced was even greater because he had no food whatsoever; in three nights of hiking through the woods all he had eaten were a few potatoes scavenged from a field. At dawn on the fourth day Allan broke cover and decided to try to hitch a lift. 'I was walking down a country road and I was very tired,' he remembers, 'when a *Kübelwagen*, a German Jeep, appeared. I thumbed it down, and then to my shock I saw two Gestapo Sturmbannführers inside. "What do you want?" Well, I had to think rather quickly. "I've left my baggage on the train," I said. "It was going to X station, and I was trying to get there and see whether I could find it in the lost property." "Get in," they said, so I did. "You're not in the Wehrmacht – why not?" I told them I was an engineering student in Hamburg. This was not the time to show off my German, so there was a limited conversation. Then, after about fifty kilometres, they said, "Can't take you any farther, get out." So I jumped out and I gave the best Hitler salute you've ever seen, I think I almost needed a new pair of shorts. Had they known who I was they might well have shot me as a spy. They drove off, and I must say I was sweating a bit.'

Riding his luck and still desperately hungry, Allan limped on towards Vienna. After eight exhausting days he reached the centre of the city, and there he went into a telephone box to look up the address of the American consulate. Despite his fatigue, he was clear in his mind how he was going to tackle this delicate audience with the consul; he was aware that this was his only chance. Allan was met at the door by a German secretary who asked him his business. She seemed satisfied with his answer and he followed her upstairs to a waiting room. 'I sat there for ten minutes and then she ushered me into the consul's office. I was very nervous and slightly light-headed by this stage. And so it all just came out. "I am an escaped British officer caught in France with the 51st Highland Division. I've escaped from Colditz – my feet are worn out and I'm hungry. I don't want to hide in the consulate nor do I want a passport. All I want is a twenty-mark note to get a meal, some beer, and a railway ticket to take me to the Hungarian border. Please help me."

'There was a silence; to this day I do not know what he was thinking. Maybe I was a stool pigeon. "No," he replied. "You have made a mistake; this is not a place to get help. Get out and forget you ever came here." Well, I was pretty shaken by this. "But just a little money?" And then he gave the rest of his spiel. "This consulate exists under diplomatic privilege from the German government, etc. etc. . . . it's no use, they'll get you in the end, they always do."'

Stunned, Allan returned to the street. He wandered into a park and fell asleep on a bench. When he awoke he was shaken by violent stomach cramps. 'I was very depressed that the Americans had refused to help me,' he remembers. 'I hadn't eaten any food for so long I was just tottering about. A park warden saw me wobbling around and came towards me. I said, "I'd like to get some food. Is there a Red Cross place near by?" "No, no," he replied. "Go in there and they'll help you." So I went in – and it was a police station. And that was it, I had no papers, nothing. I had to say I was an escaped prisoner of war, there was nothing else I could do.'

On 1 June Peter Allan returned to Colditz and spent the next three weeks in solitary. He had been out for twenty-three days. The effect on British morale was tangible, especially as the canteen tunnel had also failed. Inside his solitary cell, Allan felt the weight of expectation unfulfilled. 'I think it was the most depressing time I've ever had in my life, and I think I let down the other escapers in Colditz, because I hadn't succeeded.'

The return of Peter Allan brought home the difficulties officers faced once out on the run. Allan might have succeeded with more money, and possibly a travelling companion with whom he could have shared the burden of decision-making in a debilitated state. There was still much to learn. The Germans had plenty to congratulate themselves on. Lieutenant Eggers was promoted to captain, a well-deserved reward for being the most effective German sleuth. 'I claim some honour,' he wrote, 'for having been part of a team, a very amateur team I admit, of a German "holding" force whose clumsy efforts were nevertheless so successful that the experts had to lay on absolute masterpieces to beat us.' But the games of cat-and-mouse between the captors and captives inside Colditz Castle were only just beginning; and it would not be long before these absolute masterpieces began to be realised.

CHAPTER THREE

Co-operation

While the British reflected upon their lack of luck and the Germans congratulated themselves on keeping their unruly captives in check, the French scored another success. Lieutenant René Collin, impressed by Alain Le Ray's snap getaway from the park, had tried a variation. The door of the Terrace House which had served Le Ray so well was now locked, but there was another unlocked building within the confines of the prisoners' area – the pavilion. During an exercise Collin had managed to climb into the rafters and hide until the POWs were marched back to the castle. As soon as night fell he was on his way home. The Germans realised Collin was missing but were unaware of his method. Several of his comrades were party to the secret, including Lieutenant Pierre Mairesse Lebrun, who decided to follow suit a few days later. This tall, elegant Frenchman had already acquired a reputation at Colditz. Padre Platt, a *Deutschfeindlich* vicar who spent most of his time as a prisoner writing his diary, described Lebrun as 'a French cavalry officer of courtly appearance and manners, and the most lavishly dressed officer in the camp . . . his debonair Don Juan air gave us the impression he was at his best in the Bois de Boulogne and Champs Elysées'. At the outset of war Lebrun had volunteered for independent missions, free from the constraints of the regular army, and by May 1940 he had already won the Croix de Guerre and the Légion d'honneur. For these feats alone he held the admiration of his countrymen.

Mairesse Lebrun climbed up into the pavilion and as soon as the park was empty he slipped over the perimeter wall and strolled seven miles to Grossbothen, where he intended to catch the train to Leipzig. 'I was dressed in an impeccable grey suit, so my disguise was perfect,' he recalls 'But my problem was money. The only German money I had was a hundred-mark note that my family had sent me concealed inside a nut in a pot of jam. It was printed in 1928. The stationmaster had already issued my ticket and looked at the note. "This is out of date. Give me something else." I had nothing.'

Mairesse Lebrun made a run for it but he was cornered on the platform and sent back to Colditz. He spent the next four weeks in solitary confinement, staring at the bare wall, the water jug and the window. These long hours concentrated his mind, and it was not long before he had another plan. Prisoners in solitary confinement were also entitled to their quota of fresh air in the park, although at a different time to the rest of the POWs. 'It was the beginning of July, and I had set myself a challenge that I wouldn't remain a prisoner for more than a year,' remembers Lebrun. 'Well, the end of that year was fast approaching. Every day I ran eight hundred yards because I needed strong legs for the plan I was thinking of. I knew it was crazy, but the plan demanded it.' Mairesse Lebrun convinced a French orderly to smuggle in his 'escape kit,' which consisted of a pair of shorts, a scarf and a short-sleeved shirt. Lebrun then sewed a bit of sugar and some chocolate into the scarf, together with a razor and some soap. Each day Lebrun and his compatriot, Lieutenant Odry, were escorted down to the park by an officer, an NCO and three armed soldiers. The two prisoners were let into the wire enclosure, and left to wander about for an hour. Lebrun's plan was audacious to the point of stupidity; using Odry as a springboard he would vault over the wire fence and run for the park wall. He knew the guards would fire at him, but it was a calculated risk. 'I think it's easy to be brave in war, unless you are a complete coward. Escaping is a voluntary act of bravery, which is very difficult. Very difficult when you are risking your life. During other escapes I had never risked my life as directly as I intended to now.'

Odry agreed to help him. Both men knew this gymnastic feat could only be attempted once – there would be no time to practise. 'I said to Odry we'll mark the best spot with a pebble, and then keep walking round to tire out the Germans. After an hour I will say OK and we will do it. Every day I watched the faces of the officer and the three guards, who were armed, of course. I looked to see if they were dangerous or not. I was very much aware of the risk I was taking. On the first and second days the Germans looked as if they knew how to shoot, they didn't look stupid. And then on the third day, there was one guard wearing thick glasses. I thought to myself, he can't see very well! The officer in charge was an old second lieutenant with grey hair who didn't look like a killer. The two other guards didn't look like bad chaps. So I whispered to Odry that today was the day. We placed the pebble on the correct spot, we walked round for an hour, then I said this is it.'

Lebrun decided to make one more circuit. When they reached the pebble, he casually took a few steps away from Odry. When he turned around Odry leaned against the wire and cupped his hands as a stirrup. Lebrun ran towards him, vaulted, and flew clean over the wire. He landed ten feet from the nearest guard, sprang up and away before the guard realised what was happening. The guard shouted, and Mairesse Lebrun ducked and zigzagged, racing for the park wall. Then the shooting started. By the time the Frenchman reached the wall splinters of stone were ricocheting into him, but he was not hit. He ran up and down the base of the wall 'like a rabbit' as the sentries, only fifty yards away, tried to pick him off. 'There were three guards, and I had to let them fire their three shots each,' he recalls. 'Because I didn't want to start climbing the wall where I would be a static target.' Mairesse Lebrun counted the shots until he knew their magazines were empty. As soon as the shooting stopped he leaped at the eight-foot wall. 'I hoped that in their panic the guards' hands would be shaking, so it would take them longer to reload. It wasn't their job to kill people.'

In a few seconds he was over the wall and crashing through the woods beyond. A hail of bullets ripped into the trees and an off-duty guard set off in pursuit, but Lebrun eluded them. After an hour he entered a cornfield, careful to walk in backwards so as not to leave a trace, and waited until dark. The voices of peasants and sounds of dogs barking drew closer, and he now put his faith in a precaution he had taken before he left the castle. 'A friend taught me an old trick to put the dogs off a scent,' he recalls. 'Inside my case of belongings I had mixed up some sausage meat and pepper. When the guards opened up my case to give the dogs my scent they dived straight at the sausage and got a noseful of pepper, ruining their sense of smell. It must have worked, because they didn't find me.'

As night fell it began to rain. Lebrun, still wearing his running kit, left his hiding place and began to walk. Evading Operation Mousetrap and a German spotter plane sent out to find him, he walked through the rain for three days, all the way to Zwickau, seventy miles south of Colditz. The sugar and chocolate sewn into his scarf sustained him, and on reaching the town he was relieved to discover he could buy cake and beer without ration coupons. Having eaten his fill, he set off once more, and shortly afterwards he had another stroke of luck; he passed a bicycle leaning against a wall, unlocked. Casually he strode over to it and pedalled away, embarking on the four-hundred-mile journey to the Swiss border, which he hoped to complete in four days. The bicycle gave him confidence – he had stolen one a year earlier in his first escape – and now he set off south-west, straight down the main autobahn to Nuremberg. 'Bare-chested in the sun, like a German on holiday,' he recalls. 'It was a couple of weeks after the German Army had invaded Russia. I was all alone heading south-west, and coming up the other side of the motorway were troops, troops and more troops. Everyone was watching the army pass by; they didn't pay much attention to a passing cyclist.' Lebrun passed himself off as an Italian officer on leave, which explained his swarthy looks, his bad German – and his bicycle. At Ulm the front inner tube split beyond repair, but Lebrun continued on undeterred, riding the next fifty miles on the rim. Travellers laughed as he passed them, and Lebrun waved back. The broken bicycle was taking him ever closer to the border.

Eight days out of Colditz he arrived at Singen and aban-doned the bicycle in a wood, but decided to hold on to the

bicycle pump. 'It might be useful against farm dogs or something like that.' As darkness fell he set off in the direction
of Switzerland, and at dawn the following day he came upon
a mountain village which looked down on the Rhine and
Lake Constance. With no map to guide him, Lebrun was
unsure whether he was in Switzerland or Germany, so he
carried on up the hill until he came to a 1914–18 war
memorial. He was in Germany, having walked in – and out
– of Switzerland. Retracing his steps down the wooded slope,
he stepped on to a small metalled road. As he began walking
a man on a bicycle came around the bend up ahead of him;
it was a policeman. Lebrun looked suspicious; after all, he
was suntanned, wearing running kit, carrying a bicycle pump
and walking close to the Swiss border at six o'clock in the
morning. The policeman drew up in front of him, and without dismounting from his bicycle began to ask questions,
listening patiently to the 'Italian officer on leave' story, and
clearly not believing a word. He then asked Lebrun to return
to the station with him, and an argument began. 'I remembered a trick I used to annoy my brothers and sisters when
I was a child,' recalls Lebrun. 'There was nothing else for it.'
He grabbed the policeman's bicycle and pulled it from under
him, toppling him over. A swift blow with his bicycle pump
knocked the unfortunate man unconscious, whereupon
Lebrun stole his pistol and ran off into the woods. Climbing
to the top of the hill, he found a marker stone with the
numerals 1830 on it. Moving on, he found others, possibly
designating a frontier. But which side was which?

'I was flitting from tree to tree when I suddenly saw a
girl heading towards the chalet up ahead,' recalls Lebrun. 'I
was all alone in the woods with her so I wasn't risking a
lot. I appeared from the trees, and she was a bit frightened.
I very quickly said to her in French and then in the best

German I could manage: "Don't be afraid, I'm a French escapee, a French officer." Fortunately she understood me, so I asked: "Am I in Switzerland or Germany?" and she said: "But, monsieur, I am Swiss, you are in Switzerland!" She can't have understood the complete and overwhelming joy I felt! I said to her: "What are you doing?" She was carrying a small can of milk in her hand. "I'm taking milk to the chalet over there," she replied. I said: "What is that chalet?" It was the German border guards. I had crossed over twenty yards away! I could have run into a patrol. So I said: "Don't be frightened. Where is the nearest customs post?" "It's in my village." So I said: "Mademoiselle, don't trick me. I am armed, I'm warning you – and I will do anything; believe me. So, take them your milk as normal, then come out back here, and take me to the customs post in your village." I waited for her, and she came back.'

The girl led him to safety, and on arrival at the customs house Pierre Mairesse Lebrun had himself put in jail until the Swiss officials came and picked him up. Sensing that the Frenchman might be hungry, the local customs officer asked him if he wanted to share his lunch. 'They gave me tripe Caen-style. Tripe Caen-style! What was a dish from Normandy doing here in this Swiss enclave? I have no idea. I couldn't stand tripe Caen-style but it was the best meal I have ever eaten in my life.'

When news of Lebrun's escape reached Colditz, his portrait was hung in the French quarters, decorated with the tricolour ribbon; and his leap to freedom soon came to be regarded by all POWs incarcerated in Germany as one of the greatest escapes of the war. Even Reinhold Eggers was forced to agree. 'For sheer mad and calculated daring, the successful escape of the cavalry lieutenant, Pierre Mairesse Lebrun, will not, I think, ever be beaten.' Two weeks later,

Oberstleutnant Schmidt received a letter from Lebrun back home in Orange asking for his belongings to be forwarded. It would have been churlish for the Kommandant to have refused.

As the summer wore on more prisoners arrived. By the end of July 1941 there were over 500 officers and other ranks inside Colditz Castle: over 250 were French, with 150 Poles, 50 British and now 68 Dutchmen. These men had been overrun while in their barracks, and on capture had been asked by the Germans to sign a declaration stating that they would take no part in the war against Germany – anywhere in the world. 'How could I sign?' recalls Tony Luteyn, a lieutenant in the Royal Netherlands Indies Army. 'I mean, my parents were still in the Dutch Indies and the war was not over in the Pacific. If I signed I would have given my word of honour and then I would have been free to leave the army. But I couldn't do that.' Of the 15,000 Dutch servicemen captured, only 68 would not sign the declaration, and their refusal became a statement of intent. They harassed the Germans at a camp at Westphalian, and then continued to do so at Juliusburg on the Polish border, before the Germans lost patience with them altogether and sent them all to Colditz. On 24 July they marched into the prisoners' courtyard, immediately arousing curiosity and suspicion. The problem was their appearance. 'We were so military, we had our caps on, we were always in uniform, buttoned up, and we had the greatcoats,' recalls Tony Luteyn. 'I think there was an attitude of "Hey, is that a herd of spies or can we trust them?" Well, the only ones who cheered us were the Polish officers; there was quite a bunch of them, but the others were just looking at us, even the British.'

'They look like a bunch of bandsmen from a toybox,' remarked 'Lulu' Lawton, a British officer. In fact they looked very much like Germans. When the Wehrmacht had invaded the Netherlands they were very short of material to make uniforms, so they confiscated all the military cloth they could find. Dutch field grey was so close in tone to the Wehrmacht uniform that the Germans did not bother to change it. With the exception of a few minor details the large Dutch great-coat was identical to its German equivalent; it was a simi-larity that would prove significant in the months ahead. To understand how different the Dutch must have looked in their polished boots and overcoats it is worth recording the appearance of the French and British. Most had been captured in the clothes they stood up in, ragged from battle. To combat the chill of a Saxon winter the British effected combinations of anything they could muster; it was a common sight to see men clattering round the courtyard in a pair of wooden clogs, sporting a Balaclava, a khaki jacket, blue RAF trousers or even red Czech Army trousers. Such sartorial sloppiness in-furiated the Germans, and was positively encouraged by Guy German, the first Senior British Officer. 'As far as I'm concerned,' he said, 'you can all come down in your pyjamas and dressing gowns or anything else and the Germans can jolly well lump it,' remembers one young officer. 'I think we were typically British in that way; we weren't going to be frightfully military just for the Germans' benefit.'

This approach never failed to hit the mark. 'Oh, but the French and the British!' recorded Reinhold Eggers. 'On parade in pyjamas, unshaven, slopping in clogs and slippers, smoking, reading books, wearing the first combination of clothes that came to hand when they got out of bed, just asking to be ridiculed. They insisted on distinguishing between "parades" as on the King's birthday, when they turned out unrecognisably smart, and the daily roll-calls we held to count them. Very quickly we saw through what was superficially slipshod, though sometimes they all behaved whole-heartedly like urchins.'

The Dutch may have looked suspiciously like Germans, but as escapers they enjoyed many advantages over their fellow prisoners. All had been obliged to learn English, French and German at school, and most had travelled extensively in Germany before the war. In addition the country was full of *Arbeitsdienst*, thousands of Dutch workmen who were pressed into the service of the Third Reich. As long as they could produce work papers, Dutchmen were free to travel around Germany on their own passports.

Colditz Castle was now brimming with escapers and escape plans, and the prisoners' courtyard could not accommodate them all. A degree of co-operation was required between the nationalities, and this was highlighted by a series of incidents and accidents in which attempts were foiled not by the Germans, but by the prisoners themselves. When the British began work on the canteen tunnel at the end of January 1941, there was no sentry stationed on the patch of grass where the tunnel was destined to surface. Over the course of its construction the Poles made an escape attempt from the windows above, and thereafter a guard was placed there, whom the British were forced to bribe. This eventually resulted in the scheme's failure. Several other mishaps occurred during the spring, but events came to a head in June. 'We were coming back from the walk in the park,' remembers Kenneth Lockwood. 'And we passed this lady, perfectly turned out, coming towards us in the opposite direction. Well, nobody bothered about it very much until Brian Paddon looked down and noticed that she'd dropped her watch. So being a gentleman he picked it up and ran after her. And he was trying to give it back to her but she just kept walking along. The guards who were with us saw this scene and then it suddenly occurred to them there shouldn't be a lady walking down here, so they ran after her. It was indeed no lady.' It was Lieutenant Boulé, walking out of the camp in his own ingenious disguise. Had it not been for the gallant Brian Paddon, he would have passed out of the camp undiscovered.

This incident ushered in the international escape committee. Each nationality would appoint an Escape Officer, responsible for telling his counterparts about any attempts that were planned and when they were intended to take place. Each Escape Officer was privy to other nations' secrets, but there was a caveat; Escape Officers were not allowed to escape. Undaunted, Pat Reid assumed the role for the British. Because the castle was so small and there were limited opportunities, the international escape committee also had to act as an arbitrator between nations if they presented the same idea. This inevitably caused a certain amount of tension, especially among the French. They did not take to the more formal committee structure embraced by the other contingents, believing it would only hamper their efforts. After all, Le Ray, Collin and now Mairesse Lebrun had all succeeded in breaking out of Colditz – and then out of Germany – with no resources beyond their own wits. 'The English had the attitude that they had to obey the senior officer, and also do what the escape committee asked them to do,' recalls Dominic Corcosteguy, a young French officer at the time. 'This attitude did not exist among the French. We were much too individualistic to accept that kind of system. When someone came up with an idea that required organisation it happened through friendships. You're my friend, you help me, I ask my friend, he joins in. We did it among ourselves and we didn't like telling anyone anything. Which is why from time to time there were two French teams working on the same idea. This was a failing perhaps, but it was part of our French spirit. Everyone wanted to escape, and there were so few opportunities. It was each man for himself.'

For their next effort the British did not have to worry about stepping on anyone else's toes, as it began in their own Long Room, and extended through an eighteen-inch wall into the German lavatories of the Kommandantur. Their plan was to emerge through the hole above the cistern dressed as workmen, and casually walk out of the building. These lavatories were seldom used, and the only German on duty there throughout the night was the telephonist. While he was relieving himself one evening he was puzzled to hear intermittent scratching sounds coming from the other side of the wall. Hauptmann Priem was summoned and it became clear what the British were up to. Once again the Germans allowed the prisoners to expose their own plan. 'Let them tunnel. It will keep them busy and happy.' The door directly opposite the lavatory was locked and a tiny spyhole bored through it, allowing the ferrets to mount a twenty-four-hour watch on the lavatory. On Sunday, 31 July 1941 they noticed a minute hole appear in the plaster on the back wall above the cistern. Behind it were twelve escapers dressed as workmen, lined up in the British Long Room.

'We had cleared all the bricks out of the way and everything was set,' recalls Frank 'Errol' Flinn, a pilot who was one of the instigators of the escape. 'We chose a Sunday lunch-time when we thought there would be fewer people about. Peter Allan was first through, and I was second; we were going to travel together. The lavatories were empty. We crept around the corner and the next thing I knew was a pistol in my back. "*Hande hoch!*" We were taken into an office, our clothes were removed, and very cleverly the Germans dressed up two soldiers in our clothes, because they knew that the others would be watching from the windows to see if we'd made it through. The soldiers went down into the German courtyard and our chaps thought we'd escaped, so they sent more men through into the lavatory. And the Germans were just collecting them as they came. It sounds funny really, but it wasn't at the time.'

When the last man had emerged, the ferrets swooped on the British Long Room and confiscated even more clothes and passes hidden in a stove. It was their greatest haul so far, and ceremoniously the escapers were led back into the castle by a platoon of grinning guards. 'There were loud cheers from the French wing,' recalls Francis Steinmetz, a Dutch naval officer. '*Vive les Rosbifs, à bas les sales Boches!* Hooray for the Brits, down with the Krauts. It was a Colditz custom to give unlucky returning travellers a rousing welcome for their effort.'

For the British, these rousing returns were becoming all too familiar. By now the Germans had acquired so much escape equipment they had established an unofficial museum in the Kommandantur, which displayed every captured article. Among the key exhibits were the photographs of Johannes Lange, a local man who was drafted in to record every detail of escapes. Officers posed in their home-made clothes, tunnels and ropes were photographed *in situ*, and escapers were even made to re-enact their escapes. Eggers intended to use this extraordinary collection of photographs as a teaching aid, demonstrating to security officers of other camps the devious methods employed by Colditz officers to escape from the 'escape-proof camp'. Lange's photographs soon became a regular feature of a weekly security magazine, 'Das Abwehrblatt' (Security News), circulated in prisoner-of-war camps throughout Germany and in the offices of the OKW in Berlin, which accompanied Eggers' own articles describing the escapes. These tales only fuelled the growing reputation of the Sonderlager.

With the British, Polish and French officers all actively engaged in trying to escape, the Germans were more than relieved to regard the Dutch contingent as dormant. They seemed to be model prisoners, correct in their discipline, smart on parade, affable towards the guards – men who would not sully themselves with the 'dirty business of escaping'. So it was a shock to discover on 16 August that seven Dutchmen were missing. 'That's when the attitude of the camp towards us totally changed,' recalls Tony Luteyn. 'At the *Appell* all the other Allied officers had to move up, and the whole Dutch contingent marched between the ranks of Poles and British and French. They all cheered and applauded as we formed up in the bad boys' place.'

The numbers were counted and recounted, then a full-scale search of the prisoners' quarters ensued, conducted by the acting camp Kommandant himself. The Germans were convinced that the Dutch were digging a tunnel. But the tunnel never materialised, and neither did the Dutchmen. The seven missing Dutchmen were in fact four who had escaped over two separate days using the same method. Their escape was masterminded by the Dutch Escape Officer, Captain Machiel van den Heuvel, known to the British as 'Vandy'. Pat Reid remembered him as 'a fairly tall big-chested man, with a round face, florid complexion and an almost permanent grin. He had hidden depths of pride and a terrible temper, which was revealed on very rare occasions.' Vandy also had a gift for looking at the familiar and obvious from a different angle.

In the exercise enclosure below the castle was a large manhole capped by a wooden cover and secured by a heavy nut and bolt. Ever since the prisoners had been allowed down into the park attempts had been made to discover where the drain below led. Escape-minded officers, Pat Reid among them, concluded that it was a dead end and that the difficulties of concealment were too challenging. Once the hour for exercise had elapsed Germans with sniffer dogs entered the enclosure and made a meticulous inspection of the grounds, including the manhole cover; if it was unlocked they would notice. One afternoon that summer Vandy was sitting on the manhole watching a game of football. Idly he lowered a pebble on the end of a piece of string through one of the small airholes in the wooden cover, and was pleased to discover that it descended a full ten feet, of which half was water. This was perfect for his plan. During the next few Dutch excursions to the park, Bible readings were held around the manhole, and while these were in progress the dimensions of the nut and bolt were established. Vandy manufactured a pair of home-made spanners to release the bolt, and confident that he now had access to the drain, initiated his plan. On 13 August two Dutchmen, Dufours and Smit, disappeared into the manhole, only to be recaptured on the Swiss border. Two days later Vandy approached two young Dutch naval officers walking in the park. 'He said I have clearance for tomorrow afternoon, are you ready?' Francis Steinmetz, together with his friend Hans Larive, knew the manhole was being used as an escape route, but the details had been kept secret. Van den Heuvel now explained to them the method. During the Dutch visits to the park, the prisoners often played a form of rugby that involved wrestling a heavy medicine ball into the goal of the opposing team. It was noisy and rough with frequent scrummages, and often distracted the attention of the guards. Using the scrummage as cover, Steinmetz and Larive would be concealed inside the manhole, which would be 'locked' above them. To ensure the manhole appeared secure Vandy had made a false bolt, identical to the original, out of painted glass. This dummy bolt would convince the German guards and their dogs that the manhole was secure, and also enable the two escapers to get out; it would shatter when they made their exit. Clearing away the debris, Steinmetz and Larive would replace the real bolt on the hasp, and the manhole would appear never to have been opened.

That night Steinmetz and Larive made their final preparations for the escape, collecting railway timetables, compasses and money, and rehearsing their route across the border. This last piece of information was of particular interest to Hans Larive. Prior to Colditz he had escaped from Soest transit camp, only to be recaptured near Singen on the Swiss–German border. The border guards were convinced he was a spy, and he was detained for further questioning by the local Gestapo chief. During the course of his interrogation Larive accidentally made a discovery which would have a profound influence on the escapers from Colditz. On arrival at Gestapo headquarters, he was led into a large white office and told to wait. Then 'an enormous Bull' in black SS uniform strode into the room. 'The big brute glowered at me,' wrote Larive, 'and without any preliminaries spat out, "This is the Gestapo. You'd better speak the truth or we'll put you up against the wall, is that clear? One more or less of you does not make any difference to us."'

After several hours of persuasion Hans Larive convinced the Bull he was not a spy, but an escaped Dutch officer. The mention of his nationality touched a soft spot – it turned out that the Bull had been the chief cook in a Dutch hotel before the war, and he liked Holland. His temper subsided.

'Having described the last part of my journey,' wrote Larive, 'he [the Bull] remarked that the only clever thing I had done was getting off the train at Singen – all the rest was damn stupid.

'"Why?"I asked.

'"You must have known that Singen was the last station where anyone could get on or off the train without showing an identity card!"

'"No, that was just a guess."

'"Having got that far it was stupid to take the train instead of walking across the border," he said.

'"Well, the reason is I didn't know how to get through the defence line."

'"Defence line!" he exploded. "Defence against whom? Surely not those damned Swiss? What a crazy idea. There are no defences at all; we haven't got a single man to guard the border! You could have walked straight across." From the drawer he produced a staff map and I had to point out the route I had taken.

'"You fool," he said; "look." He indicated the spot where I had unwittingly walked past a part of the Swiss border jutting into Germany, at a distance of only three hundred yards. He asked me whether I remembered a certain house at the edge of a wood and the road leading past that house into the wood with a sharp bend beyond. Well, a quarter of a mile beyond that bend I should have turned left off the main road and followed a path. After a few hundred yards I would have been in Switzerland – just as easy as that. I asked him whether he could give me some more information.

'"Of course, of course," he said. "By all means."

'Naturally I would not manage to escape for a second time, and besides the war would be over by Christmas; it was not worth the risk of being shot for such a short-term imprisonment. I asked him questions about everything that could be of interest to an escaper, and learned a lot.'

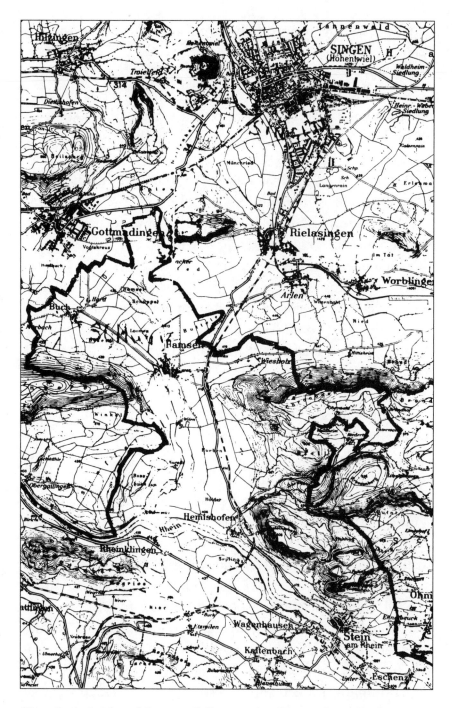

Hans Larive's Map of Ramsen Salient on the German-Swiss Border

This vital information remained in Dutch possession throughout their time at Colditz, and they communicated it to the international escape committee. It was successfully used by eight officers to make home runs, four Dutch and four British. Mairesse Lebrun and Alain Le Ray had relied on their wits and luck to make the difficult border crossing; Larive's careless Nazi made the adventure considerably less perilous.

The following afternoon the Dutch marched down to the park for their exercise. As usual they were counted when they left the prisoners' courtyard and once again on entering the park. Larive and Steinmetz began to watch the game of rugby. 'On a discreet signal from the escaping officer,' recalls Steinmetz, 'the scrum, or rather a yelling mob of players, moved quite naturally over the manhole, providing a human screen between us and the spectators. A helping hand had removed the bolt and now lifted the cover long enough for me to slip into the manhole. After half-time Larive followed. He had the real bolt in his pocket.'

Both men were now hiding in a dark shaft three feet wide and ten feet deep. At the bottom was five feet of stagnant grey water. At first they stood waist deep in the water with a blanket over their heads in the hope that they would not be seen if the Germans lifted the manhole cover. Above ground the Dutch exercise period was rapidly approaching its conclusion, and van den Heuvel knew that there would be a head count before they left the park, when the Germans would certainly discover that two officers were missing. To solve this problem he had organised a dangerous diversion undertaken by Lieutenant Gerrit Dames, known as 'the third man'. Dames had been sitting watching the game of rugby close to the barbed-wire fence. As the game continued, he edged closer to the wire until he was actually leaning against the fencepost in full view of two sentries fifty yards away. He then coolly clipped a hole in the wire and wriggled out. Ostentatiously dusting himself down, he started to walk towards the woods, hoping to catch the sentries' attention. The two guards suddenly saw him and dashed forward blowing their whistles. This was the cue for Dames to shout 'Run discovered!', directing his cries to the woods beyond. The nervous sentries levelled their guns at the escaper; fortunately they did not shoot. In the rapid head count that followed, two officers were found to be missing. Patrols with dogs scoured the park; they found nothing. The guards could only conclude that the two missing officers had escaped from the hole in the wire before Dames, and that he was the 'third man'. In fact Larive and Steinmetz were still within the Germans' grasp, practically under their feet. The diversion had worked, and Dames received three weeks in solitary for his bravery.

Larive and Steinmetz were left in the quiet of the well; they still had seven hours to wait until nightfall. After a while they took it in turns to stand in the water, holding on to rusty iron footholds cemented to the side. They both began to feel sick. 'We were breathing like fish on dry land,' recalls Steinmetz. Carefully he raised the cover a fraction with his penknife to stop them suffocating. At 10 p.m. they made their exit. 'We pushed the wooden cover upwards and in doing so broke the glass dummy bolt. I collected the broken glass and Larive inserted the real bolt which he had in his pocket. We left the manhole ready for use another time, which in fact it was.' By morning they had reached Leisnig station and there they bought tickets to Dresden. Despite their dishevelled appearance they were not challenged, and the following evening they were walking through the dark streets of Nuremberg. A Pole warned them that the train station was patrolled by the Gestapo at night, so they struck out into the town looking for a suitable place to hide. 'We came across a graveyard,' recalls Steinmetz. 'And we were not the only ones seeking the dark. It turned out to be the favourite meeting place of amorous couples, which was clearly audible. So there was nothing for it but to pretend to be one of them. I wrapped the army-issue blanket round my knees and played the female part and Larive made loud smacking noises to imitate passionate kisses.' It was 3 a.m. before the couple next to them moved off and the two Dutchmen could relax.

The following evening Hans Larive and Francis Steinmetz were walking through the woods south of Singen, following the Bull's instructions from memory. They picked up the railway line that led south-west to Switzerland; this same line had carried Alain Le Ray across the border to safety only months before. The Bull had told Larive that where the road diverged from the railway was very close to the frontier. They should follow this road for an hour, and then turn left through the fields. The Ramsen salient would be a hundred yards ahead of them. They followed his instructions, but instead of finding the border they met an armed guard walking towards them. They crossed the road and walked on, whereupon the guard crossed the road and unshouldered his rifle. Twenty-five yards from him they broke for the woods. He fired and missed, then ran back to alert the guardhouse. Larive and Steinmetz crawled into the depths of a thicket, and cautiously looked back at the road. Soldiers were now climbing on to their bicycles and heading off towards Gottmadingen village; every few hundred yards one of them dismounted and stood guard on the road the escapers would have to cross to reach the Swiss border. Larive and Steinmetz crawled back into the thicket and decided to wait.

Darkness fell and it began to drizzle; and from somewhere in the woods behind them came the sounds of shots and dogs barking, only to drift away again. At 10 p.m. the two escapers slithered out from their hiding place and across a field of beetroot close to the road. It was all quiet now; there was just one sentry standing at the edge of the forest. Larive and Steinmetz froze for fifteen minutes, waiting for him to move. The sentry turned out to be a tree. Taking their shoes off, they crept silently across the gravel road and into the fields beyond. Here, somewhere, was the border, and it was not long before they became lost. The dark fields and hedges all looked the same, and their compass told them they were walking in a circle.

'We stumbled on a cart track,' remembers Steinmetz 'There was nothing, no sound, nothing except the rain in the trees, not a glimmer of light, no sound of cattle in stables, and we found shelter in an overhanging roof of a shed. We discussed the situation in whispers: it would be best to stay where we were and not get more lost than we already were, and at first light get our bearings and make a dash for the last few hundred yards, perhaps less. We leaned against the boards of the shed. We were cold, wet and tired – it was our third night in the open without sleep. We half dozed, but I nearly jumped out of my skin when a bright beam of light shone out of the darkness straight in our eyes, and behind the light in the darkness heavy boots squelched in the mud. The beam seemed to nail us to the board like rabbits. A voice said in German from the dark, "*Wer sind Sie? Was Machen Sie hier?*" Who are you, what are you doing here? We both had the same reaction of hot anger. He wouldn't get us so close to freedom, he had come too close for his own safety, a few whispered words were enough, we would kick him where it hurt and I didn't care about his future family life. We pressed ourselves against the boards, then the beam wavered and I saw on his uniform sleeve the Swiss insignia of a white cross on a red circle. I said in German, "*Wir sind Holländer.*" We are Dutch. The Swiss guard said, "You must come with me, you are in Switzerland." In the pitch darkness we had crept just across the border. Escapers' luck had been with us. We were free.'

Francis Steinmetz and Hans Larive were taken to Geneva, and after months of planning left the country disguised as Dutch planters bound for Havana. Intercepted at Gibraltar, they found their way to England and by 18 December 1941 they had arrived in London. Here they were debriefed about conditions inside Colditz at the 'Patriotic School of London', an interrogation centre for all escapees from the Continent, and then they faced an audience with Queen Wilhelmina of Holland. 'She was a small dumpy woman, sixty-one years old and badly dressed in the fashion of some twenty years earlier,' recalls Steinmetz. 'In a clear silvery voice she asked after our experiences, and we gave her the message of loyalty of her officers who were in Colditz now, which seemed very far away, and who had not given their parole to the Germans. The Queen was visibly moved, and so were we. After the audience we turned right into the next bar and had a stiff drink.' Both men then went on to serve with the Dutch coastal services for the rest of the war.

The Germans in Colditz did not solve the mystery of the missing Dutchmen until four months later, during a Polish–British attempt, during which they witnessed the manhole being opened. Thereafter it was sealed with concrete, but the horse had already bolted; in September 1941 two more Dutchmen, Major Griebel and Lieutenant Drijber, repeated the method and, using updated information on 'Larive's route', successfully crossed the border at Ramsen. During this attempt the Dutch could not repeat the third man ruse, so they came up with an even more remarkable trick. 'Going through all the possibilities and impossibilities of the methods of escape, the Germans became suspicious of our long Dutch capes,' recalls Damiaem van Doorninck, one of the Dutch officers who helped van den Heuvel plan the manhole escapes. 'So the guards began to count our feet rather than our heads. This was a major problem, so van den Heuvel approached the Poles for help. Among them was a sculptor, who within one week succeeded in making two clay heads, whom we named "Max" and "Moritz".'

The Dutch carried Max and Moritz plus two coats and four boots down to the park to make up the numbers, and thereafter they became a regular feature of many nocturnal *Appells*. Their presence was disguised by the uniform appearance of the Dutch on parade. It was several months later, on 12 December, while Priem was counting and recounting the rigid Dutch formation, that 'Max' was asked to dress to the right. The officer did not move, and to Priem's amazement and the delight of the other prisoners 'Max' was unmasked. He was photographed and given pride of place in Colditz's burgeoning escape museum.

CHAPTER FOUR

The Stage is Set

Aside from the excitements of escaping, the daily reality of Colditz life was imprisonment, twenty-four hours a day, seven days a week. To alleviate the boredom the prisoners began to organise events in the small cobbled courtyard, and in August 1941 this draughty arena played host to the first camp Olympic Games. 'It was an expression of nationalism, I think,' recalls Jim Rogers, a former mining engineer who was one of Colditz's early inhabitants. 'The Poles organised it. I'm sad to say that the British messed it up in the first place by forgetting all about it. When all the Poles and the French and the Dutch were lined up in the courtyard for the opening ceremony, there was an empty gap where the British should have been. We were really quite unpopular, I think.' The opening ceremonies over, international competitions were held in football, volleyball, boxing and even chess.

The British turned up in any assortment of sports gear, and as Rogers recalls, cheerfully came last in every single event. 'What made it even funnier was that the other nations could not make out what the hell we were laughing at. The Poles were deadly serious, the French were exuberant – the honour of France was at stake so they went out to win for that; the Dutch were solemn too, thinking of Queen Wilhelmina, the Belgians followed the French, and we Brits just laughed. That was one of the charms of Colditz, how all these nations reacted to a particular situation.'

The closing ceremony, in which the British failed to win a single medal, was interrupted by a German fire practice. Hoses were trained on the windows above, and when a fireman climbed the extension ladder up to the attics, an officer leaned out and handed him a bunch of flowers. Everyone cheered. Colonel David Stayner, the new Senior British Officer, dutifully sat through the shambles; known affectionately as 'Daddy' by his juniors, he encouraged misbehaviour and 'goon-baiting', the practice of annoying the Germans that the British excelled at. 'I remember one incident when some of the goon-baiters were really getting wild,' remembers Lieutenant Gris Davies-Scourfield. 'Everyone was shouting and screaming, and the German riot squad were ordering us back into our quarters, but it was quite difficult for us all to get back in as quickly as they wanted us to. Then Daddy came forward and stood between us and these rather menacing-looking soldiers, wearing a very smart tropical uniform sent out from home. He undid the buttons of his tunic and he opened it, saying, "Don't shoot my officers, shoot me, shoot me!" It was very dramatic really, and because it was Daddy doing it we all thought it was frightfully funny. Of course, they didn't shoot him.'

In October 1941 Colditz received its first political

prisoner. Giles Romilly was a short dark man in his early thirties who enjoyed boxing and theatre. As a civilian journalist, he had been captured at Narvik in Norway in 1940, where he was reporting for the *Daily Express*. The Germans considered him valuable because he was the nephew of Winston Churchill, 'Nelly's boy' as his uncle referred to him, and therefore useful as a hostage. Romilly had escaped from another camp earlier in the year dressed as a woman, and the German High Command had no intention of letting him try again. The orders to Kommandant Schmidt came directly from Hitler:

1. The Kommandant and Security Officer answer for Romilly's security with their heads.
2. His security is to be assured by any and every exceptional measure you care to take.

Colditz was the obvious home for Romilly; it was the only high-security Sonderlager in the country. Yet the Dutch, French and Polish prisoners had already demonstrated that the castle was far from secure. The Germans decided Giles Romilly would have to be treated differently from the rest of the POWs; he became, in their words, a 'Prominente'. He was nicknamed 'Emil' by the guards and his photograph was posted up around the Kommandantur, so that everyone knew his face. Romilly had the freedom of the courtyard by day, but at night he was locked in a separate cell. The exterior window was picked out in white paint to provide an easier target for the sentries to aim at, should Romilly ever try to escape, and throughout the night the guard would check through a spyhole that 'Emil' was asleep. Initially Romilly protested against the cage he found himself in, flinging his boots against the door whenever the guard appeared, and covering the spyhole with paper. Having a cell to himself soon became a luxury as the camp filled up, and gradually he accepted these inconveniences, but he did not give up his desire to escape; a month after his arrival he was caught disguised as an orderly loading a coal cart. 'Mr Romilly, this is no work for a nephew of Winston Churchill,' chided Priem. 'Please don't make your hands dirty with such a menial task.'

Being a civilian was not all that set Romilly apart from his companions. During the Spanish Civil War he had sympathetically reported on the communist side, and was regarded by some of the senior officers as 'a wayward type'. However, his communist beliefs were 'very much of the parlour variety', and throughout the war he continued to write and send articles back to the *Daily Express* via the byzantine prisoner-of-war mail service. Later in the war Romilly would be joined by other Prominente; captured relations of the King and Queen, sons of generals and diplomats, and members of the aristocracy to whom the Germans attached a price. The fate that awaited the Prominente was never made clear, and the very idea of holding them is revealing of the Nazis' unusual belief that these high-born young men also had some political importance. Many high-ranking National Socialists, including Goebbels and Himmler, held the British aristocracy in particular contempt; but it seems fanciful of them to have imagined that Giles Romilly and the other hostages might protect them from assassination, or alter the course of the war in any way.

While the Germans busied themselves with 'Emil', some of the younger members of the British contingent were finding their escaper's feet. Twenty-five-year-old Airey Neave, a self-assured old Etonian and a veteran of Calais, had been inside Colditz only three months before he made his first attempt to escape. On 28 August, after the evening *Appell*, Neave boldly walked through the courtyard gate dressed as a guard. Unchecked, he gamely sloped off down the cobbled alley towards the Kommandantur. When challenged by a sentry, he replied that he had a message for the Kommandant from Hauptmann Priem, and handed over a brass pass disc he had bribed from a painter. He was let through, and it wasn't until he was choosing a bicycle from the bicycle racks that a squad of excited guards with rifles surrounded him. His home-made 'uniform' was ingenious – it consisted of an RAF tunic he had boiled green and a forage cap made out of a blanket, both of which were correct in shape if not in colour. But it was his 'unGermanic bearing' that revealed Neave's true identity. In a now familiar custom, Neave posed for Lange's camera dressed in his green uniform, which was 'an insult to the German Army', and Priem thought the photograph so amusing he posted it up in the guardroom. 'Gefreiter Neave is to be sent to the Russian front!' he announced at *Appell* the following day, to much good-natured applause.

Airey Neave was sentenced to the standard two weeks in solitary, but the punishment cells were full – indeed, there was a waiting list to get in. To cope with the demand, Oberstleutnant Schmidt had taken over the town jail for his wayward charges, and it was to these that Neave was sent. On his way out of the castle he marched across the bridge, and to his left he noticed a small wicket gate leading to some steps that descended into the dry moat. This swung around the German side of the castle and away towards the woods beyond the park. The detour avoided the gatehouse sentry at the castle's entrance, and potentially was a new route out of Colditz. While Neave sat in his town cell wondering how this information could be useful, Pat Reid stared out of his solitary cell window overlooking the prisoners' courtyard. Opposite stood the great rendered wall of the Saalhaus, the building adjacent to the main gate. Ever the civil engineer, he noticed that there was a window on the third floor which did not correspond to any room to which the prisoners had access. He wondered whether it was connected to the small *Hexengang*, the narrow witches' walk over the main gate which was thought to connect with the attic of the guardhouse. If he was correct, the mysterious window must lie under the stage of the Colditz theatre.

As soon as he was free, Reid investigated his theory. He crawled under the stage and discovered that directly below the boards there were only joists holding up the lath-and-plaster ceiling of the room below. With the help of the Canadian Hank Wardle, he cut a hole in this ceiling and lowered himself down, into the room with the window he had seen from his cell. The locked door opened easily to Reid's universal key, and revealed a corridor leading to the witches' walk over the main gate and then down into the guardhouse. Here was yet another possible exit, if an escaper had the temerity to walk straight through the German guard-room, full of off-duty NCOs. It would only be possible with perfect German uniforms, and with this specific requirement in mind Pat Reid approached the Dutch Escape Officer, 'Vandy'. He explained the route to his counterpart, and then told him he had already initiated an unofficial competition among the British to make the most convincing German uniform. John Hyde-Thomson and Airey Neave were short-listed, Neave having already demonstrated that he possessed the assurance and the tailoring skills required for such a scheme, but their chances would be immeasurably increased if they each went out with a Dutchman. The Dutch spoke

German, and they all wore their invaluable 'Wehrmacht' greatcoats.

Vandy agreed, but when he proposed the idea to his fellow officers he encountered an unexpected reluctance to press their advantage. 'Originally two naval captains were chosen, because they would be more useful when they got out and got back to the Dutch East Indies,' remembers Tony Luteyn. 'But none of us knew what would happen if we were caught in German uniform, because the Geneva Convention does not protect you if you are caught impersonating the enemy. You might be court-martialled and shot. So these two captains – who had families back home – decided that though they wanted to escape, not in that way. Then Vandy got very angry, and he said, "Very well, I'll take these two youngsters," pointing at me and Donkers. And because I had the best home-made uniform I was paired up with Airey Neave, who also had the best uniform among the British. We were to go first.'

While Pat Reid busied himself with preparing the escape route, on the boards above him the British officers were hard at work rehearsing their parts for the first Colditz pantomime. The theatre at Colditz was a curious relic of the castle's luxurious past; situated up on the third floor of the Saalhaus, it was a large dusty room with a sprung floor, opening on to a small proscenium arch at one end. There was a grand piano in the corner, chandeliers hung from the ceiling, and all around there were tatty painted clouds surrounding the laurelled names of famous German artists, whose ranks were swelled by Rossini and Shakespeare. The use of the theatre was a privilege the Kommandant was quick to remove as a punishment, and often performers could not be sure if an escape would cancel their production until the curtain rose on the first night. When it was open, all nations indulged themselves in exotic escapism, producing home-made revues, classics and comedies by Coward, Wilde and George Bernard Shaw. *Gaslight, Rope* and *The Man Who Came to Dinner* were highlights among the many.

'I used to let my hair grow down to my shoulders, because we could never get wigs or make them,' recalls Jock Hamilton-Baillie, a sapper who was one of Colditz's leading ladies. 'And I used to shave my legs, of course, but we had a lot of difficulty getting silk stockings. The Germans gave us a few old ones but they weren't very nice, so I came up with an alternative. I used to rub brown boot polish over my legs and then draw a line down the back of them in pencil, because all ladies' stockings had a seam down the back in those days. The only trouble was I could never get the boot polish off. Well, the Germans used to come to the performances, and I think they rather liked me doing this, and this was the only time I took advantage of their kindness towards me. They allowed me to have a proper bath, which was considered a real luxury as we only had showers in the prisoners' quarters. I had to have it "on parole" – in other words promise I would not try to escape from the bathroom window – but it was the only way I could get the boot polish off.'

As time went on the productions became more professional. The 'girls' were so convincing that after one memorable performance two elderly French officers even invited the leading lady back to their mess for dinner! 'They really did look like women,' remembers George Drew, one of the Colditz stage hands. 'I used to feel quite embarrassed to find myself standing behind one of these chaps in the shower. They all had long hair down to their shoulders, and one began to wonder what was going on.'

Staging these plays required huge dedication and effort. During the theatre's peak periods, particularly the spring of 1944, there were new productions every two weeks, all of which required actors, sets and costumes. The Germans encouraged this activity as it kept the prisoners legitimately busy, and as Colditz town had little in the way of entertainment anything the prisoners provided was welcomed. They allowed theatrical make-up for the *Theatermädchen* to be ordered from Berlin, provided powder paint and white lining paper to change the colour of the sets, and also lent the prisoners 'parole tools' with which to build them. 'Every morning I went down to the guardhouse to draw a set of tools in a carpenter's bag,' remembers Hugo Ironside, one of the set builders. 'We told the Germans that these tools would not be used or copied in any way for escaping purposes, and we stuck to that in true Brit fashion. And I don't think anyone ever misused that promise we made to them. It didn't seem right somehow.' Both parties abided by this arrangement, even if a saw or a chisel was exactly what the prisoners required. They were content to make their own escapers' tools out of gramophone wire, bedsteads, cutlery and anything else they could steal from around the castle. 'Parole tools' were yet another example of the value both sides placed on giving their word, and keeping it.

Like school plays, the Colditz productions enjoyed a far from critical reception. In one of his articles sent back to the *Daily Express*, Giles Romilly described a typical evening out at Colditz theatre, watching *The Importance of Being Earnest*. 'Prisoners of war are perhaps easier to please than other theatregoers,' he wrote. 'They enjoy the glamour of the theatrical evening, which makes them forget the unattractiveness of their daily existence. They like to see their companions costumed and greasepainted, for here the removal of a familiar moustache, or even a mere change of jacket, are minor sensations. They also enjoy party scenes, introductions, and anything else reminiscent of the intimacies of family life. Helped by this circumstance, by its own merits and by a most convincing Lady Bracknell, the play had a very long run of two nights to packed houses of nearly 150 people.'

The Lady Bracknell in question was played by a burly naval sub-lieutenant, Charles Elwell. 'Luckily I had seen Edith Evans playing that part at Oxford not very long before,' he remembers, 'so I had some idea of how do to it. I then played Mrs Eynsford-Hill in *Pygmalion*, and then I was asked to play yet another middle-aged lady and I refused to, because I didn't want to be permanently cast as an old bag. The only trouble with our female parts was that our dresses were made out of paper and during the winter it was exceedingly cold. But even the ingenuity of our dressmakers did not extend to making shoes, so us old bags would march around the stage in our ammunition boots.'

As a leading female, Jock Hamilton-Baillie was not content with his masculine footwear. 'Every pair of ladies' shoes I made I found the heel kept going backwards and falling off. Looking for a better way of securing the heel to the sole I took a spring out of a broken gramophone and coiled it around the heel so it acted like a spring. And it seemed to work. It was only after the war when I came home and I was looking at my wife's shoes that I realised that's how heels are constructed. Without knowing it I'd come up with the same solution.'

Many of these performances were accompanied by the Colditz band, led by Jimmy Yule, a Royal Signaller and accomplished jazz pianist. Yule put his songwriting talents to good use during the autumn of 1941 when an international competition was held to stage a Christmas show. 'We thought we would come up with the idea of something suitably British,' he recalls, 'and decided to get five of the most hirsute individuals in the camp dressed up as chorus girls, in ballet costumes and tutus, and sing this thing called "Ballet Nonsense".'

> Ballet Nonsense, Ballet Nonsense,
> Everything's just mad today.
> Ballet Nonsense, Ballet Nonsense,
> Everything will be OK.
> We are here this crazy night to give of our best.
> We will try to brighten it with laughter song and
>   jest. Oh!
> Ballet Nonsense, Ballet Nonsense,
> Ballet Nonsense all the day.

'Ballet Nonsense' developed into a series of sketches involving a large cast. From the opening number involving five brawny moustachioed ballerinas thumping around the stage, it progressed to an Indian dream, a racy public school farce, and ended in an English pub, 'At the Rose and Crown'. The constant rehearsals provided Pat Reid with ample excuses to be seen in the theatre and continue with his preparations under the stage. Few of the actors above him knew the escape was on. Two of the escapers even performed in the show; Tony Luteyn played the double bass in Jimmy Yule's band, and Airey Neave took the role of the headmaster. Pat Reid himself was the principal ballerina.

'Ballet Nonsense' premièred on 16 November to huge uncritical acclaim. 'It was primarily the production of sex-starved, virile young men, whose minds inclined towards abuse as an antidote,' recorded Padre Platt in his diary. 'There was a good deal of overacting, but each scene was thoroughly alive.' Hauptmann Priem granted it a third day's perform- ance, even attending this final showing himself, and his presence would have brought a neat irony to Pat Reid's escape plan: as the last curtain came down it was intended that Neave and Luteyn would change straight from their show costumes into German uniforms and disappear under the stage to begin their escape. Hyde-Thomson and Donkers would follow the same route the following evening. Unfortunately, the German greatcoats – which had to be immaculate – were not ready in time, and the delay gave Luteyn and Neave ample time to rehearse their new re- lationship. Tony Luteyn's German was fluent, and Airey Neave spoke very little, so he would play lieutenant to Luteyn's captain. Long hours of practice were required to improve Neave's 'unGerman bearing'. 'Normally Airey walked with his hands in his pockets, like most of the British officers at Colditz, slouching around,' recalls Tony Luteyn. 'I had to train him to be subordinate to me, so we spent a week walking in the courtyard, up and down, him walking at my left-hand side, because I was a superior, and when I turned, he had to turn around me. I'm not sure Airey liked pretending to be an upstanding, well-dressed German lieu- tenant, walking with his captain.'

Whatever Airey Neave may have felt about playing the junior officer, he knew it was Luteyn's flawless German which would carry their escape off. As Christmas approached the prisoners received news of yet another French success. On 17 December a party of five Frenchmen accompanied by two guards were sent down to Colditz town to visit the dentist. It was a dank, foggy afternoon, and taking advan- tage of the inclement weather three of them bolted; the guards gave chase, but lost the escapers in the mist, and by

Christmas Eve all three were back in Paris. Their home runs fuelled the end-of-the-year celebrations, and on New Year's Eve officers from all nations joined in a conga that snaked in and out of the living quarters and down into the yard. Eggers let it pass as a festive indulgence. In his diary he tallied the figures for the end of year, and noted with some concern that 104 prisoners had tried to escape from the escape-proof Sonderlager in 49 separate attempts. The un-official league table ran as follows:

1941	ATTEMPTS	DETECTED IN CASTLE	DETECTED OUTSIDE CASTLE	HOME RUNS
FRENCH	30	6	14	10
DUTCH	14	8	2	4
POLISH	19	10	8	1
BRITISH	35	33	2	0
BELGIAN	6	6	0	0

The French had much to celebrate, and the British were well aware that, despite their thirty-five efforts to escape, only two of them had managed to find a way beyond the prisoners' courtyard and outside the castle walls. All their hopes were now pinned on the theatre escape. The date was set for 5 January, immediately after the concert in the theatre. The Camp Orchestra played Beethoven's first symphony to an audience of prisoners and guards. Airey Neave was there, as was Tony Luteyn; playing double bass. Immediately after the performance Pat Reid and Hank Wardle joined Neave and Luteyn up on stage, and once the Germans had dispersed they slipped beneath the boards, crawling towards the camouflaged trap door Reid had made in the ceiling below. The escapers swung down into the dark room, followed by Reid. Using a cigarette lighter to work by, he then picked the lock of the door on to the corridor. The escapers padded along in their socks to the next door which led on to the witches' walkway above the main gate. As Reid struggled with the lock, Neave and Luteyn removed their battledress and stowed it in Red Cross boxes. Underneath they were wearing civilian clothes, over which they buttoned their German greatcoats and hats. Directly below them they could hear the voices of the sentries on the gate. Unable to pick the lock, Pat Reid resorted to unscrewing it from the door, opening up the way to the *Hexengang*. Prisoners and escapers shook hands silently, whereupon Reid locked the door behind them and climbed back into the theatre. The whole operation had taken eleven minutes. Neave and Luteyn waited in the dark, then lit a couple of matches to inspect each other's uniforms. They had no idea what lay before them in the guardhouse. Ten minutes passed; noiselessly they then opened the wooden hatch in the floor of the *Hexengang* and stepped down on to the spiral staircase.

'We crept quietly down the stairs,' recalls Tony Luteyn, 'which led past a room which belonged to the officer of the guard who had just taken our *Appell*. The door was ajar, and we heard German music coming out. We tiptoed past the door, and he sat with his back to us, listening to the radio. If he had turned around the escape would have ended there. We carried on down to the ground floor, and stopped outside the guardroom. We heard voices and knew guards were inside. Now if an officer comes into a room everybody has to jump up and stand to attention. So when we went in a guard shouted very loud: Attention! And all the other guards sprang up, and we walked in, me first and then

Airey – he had to keep the door open for me. And the sergeant of the guard opened the front door to let us out. Outside there was the first sentry, standing with his rifle. When an officer comes past he has to put his rifle up and shout: "Post number one, nothing to report!" And he said that very loudly, and I thought, Christ, the officer upstairs will hear it. But no, there was no reaction. So we marched down the cobbled path outside the theatre building and, looking up, I saw the faces of the prisoners watching us go.'

The two escapers marched into the German courtyard unchallenged, heading towards the bridge. As they did so two German NCOs came out of the Kommandantur and fell in behind them. It was a tense moment; all four men passed the sentry under the archway – another salute was given and returned. On the bridge Luteyn turned and opened the small wicket gate in the parapet, the gate that Airey Neave had noticed on his march to the town cells two months before. The Dutchman and the Englishman descended into the moat; the NCOs marched on across the bridge.

Once in the moat they followed the path around the castle towards the married quarters. It was dark and there was snow underfoot. Quite suddenly a soldier appeared, bracing himself against the wind. When he drew level with them the escapers saluted; the soldier stopped and stared back. Tony Luteyn realised that a rebuke was expected of him. 'I remembered that this soldier had not returned my salute, so I turned around and scolded him in German. "Why did you not salute your senior officer?" Then the soldier sprang to attention, and he marched away.' Luteyn's perfect German had dismissed any suspicions, and soon the two escapers descended into the snowbound park and reached the darkest part of the wall. Climbing up on to the eight-foot wall proved very difficult in their greatcoats, but they managed it. 'We had to be very quiet because not too far away another sentry was standing,' remembers Luteyn. 'We lay on top of the wall looking at the snowy darkness below us. Was it grass down there, or rocks? If it was rock we could break our legs or strain them. So we jumped, and it was grass.'

Like many Dutchmen before him, Tony Luteyn had memorised Hans Larive's route to the Ramsen salient from Singen. Despite getting lost in the snow, the escapers avoided the border patrols and the ever-inquisitive Hitler Youth to cross the frontier into Switzerland forty-eight hours later. Airey Neave had achieved the first British home run.

CHAPTER FIVE

Le Métro

1942 had got off to a good start with the audacious escape of Airey Neave and Tony Luteyn. It was a breakthrough for the British: they had achieved their first home run and got a foothold on the unofficial escapers' ladder. The following evening, Hyde-Thomson and Donkers left the castle by the same route. But the trick did not work a second time – at Ulm station they met the policeman who had questioned Neave and Luteyn two nights before, and the fact that they were carrying similar identity papers and were travelling to the same destination was too much of a coincidence. They were returned to Colditz on 10 January, but the escape route was kept secret in the hope that others would be able to make use of it. A week later, after several thorough searches, Eggers and Corporal Schädlich found the hole under the stage; it was filled with concrete and the theatre was closed, temporarily.

Yet these reprisals did nothing to dampen British spirits. 'It has taken the British contingent a whole year to bring off one success,' wrote Padre Platt in his diary on 28 January. 'The escape barometer has risen like a hydrogen-inflated balloon.' As the British waited eagerly for news of Neave and Luteyn, the French were also in a state of high expectation. They had begun a project which would, if it proved successful, result in the first mass break-out from Colditz. It was a tunnel – but a tunnel unlike any that had been attempted before. Work had begun on it in the spring of 1941. It was organised by a small group of French officers calling themselves the 'Société Anonyme du Tunnel' – the Tunnel Limited Company. As its name suggests, the group was an exclusive one, made up of nine officers who had spent many hours debating the possibilities of tunnelling out of Colditz.

After surveying the prisoners' courtyard, they decided that their best hope lay in the chapel on the north side of the courtyard – a building to which they had access. They had good reason to believe there might be a crypt beneath the chapel floor. They knew that the Kellerhaus – which lay adjacent to the chapel on the west side of the courtyard – contained a wine cellar, and they reasoned that the cellar might well connect with a crypt; they also knew that the British had been sent an ancient ground plan of the castle which showed a small spiral staircase beside the altar – could this be a bricked-up entrance to the crypt? If the crypt did exist, they hoped it might contain a passage leading under the walls of the castle to the terraces below – and if there was no passage, then it would be easy to burrow outwards from the crypt, which would, presumably, lie below the foundations of the exterior walls. But the first challenge was to find a way into the crypt undetected. They could not begin a tunnel from the chapel itself – although it was regularly opened for services given by the prisoners' chaplains, it was also visited regularly by the German ferrets.

The first of the French tunnel's unique features was its entrance. Adjacent to the chapel, in the north-west corner of the prisoners' courtyard, was a clock tower. Inside it, there was a stone spiral staircase which gave access to all three floors of the Kellerhaus, which were occupied by prisoners. At the top of the staircase, above a flat roof, there was a small room containing the inner workings of the clock; and above that was another attic, directly beneath the pepperpot roof of the tower. From the small room containing the clock, two sleeves had been constructed which descended between the spiral staircase and the rooms below to ground level; these thin, curved shafts contained the ropes and weights that provided the clock with its momentum. The sleeves were accessed through a small compartment on each floor, which the Société Anonyme du Tunnel had discovered in March 1941. They realised that the sleeves ran the entire height of the clock tower, but unfortunately their investigations were immediately discovered by the Germans, who bricked up the access doors and removed the weights and ropes that hung inside the sleeves. Eggers now believed the shafts were impenetrable, and congratulated himself on stopping a hole before it could be used. But the Frenchmen had seen enough to realise that the sleeves might provide them with an exit – if they couldn't gain access from floor level, they would get over the top of the tower and make their entry from the clock tower attic. The stairs up to the attic were barred by a reinforced door, but the expert lock-pickers in the French contingent made light work of it. Once inside the attic, they made a camouflaged trapdoor and descended into the sleeve. They were now eighty-five feet above the prisoners' courtyard – the last place any ferret would look for the entrance to a tunnel. It was the perfect place to begin.

Each evening the French broke into the clock tower attic, and dropped down into the sleeve. They made a series of holes in each floor and built home-made ladders to connect with the floor below. The work progressed quickly, and within weeks they had descended to the ground floor undetected. Their aim now was to get into the German wine cellar, which was dug into the basement of the Kellerhaus, adjacent to the base of the clock tower.

One of the principal tunnel-diggers was Bernard Cazaumayou. He was an officer in the French Foreign Legion and a champion weight-lifter; he was short and stocky and his friends nicknamed him 'the Mole'. 'Our first objective was the wine cellar,' he recalls. 'But how were we going to reach it? It was dug out of the subsoil like every wine cellar worthy of the name, and it included an air duct which was quite wide and a few metres long. With a gradient of about forty-five degrees, the duct led up towards the surface through a thick wall and came to an end at a small grille which opened on to the inner courtyard right by the chapel door. It goes without saying that there was no question of going about our business by day, since the Germans sometimes went to fetch bottles of wine. But at night, there was still a *Posten* [sentry] permanently on guard in the courtyard who moved about whenever he pleased. So it would be necessary to take the utmost care: not the slightest sound, not a single flicker of light.'

Despite the fact that the Germans made use of the wine cellar, Cazaumayou and his fellow diggers decided to gain access to its ventilation shaft. Before them lay an enormous concrete slab. The tunnellers dismantled parts of the now defunct clock to make several iron levers, and on 15 August Cazaumayou, Godfrin and Barras – 'the strong-armed boys' – inched the slab from its hole. When night fell, a Frenchman slipped down the ventilation shaft and into the German cellar. What he found was disappointing: the cellar did not connect to the crypt – or to anywhere else. 'It wasn't an end to our difficulties, but we had at least achieved our first success,' recalls Cazaumayou. 'All of us thought it only right – since effort should not go unrewarded – to sacrifice one or two bottles of Tokay, that lovely Hungarian white wine. This bucked everyone up and we decided that our Gallic palates were in a much better position to appreciate the Teutonic taste in wine. The whole manoeuvre was carried out so cleverly that there was not the slightest trace of our having helped ourselves, and even the number of bottles remained unchanged.'

Having gained access to the cellar, the French now had to dig their way out of it, through the foundations of the tower towards the chapel. The five boulders in the cellar wall closest to the chapel were carefully removed, and the tunnellers began digging through the rubble and rock which lay beyond them. The French knew that the Germans visited the wine cellar frequently, and at the end of each shift the five stones were replaced and carefully camouflaged. It was now that the real work began, for the prisoners were tunnelling through the medieval foundations of the castle. The only digging implements they had were table knives and pieces of iron bedstead, broken and fashioned into crude hammers and chisels. More parts of the clock mechanism were stolen to help them create the implements they needed. If they were unable to move a piece of rock they would try to crack it, placing a fat lamp on its surface to heat it and then splashing the stone with cold water. This time-honoured method met with partial success, but it was often quicker to scratch around the boulders, and dislodge them one by one.

Digging a tunnel took patience and perseverance, but the French knew that if they managed to complete it, a mass break-out would be on the cards – as many as two hundred French officers would be able to escape the castle. They had set their sights on getting out in time for the Leipzig Trade Fair in September 1941. Leipzig was only twenty-four miles from Colditz, and the trade fair would attract hundreds of foreigners from all over Germany – many of them would be French-speakers, and the officers would be able to mingle with the crowds. With this date uppermost in their minds, the tunnellers struck out into the castle's ancient foundations.

Progress was slow – some nights, they got no farther than eighteen inches. Aside from a handful of fortress prisons at Tittmoning, Spangenberg and Laufen, most POW camps in Germany were purpose-built. They were collections of huts laid out on a large flat area, ringed by wire fences; the earth on which they stood was comparatively easy to tunnel through – it could be dug with primitive shovels and the spoils dispersed with relative ease. Maintaining the air supply, and avoiding the risk of the tunnel flooding or its roof collapsing, were the greatest dangers, for the tunnels had to be long enough to allow the escapers to emerge well beyond the perimeter fence. But the French officers soon realised that Colditz Castle was a different proposition: it was built on rock, and its foundations – a mixture of boulders, rubble and concrete – had lain undisturbed for centuries. 'If I had known how difficult it would be,' remembers Cazaumayou, 'I would never have started.' He was not alone – over the summer, news filtered back to Colditz that Alain Le Ray had made a home run, and he was soon followed by Mairesse Lebrun; it was clear that there were easier ways out of Colditz.

After tunnelling through twelve feet of foundations, the tunnellers found themselves underneath the chapel, where they came up against another obstacle – a huge boulder four feet wide and weighing 150 kilos was wedged into the rubble before them. With extreme care, Cazaumayou and Barras dug out a hole beneath the boulder; they then had to find a way of removing it, without being crushed beneath it. It was a delicate task, and it was an Englishman – Frank 'Errol' Flinn – who unwittingly provided the solution.

Flinn had been walking around the courtyard watching a workman carrying out some repair work. He saw that the German had left his crowbar on the ground beside his feet, and he made a lightning decision – in full view of the guards, he ran up to the workman, grabbed the crowbar and escaped up a staircase. The bar was passed from hand to hand and secreted in a hide. 'I didn't know anything about the French tunnel,' recalls Flinn. 'I just thought it would be useful. It turned out that this crowbar was a godsend to them, and in fact when they loosened the boulder, with great risk to themselves, it came down with such a thump the whole castle seemed to shake.' Later, Flinn learned from a French friend that he would have a place on the tunnel break-out, should it take place – the only officer outside the French contingent to be thus honoured.

The boulder was safely beneath them, and now Bernard Cazaumayou came face to face with the underfloor of the chapel. A three-hundred-year-old oak joist barred his progress. 'It was about twenty centimetres thick, and very very hard,' he recalls. 'So we made some saws out of kitchen knives, cutting teeth into them as best we could. They were very bad saws. We lay on the cold stone floor cutting away. It was dark, cramped, hellish work. And it took for ever. I remember thinking I must have gone mad.'

As Cazaumayou scratched at the massive oak beam, he was still hoping that the chapel crypt would lie beyond it – if so, they would advance forty-five feet at a single stroke to a point where they could resume digging into the castle's external wall. It took him several nights to cut a two-foot hole in the massive joist, but when he levered it clear, he did not discover the long-hoped-for crypt – just another beam, and then another. But Cazaumayou stuck to his task, despite the noise of his sawing. 'Just imagine how the chapel floor acted as a resonance chamber to amplify it! We had to be very cunning and clever to make noise just a few decibels louder than that created by the resonance chamber in order to completely drown it. The hymns during Sunday morning mass and certain other services during the week were just the ticket! We sang along at the top of our voices:

> Let us go forward into the glorious battle.
> Let us walk in the footsteps of Jesus.
> We shall be victorious.
> And be crowned the Chosen people,
> And be crowned the Chosen people.

Hats off to the Poles whose half-patriotic, half-religious hymns were particularly loud, especially when the singers accentuated the rhythm by stamping their feet on the chapel floor.'

It took Bernard Cazaumayou a month to cut holes in the twelve oak beams under the chapel, while others dug out the tunnel around him. The Leipzig Trade Fair came and went, and still there was no crypt. They were forced to admit that it did not exist. But they persevered, and by the end of September 1941 had reached the far wall of the chapel. It had taken three months of extraordinary effort to get this far, and they were now faced with an even larger obstacle – the exterior wall of the castle itself. Fortified by the electors of Saxony four hundred years earlier, it was seven feet thick, and it presented a challenge even to the intrepid French and their table knives. They decided that the wall was too hard to tunnel through, and they took the easier option of burrowing underneath it instead. It was now that the members of the exclusive Société Anonyme du Tunnel realised that they needed help: the original nine members expanded to thirty, and many more volunteers were turned away. The fresh blood brought new enthusiasm to the scheme, and work began on a vertical shaft, parallel to the outside wall and sunk into the rock upon which the castle was built.

By now, it had become apparent to everyone that the French were digging a tunnel. 'The German microphones were quite sophisticated for the time, and I don't understand how they never discovered the origins of the sound,' remembers Jean Chaudrut, a burly French officer who was one of the tunnellers' new recruits. 'The first evening I spent in Colditz I was astonished, because there seemed to be scratching and grating noises coming from everywhere. A German guard was out in the corridor, listening and watching, but he didn't do anything. When we were sawing through the beams there was a noise, when we cleared the spoil there was a noise, and when we resealed the German wine cellar after each shift there was a noise – some people thought that the Germans were well aware of what we were up to and let it continue.'

In fact the Germans were very keen on discovering the tunnel. Sergeant-Major Gephard – otherwise known as 'Mussolini' – recorded in his diary that the tunnel was causing concern: 'We had known for a long time that something was going on, but to discover where was extremely difficult. Our sentries on the inside and the outside of the castle reported almost daily scraping and knocking noises, but could not pinpoint the exact locations – particularly at night, the noises spread over the entire wall. Our search parties were sent out day and night, but they were always unsuccessful – the moment they got anywhere near the "site", the excellent POW warning systems took over; everything was quiet and all we were met with was a dirty grin on the POWs' faces.'

To shorten the tunnellers' day, three *Appells* were introduced during daylight hours, and lightning searches became more frequent, but the work continued as steadily – and as noisily – as before. Soon, the fat lamps inside the tunnel were replaced with electric lights: three new arrivals – Madin, Vidal and Frédo Guigues – had managed to draw a supply from a switchbox inside the sacristy. They also rigged up an electric alarm system; a flashing light warned the tunnellers when the Germans approached sensitive points near their route. The French chaplain, Abbé Jean Jean, contrived to spend as many hours as he could in the chapel, so he could act as a lookout; he also had to spend a great deal of time 'hearing the confessions' of the three electricians in the sacristy. 'I can still see Vidal on his knees and Father Jean Jean hearing his confession,' remembers Guigues. 'There was a whole jumble of electrical wires lying at their feet, less than a metre away from a German ferret who was apologising for having disturbed their spiritual exercise. All of us received crash courses in the catechism, because of our "conversion". Absolutely genuine, of course.' At one stage, the Germans closed the chapel, suspecting that it was being used illicitly, but the Abbé protested, and he was allowed in alone for a couple of hours a day. He continued to stooge for his comrades.

The disappointment of not finding a crypt was compounded by a more serious problem: the disposal of the spoil. The tunnellers had hoped that, had they dug their way into the crypt, it would be a perfect place to dispose of the rocks and rubble they were removing from the castle foundations. But without a hiding-place close to the tunnel face, the spoil had to be carried to the top of the tower and dumped in the attics — a distance of fifty feet horizontally, and one hundred feet vertically. Disposing of the spoil was an arduous task, which involved all thirty-one members of the Société Anonyme du Tunnel. Bernard Cazaumayou remembers the ritual that began after evening roll-call: 'As soon as it was over, the entire group donned battledress — old articles of clothing put on one over the other as protection against the cold and numbness, a scarf over the mouth to prevent the dust from being inhaled, and a scarf swathed about the head like a kind of turban — we had no hard hats, or very few. The two comrades who would be spending the night at the face were the first to enter the tunnel, in a well-defined order — the one who had the best pair of hands leading the way. Once they had reached the Boche wine cellar, they removed the five stones from the blank wall, climbed into the vertical shaft and then made their way beneath the chapel to the bags of rubble stacked there by the previous night's work party.

'The rubble was stockpiled in sacks made from straw mattress covers and sewn up with electrical wires salvaged from an old telephone installation. The sacks were brought up in a sort of hand–to–hand Persian wheel as far as the attic above the chapel, which was, it goes without saying, *streng verboten* – absolutely out of bounds. Each sack weighed between twenty and thirty kilos. It was exhausting work. The most dangerous part of the operation was getting the rubble through the skylight in the chapel roof. The bars of the skylight had been cut with a razor blade, but gaining access to it was difficult, for it was on the fourth storey, overhanging the prisoners' courtyard. One of us had to stay outside, balancing on the rooftop, out of range of the searchlights – and therefore in darkness – to take final delivery of the sacks arriving from the cellar. Then, he had to clutch them in his outstretched arms in order to pass them up through a small skylight, about two metres above him in the gable of the chapel attic. It took a real athlete to succeed in this feat of strength, and only one of us was capable of carrying it off successfully – our comrade Edouard Barras. He could hold a volleyball in his hand as if it were a tennis ball! But he couldn't afford to get it wrong: he couldn't let go of a sack or fall, on pain of being dashed against the floor of the court-yard, or crushing one of the human "buckets" in the chain. Once the rubble had been removed, the two fellows who were to spend the night at the face were "walled up alive" in the cellar by those going back up. Believe me, it is impos-sible to know how we felt without having lived through the experience. It was a nervous ordeal which certainly left some of us suffering from claustrophobia even after several decades of normal life. Finally, at about five in the morning, the two men who had been working all night to fill the sacks would "down tools," retrace their steps back to the cellar wall and wait for the morning shift to dismantle the wall and let them out. The wall was always rebuilt before we left the cellar because the Germans visited it as much as the French.'

Tons of spoil were being spread across the attics. Every night, without fail, the sounds of digging were heard, mocking the Germans' efforts to put a stop to it. Their searches became more and more frantic, but still they were unable to locate the source of the sound. The scratching noises appeared to be coming from all over the north-west side of the prisoners' courtyard. Even the prisoners began to marvel at the French tunnellers' audacity – the British nicknamed the enterprise 'Le Métro', and were convinced that the French were at work with a seven-pound hammer. It seemed inevitable that the tunnel would eventually be discovered, yet the French remained confident. Then, during a search of the prisoners' quarters in November, one of the guards noticed that the ceiling was bulging; Gephard explored the attics, and discovered the spoil. 'Nearly 8 to 10 horse cartloads of it,' he recorded in his diary. 'At one spot so much rubble had been pushed into the ceiling that it came down. This fractured the main water pipe which was installed inside the attic, and, to the great enjoyment of all the prisoners, rubble and water poured down the stairs like a waterfall.'

Eggers was concerned to find samples of porphyry in the spoil – a stone which originated deep below the castle's foundations. He was even more alarmed when traces of mud were found, suggesting that the tunnellers were already beyond the castle walls. Clearly, this was an enormous operation, involving a large number of prisoners. The spoil was only part of the problem – the castle was being systematically 'stripped'. 'From the staircases, corridors and other rarely used rooms, gradually all the electric lights, switches and cables "disappeared,"' wrote Gephard in his diary. 'From the Fürstenhaus attic 300 wooden planks, metal supports and screws were taken off the military beds stored up there, although the doors to these rooms were very securely locked.'

But the entrance to the tunnel was still a mystery. The security officers had to endure not only the taunts of the prisoners, but also sarcastic remarks made by the regional command in Dresden, and even the Wehrmacht High Command in Berlin – both sent security and police to help the beleaguered gaolers of Colditz, but all the searches revealed nothing. The French had been careful to cover all traces of their unlikely entrance, and they had made sure that the other vulnerable point in their scheme – the German wine cellar – looked exactly as the Germans had left it. The chamber was used every day by the Germans, and yet tons of rubble were shifted through it undetected, passed from hand to hand during the night. 'Once a week, in fact, we cleaned all the wine bottles,' recalls Cazaumayou. 'Each time we carried out "Operation Rubble Removal", they became coated with a slightly reddish dust not usually found in a wine cellar. We carefully wiped them, and sprinkled authentic dust on the bottles and the five crucial stones of our tunnel entrance. This dust had to be the right colour, and we collected it from the numerous beams in the attics we controlled.'

By New Year's Day 1942, the French had completed their vertical shaft; it sank fifteen feet below the castle found-ations, at which point they turned and dug horizontally into the earth beyond the exterior wall. Now all that lay between them and their destination – the top of the ravine, beyond the terrace wire – was a few metres of soft soil. By now, hasty preparations were under way to equip all two hundred French officers with civilian clothes, papers, maps and money. They were going to escape *en masse*. A rope was made to carry the escapers down the ravine, and lots were drawn to decide the order in which they would exit. Most of the equipment was hidden deep in the tunnellers' domain – though there was a scare early in the new year, when a German search of the chapel revealed the lower register of the organ pipes to be stuffed with civilian clothes. Abbé Jean Jean protested his innocence, but the Germans scented blood: the ferrets, led by Sergeant-Major Gephard, were in a bullish mood, for they had just discovered the exit under the theatre used by Airey Neave and Tony Luteyn. The French closed the tunnel for three days, and laid low; then they started work again. They were now within twelve feet of the ravine, and the break-out was imminent: it was planned for 17 January.

On 15 January, Gephard paid a surprise visit to the top of the clock tower. He opened the sleeve that housed the balance weight of the clock. He shone his torch down into the darkness, but he could see nothing. He dropped some pebbles down into the shaft, and heard them hit a board on the floor below – camouflage the French had erected to prevent anyone looking down into the shaft and seeing their ladder ropes and pulleys. But the sound of the pebbles landing on the board was curiously hollow, and Gephard decided to investigate further: 'I dropped one of the clock weights, about thirty or forty pounds weight, down the shaft, and it landed somewhere in the darkness with a terrible noise. We now lowered the lamp once more and discovered that there was a ladder there that had not been in the shaft before. It was now clear to us that we were on to something. But how could we get into the shaft? As the electrician and I were too big for the narrow shaft, the skinny electrician's apprentice – who was a young boy – offered to go down. We got hold of a fire hose and tied him to it, and then – very slowly because of the many nails protruding from the wooden casing – lowered him into the shaft. When the apprentice reached the second floor he suddenly called to us: "There are prisoners here!"'

The three prisoners were stitching sacks when the terrified boy appeared, suspended above their heads. Wisely, they did not descend into the tunnel. Instead, they took a length of chapel beam and used it as a battering ram to attack the side wall of the shaft. Gephard and the two guards, who were hauling the screaming boy up through the hole, could do nothing about the frantic battering below. The prisoners crashed through the wall into a bathroom. The bath's occupant – a Belgian called Major Baron de Liedekerke – sensibly got out before the three French tunnellers burst through the wall; they escaped, covered in rubble and sweat, but the tunnel from the clock tower to the wine cellar had been discovered.

Soon, Germans were swarming up and down the ladders of the clock tower, examining the pulleys and sacks. Gephard found it hard to believe that the wine cellar was the place where the tunnel ended, but the tons of rubble in the attic suggested that it was. The Germans spent four days tapping every stone in the cellar, and eventually one of the five camouflage boulders gave way; beyond was the gaping hole that the Germans had been looking for for seven months. It was half a metre wide. A ferret crawled into it, tentatively. He was armed with a torch, but after the first bend he didn't need it: before him were forty-four metres of tunnel, lit and ventilated. The tunnel travelled through the bedrock to the chapel and ran the entire length of the building, passing sawn beams and warning lights; it was 2 feet 4 inches square, and its sides had been worn smooth by the bodies of the tunnellers. A small trolley carried spoil from one end to the other. At the end of the chapel, a shaft equipped with a rope ladder descended fifteen feet under the foundations of the castle, and then the tunnel struck out horizontally, travelling beyond the castle walls and into the soft brown earth of the hillside. At the tunnel face, the ferret heard the guards talking on the terrace above; the French had almost made it.

The Germans estimated there were 1,200 square metres of rubble in the attics: they said it would cost 12,000 Reichsmarks to remove it — a sum they wanted to deduct from the profits of the canteen. More importantly, the Germans closed the chapel indefinitely, and its door remained shut until mid-1943. For a while services were held in the yard. The Germans also installed more microphones around the outer walls of the prisoners' courtyard, in order to help them detect future excavations. Many new tools had been discovered inside the shaft, and the security officers suspected guards and German workmen of providing them. The evidence of large-scale bribery was not lost on the Kommandant, who replaced the entire guard company.

For Eggers and Gephard, discovering the tunnel was a high point: both received a spell of leave as a reward. Eggers was so proud of his achievement that he commissioned a scale drawing of the tunnel, complete with prisoners at work removing the rubble via trolleys and sacks. He saw it as a vindication of his methods. 'This was one of those lucky chances that happen occasionally if one follows a sound principle long enough. In this case, our rule was to close in slowly and methodically upon a suspected danger spot, and ignore lack of results until the job was finished, either successfully or unsuccessfully.'

The French did not share his view: at first, they suspected that the entrance to the tunnel had been revealed by a traitor. Eggers vigorously denied that he had received a tip-off, but the French never forgave him: they nicknamed him 'Tartuffe', in response to his fixed grin and 'diabolical cunning'. Every time he entered the prisoners' yard, he was jeered and whistled at – and the mockery hurt: 'French ingenuity and energy were something to be wondered at, but why so often did they, if I may say so, let themselves down, with stupid and empty personal attacks, on myself and other members of the German staff? Could not the French company have been satisfied with their great contribution to the common stock of prisoner successes, without indulging in childish and, as it turned out, utterly ineffective reactions, which served, surely, only to reaffirm the legendary hate complex between our two countries?'

For Bernard Cazaumayou the price of failure after all his immense labours was particularly hard to take. But he remains philosophical. 'What did we achieve? We succeeded in building a tunnel forty-four metres long, from its starting point twenty-seven metres above the courtyard, to its end point located a few metres from the likely exit eight and a half metres outside the castle wall. We dug it in the space of two hundred and fifty days, and transported and made tons of rubble *virtually* disappear. It required a superhuman effort only dashed at the last moment. But it is still there.'

The French tunnel can indeed still be seen inside Colditz Castle. It was the largest and most ambitious 'alteration' made to the castle during the Second World War. No other tunnel rivalled it in length – and, had it succeeded, no other scheme would have got as many people out.

CHAPTER SIX

Running the Jail

During the winter of 1941/2 there were heavy snowfalls. Exposed on its hilltop, Colditz Castle was a bitterly cold place – the temperature was regularly twenty degrees below freezing. But the arctic conditions did not dampen British spirits. Despite the failure of the French tunnellers' audacious scheme, they still believed there were ways out of the castle which had yet to be discovered. As Pat Reid stared out of the window at the falling snowflakes, he realised that the weather had provided a possible means of escape. On the other side of the courtyard, above the canteen, was a small flat roof; it lay beneath a blanket of snow three feet deep, which nudged against the windowsill of the British quarters. The other side of the flat roof met a buttress which was in the German part of the camp. The buttress contained a room which Reid knew was sealed – the adventurous Poles had told him as much in their early tours of the castle. Yet there might be a way out and into the Kommandantur – and the weather had provided the perfect opportunity to find out. Reid cut through the window bars and burrowed into the snow heaped on the roof, making a tunnel through which he could crawl. 'It was shaped like an arch, one foot nine inches high,' he wrote. 'The snow caved in at one point but a little cardboard helped to prop it up. The tunnel did not melt with my body heat but, on the contrary, formed a compact interior ice wall.'

When he reached the buttress, Reid scraped a hole in the exterior wall and crawled through into the sealed room. But while he was searching for a way out his luck turned – Hauptmann Priem and the Ferret decided to make a snap inspection of the British quarters. Reid's cut window bars had not been disguised, and minutes later the Ferret drew his pistol and entered the snow tunnel. Reid could see him approach. He forced open a window that overlooked the yard. 'Tools coming,' he shouted, and threw saw, file and skeleton keys into the snowbound yard. Kenneth Lockwood, who was loitering with intent below, gathered up the precious objects and shortly afterwards their owner appeared: he slid down the roof and tumbled over the edge, falling fifteen feet into the yard. Reid's Balaclava and the soft snow cushioned his fall, and the Ferret went away empty-handed. It was an inspired attempt – albeit an aborted one – and it set the tone for the rest of 1942. Many of the Allied officers had spent over a year in captivity, and they had no idea how long the war would last – escape by any means possible was the order of the day. As Eggers himself acknowledged, 1942 would turn out to be 'a peak year'.

The mood of the prisoners inside Colditz was in sharp contrast to Allied fortunes in the war. Throughout January,

Iditz castle by daylight, and searchlight. Photographed circa 1943.

The Laufen Six: *(left to right)* Harry Elliott, Rupert Barry, Pat Reid, Dick Howe, Peter Allan, and Kenneth Lockwood

The Polish contingent

The first men out: Alain Le Ray *(left)* and Pierre Mairesse Lebrun *(right)*

The Toilet Escapers in their home-made civvies: Peter Allan *(standing far left)* and Frank Flinn *(standing second right)*

OPPOSITE PAGE
Home-made impersonations:

Top left Perodeau and little Willi

Top right 'gefreiter' Airey Neave

Bottom left Max the Dutch dummy

Bottom right Lt. Boulé

THIS PAGE
Testing the boundaries:

Left Peter Allan posing in costume at his point of exit

Below left The canteen tunnel emerges

Below Part of Miki Surmanowicz and Mietek Chmiel's 120-foot rope descen

Colditz entertainment:
Above The cast of *Ballet Nonsense* with Jimmy Yule at the piano.
Below The Dutch Hawaiian guitar band with Tony Luteyn *(third left)*

e German team 1941 with Colonel Schmidt *(at centre)*

rporal Schädlich a.k.a. The Ferret

His boss Reinhold Eggers

Left The yard – with prisoners leaning out of their solitary cells

Below An unusual sight – the French are unrecognisably smart for a Bastille Day *Appell*

Rommel's Afrika Korps forced the Eighth Army to retreat towards Tobruk, and by February Singapore had fallen. The Royal Navy had suffered heavy losses in the Mediterranean, and from their bases in northern France, the German U-boats were wreaking havoc among the Atlantic convoys. There was very little for the Allied officers to celebrate, and yet the steady trickle of new inmates were struck by the prisoners' high morale. Corran Purdon, a twenty-year-old Commando captured at St Nazaire, whom the Germans had labelled *Deutschfeindlich*, first encountered Colditz folk during a spell in solitary at Spangenberg. 'They had been caught escaping and were being sent back to Colditz, and I was told I would be joining them,' he recalls. 'Black Campbell and Jimmy Yule were in the cells next to me. I got an idea of the Colditz mentality because they had managed to take a door off its hinges, release us from our cells, and the four of us were rather ostentatiously sitting playing cards on the door when the German came in!' Closely guarded, the party returned to Colditz. 'My first impression was that we were walking across the bridge from the railway station and there was this grim-looking castle in front of us, and as we were crossing the bridge there appeared to be a hell of a lot of noise coming from the castle. The nearer we got to it the louder the noise became. Once inside the castle we came to a great wooden gate which was thrown open and inside was a small cobbled courtyard. And I noticed that all the windows were barred and there were all these grinning faces at the windows, shouting and yelling. And underneath the windows were tables where us new arrivals were going to be documented. And as we stood there, water bombs rained down on to the Germans – the ink and papers flying every-where. Then finally a blazing palliasse was stuffed out of a window, and with that a riot squad doubled in wearing

coal-scuttle helmets and took aim up at the British prisoners. And I thought, My God, the people here obviously treat
the Germans with complete disdain – the morale here is
first-rate!'

Locked in a castle hundreds of miles from the theatres of
war, the prisoners were engaged in their own private battle:
it was known as 'goon-baiting' – annoying the Germans.
Goon-baiting was practised in other camps, but not with
the same zeal or frequency as at Colditz. In many Oflags,
officers were wary of upsetting their captors for fear of
reprisals – the practice of 'comfort before country' gave rise
to 'vigorous knitting and tatting circles', where any baiting
or escaping activity was frowned upon. Allan Campbell,
known as 'Black', was a young Territorial gunner captured
in France in 1940. He recalls his conversation with the Senior
British Officer at Spangenberg Castle:

'"Are you intending to escape?"

'"Maybe."

'"Please do not. We are comfortable here and do not wish
to lose our privileges, our parcels, our walks. That is an order."

'"I may disobey it."'

Faced with such attitudes, those who did want to escape
would go about their business quietly, trying not to draw
attention to themselves. But at Colditz, it was different: the
officers were younger than in other camps – most were in
their twenties or early thirties – and they resented both
captivity and the privations of prison life. It was an officer's
duty to escape, but in the meantime, 'annoying the Germans
was seen as a good thing', too.

Goon-baiting had been practised at Colditz ever since it
was first used as a Sonderlager. When the Laufen Six walked
into the courtyard in November 1940, they were heartened
by the spirit of defiance exhibited by the Polish officers

imprisoned in the castle. It was a tradition which both the British and the French arrivals did their best to uphold. Mairesse Lebrun remembers one warm May night in 1941, when the Germans imposed an unexpected roll-call: 'There was no reason for it – other than to be a damned nuisance. All twenty-five of us in the French barrack room decided that the next time they had a night-time roll-call, we would have some sport. Normally, they would run up the stairs with their boots and guns clattering, and come into the room – a whole group of soldiers and one or two officers. We would stand to attention beside our beds wearing our pyjamas and be counted. So the next night we heard them thundering up the stairs someone shouted, "Everybody, get 'em off!" The Germans came in as they usually did to find us all stood to attention at the foot of our beds, completely naked. The German soldiers couldn't prevent themselves from laughing – it was completely ridiculous. The officer found himself in a ludicrous situation and finally, after five minutes, he said: "Let's go". They couldn't take it. What we had done wasn't bad, but they couldn't take it.'

The guards were easy targets, for they were literal-minded, rigidly disciplined and puffed with pride at their country's military prowess – since for the time being, at least, the war was going well for the Germans. Within the walls of the prisoners' courtyard, where the captors and the captives met, goon-baiting became an art form. It was often at *Appells* – which they had to attend four times a day – that the prisoners expressed their collective dissent. Jimmy Yule recalls the events of a winter night in 1942, when the snow lay thick on the ground in the courtyard: 'The Germans were given to turning us out any old time of day to have a search. Priem, the security officer, had had a few drinks, and when he had a few aboard he was unpredictable. He turned us out at one o'clock in the morning to search our quarters. There was snow on the ground, so we just got out of bed, put our overcoats on, and before we left the room we each grabbed a handful of ash from the fire. Then we arranged ourselves in the courtyard in rows of five, and when we left there was a nice V for Victory in the snow. That confounded the Germans – they couldn't understand it, but everyone was looking out of the windows in the courtyard, whooping and cheering.' Yule recalls 'a wretched guard' trying – and failing – to kick the ash away: 'It was quite a successful evening.'

All the different nationalities in Colditz enjoyed goon-baiting, and they went about it with varying degrees of subtlety. They were fascinated by the methods that other nationalities employed to push the German guards to the limit. The British reserved their greatest admiration for the French, who would murmur a call-and-response chant without moving their lips: '*Où sont les Allemands?*' '*Dans la merde!*' '*Enfoncez-les?*' '*Jusqu'aux oreilles!*' Sustained throughout an *Appell*, the chant would drive the German NCOs wild with frustration.

One of their greatest moments came at the end of a particular parade – as Gris Davies-Scourfield remembers. 'The French just knew how to really get at the Germans. I remember when Püpcke was taking this *Appell* and at the end he suddenly addressed us in German, which we all understood well enough by this time. "Gentlemen, I have a special announcement to make," he said. "You will understand that I'm a soldier like all of you are and I have my orders to carry out, the same as you have, and I'm carrying out one of those orders now – I hope you'll understand that. I'm not sure if you will like what I'm going to say, but the German government has decided to make a very special

offer to officer prisoners of war. Anyone who is a civilian
in normal life, who may have some special profession which
could be useful to the great German crusade against communism in Europe . . .Volunteer, give your name to me and
we'll see what can be done . . . Thank you, gentlemen." He
turned as if to leave, hoping that there weren't going to be
brickbats and catcalls; but we were all so astonished that
there was silence. And then a Frenchman suddenly clapped
to attention and marched forward. The silence intensified.
We thought, Well, surely no one's going to volunteer. We
were wrong. "I would like to be a volunteer," the Frenchman
said. Püpcke could hardly speak, he was so astonished. "You
mean to say you wish to help us?" "Yes, indeed. And what's
more, I hope that you'll give me a maximum amount of
work – the more work you give me to do the prouder and
happier I shall be!" So Püpcke said, "What is your profession? What technical qualifications have you got to offer?"
"Sir, I am an undertaker." There was a slight pause and then
everyone burst out laughing; there was cheering and clapping, and he was marched away to the cooler.'

If the French employed their Gallic wit to great effect,
then the Polish had a very different way of demonstrating
their defiance. The Polish Senior Officer, Lieutenant General
Piskor, had set the tone from the beginning: 'Never show
the Germans you are defeated, be smart at all times. Keep
discipline, and no one must speak to a German except
through an interpreter. No Pole must ever be photographed
with a German.' It was an attitude that manifested itself in
open hostility on parade, as Davies-Scourfield remembers:
'If a German even touched one of them, two Polish officers would immediately come and dust him down where
he'd been touched. They were very offensive – but one can
understand why.'

There was more tension between the Poles and the Germans than there was between the Germans and any other nationality. The guards would constantly remind the Poles that they were an 'inferior race' because their country had been subsumed into Germany. On one occasion, a drunken Priem so insulted the Poles that their adjutant broke ranks and struck him in the face. The antipathy between Poles and Germans was graphically illustrated at the end of Colditz's Olympic Games, which were held in the summer of 1941. Each nation had made a crude flag which they kept in their mess-rooms when the competition was over. The Poles had made a double-headed eagle, and placed flowers in front of it as a remark of respect. But as soon as the ferrets saw the Polish flag, they ripped it down: 'There is no longer a Poland,' they insisted. The Poles were outraged: they went on hunger strike for three days, but to no effect.

Though Colditz's international population served to protect them to some degree, goon-baiting was a dangerous pastime for the Poles. As POWs, they enjoyed a degree of protection under the terms of the Geneva Convention, but the Germans never let them forget that the treaty was only binding between recognised states, and they were soldiers of a country that no longer existed. In some of the other camps in which they had been imprisoned, the Polish officers had been beaten or lined up before firing squads – brutal reminders of their diminished status in the eyes of the Germans. Jewish officers had seen their families dispatched to an uncertain future, and through their secret contacts with Warsaw they knew that the Germans were perpetrating atrocities in Poland.

The British, on the other hand, acknowledged that they had far more licence to insult the Germans. In the first place, their country had never been invaded: 'The British liked to think they were always more cocky than everyone else but that's because they could afford to be,' recalls David Hunter. 'If you were Polish – or even French or Dutch – it must have been worrying to know that if you irritated somebody here, the Gestapo could knock on the door of your house a few days later, and your wife or your sister might get a very rude surprise.' The British officers never believed that they would be on the losing side: it was an item of faith that 'Britain always won wars'.

The British knew the Germans respected them, for they were 'fellow Aryans' – members of the Nordic race with whom they happened to be at war; indeed, many of their military traditions belonged to a common source. They also sensed that they were able to intimidate their guards by virtue of their rank. Most of the guard company at Colditz were either veterans of the First World War or young soldiers not fit for the front, but they had been trained to respect and obey officers, and the British prisoners felt that the guards concealed a secret admiration for their captives. After all, it was the duty of every officer to escape, and the British POWs were young men who had attempted to fulfil their duty. Unlike the other prisoners, the British enjoyed a sense of invulnerability which found its expression in the time-honoured pastime of goon-baiting.

Many of their antics seemed more suited to the school-yard than the parade ground. David Hunter – then an ebullient twenty-two-year-old in the Royal Marines – became adept at making water bombs. 'It was a knack, but I got the hang of it pretty quickly. We made them like a milk carton, to be released if a German sentry was standing with his back to the wall, and wasn't prepared – if he hadn't looked up, or his friend across the courtyard wasn't looking at the window above him. We made water bombs and solid bombs. The solid ones were usually filled with excrement.'

The Germans reserved their greatest respect for Douglas Bader – one of the greatest goon-baiters of all. Bader, the legendary legless fighter pilot, had been shot down over occupied France and sent to hospital at St Omer. In Germany, Bader had already aquired a status similar to that of the Red Baron, and the ruder he was to his captors the more they liked him. He was fêted by a party of Luftwaffe pilots who entertained him in their mess, then they allowed him to sit in the cockpit of an ME 109. Bader escaped from the hospital on a bedrope, and having been recaptured he was sent to Warburg, where he escaped again, only to be discovered on a work party near an airfield. His constant escaping and aggressive attitude towards the Germans ensured his arrival at Colditz; and when he walked into the courtyard the German sentries saluted. He seemed to embody an ideal of conduct – this was the way in which a soldier should treat his captors. His magnetic personality had a similar effect on the other nationalities, who marvelled at the way this tin-legged man intimidated the Germans. The senior British officers were not so easily seduced: they held him in high regard as a courageous pilot, but watched his boisterous antics with appalled fascination. Bader knew this and cared little. 'I know you British officers think I am stupid,' he once told an *Appell*. 'You think I know fucking nothing – but actually I know fuck-all.' It was an uncharacteristically perceptive remark.

But Bader was the senior RAF officer, and there were several young pilots eager to impress him. Invariably, it was Flight Lieutenant Pete Tunstall who executed Bader's orders: once, at Bader's prompting, he dropped a bucket of water on Eggers, and on another occasion, he put a birdcage out of a window containing a dummy of Hitler on a noose, holding a censored anti-British cartoon cut from a newspaper. He wrote letters praising the bombing of German cities and insulted the ferrets. Tunstall was a relentlessly dedicated

goon-baiter, and he believed his wild behaviour was justi-
fied: 'Primarily, I was obeying my orders – which were to
create as much bloody trouble as possible. Before we went
on operations, we had been given a lecture by Johnny Evans,
a famous escaper in the First World War, when he got out
of various prison camps in Germany. He said that the first
duty of a captured officer was to escape – and if escape was
impossible, then you had to create trouble. Dick Howe would
ask me to create diversions during the *Appells*, because they
needed to disguise the fact that someone had escaped. So I
used to blow raspberries in the British ranks, then go over
to the French ranks before they could catch me, and blow
raspberries there; when they came after me, I would hide
somewhere else. But it was no good creating mayhem only
when there had been an escape. To make it seem normal, I
had to do it all the time, so the Germans thought, Christ,
it's Tunstall making trouble again. And I paid for that dearly
– four hundred and fifteen days in solitary, the record for
Colditz, and five court-martials, more than any other prisoner during the Second World War. But it was my job.'

Pete Tunstall's persistently bad behaviour made him an
enemy of Eggers, who, despite being a surreptitious anglophile,
could not abide his jibing and taunts. It also divided opinion
among the British, some of whom did not find his antics
amusing – nor see any point to them: it was not the way officers and gentlemen were supposed to behave. 'I personally
felt rather embarrassed by "the men of spirit", as I think we
called them,' remembers Lieutenant Michael Alexander. 'I
remember once when there was a morning parade and people
were teasing the Germans. There was quite an amiable officer
running the parade, and for some reason he got up against it
and everybody was baiting him. He screamed, "Are you officers or children?" There was a certain element of Brittery –
a sort of ya-booism against the only authority that there was.'

Key
1. Theatre
2. Senior Officers' quarters: British, French, Poles and Dutch
3. Boiler room
4. Shower baths
5. Entrance
6. Punishment cells
7. French quarters
7A. Belgian quarters
8. Parcel office
8A. Parcel office and hospital entrance

THE PRISONERS' QUARTERS

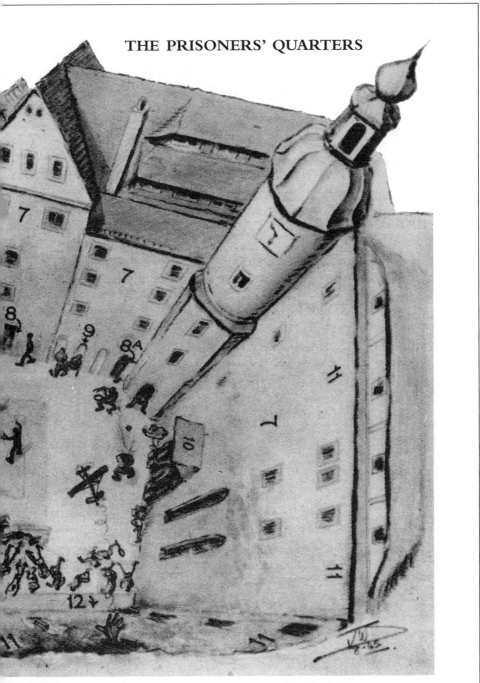

9. Cellar door
10. Chapel
11. British Officers' quarters
12. Medical inspection and dentist's rooms
13. Barber's shop
14. Polish quarters

15. Dutch quarters
16. Canteen entrance
16A. Evidence room
17. Kitchen
18. Orderlies' quarters

Yet few of the senior officers did anything to restrain the antics of the most rebellious men. 'You couldn't control people's high spirits,' remembers Frank Flinn. 'You're stuck in there – three hundred of you – all milling around. It's rather like being at a party, and popping somebody's balloon. You just have to show defiance.' Tunstall and the other 'men of spirit' stuck to their tasks, and enjoyed some success: they confused counts at *Appells* or created trouble to cover the noise of a tunnel being built. But their main function was to keep morale high: 'When I instigated a bit of trouble, the rest of the guys would be wetting themselves with laughter – if there was one thing that everybody loved it was annoying the Germans,' says Tunstall. Reprisals were common: electricity supplies 'failed', hot water 'ran out', and the chapel and theatre were sporadically closed, but the punishments, irritating though they were, did not deter the prisoners. Goon-baiting made the prisoners feel they were running the jail – and in many ways, during 1942, they were right.

The first months of the year saw a goon-baiting campaign which became known as the Great Saluting War. Under the Geneva Convention, POWs were required to salute enemy officers of senior rank, just as they would those in their own army. The regulation caused a great deal of friction in the often strained atmosphere in the prisoners' courtyard: POWs omitted to salute, or delayed before saluting a senior German, and the result was a week in solitary. 'Let's face it, we were bored to death,' remembers David Hunter. 'We had no movies, no news, we didn't know accurately what was going on, and one way of relieving one's boredom was to start some form of internecine warfare. It was deliberately intended to irritate the people who were known to have weak tempers.' Major Rahm, the medical officer, and one of the most irritable Germans in the camp, was a favourite target. Rahm's nickname was 'Tierarzt' – the animal doctor – in ironic recognition of his medical expertise. He would often wander into the courtyard to elicit a salute – or to see those who did not oblige punished.

After the discovery of the French tunnel, a campaign of calculated insolence began. On 19 January, a Belgian, Lieutenant Verkest, crossed the path of Captain Eggers on his way to an *Appell*; Verkest did not salute, and Eggers stopped him and asked him to do so. Verkest refused. Eggers reported the offence to the Kommandant, who ordered Verkest into a cell pending a court-martial, on the charge of disobeying an order. The court-martial was fixed for 24 March. The Belgian pleaded guilty to disobeying an order from Eggers and received a three-year prison sentence, but during the proceedings he had revealed that the whole Belgian contingent had agreed it would no longer salute German officers. The evidence was taken to mean that Verkest was party to mutiny, and on this count he was sentenced to death. The verdict was suspended for three months while confirmation came from the head of state – Hitler himself.

News reached Colditz of the court-martial's verdict on 25 March. On the same morning, Major Rahm entered the prisoners' yard on his way to the sick bay. He saw a group of French and Polish officers and headed straight for them, hoping to harvest their salutes. Instead, the officers split into two groups: one group went to the left, and the other to the right. Rahm pursued one party, and the other turned and followed him, shouting and catcalling: 'Tierarzt, go to Moscow!' When the first group of prisoners left the yard, Rahm turned on the second group, who promptly escaped indoors; then the first group emerged, and began jeering at him again. Soon, the windows of the courtyard were filled with POWs mocking Rahm: 'Tierarzt, Tierarzt!' It was not long before the riot squad arrived, bayonets fixed, to clear the yard. Rahm retreated to the sick bay.

The Kommandant banned visits to the park in response to the demonstration. On this occasion, the Senior British Officer, 'Daddy' Stayner, did not approve of his juniors' actions, and he remonstrated with the Kommandant on the grounds that the British had not taken part. The Kommandant rescinded the ban on the British, whereupon some of the junior officers insisted that they had, in fact, taken part and should be punished with everyone else. Stayner was forced to withdraw, but he pleaded with the British to refrain from such behaviour.

In due course, news came through that Hitler had not upheld Verkest's death sentence: 'Loss of freedom sufficient,' said the Führer's note. In the end, Verkest was sent to Graudenz military prison for two years, and the Great Saluting War died down. It had resulted in one casualty on the German side – Hauptmann Priem, the easy-going, drunken chief camp officer, was replaced by the cunning teetotaller Reinhold Eggers. He believed that his pre-war experience as a schoolteacher was invaluable in helping him run the 'bad boys' camp': 'I knew that the first aim of an unruly class is to make the person in charge angry, what-ever the consequences, and I also knew that if I lost my temper in the position I held in Colditz I had lost the day and possibly the years to come as well,' he wrote. 'I told the Senior British Officer once, "I will never allow you gentle-men the honour of getting me rattled. Correct behaviour under the convention or under our own disciplinary code is my line. Anything your officers do to offend I shall report the fact. What happens then is not my affair." I was provoked beyond belief, time and again for four years on end, by the hotheads among hundreds of officers of all nationalities, ages, ranks and background. Time and again I would start to react and then control myself.'

Eggers' attitude was not shared by all the guard company. There were several officers who firmly believed that strict measures were called for: shooting a few prisoners would quieten things down immediately. But the prisoners were well aware that Colditz was a Sonderlager — a special camp — and the senior officers were in regular contact with Geneva in the hope of improving their conditions. Since Colditz contained high-profile prisoners such as Douglas Bader and the hostage Giles Romilly, the prisoners believed it was under closer observation than other camps. As 1942 wore on, it seemed increasingly clear that the Germans had chosen to treat the prisoners at Colditz fairly. Peter Hoffman, who joined the guard company when he was eighteen, having been declared unfit for military service, recalls the relationship that prevailed within the castle: 'There was a notice on the command post. It said: "It isn't the captured officers who are at fault in trying to escape, but it is the duty of the German Army to prevent these break-outs". They were doing their duty and we were doing ours. We all knew the rules, and we stuck strictly to the Geneva Convention.'

Respect for the letter of the law ensured that the prisoners were never treated brutally. What's more, some of the guards did not seem to care particularly if their prisoners escaped. 'The night before I was planning to escape I left my civilian disguise — cap, boots, jacket: everything — in my cupboard,' remembers Jean Chaudrut. 'After the lights had gone out a German guard, whom we happened to know well, came into the quarters. I was lying down in my bed, hoping he would just count me and move on. But he stopped just by my cupboard, opened it and felt my escape kit hanging there. He paused for a moment, and then left. I could not understand it: did he have no common sense – or did he not care? Or was he just going to wait until my escape happened? It occurred to me that he was wilfully indifferent – he was an old soldier, he had spent years away from his family and he just didn't care. Many of the older guards were like that. They were not aggressive, and you had to really push them to get a rise. They were just doing their job.'

Other prisoners suspected that the guards were under specific orders not to allow themselves to be provoked. '*Dienst ist Dienst, und Pflicht ist Pflicht*' – service is service, and duty is duty – was the cliché often repeated to the offenders as they were marched off to the cells. If Eggers felt that a misdemeanour was worthy of higher punishment, as in the case of Verkest, the prisoner would be recommended for court-martial. In its conduct of the court-martials, the Wehrmacht behaved with scrupulous regard for the Geneva Convention as well: the prisoner was allowed to prepare a careful defence, and engage a lawyer from among his fellow POWs. The chief British defence counsel was Black Campbell, who had just qualified as a barrister at the outbreak of war and handled most of the cases involving British offenders. He would go over their cases in meticulous detail, conducting interviews with defendants and witnesses in quiet corners of the castle – often in the dormitory. Campbell was not always allowed to accompany his 'clients' before the district military court in Leipzig, but he was able to instruct a German civilian lawyer, Dr Naumann, who practised in Colditz town and understood the POW predicament up at the castle – he himself had been a prisoner in Britain during the First World War. The POWs trusted Naumann and were allowed by the Geneva Convention to pay him proper fees. All the prisoners who encountered the military court were impressed by the fairness of the senior German officers who sat on it.

The prisoners inside Colditz took comfort from the knowledge that the Wehrmacht would treat them with scrupulous impartiality. But they could not close their eyes to the chilling evidence of how POWs not protected by the Geneva Convention were treated. During the spring of 1942, groups of Russian prisoners were brought into the prisoners' courtyard to be deloused. They came from the Schützenhaus, another camp in the town where several hundred were employed as workers. Dressed in tattered green uniforms and clogs, they were little more than ragged skeletons. Their ghoulish appearance shocked the Allied officers.

These Russians fared no better than millions of others taken prisoner by the Germans during Operation Barbarossa in the summer of 1941. The Soviet Union had not signed the Geneva Convention in 1929, though it was a signatory to the Hague Convention in 1908, which included some protection for POWs. The Germans were prepared to recognise the Russian POWs as covered by the Geneva Convention, provided the Russians behaved in the same way towards their German prisoners. But Stalin never granted this reciprocity – indeed, he broke off negotiations with the international committee of the Red Cross, granting the Nazis licence to treat the Russians as the inferior beings they believed them to be.

Russian POWs were marched hundreds of miles from the Eastern Front, with little food or shelter; they were reduced to eating grass and worms, and thousands died on the march. Those who survived to reach the German camps were treated little better – they were assigned the heaviest labour, punished for the slightest misdemeanour, and often shot for trifling offences. By the end of 1941 over 2,000,000 of the 3,350,000 captured Russian soldiers had died. Faced with the plight of the 300 Russian POWs in the town camp, the Senior British Officer, Daddy Stayner, approached Kommandant Oberstleutnant Schmidt and asked whether the British could send some of their Red Cross food parcels to the Russians. At first, Schmidt agreed; but then he checked with the Wehrmarcht HQ in Berlin, and withdrew his offer. 'Befehl ist Befehl' – orders are orders – came the reply. The Wehrmacht could tolerate water bombs and high jinks up at the castle, but the Russians were left to starve in the town.

CHAPTER SEVEN

Contact with the Outside

The Geneva Convention ensured that the prisoners of Colditz were treated fairly by their guards, and it also ensured that they enjoyed contact with the outside world. German rations remained as scant and shoddy as ever, but throughout 1942 the thin soup and ersatz coffee were supplemented by a steady flow of Red Cross parcels, which each man consumed at a rate of one a week. Even Eggers was forced to acknowledge that the prisoners were now better fed than their guards.

Gris Davies-Scourfield, who had spent months on the run in Poland before he was recaptured and sent to Colditz in 1942, was struck by this strange prosperity: 'The very first morning I arrived, I was taken under guard into the court-yard. It was very early in the morning. There was no one about. I was taken into the showers, and my clothes were taken away and cooked up. And while I was standing under the hot shower, who should come walking through the steam towards me but Mike Sinclair, who I'd last seen in Warsaw ten months earlier. I had no idea what had happened to him – I didn't know whether he had got home, or been shot. He was standing there holding a large slice of bread thickly covered in margarine and German jam. "I've brought you some breakfast," he said. And my immediate reaction was that I couldn't possibly accept it. The thought of eating one slice of bread just like that was anathema to me. It seemed a really wicked thing to do. "But there's plenty of food here, you know," he said. "The Red Cross parcels come in every week."'

With the food parcels came letters, which were censored before they were passed on to the prisoners. There was no limit to the number of letters a POW could receive, but they were only allowed to write one letter a week, on special forms provided by the Germans. The *Kriegsgefangenenlager* forms were printed on glossy paper, which was designed not to take invisible ink, and letters had to be written in pencil, on the lines provided. If the German censor noted anything suspicious, such as figures and place names, they would be rubbed out before the letter was dispatched to the international postal service in Switzerland or Sweden. The system was overseen by the Swiss government, and it could take up to two months, sometimes longer, for a letter to reach its destination. German families often complained about the length of time it took to receive mail from German POWs held in Canada, and as a result letters to the Canadians imprisoned in Colditz were often delayed; on average, they were six months old by the time they received them.

The censors ensured that intimacy was impossible, but letters were highly valued, and from a very early stage in the war captured officers attempted to convey information to their families through hidden codes. Pat Reid was one of the first to attempt to pass on secret messages during an avid correspondence with an Irish girlfriend, Biddy O'Kelly; unfortunately, she did not realise that he was writing to her in code, and she never understood the true meaning of his surreal billet-doux. Another of the Laufen Six, Rupert Barry, enjoyed more success. Barry knew that his wife, Dodo, was keen on crosswords, and he sent her a letter made up of crossword clues: 'My wife's immediate reaction on receipt of this letter was that I had gone mad – "Poor old Rupert, they've got him down already!" At the time, she was working as secretary to the head of a firm making aircraft valves in Maidenhead, Berkshire. She showed him the letter but he was unable to offer any immediate advice. Then, that night, lying in bed thinking, she suddenly hit upon the clue. She got up and started working on my letter. She was able to get as far as "Go to the War Office . . ."'

Dodo duly presented herself at the War Office, where the rest of the code was deciphered. Barry had asked for diplomatic passes to enable him and other officers to travel in Sweden, but the request was turned down. It was a classic example of communication via a 'dotty' code – so called because the punctuation provided the clue as to how to read it. Dotty codes were in use between many officers and their families during the course of the war. Official sources encouraged their use in certain circumstances, though they felt they should not be used to transmit vital information – they were too easy to decipher.

What was required was a system enabling every officer to use the same easily decipherable code. The War Office came up with an ingenious solution: employing Barry's own crossword code, it wrote back to him to say that Peter Allan and

Kenneth Lockwood had been sent some handkerchiefs and clothes by a 'good works' institution called 'The Prisoners Welfare Fund'. Among the various handkerchiefs was a set of six with coloured borders, and concealed within the clothes was a small packet of sugared almonds. Barry was instructed to drop the yellow almond into a mug of water, and then add the green-bordered handkerchief; he did so and before his eyes the yellow dye 'developed', and the hand-kerchief revealed detailed instructions for a code. Barry memorised the instructions and destroyed the handkerchief. He was now the Colditz proprietor of the 'HK code' – the official system used to communicate with POWs in camps throughout Germany.

Though their knowledge of the outside world was limited, the constant trickle of new arrivals meant that Barry could send back information about troop movements, bomb damage and the whereabouts of certain prisoners. His reports had some value, even if the information was out of date by the time it reached England. In time, Barry taught eight other officers how to use the code, so that long messages could be transmitted via several different letters. When it arrived in Britain, the censor could tell immediately whether the letter was written in code or not by the way the date was expressed, or by its greeting: 'Dear Dad' might be a normal letter; 'Dear *Daddy*' was in code. Each letter-writer had his own system of correspondence. Sometimes, the deception was very simple: Rupert Barry's wife was instructed by MI9 to remind him to correspond with a fictitious old aunt named Christine Silverman who lived in Leeds, and every time he wrote to her the letter was sent straight to the War Office to be decoded. Another of the coded letter-writers in Colditz was Julius Green, an army dentist. He wrote the following coded letter to his mother:

Dear Mum,

How are you keeping?

I will not be home as soon as I thought. Escorted by guards I got out of the train near here and was glad after almost two-days travelling to arrive and meet some English fellows again. Submarine, destroyers, merchant ships, even merchant raiders are represented. Seeing sailors disguised as soldiers is a bit grim when you think of how they have lost their own togs . . .

The letter contains the following message: 'Disguised raiders meet submarine two days out and escorted home'. In this instance, Green was using the HK code frequency 5, 6. 'One had to ascertain the number of words in the message,' he explains. 'This was determined by multiplying the number of letters in the first two words of the first line. "Dear Mum, How are you?" The first two words are: "how" and "are" – both three-letter words. 3 × 3 = 9. Nine words. So a grid was drawn up with nine squares.

	H	**O**	**W**
A	HOME	ESCORTED	OUT
R	AND	TWO-DAYS	MEET
E	SUBMARINE	RAIDERS	DISGUISED

'Then, starting on the second line, we count the words and the fifth word – "home" – is put in the first square, on the top left; the sixth word after it is "escorted", which goes alongside it; then the fifth word after that is "out", the sixth word "and", which goes below "home" in the second row – and so on . . . Every fifth and sixth word gives us

"two-days", "meet", "submarine", "raiders" and "disguised"
... This gives nine words and the message is read by starting
at the bottom right hand corner of the grid, and reading
the words going up diagonally: "Disguised raiders meet
submarine two days out and escorted home."'

Green had to hyphenate 'two-days' to make the word
count correct, and hoped that the censors would not realise
the significance of the misspelling. This kind of discrepancy
usually passed unnoticed. The Germans remained suspicious
of the prisoners' letters, but despite the widespread use of
the HK code across Germany, they were never able to decipher it. This was due, in part, to an additional spelling code
often used in conjunction with the counting code that
allowed the writer to vary the frequency and spell out words
that might catch a censor's eye, such as figures or place names
which would automatically be scrubbed out.

Writing coded letters was a cumbersome business, and the
officers who practised it regarded it as a sacrifice – after all,
they were donating their precious contact with their families
to the escape industry. 'Letters were very important to us,'
recalls David Wheeler, another coded-letter-writer. 'The
letter forms we had to use weren't very large, and in order
to please our German hosts we had to add our names and
addresses as well, so after that there was very little opportunity to write anything. Writing the coded message wasn't
something I enjoyed doing. It took hours and hours, and
one had to make the letter seem authentic – one had to
sustain one's normal style, while making sure, of course, that
the contents meant something quite different. The fact that
it was in code meant that it went to the War Office first,
and when the letter finally arrived at home, it was very late.'

The labour of sending a long coded message home
encouraged officers to think of ways of avoiding the censor.

Peter Tunstall – the goon-baiting scourge of the Germans – had arrived at his own ingenious method before he was sent to Colditz. 'We were allowed to send the odd photograph home stapled to a letter. The Germans would take these snaps and we would pay for them in our camp money, but we were not allowed to write on them. But I had a plan. First, I made a light-box. Then, with a lot of trial and error, I found a way of splitting the photograph open with a razor blade. My plan was to write on the inside, behind the black part of the photograph. Unfortunately, it didn't work – you could see the writing if you held the photograph in front of the light-box, as I knew the Germans did. So I tried something else. I got a piece of bog bumpf and cut it to the size of the photograph. I then carefully made holes in it that corresponded with the light parts of the photo. I used this to write my message in tiny handwriting, and managed to get about five hundred words down. As it was already disguised I could write in straight English. Very carefully I stuck it into the split photo and sent it to my girlfriend with a message: "Split open this photo with extreme care". She got the message and passed the photo on to the War Office.'

During an escape, Tunstall had come across a camouflaged engine-testing site hidden in thick forest. He sent details of its location in a message concealed in one of his carefully doctored photographs. He also sent back details of the movements and methods of U-boats in and out of St Nazaire – information which a downed bomber crew had learned from an indiscreet German coastguard. Both messages were received with interest in London. By the time he arrived at Colditz, Tunstall had shown his patented method to Douglas Bader, who asked him to send a message on his behalf: 'Message from Wing Commander Bader . . .' it began; and ended, 'Bomb the bastards to hell!' Tunstall was eager to help his senior officer, but was understandably reluctant to spend the considerable time and effort involved in doctoring the photograph for such a frivolous message. As fate would have it, he did not have to; during a lightning search of the British quarters, Tunstall threw the photograph and message out of the window to avoid capture. They floated gently down into the yard and landed on Eggers' shoulder. The method was revealed.

The department of the War Office that communicated with POWs was a new branch of the secret service. MI9 had been set up in December 1940 specifically to aid 'escape and evasion'. It began life in Room 424 of the Metropole Hotel, Northumberland Avenue, but later moved to Wilton Park, Beaconsfield, where an extraordinary group of staff officers gathered under Colonel Norman Crockatt, a former head of the London Stock Exchange. They included the legendary Johnny Evans, who had escaped several times from POW camps in Germany during the First World War. Evans was the author of *The Escapers Club* – a classic account of his adventures which many of the inmates of Colditz had read and enjoyed as schoolboys. Evans set up a school in Highgate to teach the art of escape and evasion. His pupils included officers from all three services, who returned to their units to pass on Evans' gospel. His catch-phrase was simple: 'The faster the getaway, the better'. He reminded officers that once behind wire in the middle of Germany, escape would be much more difficult. At first, Evans' advice fell on deaf ears. The Navy in particular, was reluctant to train its men in the art of escape, because it presumed they would not be captured – sailors went down with their ship. This attitude soon changed.

Evans drafted in other successful escapers to spice up his

lectures. Airey Neave, who joined the small staff of MI9 shortly after his return to London in 1942, was able to offer invaluable practical advice. Neave warned his fellow officers that, while escaping, POWs should on no account smoke English cigarettes or offer chocolate to strangers – he had done so, forgetting that the civilian population did not have access to such luxuries, and had almost been recaptured as a result. There was another popular – and almost certainly apocryphal – story about a pilot who was shot down close to a French convent; the helpful nuns gave him shelter, and disguised him in a habit. The following morning, he found himself sitting next to a particularly attractive nun who caught his eye. He attempted to strike up a conversation, and received a sharp rebuke: 'Don't be a bloody fool, man – I've been here since Dunkirk.'

To be prepared for escape, soldiers, sailors and, in particular, airmen had to carry three essentials into combat: a map, a compass and enough food to see them safely home. Each item had to be disguised, for they would be searched when they were captured. If an immediate escape was not possible, MI9 planned to help by sending tools and equipment into the POW camps. What MI9 needed was nothing less than a magician – a man with an ability to conceal escape aids within everyday objects which could be delivered to prisoners by post.

Major Russell of MI9 interviewed candidates for the job in Room 424 of the Metropole Hotel. Here he met a bespectacled middle-aged man in a dark brown suit, who told him he had challenged the great escapologist Harry Houdini to break out of a wooden box of his own design. Houdini accepted the wager, and the box was assembled on stage at the Birmingham Empire. On 2 May 1913, the great escaper was nailed into the box, and only managed to escape because he had bribed the carpenter who made the box to use false nails. The candidate had proved his credentials. 'We are looking for a showman with an interest in escapology,' said Major Russell. 'You appear to fit the bill.' And so Christopher Clayton Hutton joined MI9. Colonel Crockatt immediately recognised that 'Clutty' was not one to do things by the book: 'This officer is eccentric,' he said. 'He cannot be expected to comply with ordinary service discipline, but he is far too valuable for his services to be lost to this department.'

Clayton Hutton had been a pilot in the First World War, and had gone on to work in public relations in the film industry. He could see extraordinary potential in ordinary things – an ability he shared with many of the men for whom he was designing escape aids. He began by making compasses, maps and food parcels. His compasses were hidden inside a pen or the button of a tunic. They were soon discovered by the Germans, so he made others that worked only with a left-hand thread – the more the button was 'unscrewed', the tighter it became. Clutty found other hiding-places for compasses, too, such as bars of soap and walnuts. He magnetised pencil clips – if removed and balanced on the point of the pencil, the magnetised steel swung north – and discovered that maps could be printed on silk; the fact that they would not rustle meant they would survive a search. They were sewn into the lining of flying tunics or disguised as handkerchiefs.

Airmen were especially vulnerable to capture as many were shot down over occupied France and Germany. So Clayton Hutton designed special flying boots: they had hollow heels which contained packets of dried food, and detachable leggings which meant they could easily be converted into civilian brogues. Initially, he was regarded with suspicion within the War Office, but once his aids began to prove their worth in the field, his office was regularly burgled by officers in search of new gadgets. In 1942, to escape unwanted attention, Clayton Hutton built himself a secret underground bunker in the middle of a field, where he could work through the night undisturbed.

But the greatest challenge faced by Clayton Hutton and MI9 was not inventing escape aids: it was smuggling them into POW camps. In Colditz, all the Red Cross parcels and other parcels for the prisoners were stored inside the parcel office, on the ground floor of the prisoners' courtyard. Here, they were counted and handed out across a large counter. Every parcel was opened and searched in the presence of the recipient, so that nothing of any use to an escape could find its way into the camp. With some advice from 'Maskelyne the Magician', a famous conjuror, Clayton Hutton devised numerous hiding-places for his escape aids: a screwdriver was hidden in the handle of a cricket bat, a hacksaw blade inside a comb or a toothbrush, and cheese wire for cutting iron bars was concealed inside shoelaces; he hid maps on the back of playing cards. But Clayton Hutton's masterpiece was the escaper's knife – a complete escape kit in itself, with a strong blade, a screwdriver, three saws, a lock, a forcing tool and a wire cutter.

Clayton Hutton went about his business with vigour, bull-dozing firms into making his escape aids – as reward, they were told they were helping the war effort. He had an arrangement with Waddington's to produce Monopoly sets concealing money, and Gillette, making razors that concealed compasses. MI9's operations created a small industry in 1941 and 1942: as many as 1,642 'naughty' parcels were dispatched to POW camps in Germany, all with Clayton Hutton's escape equipment hidden in their contents. Some of the parcels even surprised their recipients: 'We were sent HMV gramophone records,' remembers Jock Hamilton-Baillie. 'In those days, they were brittle wax and you had to be careful with them. One day, somebody dropped one and it broke, and in the middle of it was a very thin map. So there followed an orgy of breaking all our very precious gramophone records to see if there were any other maps. But there were no other maps and we'd broken all our records, which was rather sad. In fact, we needn't have done it because a more careful prisoner looked at the bits of the record that had the map in it, and it had a dot after the number, whereas the others hadn't; if it had a dot on it, it had got a map behind it, but we found out too late!'

Prisoners were usually tipped off via a coded letter if they were to receive a 'naughty' parcel, but often the clue was in the label. When Kenneth Lockwood began to receive parcels from a clergyman whom he had never heard of, he noticed the sender's address − *Bolt* Court, Fleet St − and thought it might be significant; the parcel contained Reichsmarks and maps printed at a small printing school at Bolt Court − a nondescript institution which MI9 used to manufacture all sorts of contraband. Others received board-games from a certain 'Mrs Mappin' (Map-in), but the most common labels were those of a number of fictitious charities set up to help prisoners of war: 'The Welsh Provident Society', 'The Licensed Victuallers Association', 'The Lisbon Book Fund' − all had distinctive labels that told the observant recipient what they contained. Red Cross parcels were never used by MI9 to conceal escape aids: the food they contained was the prisoners' lifeline, sanctioned by the Geneva Convention, and their status was never put in jeopardy.

Clayton Hutton's concealed escape aids did not pass unnoticed for long: as soon as the Germans began to find objects, every parcel was searched. Early in 1942, Eggers noticed that the hardback covers of books from the Lisbon Book Fund varied in thickness; ripping one open, he discovered a map inside. From then on, all covers were ripped off before the books were handed over to the prisoners. When the guards discovered maps and money inside records, they were routinely broken.

The Germans were forced to admire the ingenuity the British brought to bear on the task of smuggling equipment into Colditz. In 1942, Corporal Schädlich – 'Dixon Hawke', the most feared ferret at Colditz – recorded the following entry in his diary: 'A while ago, five dress uniforms for English officers arrived here. They are made of blue civilian cloth with stiff, high collars, sewn-on pockets and brass uniform buttons. They have an almost civilian appearance and have not yet been handed over to the English, despite repeated requests for them. Fraülein Grunert has made a detailed inspection of them and found nothing suspicious. However, the Mail Inspection had found, hidden in a game, quite a number of civilian buttons. What do they want with these buttons in a POW camp? There has to be a connection between these and the dress uniforms! When we made another detailed search of the latter, we made the following discovery: when the front seam of the collar was opened and the stiffening material pulled out, the collar immediately turned into a soft fold-over civilian collar . . . Pockets and epaulets were only very lightly attached and could be pulled off easily. Within a minute the uniform turned into a civilian suit. A really clever piece of work, proving to us, in connection with all items we found hidden in things sent to the English, that there was an entire industry at work over there that produced escape items and sent them, masterfully hidden, to their POWs.'

Security officers in camps across Germany shared news of their discoveries, and Clayton Hutton was forced to find ever more ingenious hiding-places for his 'toys'. When he learned that every tin of food was pierced top and bottom to reveal its contents, he designed a tin made of two thin sheets of metal; the sleeve in between contained a silk map, so the tin could be pierced and the map would remain hidden. Some of his inventions were foolproof. The magic handkerchief, which had so effectively revealed the HK code to Rupert Barry, provided airmen with diagrams of German military aircraft, in case they were able to steal one and fly it home. Innocent-looking blue blankets were treated with the same chemical, so that when they were washed they revealed the pattern of a German jacket – the prisoners simply had to cut out the pattern and stitch it together; elsewhere in the camp was a collection of dyes to create the exact shade of grey required. But perhaps the most valuable document smuggled into Colditz in this manner was a complete ground plan of the castle – the escapers had asked for it in the hope that it might show them where ancient drains and cavities lay in the massive castle walls. MI9 scoured libraries and collections, and eventually found a large nineteenth-century example in the vaults of the British Museum.

As Clayton Hutton stepped up his efforts, POW camps across Germany responded by introducing new security measures. In October 1941, an X-ray machine commandeered from a hospital in Leipzig was installed in the parcel office at Colditz. It was a primitive piece of apparatus, but it revealed many of Clayton Hutton's ingeniously hidden implements. As a result, a safer system was introduced: MI9 told the prisoners via coded letter that a 'naughty' parcel was to be sent into the camp, relying on the prisoner to steal it before it was X-rayed and opened. When a parcel was delivered to the castle, it was deposited in the parcel office, registered and distributed the following day; fore-warned of its arrival, the officers had to find a way into the parcel office, which was separated from the courtyard by two internal doors and guarded by a sentry. Breaking into the parcel office was a formidable challenge even by Colditz standards; and the British took their lead from the French.

French prisoners of war at Colditz were not as well cared for as their British counterparts. Though they received a certain amount of food and comforts from home, there was no French equivalent of MI9 – given the Vichy govern-ment's ambiguous relationship with the Germans, they could not expect escape help from that quarter. The French had to devise their own supply instead. Each officer was allowed four parcels a year, and the French prisoners began sending messages to former inmates of Colditz – elderly officers who had been repatriated – and to their wives and families, requesting that escape aids and other forbidden items be included in their parcels. The French knew when the parcels were going to arrive, which meant that they, too, faced the challenge of entering the parcel office, identifying which parcel contained the contraband, removing it and replacing it with a fake which could be inspected with impunity the following morning. The battle for the parcel office was led by one of the most talented escapers in Colditz – Frédo Guigues.

Guigues had received the perfect training for an escaper. The other French officers referred to him as one of the 'gaz d'arts' – 'blokes from the Poly', for he was a graduate of the Ecole des Arts et Métiers in Paris. His course had combined instruction in the theoretical principles of engin-eering with practical training, and he could turn his hand to almost any craft. Guigues, who was half Egyptian and bore a deep scar across his left cheek, cut a distinctive figure among his countrymen. The amateur locksmiths of Colditz recognised him as the master. Yves Desmarchelier recalls: 'He was our God.'

The Germans knew that the traditional nineteenth-century lever locks in the castle were child's play for the prisoners – their wanderings through the 'locked' corridors and rooms of the castle testified to the fact. In the middle of 1941, they began fitting high-security doors with an additional cruciform lock – a precision mechanism made by Zeiss Ikon. These cylindrical locks fitted into the existing nineteenth-century keyhole, and were the most secure lock available in Germany. A cruciform lock had recently been fitted to the door of the parcel office; Guigues rose to the challenge of picking it. He was able to study the workings of the lock from a door that had been taken off its hinges in the Saalhaus. He also made an enlarged cardboard model of the lock in order to study its workings. The lock was cross-shaped, and when a key was inserted it moved several tiny pistons in their cylinders. Each piston moved a certain distance, the accuracy of which was gauged to a thousandth of an inch. When all the pistons were moved accurately a circular drum could be rotated by the key to operate the lock. For the blank of his skeleton key, Guigues used a spindle stolen from the clock tower. He prepared a precision saw, fashioned from razor blades, and waited for an opportune moment to steal the cruciform lock from the parcel office door. It arose when a German general visited the camp – the lock was removed, and in the short time available, Guigues etched in his blank key the exact depth of the notches required to fit the lock. The two internal doors, which were fitted with traditional locks, presented no problems for him.

The stage was set for Frédo Guigues' first visit to the parcel office. Seventeen men were used as decoys in the yard. 'We were all standing around in the yard talking away,' recalls Bernard Cazaumayou. 'Several of us would distract the attention of the guard, who stood in front of the parcel office. He would walk over to us and we would have a long chat. In broad daylight, Guigues casually wandered over to the door and, holding the skeleton key behind his back, unlocked it. He waited for a signal from one of the other officers, and then he went inside. Another officer would take the cruciform key and lock the door behind him.'

Guigues negotiated the internal doors that separated him from the parcel office storeroom, and picked up his 'dynamite' parcel: it contained five kilograms of tools sent by Madame Guigues. He replaced it with a double, resealed the sack and relocked the doors that led to the courtyard. He signalled that he was ready to leave by pushing a small piece of paper under the door. At the given moment, he reentered the courtyard, was handed the cruciform key and relocked the door behind his back. Using this method, Guigues began to 'abstract' contraband organised by other husband-and-wife teams, including that of his friend Pierre Boutard. 'While at Colditz my husband asked me for a hand-cranked generator,' recalls Madame Boutard. 'Well, I found a chap in Vincennes to make it in two parts. It was so heavy I had to make a second trip on my bicycle to bring the handle. The pork butcher – a trustworthy fellow – sealed it up inside a ham tin for me and I put black wrapping paper on it so that Guigues would be able to recognise it.' The generator arrived safely, as did another set of tools from Madame Guigues; and finally he received two radios.

Yet Guigues was aware that his method was dangerous, and in time he discovered an equally ingenious but far safer

way of stealing the parcels. 'After a parcel had been carefully examined by the German guards, we had the choice
of either retrieving the tins of food straight away, or leaving
them in the store,' he wrote. 'In the latter instance, we were
allowed to read the contents on the label. At this point in
the distribution process, the serving hatch which separated
the searcher from the prisoner was locked in the open position. We were allowed to pick up the tin to read the label
on the "home-made" food. I prepared, in advance, a tin identical to the one I wanted to spirit away. I filled it with
spinach from the kitchen – peelings from swedes – and then
we peed in it. A comrade resoldered the lid – I did say we
were superbly equipped – and stuck on the label we had
salvaged from the previous tin. The wording was always the
same: "Wild boar in sauce", in a one-kilo tin. "Wild boar
in sauce" contained a small box welded shut and in this was
hidden a lot of our underground mail, German marks, money
and addresses of people who could get us across borders. In
our coded language, it was a "dynamite" tin, and we had to
"explode" it. I would go into the parcel office to pick up
the tins of home-made food sent to me. While I was waiting,
one of my comrades would sneak down between my legs
holding the false tin we had made. At the exact moment
when I picked up the tin to read the inscription, I clum-
sily let it slip from my grasp – it didn't even have time to
reach the ground before my comrade gave me the false tin
which I handed back to the searcher with an apology. This
solution made it possible to avoid having to brave getting
into the parcel room just to "explode" a single parcel. It also
meant that if there was a snag of some kind, we could leave
the tin in the store as usual and retrieve it the next time
we were inside the parcel room. Another way of working
the system was to get the tin thrown away. Back in France,

my wife deliberately failed to take the usual precautions for sterilising the contents. As a result, they began to go off *en route* and the tin would be swollen when it arrived. The German stuck his bayonet into it and a foul-smelling gas escaped. Sickened by the smell, he signalled for the tin to be taken out and thrown in the bin. We could retrieve it later. The Wild Boar trick was never discovered.'

Through the skill of Frédo Guigues and the courage of the French officers' wives and girlfriends, they managed to smuggle into Colditz as much contraband as MI9 – though their system was not without its difficulties. In May 1942, a snap *Appell* was called while Guigues was inside the office. Just as he was relocking the internal doors, he noticed that a cat was nursing her kittens in the first room; when he approached, the cat ran off into the parcel office. Knowing that his absence would be noted if he did not attend the *Appell*, Guigues was forced to lock the cat in one room and her kittens in another. The next day, when the Germans saw that the cat had been separated from her kittens, they realised that someone must have been inside the parcels office, even though nothing was missing. Puzzled and concerned, they installed an alarm on the outside door which alerted the guardroom if the door was opened unofficially. But Guigues knew what the Germans were up to, and before the installation was complete the wiring had been intercepted and extended to a switch in one of the dormitories above. Now, as well as being able to enter the parcel office, the French could raise the alarm or shut if off, at will.

Guigues' switch was soon put to bizarre use. Frank 'Errol' Flinn was one of several officers who was beginning to feel the effects of long-term captivity. He had been involved in numerous failed escape attempts, and had paid for his trouble with long spells in solitary. He was well known to the French for providing 'Flinn's bar' – the large tool that had been so useful in removing boulders in the French tunnel. One afternoon, Flinn walked up to the door of the parcel office and began picking the lock in broad daylight. It was only a matter of time before he was spotted by a guard. Guigues alerted Dick Howe and asked him to stop Flinn – the last thing the Frenchman wanted was the Germans to change the cruciform lock. Moments later, they rang the door alarm, and the riot squad rushed into the yard. Frank Flinn was dragged off for another spell in solitary – his tally was 142 days and counting – but the Germans did not change the lock.

The most extraordinary incident to result from the French access to the parcel office has only recently come to light. One of the German NCOs in the camp was from Alsace – the border province that lies between France and Germany. He was well known to the French prisoners because he spoke both French and German. He was often observed hanging around the parcel office, and once or twice he was even seen entering it at night. His activities began to arouse the curiosity of the French – in the paranoid atmosphere of Colditz, they suspected that he might be poisoning the contents of their food tins. To find out what he was doing, Guigues left one of his gang, Yves Desmarchelier – 'Le Petit' – hidden in the store. 'It was the dead of night and I was hiding behind some sacks,' he remembers. 'I saw the Alsatian come in and start tampering with the tins. He looked in a tin, then closed it up, several times. Then he turned around and he saw me move. I rushed at him and we began to wrestle. I tried to strangle him but being rather small couldn't do it properly; Guigues, who had been waiting outside, then appeared, and he had enormous hands and finished him off. When I attacked him the guard had said, "*Fais pas le con.*"

(Don't be a bloody fool!) He spoke to me in French, and at that moment I knew he was a traitor. The next day the Germans found his body and hung him up and said he killed himself.'

According to Eggers, the Alsatian was found dead in the parcels office the following day; apparently he had committed suicide. Either he never suspected what Desmarchelier claimed happened, or he chose to ignore it. If Desmarchelier's story is true, it is the only time that physical violence was directed at a member of the guard company throughout the four and half years Colditz was used as a Sonderlager. And the deed was so well disguised that no one suffered the inevitable consequences of murdering a guard.

The French mastery of the parcel office was one of the great breakthroughs in the internal battles at Colditz. They collected parcels for other nationalities in return for escape opportunities, and other perks. But in time, other nationalities mastered the cruciform lock. Through their ace lock-picker – the Australian fighter pilot 'Bush' Parker – the British continued to enjoy access to the parcel office until the end of the war.

CHAPTER EIGHT

Open Season: Summer 1942

Spring 1942. As the winter ended, the escaping season began. The prisoners were now better equipped than ever before, for there were large stores of contraband inside the camp, as the discovery of the Dutch tunnel in March revealed. The Dutch had long believed there was an ancient connection between a lavatory leading off their quarters on the third floor and a buttress on the outside of the castle. They were right: a preliminary investigation from the lavatory revealed that the buttress was hollow and contained a shaft that once served as a medieval 'long drop', ending in a pit below ground level. The Dutch constructed a rope ladder fifty feet long, and clambered down the inside of the shaft to the pit, where they began to tunnel outwards, under the terrace.

But Eggers also had his suspicions about the long drop,

and it was not long before an attentive guard heard the sounds of scraping from an adjoining ground-floor room. Hacking a hole into the buttress, the German ferrets startled the Dutch tunnellers. They beat a hasty retreat, but not before the ferrets glimpsed the rope ladder disappearing through a hole above them; as the ferrets climbed the shaft, two Dutchmen, Hagemann and Dames, set fire to their precious stores of equipment, but the smoke soon forced them into the open, revealing the tunnel entrance. A great deal of Dutch escape equipment was recovered, including home-made passes, money, uniforms, ladders and 'Moritz' himself – the second of the two dummies that the Dutch had so successfully used to make up the numbers on parade. The cache was another significant addition to the Colditz escape museum.

The Dutch store was one of several large hides used by the escape committees of different nationalities to secrete their communal kits. There were also scores of smaller hides maintained by individuals for their own personal use. Equipment was hidden all over the castle: above door frames, underneath stoves, inside walls and under the floorboards – a particular favourite, as the gaps between each floor were filled with earth and rubble. The earth had provided the Electors of Saxony – the original occupants of Colditz – with insulation and soundproofing; it was over a foot deep and could easily conceal bags of uniforms or boxes of passes and tools.

The Germans employed several tactics to try to find the prisoners' hides. Often, the ferrets sneaked about the prisoners' quarters in their rubber-soled boots and attempted to catch them using a hide red-handed. Alternatively, a riot squad suddenly appeared from the gate and rushed towards a staircase. But their efforts were often fruitless, for the prisoners now had an effective system of 'stooging' which operated day and night. Whenever a German entered the yard, the cry of 'goons up' echoed through the quarters. The system depended on a sophisticated set of signals: men spent hours leaning out of windows appearing to read or smoke; if they closed their book or took off their cap, it sent a signal to another window indicating which staircase the Germans were heading for, and any illicit activity in those quarters promptly ceased. The system was not foolproof, but it worked well. Even those not interested in escaping did their turn – there was little else to do all day. Stooging was a part of Colditz life, and Reinhold Eggers was unable to do anything to prevent it.

Since they could not arrive in the courtyard unannounced, the Germans employed another technique. The prisoners were counted four times a day at *Appells*. There used to be a twenty-minute interval between the bell and the beginning of the parade, but Eggers cut it to ten; he hoped to catch absent officers at work in tunnels or in the attics. Once everyone was assembled, sentries were posted on the doors. 'The German officer would announce that we were to stay in the courtyard as there was going to be a search carried out in some of the rooms,' remembers Gris Davies-Scourfield. 'Search parties would go up into the quarters and then they'd really set about the rooms. They'd tear up most of the floor, they'd drill holes with electric drills into the stone and the concrete walls, they'd empty all the straw out of every palliasse and take the beds apart. If there was anything there they were likely to find it, unless it was very well concealed. And if they didn't find anything, they just turned the place upside down and left it. This would sometimes happen in the middle of the night.'

At 6.30 a.m., on 16 April, the Germans mounted their

biggest search to date. The prisoners were marched down into the courtyard while their quarters were ransacked. The search also involved a full body inspection. At 10.30, each prisoner was stripped naked, their hair examined with a torch and their mouth prodded for any sign of contraband in a false tooth. The British were well prepared for such a rigorous examination. 'Pat Reid had some cigars sent to him by some university friends,' recalls Kenneth Lockwood. 'They all arrived in their cases, each in a little cylinder with a screw top. They were Upmann cigars. The name gave us the clue as to how to secrete our false papers and money. They became known as "arse creepers".'

On this particular occasion, the British had the advantage of the French, who were also subjected to the '*codette du légionnaire*'. Lockwood remembers the scene: 'The French didn't have the cigar cases and they used to wrap their contraband up in a sort of foil. But they were a little bit more fastidious than we were, and they attached a piece of string to it. We were all strip searched, and of course the Germans asked the French to bend over. The guard noticed a little bit of string hanging out from their rear department, and he pulled it and out came the contents . . . It rather gave the show away. Now, when it came to the British turn to be strip searched, Monty Bissell stood in line and they asked him to bend over. Monty replied he was not going to bend over without the presence of a padre and a doctor! The Germans were livid, of course, at the implication – so they let him off!' When the British returned to their quarters they found the place ransacked. The Germans had found nothing, and the chaos they left behind was evidence of their frustration.

Occasionally, Gestapo men from Dresden tried searching the castle, thinking, perhaps, that the guard company was not thorough enough. The prisoners regarded their attempts with derision, but it gave them an opportunity to observe the acrimonious relationship between the Wehrmacht and the Nazi policemen. 'Dick Howe and I were standing in this room while Gephard watched the Gestapo turning it upside down,' remembers Kenneth Lockwood. 'We noticed that the searchers had left their keys on the table. I looked at Dick and then moved in front of Gephard while Dick swiped them. He nipped out, gave them to someone else and returned. When the search was over the Gestapo men saw their keys were missing. They asked us, then they asked Gephard, and he just stood there and shrugged his shoulders. Then he turned to me and he gave me a look; he knew damn well we'd pinched them, but he was never going to let on to the Gestapo boys. He liked to see them defeated.' Unknown to Kenneth Lockwood, Gephard was already trading with the prisoners, and storing contraband in his office; Eggers had discovered his treachery, but had chosen to do nothing about it.

In the summer of 1942, Dick Howe took on a more significant role in the British escaping fraternity when he became the new Escape Officer. Pat Reid, who had successfully masterminded the escape of Airey Neave and Tony Luteyn, as well as assisting in many other attempts, had become increasingly frustrated by the rule that bound him; as Escape Officer, he was not allowed to escape himself. Howe, another member of the original Laufen Six, was a worthy successor. He was a captain in the Royal Tank regiment – an approachable and enthusiastic man. The fact that he had set up his own radio company before the war was another advantage, for his knowledge of electricity was to prove invaluable. Finally, Howe played the drums in Jimmy Yule's theatre band, which he believed often put him above suspicion; the Germans did not expect a lowly drummer to be running the British escape operation.

Pat Reid's decision to attempt to escape himself was indicative of the mood of the camp in the summer of 1942. In all, thirty officers attempted to escape during this period, often on consecutive days from different parts of the castle. 'The prisoners and we were engaged in a permanent game of leap-frog,' wrote Eggers. 'First we were ahead with our security barriers, then they were, scheming around them.'

Realising that German security measures were less effective outside the castle, many officers began to attempt to escape while in transit. At the end of April, two Poles, a Belgian and a Briton, Brian Paddon, escaped from a military hospital at Gnaschwitz. All were picked up, except the Belgian, Captain Louis Rémy, who eventually reached a British ship off Algeciras and made a home run. In May, a Frenchman, Raymond Bouillez, was on his way to Stuttgart for a court-martial when he leaped from the train. Train-jumping was a dangerous art which many officers who arrived at Colditz had attempted. Unfortunately, Bouillez hit a concrete post and was found unconscious and bleeding beside the track the following day. He was taken to hospital, where he quickly recovered. Remarkably, he eluded his captors once again and returned to France successfully.

Mike Sinclair was a new arrival who had escaped from Germany once already − he had reached Poland, before fleeing south through Slovakia, Hungary and Yugoslavia, only to be recaptured on the Bulgarian frontier. In June, he made his first attempt to get out of Colditz; he was sent to hospital in Leipzig for treatment for sinusitis and, jumping from a hospital window, escaped to Cologne. But Sinclair was unlucky: the city had just survived its first thousand-bomber

Train Jumpers

raid, and he was caught in a civilian witch-hunt for a downed aircrew who had parachuted into the surrounding woods. He was sent to a Stalag, from where he escaped yet again, before being recaptured and returned to Oflag IVC.

All these escapades provided succour to the prisoners inside the castle. Each escaper was aware that he carried the hopes of the prisoners with him: 'Returning escapers were bad for morale,' wrote Pat Reid. 'Each successful getaway was like a tonic for the rest of the prisoners, even though it usually meant one less bolt-hole for those who remained . . . It was becoming obvious to everybody that once out of the castle, it was an escaper's duty to take very heavy risks rather than return to the fold within the oppressive walls of Colditz. I resolved I would not come back if I ever escaped again and I know it was the decision which many others made as the months of 1942 dragged on.'

Colditz Castle was indeed an oppressive place, and some of its prisoners began to feel the strain of captivity. Don Middleton – a Canadian flyer, and one of the three original inmates of Colditz who welcomed the British in 1940 – became haunted by letters he had received from his wife. He was the first of several to receive a 'Dear John' letter, and it affected him deeply. Believing he should release his wife from their marriage, he slit his wrists, and only an alert friend saved his life; then he tried to provoke the guards into shooting him by throwing a bottle at a sentry, and when he failed, he attempted to cut his throat. Don Thom, another Canadian pilot, maintained a close guard on his friend. Eventually, Middleton was removed to a mental hospital. But the deteriorating mental state of men like Don Middleton increased the pressure on their fellow prisoners. Before the war was over, Don Thom was also certified insane, and sadly he never recovered. They were the first casualties of long-term confinement inside Colditz, and they would not be the last. Watching their brother officers descend into madness provided Pat Reid and others with a greater spur to get out; they did not want to suffer a similar fate.

As summer approached, and the sun began to penetrate over the high walls of the prisoners' courtyard, the usual high jinks began. The arch goonbaiter Pete Tunstall set fire to a pile of wood shavings which were meant to be used to refill the British palliasses; the flames quickly spread to the dormitories, bursting the window panes and filling the British quarters with smoke. Hoses were summoned and water bombs were helpfully aimed by the onlookers, but it was late in the evening before the fire was finally extinguished. 'Lord! How empty of amusement life must be for grown men to welcome fire as a diversion!' lamented Padre Platt. The 'caper' had a dramatic conclusion: the

following week, a water fight was in full swing when the
riot squad entered the yard. The noise was so loud it had
alarmed the people in the town. The NCO ordered the
horseplay to stop – a command that provoked chanting from
the spectators in the windows. The NCO gave another order
– incomprehensible above the din – and the riot squad raised
their rifles to the windows. 'Higher! Higher!' shouted the
prisoners; but the riot squad heard the command to fire –
'*Feuer!*' A fusillade cannoned into the windows of the French
quarters, shattering glass and masonry, and ricocheting into
the neck of Lieutenant Maurice Fahy – a Frenchman who
was leaning out of the third-storey window. When he recovered, the fingers of his left hand were paralysed.

The incident was remembered long afterwards. It was
widely felt that the Germans had overstepped the mark:
their response to the prisoners' high jinks was heavy-handed.
Though the riot squad often doubled into the yard, bullets
were rarely fired, such were the rules of the camp. The officers relied upon the Geneva Convention to protect them.
Shortly after the shooting incident, the Kommandant was
touring the British quarters when he saw a slogan scrawled
on the wall: 'Remember Holzminden'. He asked what it
meant, and was told that Holzminden was a POW camp in
the First World War in which the Kommandant had murdered a prisoner; he was hanged for it after the war. At
Colditz the shooting incident was not repeated and at the
end of the war it was the only occasion that the prisoners
cited for investigation by the war crimes tribunal.

On the morning of 6 July, the camp received a genuine
surprise during the morning roll-call. 'Colonel Kowalczewski
[the Senior Polish Officer] called his men to attention,' recalls
Kenneth Lockwood. 'He marched up to Hauptmann Püpcke
to report the number of Polish officers on parade. In a loud

voice he said, 'Forty-seven officers present – and one traitor.' Ryszard Bednarski – the traitor – was immediately removed by the Germans. The other nationalities were astonished, but it appeared that the Poles had held Bednarski under suspicion for some time. Originally imprisoned in the camp at Murnau, where he was already in the Germans' pocket, Bednarski had been ordered to simulate an escape, so that he might legitimately be sent to Colditz. The Gestapo wanted him there because they suspected that the Polish officers were corresponding with the Warsaw underground; they hoped that Bednarski might be able to discover the names of their contacts.

Bednarski was not a Polish officer – he was not even in the army – and he was unaware that he had been under suspicion since April 1941, when several escape schemes had gone badly awry. At one point, four officers had come up with a plan to escape at night through the prisoners' courtyard. But when the time came, one of them was ill in bed; undeterred, the other three made their bid for freedom. They were caught easily. 'Only three?' said one of the guards who apprehended them. 'Where is the fourth?' The Poles realised that their plans had been betrayed, and other incidents confirmed that there was a traitor in their midst.

Tensions arose because some of the Poles had divided loyalties, as Anthony Karpf, a young Jewish cadet officer at the time, attests; his attempts to escape from a previous camp had been foiled when a group of *Volksdeutsche* – Polish officers of German origin – told the Germans of his intentions. Yet Karpf sympathised with the plight of men like Bednarski: 'We all knew that the Germans had some hold over his family, and that he was in a compromised position, and it is difficult to judge what a man does in that situation. Polish Jews sometimes gave their fellows away, and we knew Jewish police ran the ghettoes and handed men over to the Gestapo. We had been in other camps where there had been Polish informers. But as far as the officers at Colditz were concerned, Bednarski was only worth a rope. It was an officer called Hauptmann who eventually denounced him.'

That night, a hasty court was convened in the Polish Long Room, and the Polish officers gathered to witness Bednarski's humiliation. Once they were all assembled, Captain Lados ordered the traitor to step forward. Colonel Kowalczewski accused Bednarski of treachery, collaborating with the Germans and betraying his country. Another officer stood up and ceremoniously ripped off his epaulets, to shouts of condemnation. Several of his countrymen planned to push him out of a window to simulate a suicide. Kowalczewski then asked the camp Kommandant to remove Bednarski as he could no longer be responsible for his life. Schmidt acceded to his request. But the story of Bednarski has a final macabre twist: after the war, he met fellow Colditz inmate Colonel Mozdyniewicz in a city street in Poland, but by the time the colonel had informed the public prosecutor who he was, Ryszard Bednarski had committed suicide.

The revelation of the Polish traitor did not interrupt the escaping season: there were fourteen separate attempts in July and August 1942, using methods both new and old. Some inmates attempted to change identities, so that they would be sent to other camps; others posed as orderlies; a Frenchman attempted to walk out dressed as a painter; and in an inspired 'snap escape', Bag Dickinson leaped over the wall of the exercise yard in the town cells, stole a bicycle and pedalled forty miles south to Chemnitz before he was recaptured. And there were tunnel schemes galore: Dutch, Polish and British tunnellers set to work, but this time they were not looking for a way out of the castle – they were looking for a way into the German courtyard. A joint Polish and Belgian effort began in the Saalhaus: they hoped to enter the medieval sewers believed to run out underneath the main gate. Pat Reid had the same idea but he had firmer evidence that the drain existed. It has been provided by the unlikeliest of sources – Johannes Lange, the diligent German photographer, sold Reid a pre-war photograph of the prisoners' courtyard, clearly revealing a manhole cover that had since been cobbled over. Following the drain from the delousing shed down to the centre of the yard, Reid discovered the original courtyard drain, on to which the manhole had once opened. But before him stood a brick wall blocking his path. The wall had evidently been built before the war, during the castle's days as a prison – a reminder that they were not the first inmates to attempt to escape from Colditz Castle.

To get round the wall, Pat Reid and Rupert Barry began digging another tunnel that would meet the drain closer to the main gate, but they had not got far before they were caught red-handed. The Poles and Belgians fared little better – nor did the Dutch, who had attempted to enter the Kommandantur by tunnelling into the seam wall that divided the courtyards. The failures were yet another reminder that tunnelling out of Colditz had become extremely difficult since the discovery of the French tunnel – the guards were alive to the prisoners' techniques. The Poles were particularly unfortunate: hidden inside their tunnel was a home-made typewriter and some brand-new tools; the bills for their purchase and a Leipzig telephone number were also discovered. Eggers investigated, and traced the tools back to a former member of the German guard company. The man was found, court-martialled and shot.

But it was not all bad news. Bag Dickinson proved that

snap escapes executed beyond the confines of the castle had at least one advantage – that of surprise. Brian Paddon adopted the same approach. Earlier in the summer, when he had escaped from the military hospital in Gnaschwitz, he had been on the loose as 'a tourist'; he had been recaptured in a train station, but might have succeeded in bluffing his way through the police interrogation had his briefcase not contained a small saw and a wrench for prising bars, and had his travelling companion not been Josef Just. Just was an eccentric Pole who spoke perfect German; his wife had recently been sent 'to the factory' by the Gestapo, and perhaps for this reason he had become a daredevil – even by Polish standards. In April he had jumped from an express train and narrowly escaped death; after a spell in hospital he was returned to Colditz and then he escaped from the solitary cells again, only to be hauled out of the Rhine near Basle several days later. He had become ensnared in the rolls of barbed wire hidden under the surface of the river. This time Just breezed through the busy train stations with Brian Paddon in tow, cracking jokes with strangers and wearing a distinctive khaki-green overcoat, which alerted the railway police. Any further doubts about his identity were removed when he was arrested and asked to take off his underpants; the label on the back read, 'Lt J Just, Oflag 4C'. This proved to be his – and Brian Paddon's – undoing. Later, Eggers discovered Paddon's 'escape rules' scribbled in an exercise book during a search of Colditz. Rule 12 said, simply, 'He who travels best travels alone.'

Paddon, whose endless escape attempts earned him the nickname 'Never a dull moment', had learned his lessons well, and he did not have to wait long for his next opportunity. He had been called to face a court-martial at Thorn, his previous camp, where he had insulted a sergeant-major and accused him of theft. He was escorted out of the castle under heavy guard. He had been thoroughly searched and his possessions had been X-rayed before he left, but Paddon was prepared: his 'creeper' was in place and in the odd collection of smart clothes he had assembled for the court-martial, he could almost pass for a civilian.

He travelled north by train and arrived at Thorn on a Sunday afternoon – the day before his courtmartial was due to begin. 'Pinkerton', (Paddon's own name for Corporal Schädlich) had accompanied him from Colditz, and he warned the guardroom that his prisoner was a '*sehr gefährlicher Ausbrecher*' – a very dangerous breaker-out – and gave Paddon 'a very old-fashioned look' as he was deposited in the camp. The Englishman was determined not to disappoint him. Each morning gangs of prisoners set out from Thorn to work in the fields, and Paddon knew that if he could join one of these lightly guarded parties he would be able to slip away. The soldiers assembled at the camp gates at 7 a.m. and his court-martial began at nine; he had a couple of hours to make good his escape. At Thorn, none of the tactics practised at Colditz were in place: there was no one to help him fudge a count, and no dummies or foolhardy goon-baiters to throw the Germans off the scent. But morale was high – unlike the last time he had been a prisoner here – and he thought the notice on the guardroom door might be significant: 'In future, British prisoners are not to be treated as criminals but as POWs and a more friendly attitude observed towards them'. His fellow prisoners gave him some rations, a slim 'Mappe' briefcase, and an outsized battledress to smuggle him on to the work party: the rest was up to him. He did have one advantage: he knew that 'Pinkerton' was still in the camp, and guessed that he would inform the search party that Colditz men always made for Switzerland.

If so, the guards and dogs would comb the woods to the south of the camp; but Brian Paddon was preparing to go north, to Danzig.

The next morning, Paddon joined the soldiers' work party and slipped behind a haystack at the first opportunity. He changed his outsized battledress for a brown golf windcheater and blue RAF trousers, and struck out into the forest. He was wearing an 'engine driver's peaked hat' and carrying his briefcase, and he cut a conspicuous figure hurrying down the aisles between the trees. In his pocket was the address of a Polish officer's girlfriend in Danzig and a detailed map of the port drawn up by another Polish merchant seaman; his plan was to stow away aboard a ship bound for Sweden. Once the ship had reached the neutral waters of the Baltic Sea, he would reveal himself to the captain, who would, he hoped, protect him until they reached the Swedish coast.

Paddon slipped into character as a Belgian worker called 'Philippe de Raeymakers' – the identity he had assumed before. He was perfectly at ease in his new role – he chatted naturally with curious Germans and once or twice he made a point of helping an old lady off a train. The shadowy world of the escaped prisoner held no fears for him; travelling on local trains and sleeping in waiting rooms, he arrived at the Baltic port without mishap. Mighty German battleships, including the *Scharnhorst*, lay at anchor in the harbour, but Paddon's confidence was undaunted. He sat outside a pub all day talking in garbled German with sailors and stevedores, and keeping a weather eye on the docks. When it was dark, he found a Swedish merchantman moored five hundred yards away from a German sentry. He took his chance and slipped aboard, secreting himself in the coal hold. Unfortunately, the chosen vessel had not yet unloaded its cargo of iron ore in Danzig, and Paddon spent three dark days hiding in 'a shallow grave' he had dug for himself in the corner of the black hold. Each night, he stole up to the engine room to fill his water bottle from the boiler.

On the morning of the fourth day the merchantman finally left port, and six hours later Paddon gathered his courage to present himself to the captain. Black with dust from head to foot, he appeared on the bridge and, revealing his true identity, asked the captain in his best German to guarantee him a safe passage. But the Swedish skipper was taking no chances: a week earlier, another vessel had arrived in Stockholm with eleven French stowaways, and now the Germans would not allow it to 'coal' in Danzig. Angry that Paddon had not waited till they reached Sweden to declare himself, the skipper swung the vessel around; soon, it was steaming back to Germany. Paddon tried every trick he knew – he cited international law, he attempted bribery, and he even threatened to stop the ship's registration at Lloyd's when he returned to England, but the master remained adamant, and held his course for Danzig. Realising this was his final throw of the dice. Paddon appealed to the captain 'as a sportsman': he assured him that nothing less than his life was at stake. His plea was met with silence; then the captain disappeared below to talk to his brother-in-law, the second mate. Paddon stood on the bridge, waiting to see Danzig hove into view again. But when the skipper returned, he had an altogether different air. Approaching the coal-blackened Paddon, he asked him conspiratorially, 'Do you speak Polish?'; Paddon replied with a few words in the garbled Polish he had picked up in POW camps, and the skipper seemed satisfied. He agreed to take Paddon across the Baltic on one condition: when they arrived, Paddon must declare himself a Polish refugee and remain in prison until the captain had left port. Brian Paddon – now 'Stanislaw

Rawinski' – agreed. The ship altered its course once more, and headed for the open sea.

Two days later, the ship berthed at Gëvle, one hundred miles north of Stockholm; it was twilight, on a midsummer evening. Two Swedish policemen came aboard, and Paddon, declaring himself to be a Polish refugee, was removed to the town jail. He attempted to keep his side of the bargain, until he realised the plan had one fatal flaw: as a civilian refugee he would have to return to the vessel until it reached its final destination, which happened to be Hamburg. The thought of reentering Germany to face the wrath of the Gestapo and the bombs of the RAF was too much for him: unable to sustain the charade any longer, Brian Paddon declared his true identity. He had lied to the Swedish police, but the elderly British consul chose to believe his improbable story – that he was not Stanislaw Rawinski, nor was he Philippe de Raeymakers, but a British officer who had escaped from Colditz via Thorn. Paddon was flown to Scotland and then to London, where he enjoyed a private audience at Buckingham Palace. His adventures were received with polite attention, for he was only the fourth British officer to escape from Germany – and at that stage the most senior of the escapers.

For weeks, the prisoners at Colditz knew nothing of Paddon's adventures. Fearing that he might have been executed, the Senior British Officer, Daddy Stayner, pressed the Germans for an answer. Eventually, they reluctantly admitted that Paddon had indeed eluded them, and escaped to Sweden. The effect on British morale was tangible. With two 'home runs' they remained at the bottom of the escapers' 'table', but Brian Paddon had found a new way out of Germany. It would not be long before others attempted to follow in his footsteps.

CHAPTER NINE

Month of Escapes

It was September 1942, and the prisoners realised that their chances of escape were diminishing. Since April, there had been a flurry of attempts, but only the Belgian Louis Rémy, the Frenchman Louis Bouillez and Brian Paddon had made home runs – and all three had escaped from outside the confines of Colditz. Twenty-eight others had tried and failed to escape from the castle itself, and every failure closed another potential hole which would be very difficult to reopen.

Throughout Germany, Allied officers were resorting to more and more audacious tactics in order to escape – earlier in the year, the Frenchman General Giraud had escaped from Königstein Castle by climbing out of a window and clinging to a telephone wire. To make matters worse for the prisoners at Colditz, Eggers had spent the summer at Königstein investigating Giraud's escape, and he had returned with new ideas for improving security.

At first glance, the geography of Colditz castle was simple: the garrison lived in one courtyard and the prisoners in another. But by a curious anomaly, there was one room in the prisoners' courtyard that was used exclusively by the Germans; Stabsfeldwebel Gephard – or 'Mussolini' – had his office adjacent to the sick bay on the north side of the prisoners' yard. The office was as secure as any in the camp, for the door was fitted with a cruciform as well as a standard lock. But the British officer 'Lulu' Lawton, who was also cheerfully known as 'The Black Bitch' on account of his swarthy looks, decided this was the perfect place from which to begin an escape attempt. By the standards that prevailed within Colditz, his logic was flawless: he argued that the Germans would never dream of anyone attempting to escape from Gephard's office – it was far too brazen.

Frédo Guigues – the master of the complex cruciform lock – had one equal in his understanding of its complex mechanism: the Dutch officer van Doorninck. Damiaem van Doorninck was forty – older than many of the officers at Colditz – and his venerable air was enhanced by a full-length red beard. He was something of a scholar; he lectured the English – in English – on cosmography, and the Dutch on higher mathematics, but his greatest skill was repairing watches. Prisoners would take their broken watches to him, and his reputation ensured that the German guards followed suit. Soon, he had assembled a 'parole' tool kit. One tool that van Doorninck had invented was a measuring instrument attached to a micrometer, which he used for gauging the teeth in a cruciform lock. It was accurate to within a tenth of a millimetre. His home-made micrometer measured the distance each piston was required to move, and then he cut a key to fit the lock, filing the four lifting faces and checking them against his gauge. 'I was able to gather all the specific data to make a key for a lock very quickly,' he recalls. 'But my measuring instrument was so weak that a very delicate feeling was required to get the correct indication. Until I had taught somebody else how to do it, I could not escape myself.' It took six months to train his apprentice to his satisfaction – and by the time he was ready to go, Lulu Lawton's plan was nearing fruition.

Van Doorninck's instrument meant that the prisoners could now open every cruciform lock in the castle – including the one on Gephard's office door. Dick Howe asked Pat Reid to mastermind the escape. One evening, Reid broke into the office and assessed its potential. There was a barred window looking out over the terrace to the north; it was directly in the line of sight of the sentry outside, but beneath it Reid noticed the roof of a shed used by the garrison for storing odds and ends of military equipment – old uniforms, underclothes and wooden clogs. They could tunnel into the storeroom from Gephard's office. Reid saw only one potential hitch: they did not know what type of lock was fitted to the storeroom itself. A stooging roster was introduced in the windows above. For days, the prisoners studied the guards' movements on the terrace, until a soldier was seen approaching the door with an ordinary lever key in his hand. The exit was clear.

The prisoners planned to escape as soon as possible – bitter experience had taught them that the longer the preparations took, the higher the chances of discovery became. 'The plan was designed to be executed over two nights,' recalls Kenneth Lockwood. 'On the first, I would pretend to be ill in the sick bay. Pat Reid and Derek Gill would be hiding under my bed, and when all was quiet I would let them out of the sick bay and into Gephard's office. I would lock them in, and they would make a hole into the clothing store – but they weren't to complete it. The following evening, I was to let them and the six escapers into the office, and they would break into the store.' The escape party consisted of three Dutch officers – van Doorninck, Ted Beets and Lieutenant Donkers – and three British: Lulu Lawton, Bill Fowler and Jeff Wardle.

On 8 September, Reid and Gill entered Gephard's office. In the darkness, they removed the floorboards beneath Gephard's desk, which gave them access to the outer wall of the castle; the mortar between the stones was soft, and by morning they had burrowed through to the plaster lining of the storeroom. They also cleared space under the floor so that the escapers could lower themselves down with ease. Depositing all the spoil in a sack, they replaced the floorboards and carefully refilled the cracks with dirt; Lockwood let them out of the office, and the two men crept back to the sick bay, where they hid under the beds until the orderly had made his morning round.

The date chosen for the escape was 9 September. Coincidentally, the first party of Royal Navy officers to enter Colditz arrived on the same day: 'It was really quite a fraught arrival,' remembers submariner David Wheeler. 'We'd come from a troop camp in Silesia and it was late in the evening when we arrived. The inhabitants weren't particularly used to naval officers, so they thought that they'd make it a special occasion. One of our party had hidden himself in the train lavatory, and when the Germans discovered that there'd been an escape on the way, they were bad-tempered and fretful. When we walked into the courtyard, we thought we'd reached some sort of madhouse – the inmates were demonstrating and the German guards were rattling their bullets and shouting and screaming as only Germans can. In the middle of this, Geoff Wardle – a friend of mine who I hadn't seen since the beginning of the war – came up to me and said, "David, I'm terribly sorry I wasn't there to welcome you but the fact is I'm escaping this evening." I thought he was pulling my leg.'

It was exactly the diversion the escapers needed. When the camp finally settled down, nine officers ambled into the sick bay corridor, Kenneth Lockwood told the sick bay's other inmates of the plan, and the escapers hid beneath their beds. As soon as the German orderly left the yard, Lockwood let them into Gephard's office and locked the door behind them. It was 9.45 p.m. They waited in silence – Reid, whose task was to conceal the escape route, did not want to break through the storeroom wall until the small hours of the morning. Just after midnight, the men hidden in Gephard's office heard a door being unlocked: Priem and the Ferret had gone into the sick bay. 'I heard them coming down the corridor and I knew that all eight of them were locked inside the office,' recalls Kenneth Lockwood. 'But there was nothing I could do. Schädlich stopped beside the door and said, "Do you want to look inside the office?" There was a pause. Priem must have been looking at all the locks on the door. "No," I heard him say, "There are so many locks on this door, it's safe." I heard the boots disappear down the passage, and that was that. Luck prevailed.'

At 3 a.m., Reid began to cut through the plaster into the storeroom. Van Doorninck was lowered into the hole and checked that his skeleton key opened the storeroom door. The five others dropped into the storeroom behind him. They had three hours to complete their preparations. During the course of the day, they had smuggled large wooden boxes into the sick bay in sections. The pieces of wood were passed through the hole, and the boxes reassembled. The six men then changed into civilian outfits, and pulled uniforms on top. The plan was simple: they hoped to pass for one of the fatigue parties that were sometimes sent to the storeroom to remove equipment. Van Doorninck, who spoke fluent German, was to play the part of a German NCO – he had shaved off his long red beard and was almost unrecognisable – and Donkers was to act as his private; the other four would pose as Polish orderlies. They knew the guards were changed at 7 a.m. – when they emerged shortly afterwards, the new guard would assume they had entered the storeroom earlier. 'Of course, we could only leave after the changing of the guard – otherwise, the guard would be rather startled to see an escort party emerge from the store knowing that none had been let in!' recalled van Doorninck. Once beyond the terrace gate, they would march down the park road to the gate that gave access to Colditz town. Van Doorninck was trusting to his skeleton keys – or to luck – to get them through the gate. He made three keys of different sizes in the hope that one of them would fit.

One task remained: they had to seal the hole in the wall to cover their tracks. Reid and Gill replastered the hole in the wall in Gephard's office, and van Doorninck repaired the storeroom wall. Before the hole was finally sealed and repainted, Geoff Wardle handed Reid a package wrapped in newspaper: he was keen to leave no traces behind. Lockwood unlocked the office door, and they returned to the sick bay. 'Once inside Pat pulled out a bundle of newspaper and handed it to me,' he recalls. '"Stooge Wardle says this is for you," he whispered. I took it; and it was still warm.' At 7.30 a.m., the orderly came to unlock the sick bay, and Reid and Gill left shortly afterwards.

Sealed in the storeroom, the men of the escape party had

been trying to get some sleep as van Doorninck kept watch. 'Normally the guard was changed at seven a.m. but there was a delay, and it was not changed until seven-twenty. At seven-twenty-five, I opened the door and we all went out in routine formation. I locked the door behind me and we walked past the sentries, who saluted me smartly.' To leave the terrace van Doorninck had to open one more wicket gate, but it posed no obstacle: the key was hanging beside it. The party then marched down through the park to the massive gate in the wall, but the lock proved to be much larger than van Doorninck had anticipated: none of his three keys would open it. 'I turned around and immediately spotted a German NCO holding a huge key in his hand,' he recalls. 'I shouted at him: "Have you got the key?" "Yes – didn't you know that?" he replied. "No, we have only been in Colditz for a few days and at the main guard they told us we could get out by a shorter route through here."' To van Doorninck's surprise, the NCO accepted his explanation: he seemed to understand that newcomers would not be told about short cuts out of the castle. 'He grinned broadly. "Yes, but I live here in the sick bay quarters, and when you want the gate opened you only have to call me." "Thanks," I replied. "Now we know for the future, but could you open the gate?" He took his key and did just that!' As they made their way down to the town, van Doorninck glanced back a few times and saw the NCO standing by the gate, looking after them. 'Apparently he was not quite sure of himself. Once around the bend we vanished into the bush, stripped off our uniforms and dressed neatly in civilian clothes. We then split into three groups, shook hands, said goodbye and wished each other well.'

Their fellow prisoners in the castle tried to cover their escape for as long as possible. At 8.30 a.m., the first *Appell* was called. It revealed ten officers missing. The parade was recounted again and again, but each time it came up with the same number. The guardhouse had reported a night without incident, and at first the Germans thought it was an elaborate joke at their expense. The officers were kept standing in the courtyard while search parties scoured the POW quarters. When two officers were found, the Germans began to lose patience. Reprisals were threatened, and the *Appell* turned into an identification parade. Pete Tunstall was one of the officers found hiding in the prisoners' quarters. He was locked into one of the upstairs rooms while the rest of the officers were held down in the yard. Dick Howe instructed him to create a 'diversion', and he began throwing buckets of water out of the window. Soon, a riot squad came clattering up the stairs to arrest him. Tunstall was dragged off to the cells for yet another court-martial, but the delaying tactics had worked — it was 11 a.m. before the Germans dispatched the first search parties: the escapers had enjoyed a four-hour head start.

In the afternoon, Eggers was told about the 'fatigue party' of Polish orderlies who had been seen leaving the castle. He retraced its steps to the storeroom, where he found van Doorninck's wet plaster. When it was discovered that the hole began under Gephard's desk, the hapless sergeant-major became a laughing-stock, and Priem was furious at having missed such a catch. Once more, Lange was on hand to photograph the escape attempt, but since the original group of 'Polish orderlies' were nowhere to be found, in a bizarre ritual the escape was reconstructed with the German soldiers playing the parts of British and Dutch officers pretending to be Poles.

So far, the plan had worked perfectly. But the escapers knew they would soon be recaptured if luck was not on their side. Operation Mousetrap – the standard response to any escape from Colditz – was set in motion, and a cordon was thrown up around every railway station within a twenty-five-mile radius of the castle. At nightfall, Lulu Lawton – the originator of the scheme – and his Dutch colleague, Ted Beets, were captured at a nearby station, and Donkers and Wardle were recaptured the following morning; only Bill Fowler, an Australian airman, and van Doorninck managed to evade the net.

Van Doorninck was posing as a German architecture student, and Fowler as a Belgian forced labourer. They had already agreed their cover story: they had met by chance, and when they discovered they were going to the same place, they had decided to travel together. They encountered few problems on their journey to the Swiss border, for they were following Larive and Steinmetz's well-documented route. Van Doorninck was so confident that he knew exactly how to cross the Ramsen salient and enter Switzerland that he was prepared to risk recapture in order to help the men they had left behind in Colditz. Before he left the castle, van den Heuvel, the Dutch Escape Officer, had asked van Doorninck to find out if special permits were required near the Swiss frontier. There was only one way he could obtain the information: he had to ask a policeman. It was a dangerous mission and it could very easily result in their recapture; van Doorninck did not tell Fowler that he intended to carry it out.

On a small country road south of Singen, the two men came across a pub beside a stream. There was a motorbike parked outside it. 'I knew that motorbikes in Germany were only used by the Gestapo and other policemen,' recalls van Doorninck. 'If I had not given my promise to van den Heuvel we would have hidden in the wood near by until the bike owner had gone. But this was an ideal opportunity to be confronted by a Gestapo chap at a spot very near the Swiss border, without arousing too much suspicion. Bill's papers stated that he was permitted to spend his leave at a farm near Hilsingen – allegedly, Belgian friends of his were working there under a forced labour scheme. We entered the pub and there indeed was a Gestapo man, taking the fingerprints of the barmaid. The law stated that all people working in public places near the border had to be finger-printed. He gave us a searching glance as we came in, and as soon as he had finished with the barmaid, he came straight over to our table. "Have you any papers?" he asked. "Of course," I replied, and handed him my Dutch passport – the only document I had. After careful scrutiny, he handed it back to me. "That's in order," he said.'

Van Doorninck told Fowler in French that the Gestapo wanted to see his papers. Fowler handed over his identity card and the special leave document – both forgeries made in Colditz. The Gestapo man inspected them, and handed them back; he was perfectly satisfied. But when he left their table, van Doorninck got up and pulled him aside. 'I said that I had found Bill on the platform in Tuttlingen, where he was at a complete loss, because he could speak no German. I told him I had taken it on myself to bring him to what he said was his destination; I asked the Gestapo man whether Bill's story was true, as I did not, of course, want to do anything that would harm the Reich. He said the papers confirmed the story Bill had told me.' Fowler sat drinking his beer; he did not realise that van Doorninck had put his liberty at risk – but at least he had discovered that no special permit was required near the border. That night, both men crossed safely into Switzerland.

The success of van Doorninck and Bill Fowler provided

a much-needed boost to morale within Colditz; it also proved that there were still holes to be exploited. Throughout the summer there had been a change in the composition of the POW contingent inside the castle – parties of Polish, French and Belgians officers had been moved to other camps, making way for more British prisoners. The new arrivals – and in particular the growing RAF contingent, led by Douglas Bader – were to make a special impact on Colditz life. The newcomers appraised the castle with fresh eyes: they were quicker to recognise an escape opportunity than the old boys, who were becoming jaded after years of imprisonment.

One of the new RAF officers was Dominic Bruce, affectionately known as the 'medium-sized man'. He was, in fact, extremely small, and his size had allowed him to attempt escapes that were impossible for anyone else. On one occasion he teamed up with six-foot-five 'Rex' Harrison with the intention of hiding down in the park. Bruce stood on stilts cut into Harrison's trousers, clung to a harness underneath his overcoat, and stuck his head out under Harrison's arm, which was concealed inside a split-football. Unfortunately the scheme was conceived in the British quarters on the second floor, and when, after weeks of practice, the chosen day arrived, Harrison discovered he could not walk down the spiral stairs with Bruce hidden inside his overcoat. At *Appells*, Dominic Bruce's size allowed him to regularly be counted twice: he would stand at one end of the line, and when the German guards counted him and moved on, he would drop behind his fellow officers' backs, run along the line and reappear in the place of a missing man. The tactic was not unique to Colditz, but it was practised with remarkable success, given that the courtyard was overlooked from all sides – any casual German observer stationed in one of the windows above the courtyard would have seen immediately what Bruce was doing. The tactic had proved invaluable for concealing absentees, but it was Bruce himself who was presented with the next opportunity to escape.

At the end of July 1942 Colonel Schmidt reached the age of seventy and retired as Kommandant. He was replaced by Colonel Edgar Glaesche – an officer who was even more self-important than Schmidt had been. He was rarely seen in the prisoners' yard, but he made his presence felt by instituting highly unpopular midnight *Appells* – a measure that provoked another goon-baiting war. He also enforced a High Command order that POWs were only allowed a minimum of personal belongings in their quarters; any surplus was to be removed for storage elsewhere in the castle. On 8 September a squad of guards arrived with an an assortment of boxes for the purpose – and some of them were Red Cross tea chests, three foot square. Soon the courtyard was filled with boxes and kit-bags; it was a perfect opportunity for a snap escape.

Within minutes, the 'medium-sized man' was packed inside one of the boxes, equipped with a rudimentary escape kit – a knife and a forty-foot length of rope made from bed-sheets. The boxes were loaded on to a lorry and transferred to the German Kommandantur. The guards carried Bruce up the spiral stairs to a third-floor room and dumped him on the floor. Fortunately, they did not stack anything else on top of him. Once the room had been secured and the guards had dispersed, Bruce emerged from his box. He discovered that the room he was in overlooked the dry moat on the south side of the castle. When darkness fell, he made his exit.

The following morning, a housewife spotted the bed rope

dangling from the window and reported it to the duty officer. The Germans entered the storeroom and found the empty box on which Bruce had inscribed his parting shot: *Die Luft in Colditz gefällt mir nicht mehr. Auf Wiedersehen!* – The air in Colditz no longer agrees with me. Farewell! Bruce followed Brian Paddon's route to Danzig, pedalling part of the way on a stolen bicycle. But when he reached the port a week later, his luck ran out – he was recaptured trying to stow aboard a Swedish ship, and he returned to Colditz for a spell in solitary confinement. *Auf Wiedersehen* was tempting fate.

Coincidentally, two more newcomers to Colditz also planned to try to escape through the German courtyard. Ronnie Littledale and Billie Stephens had approached Dick Howe with their plan: they hoped to climb through one of the windows in the POWs' kitchen, out across the flat roof of the German kitchen, which was, in effect, a floodlit stage, overlooked by several hundred windows, and then drop down into the courtyard. Here a sentry paced his beat, so they would have to cross the cobbles while the German sentry's back was turned, and then hide in a shallow pit on the south side. What happened next they had no idea – there were only two points of exit from the courtyard, and both were closely guarded. It was a wild scheme – and to the old boys of Colditz, it was wildly unoriginal. In his time as Escape Officer, Pat Reid had heard similar ideas, and had rejected them all; but when Dick Howe asked Pat Reid to help Littledale and Stephens with their scheme, he was tempted. The scheme was mad – so mad that it might even work.

Dominic Bruce had proved that if a prisoner could get into the Kommandantur building undetected, then he could get out the other side undetected. There was one drawback: the dry moat was likely to be closely guarded after Bruce's escape attempt. But Reid did not care – he had just completed two spells in solitary after two failed escape attempts, and he was desperate to avoid another freezing winter inside Colditz. He had been a prisoner in the castle since November 1940, and its crowded rooms, monotonous *Appells* and endless searches were becoming very tedious; he was beginning to think that the German quarters might be the best way out after all. He agreed to join Littledale and Stephens's escape attempt and suggested that a fourth man – the Canadian Hank Wardle – should also be enrolled. Four was a good number: if they succeeded in escaping from the German courtyard, they would travel in pairs.

Reid set his mind to the task in hand. He sent a message to Dominic Bruce in solitary confinement asking about the workshop building of the Kommandantur. The reply was encouraging: the top two floors were unoccupied, though there were Germans below. The door through which he had been carried led to an occupied staircase, but it was kept locked. Reid could see the door from the prisoners' quarters: it was only a couple of yards from the path used by guards coming and going from the Kommandantur, but at night it was thrown into shadow, so a man picking its lock might melt into the darkness. The only other cover was a flower-bed. To reach the German courtyard, the escapers would have to enter the prisoners' kitchen first. But the kitchen was in use all day, and locked at night. Reid found a way into the kitchen through an unlocked window, and examined the bars on the windows that overlooked the German courtyard; one was weaker than the rest, and during the next four days Reid returned to the kitchen and cut through it gradually. On the fifth day he was able to remove the rivet that secured the other end of the bar using a home-made, high-powered punch,

whereupon he replaced the bar in its socket and camouflaged his labours.

Now the exit was prepared, the four escapers gathered
their equipment. They had to move silently and invisibly, so
they wore socks over their shoes, and Balaclavas and gloves
to conceal their skin. Pat Reid had never left the confines
of the castle, but in the course of his many failed escape
attempts he had perfected an elaborate disguise: he would
travel as a Flamand worker; so would Hank Wardle. They
hoped that two Dutchmen, who spoke a mixture of bad
French and worse German, would not incur too much suspicion. Like every escaper who made for Switzerland, Reid
knew Larive's Ramsen border route by heart. They planned
to travel by train, and they had German money to pay for
their tickets. At the last moment, Reid decided to carry a
small suitcase containing spare clothes and a shaving kit.
Carrying the suitcase out of the castle would not be easy,
but he hoped it would make him less conspicuous in the
busy train stations.

On 14 October 1942, Reid and his accomplices entered
the prisoners' kitchen an hour after sunset. They threw off
their uniforms, and prepared to clamber on to the German
roofs. Reid removed the bar he had cut. Gingerly, he opened
the window and climbed out into the glare of the lights; in
full view of hundreds of windows, he crept along the roof
into the shadow of a ventilator chimney. The sentry below
did not break his step. All was well. He dropped into the
shadow of the German storeroom. Moments later, he was
joined by Hank Wardle. The other two men followed. All
four officers were hiding in the elbow of the building,
protected by its shadow. Ten yards in front of them was a
shaft of floodlit cobblestones. They could see the shadow of
the sentry pacing his beat. Now they had to cross the German

courtyard behind the sentry's back. It was the most dangerous part of the plan – and they could not hope to manage it alone. 'From where they hid, Pat and the others could not see the sentry who walked up and down the middle of the courtyard,' remembers Reid's friend Kenneth Lockwood. 'But he could be seen from the rooms of the theatre block which overlooked the German courtyard. Up there, an orchestra was playing, and Douglas Bader was the conductor. They practised for a few days to get the Germans used to the idea. Bader would watch the sentry through the window, and every time the German sentry turned his back, the orchestra would stop playing.'

In one of the breaks in the music, Reid crept to the edge of the storehouse and peered beyond the wall. The sentry was walking straight towards him; by some chance, he did not see him, but it was clear that the orchestra scheme was not working. The music started up once more and then stopped abruptly; this time it did not start again. Evidently the Germans had become suspicious of the orchestra, and its peculiar stop-start rhythm, and had gone to investigate. The four men huddled in the shadow of the German yard now had to take their chances alone.

Reid went first. He listened to the sound of the sentry's boots turning on the cobbles, and made his dash when his back was turned. He ran towards a shed on the other side of the courtyard and dived into a flower-bed. He waited until all was quiet again, and then he crawled slowly along the edge of the flower-bed, across a path and towards the Kommandantur building. His target was the pit they had seen from the prisoners' windows, which was close to the locked door. The pit was not deep, but it provided a little cover. Emboldened by Reid's success, the other three escapers timed their dashes and crossed the courtyard when the sentry's back was turned. All four now lay concealed in the pit; it had taken them three hours to get this far.

Reid crawled along the wall of the Kommandantur to the door that Dominic Bruce had been carried through. In the darkness, he set to work with a key he had specially made for the task of picking the lock. 'I had one unnerving interruption when I heard Priem's voice in the distance returning from the town,' he wrote. 'I had just sufficient time to creep back into the pit and hide before he came around the corner. We laughed inwardly as he passed by us along the path, talking loudly to another officer. I could not help thinking of the occasion when he stood outside Gephard's office and did not have the door unlocked!'

Reid went back to work, but after an hour he gave up: the key he had made would not work. He retreated back to the pit and reported the bad news. It was now 11 p.m., and they were unable to turn back; recrossing the courtyard would be even more difficult than crossing it had been, and the window they had escaped through had been locked behind them. They could not try to escape through the main gates which were guarded and floodlit. They were trapped inside a floodlit courtyard that was home to two hundred German soldiers. Reid's earlier misgivings seemed well-founded.

Their only hope was to find an underground storeroom that connected the yard with the outside wall. It was not a vain hope – such a storeroom might well exist, for Colditz Castle contained seven hundred rooms and countless nooks and crannies. Still carrying their suitcases, the four men crawled along the south side of the garrison building to its farthest corner. Here, in deep shadow, they found steps leading down to a doorway – a feature that Reid thought he had seen from the windows of the theatre block. The door was not locked. Inside, the escapers found themselves in a cellar. It was completely dark. The only glimmer of light came from the far end – on closer inspection, it proved to be an air vent. It curved four feet upwards, to an outside terrace of the castle. Wardle pushed Reid up as far as he could, and Reid saw that the flue narrowed and emerged as a barred slot nine inches wide.

He dropped to the ground again, and they held a hurried conference. Various schemes for finding another way out of the Kommandantur were discussed, but they were all hopeless – the flue was the only way out. Reid was forced to try again. 'This time I removed some of my clothing and found I could slide more easily up the shaft,' he wrote. 'I examined the bars closely and found one was loose in its mortar socket. I succeeded in loosening one end of the bar and bent it nearly double. Slipping down into the cellar again I whispered to the others, "There's a vague chance we may be able to squeeze through the flue. Anyway, it's worth trying. We shall have to strip completely naked." . . . After a tremendous struggle I succeeded in squeezing through the chimney and sallied forth on to the path outside. Bending down into the flue again, I could just reach Hank's hand as he passed me up my clothes and my suitcase, and then his own. I hid the kit in some bushes near the path and put on enough dark clothing to make me inconspicuous. Hank was stripped and struggling in the hole with his back towards me. I managed to grab one arm and heaved, while he was pushed from below. Inch by inch he advanced and at the end of twenty minutes, with a last wrench, I pulled him clear. He was bruised all over and streaming with perspiration. During all that time we were at the mercy of any passer-by. What a spectacle it must have been – a naked man being squeezed through a hole in the wall like toothpaste out of a tube!'

By 3 a.m., all four escapers, their clothes and suitcases had squeezed out of the flue and assembled on the narrow terrace on the outside of the castle. Using the ropes inside their suitcases, they descended the three twelve-foot terraces into the dry moat. At the bottom, they reached the path that led to the married quarters. They picked their way around it, until they reached the road that led down to the park. Since the Dutch and French escapes of 1941, the park wall had been crowned with barbed wire, but it proved only a minor obstacle to the determined men. In the safety of the bushes on the other side of the wall, they shook hands and parted company. 'See you in Switzerland,' they whispered. For once, their optimism was not misplaced: Reid and Wardle made it in less than four days; Littledale and Stephens took twenty-six hours longer.

As the days turned into weeks, the inmates at Colditz began to believe that the escapers had made a home run. On 9 November, Rupert Barry received a postcard from Switzerland: 'We are having a holiday here (in Switzerland) and are sorry you are not with us. Give our dear love to your friend Dick.' It was signed *Harriet* and *Phyliss Murg-atroyd*. It was the news the British had been waiting for.

In the past six weeks, twelve officers had escaped from the high-security Sonderlager, and six had made a home run. It was a remarkable achievement, and the Germans admitted they were at a loss to discover how Reid and his fellow escapers got away. Sniffer dogs traced their path to the air vent, where they discovered the bent bar; inside, a few English toffee papers were found on the floor, but Eggers refused to believe they had been left by escapers. He preferred the theory that the sweets had been given to a guard who had surreptitiously eaten them in the cellar. As far as the Germans were concerned, the four escapers had followed the same route under the theatre as Neave and Luteyn had used ten months earlier. Eggers believed that it was physically impossible to enter the German courtyard under the glare of the searchlights and cross the path of the guard; it was not until 1952, when Pat Reid published *The Colditz Story*, that he discovered that he was wrong.

CHAPTER TEN

Legend and Life

Pat Reid's daring escape typifies the legend of Colditz Castle – a legend that Reid himself did much to create. After the war, he wrote three books about Colditz which are largely responsible for fashioning its enduring mystique. Colditz has become synonymous with old-fashioned feats of daring – the very mention of the name conjures up stirring images of the Allies' finest young officers pitting their collective wits against the organised might of the German Army in a bid to escape their fortified hilltop castle. Given the appalling atrocities committed elsewhere in Nazi Germany and its conquered territories, the Colditz story is all the more remarkable. The Nazis treated their enemies with ruthless brutality: foreigners, dissidents, Jews and other 'undesirables' were transported to labour camps or murdered in their millions during the Second World War. These officers, who all had their cards marked *Deutschfeindlich*, anti-German, could easily have suffered the same fate. But the events in Colditz seem to belong to another era – a gentler age when both sides behaved with honour, and adhered to the 'rules' of engagement. There was remarkably little animosity between captives and captors – the notice on the guard-house door reminded the Germans that the prisoners were only doing their duty in attempting to escape, and it was the guards' duty to keep them in.

The Saxon regiments of the Wehrmacht were proud of their warrior traditions, and similar codes prevailed among the prisoners of war. Many of the officers were young men when they were captured: most were in their twenties; many had recently graduated from Sandhurst and other military academies. By the standards of their own generation, they were traditional, old-fashioned even. They placed great faith in the British notion of 'fair play': it never occurred to them that they might be shot for attempting to escape. What's more, they never doubted that Britain would win the war. Their natural arrogance seemed to elicit respect from their captors: 'The Germans wanted to beat us,' remembered one, 'but beat us with our permission.'

They had much in common with their captors: their armies were organised in the same way, and the punishment meted out was in accordance with what they might expect in their own country. 'It is very wrong to think of Colditz as a hell camp,' remarks Micky Burn, a Colditz prisoner and veteran of the St Nazaire raid. 'Given the atrocities that were happening all around us, the concentration camps and even the labour camps full of Russians and Poles, Colditz was very, very privileged. The Germans by and large stuck to the Geneva Convention, which meant we had food, we had letters and we could say what we liked. Of course it was cold, crowded and we were locked up, but compared to the real hell camps out in the Far East, Colditz was a bad hotel.'

In the autumn of 1942, Colditz began to receive guests who had a very different experience of Nazi Germany, and who were destined for a worse fate than a spell in uncomfortable accommodation. During the previous months, the British had launched a series of daring undercover commando raids on Vaagso, Brunevald and St Nazaire; the raids had given the British hope at a time when they had little else to cheer about, but German propaganda had painted the highly trained troops who conducted the operations as ruthless, violent thugs. On the evening of 7 October, seven British commandos arrived at the castle. The Kommandant, who had been warned of their impending arrival, telephoned the OKW in Berlin for instructions. They were locked in the guardroom for the night, and early the following morning they were taken into the prisoners' yard to be photographed by the ever-present Herr Lange. 'These guys were just milling about in the courtyard very early in the morning. There was no one else about,' recalls Pete Tunstall. 'We talked to them from a window above their heads – we told them not to look up, but just to answer our questions as if they were talking to each other. They told us they were commandos on "Operation Muskatoon". They then told us that they were worried about getting shot.'

The men were marched away to the town cells, but their arrival had excited the curiosity of prisoners and guards alike. 'Three of the men are only 20 years old, one is 27 and the staff sergeant only 28!' wrote Thomas Schädlich in his diary. He was fascinated by their story. 'The seven Commandos were dropped from an English submarine on the Norwegian coast and blew up a power station, killing a German guard.

They tried to escape into the Norwegian mountains but were caught. During their interrogation, they stated that they would grab any opportunity to escape – that's why they have been sent to Colditz under very heavy guard.' Schädlich added that the commandos had been sent food from the camp. 'In a box of cigarettes we found the following message: "Which regiment, where caught, who are you? Send reply under leaves in the tea pot." After we translated this message we let it get into their hands, inside a book.'

Once they could be sure that they were talking to fellow prisoners and not spies, the commandos gave their names and ranks, which Rupert Barry passed on via coded letter to MI9 in London. The following day they were allowed to exercise in the park, and while they were out Schädlich searched their cell. 'We discovered that the iron grille on the outside of the window has been cut through in three places,' he wrote. 'The cuts were filled with chewed bread, very neatly, and hardly visible. The five were immediately fetched back from their walk and searched very carefully. This produced a steel saw blade inside a comb sheath and a map of Germany inside a waist band. This unit has obviously been really well trained and instructed for the eventuality of being taken prisoner, and were probably equipped with the necessary items as it was totally impossible that they were smuggled to them from the camp.' The commandos were also wearing special boots, courtesy of Clayton Hutton at MI9. When Captain Grahame Black – the leader of the raiding party – was captured, a thorough search revealed that the heels of his boots were hollow; they contained an escaper's pack, consisting of a map, a compass, a phial of Benzedrine and some chocolate. The commandos were, indeed, well equipped to 'escape and evade'.

That evening, the seven commandos received a Red Cross

parcel, courtesy of the officers in the castle. 'What a sensation,' recorded twenty-year-old Private Curtis. 'TEA and English food. Marmalade, butter, chocolate, milk, sugar. We feel really happy as if we were on holiday.' On 10 October, Captain Eggers was seen escorting four Gestapo men to the town jail. Two of the commandos were removed. Three days later, a bus arrived and the rest of the party left Colditz under heavy guard. They were taken to Berlin, and interrogated at the infamous Reich Central Security Headquarters. What happened there remains a mystery, but a week later they reached Sachsenhausen concentration camp, where they were interred in the medical block. At dawn on 23 October, they were led out and shot in the back of the neck by SS guards. Their bodies were burned in the crematorium.

A few days before the commandos' murder, Hitler had signed his infamous *Commandobefehl*: 'From now on all enemies on commando missions, even if they are in uniform, in battle or in flight are to be slaughtered to the last man,' it said. 'If it should become necessary to spare one or two for the purposes of interrogation, then they are to be shot immediately after interrogation. I shall bring to trial any commander or other officer who has failed to carry out his duty instructing troops about this order or who has acted contrary to it.'

The execution of captured soldiers in uniform was a flagrant breach of the Geneva Convention. The German authorities told the Swiss government that the commandos had escaped, and ordered the Kommandant at Colditz to return to the sender any letters addressed to the men: they were to be marked *geflohen* – 'fled'. Six letters were returned in this way. Eggers and the other officers in the garrison must have known of the commandos' impending fate, but they were unable to save them. It was only at the end of

Returned Letter to Joe Houghton from his Sister

the war that the prisoners found out what had happened to the commandos. At the Nuremberg trials, Rupert Barry's coded letters were cited as evidence that the Germans had tried to conceal the deaths of the seven men. The general who signed their death warrant was sentenced to be hanged. It was a grim episode, and it tarnished the reputation for 'correctness' of the Wehrmacht garrison at Colditz.

In November, four British officers arrived who had suffered at the hands of the Gestapo. They had been held in Warsaw as spies. Among them were two men – Kenneth Sutherland and Kit Silverwood-Cope – who had escaped from Stalag XXID and made their way to Warsaw, where they made contact with the Polish underground. For fourteen months, they were passed from family to family under the watchful eye of the formidable Mrs M – a Scottish woman who had married a Pole. Mrs M (aka Miss Jane

Walker), an apparently harmless old lady, was in fact a tyran-
nical patriot, 'breathing with her every breath fire, slaughter
and defiance of Britain's enemies,' who looked after twenty
British officers, hiding them with families in various parts
of the city, while she tried to engineer their escape.

In the autumn of 1941, Silverwood-Cope had contracted
typhus, which was then endemic in eastern Europe. A Jewish
doctor saved his life. The following spring, Silverwood-Cope
was living with the doctor and her daughter, while he gradually regained his health. He was now also playing a key
role in running the escape lines out of Poland, but once the
Gestapo infiltrated the organisation Silverwood-Cope was
arrested. He was sent to Pawiak civilian prison, and the
doctor and her daughter were sent to a concentration camp.
Silverwood-Cope's fellow inmates were Jews and Poles of
all classes who had been accused of various 'crimes', such
as reading a foreign newspaper, listening to the radio or
communicating with someone in a concentration camp.
Realising that his predicament was serious, Silverwood-Cope
revealed his identity as an escaped British officer on the first
day of his internment, but the Gestapo chose not to believe
him: they knew there was much he could tell them about
the Polish underground organisation. Over the next seventy-
one days, he was interrogated repeatedly. Conditions were
horrendous: in the intervals between interrogations, he was
forced to stand in a darkened cell all day; he was given little
to eat, and as the weather turned colder he rapidly lost fifteen
kilos in weight. His only luxury was a handkerchief he
happened to have in his pocket when he was captured. He
found sixteen different uses for it – it served as towel, a
pillow and much else besides.

If he attempted to look out of the window in his cell, he
was shot at, but nonetheless, Silverwood-Cope witnessed

appalling scenes in the prison: 'By day the screams of agony from prisoners being flogged was incessant,' he recalls. 'In the baths the scars on their backs showed that few prisoners escaped this treatment. On four different occasions when I was taken to Gestapo HQ, I saw a certain Jew lying sense-less after being flogged. On one occasion, blood was flowing from a wound in his head. An SS man was kicking him. He was at length forced to his feet and scarcely able to stand, was made to crawl under tables and over chairs until once again he was unable to move. The SS men present clearly showed their delight in his distress. On his return to the prison office this unfortunate man was twice knocked to the ground. The reason given was that he had tried to support himself against the wall.' On another occasion, he watched as a guard armed with a whip and a police dog tortured a prisoner: 'The man was stumbling with weakness, but he was ordered to run. He protested with cries of terror and he was flogged into action. As soon as he began to run, the dog was released. Howling with excitement, the dog pulled him to the ground, mauling him terribly. The cries of both man and dog were indescribable. When the man's bleeding wounds began to show through his torn clothes, the dog was called off, and the process repeated again and again. It lasted about twenty minutes.' Silverwood-Cope had no doubt that it was common practice in Pawiak jail.

Kenneth Sutherland received slightly different treatment. After his arrest he was hung from hooks on the ceiling and beaten with a rubber truncheon. When he finally admitted he was an officer prisoner of war he was let down and left in an adjoining room next to the street. 'I was unguarded,' he recalled, 'except for a Polish policeman pacing up and down outside. I ran out and made for the station where I arrived – without interference – and took the train out of town. It was clear that I had been purposely allowed to escape in the hope that I would lead the police to my friends. So I tried to shake off my pursuers and continued on away from Warsaw for several days. On the second day my shoes were stolen while I was asleep. Eventually I found it impossible to escape without them, and I gave myself up at Radom station, after covering seventy miles on foot and by train.' Sutherland was eventually returned to Pawiak, where the Gestapo told him that Silverwood-Cope and the others had already signed statements confessing all they knew and that his silence was only harming himself. Wisely, Kenneth Sutherland chose to disbelieve them.

After ten weeks' imprisonment, Silverwood-Cope, Sutherland and the other officers were 'rescued' by the Wehrmacht. All had survived their ordeal without revealing what they knew of the Polish underground. When they arrived at Colditz on 3 November 1942, their appearance so shocked their fellow prisoners that they were immediately transferred to the sick bay. They were among the first foreigners to witness the horrifying events taking place in the Warsaw Ghetto, and they asked Padre Platt to take statements of their experiences to present to the Swiss government. Eggers refused to believe their stories until they were signed by the prisoners.

Silverwood-Cope and his fellow officers were not the first to bring tales of Nazi brutality into the camp, but they were the first British officers to have experienced it directly. Others had been beaten or threatened after attempting to escape, but none had ever been captured by the Gestapo in civilian clothes – and forced to endure the consequences. During one of Silverwood-Cope's interviews in Warsaw, the Gestapo interrogators had made their position quite clear. '"It is useless trying to protect yourself in your capacity as an officer as we do not recognise it,"' he recalled being told. '"You do not take your position seriously enough. We have complete power to kill you or to set you free. The Wehrmacht know nothing of your arrest and need hear nothing if we are forced to shoot you."'

Silverwood-Cope's experience in Pawiak prison convinced him that the Gestapo officer meant what he said. The Gestapo and the SS were operating outside the rules of the Geneva Convention, and they would enforce Hitler's *Commandobefehl* without hesitation – indeed, though the officers inside Colditz did not know it, the seven commandos on Operation Muskatoon had already been executed. The escapers from Colditz could only hope that if they were recaptured in civilian clothes, they would be able to convince their captors they were not spies but Allied officers – and as such, the responsibility of the Wehrmacht. The stakes had been raised: Germany was an increasingly dangerous place for an escaped prisoner.

Meanwhile, within the comparative safety of Colditz, autumn arrived and both sides were still playing things by the book. The arch goon-baiter Peter Tunstall was sent for a court-martial in Leipzig – his third. He was on trial for throwing buckets of water out of the window during an *Appell*, in an attempt to delay discovery of the clothing store escape. Black Campbell acted as his defence, and succeeded in getting Tunstall off with a month in solitary confinement.

On 26 November, Lieutenant Mike Sinclair made his second attempt to break out of Colditz. Somehow, he managed to escape through the German kitchens after lunch break in the company of Dutchman Charles Klein, but they were recaptured two days later at Immendingen, close to the Swiss border. Once again the Germans were baffled: how could any prisoner leave the castle from the German courtyard? They had introduced a system of passwords that were changed on a daily basis in order to improve security. The next day, Rupert Barry and Lieutenant Aulard attempted to follow the same route, but were caught during an accidental inspection. It was the fourth time Barry had been caught – he was yet to make it beyond the castle walls.

In December, the French discovered for themselves that brutal treatment was regularly meted out beyond the castle ramparts. Frédo Guigues – the master locksmith – was one of a party of thirty-one Frenchmen sent to Lübeck camp in October. On 1 December, he and seven others had escaped; three of the party made home runs, but Guigues and Pierre Boutard had fled into the forest, where they were recaptured in the middle of a wild boar hunt. Both were so savagely beaten that they were hospitalised at Soest. Guigues slowly recovered; by Christmas he was back in the Colditz yard, but Boutard never regained his strength and died in a Parisian hospital a year later. The return of Frédo Guigues bolstered French morale, and it was the French who rounded off the year with another ingenious escape attempt.

On the evening of 28 December, the French fused the lights in the prisoners' courtyard. The German response was predictable – Willi Pöhnert, the camp electrician, appeared with his toolbox to attend to the problem. 'Little Willi' was such a regular visitor to the castle that he rarely had to show his pass – a fact that was not lost on the prisoners. While Willi was up in the courtyard, Lieutenant Perodeau – a short, bespectacled French officer – walked coolly towards the main gate. He was wearing overalls and a yellow armband and carrying a toolkit – just like the real 'Little Willi'. Perodeau passed the first checkpoint unchallenged, but the guard on the main gate was more thorough – and once he was challenged for his pass, the game was up. At midnight, Herr

Lange was summoned to photograph the two Willis, side by side – the final addition to the bulging dossier of escape attempts in 1942. It was, said Eggers, 'a peak year': '88 men involved in 44 escapes, 16 successful. 39 caught while getting out of the castle. 19 escaped in transit/hospitalisation, of whom 3 made home runs.' Of the sixteen home runs, seven were British, five French, three Dutch, and one Belgian.

It was a considerable achievement for the officers inside the high-security Sonderlager, and Christmas was celebrated in style. 'We faced tomato soup . . . Christmas pudding and custard, sardines on toast, dessert, coffee and wine – Chateau Colditz,' wrote Padre Platt in his diary. 'Tonight's celebration had nothing new in it: it was just a repetition of last year and the year before – but with more hope. The singing of national songs in the Hof [yard] at midnight was less fierce but more prolonged and harmonious than previous years. The human crocodile sprang to life, and three hundred men roared through all quarters. The New Year was well and truly let in!'

The escape record of 1942 would never be bettered. But 1943 opened with both good and bad news for the prisoners of Colditz. It was clear that outside the claustrophobic world of the prisoners' courtyard, the war had reached a turning point. The British Eighth Army was advancing through North Africa, and reached Tripoli on 23 January; meanwhile, on 18 January, the Red Army had broken the siege of Stalingrad, and by the end of the month Field Marshal von Paulus had surrendered. Since August 1942, 110,000 German soldiers had been killed, 50,000 wounded and 107,000 taken prisoner. The Russian armies now began a long counter-offensive which would eventually bring them to the streets of Berlin. Every day, the official High Command Report was printed in the German newspapers, which the prisoners were allowed to read. Though it was full of propaganda, the prisoners soon learned how to sift out the real news. 'On Monday one would read that the German forces were heroically fighting back the Russians east of Veriye Luki,' remembers Jimmy Yule. 'And then a few days later there was the same news – except the German forces were now heroically fighting back the Russians fifteen miles west of Veriye Luki. We realised what was happening.'

The reports were soon confirmed by the evidence of their own eyes. In January, the RAF bombed the synthetic petrol plant at Leuna, a few miles west of Colditz. From their high vantage point, the prisoners could see the columns of acrid smoke rising in the distance. It was the first tangible sign that the war was coming closer to Colditz. But the Allied bombing had an adverse effect on the prisoners' lives: it put greater strain on the German infrastructure, which meant that the Red Cross in Geneva could no longer guarantee a regular supply of food parcels. The prisoners cut their consumption from one parcel per week, to half a parcel. The new regime had an immediate effect: the fact that they were lacking food resulted in far fewer escape attempts, and the early months of 1943 brought little in the way of excitement or interest. The effects of malnourishment became more visible in May, when innumerable skin complaints broke out among the prisoners, largely due to vitamin deficiency.

But it was not just the lack of food which brought a change to the rhythm of the camp. Kommandant Glaesche had begun his term of office in August 1942 by antagonising the prisoners, and he had continued in much the same vein. In January, he reminded the prisoners of their obligations under the Geneva Convention to salute officers of senior or equal rank. Camp Order 38 provoked a renewed outbreak of goon-baiting – evidently, the lessons of the Verkest affair had not been learned. Glaesche also demanded a new level of punctuality and discipline at *Appells* – another highly unpopular move. On 8 January, Eggers walked into the yard and ducked as a large snowball crashed into the door behind him. He found a large piece of glass hidden inside it. In retribution, Glaesche began taking photographs of *Appells* from a window over the kitchen, and installed a machinegun above the yard. Neither photographer nor machine-gunner was visible but it was not long before Father Congar – a French priest – discovered their existence and lodged a protest. Glaesche unwisely admitted that the photographer was in place to provide evidence of mutinous behaviour. From then on, smoking, whistling and catcalls punctuated every *Appell*; names were taken, arrests made and the solitary cells were booked solid for months. Even Eggers was disconcerted – it was clear that Glaesche could not keep control. On 15 February, less then six months after his appointment, he was sent to take charge of the prison camps in the Ukraine.

His replacement was Colonel Prawitt: he was only forty-three years old, and quite unlike his predecessors. He had fought on the Eastern Front and, though he was no longer fit for combat, he had the energy and zeal of 'a typical Prussian martinet'. From the outset, Prawitt attempted to take a much tougher line, both with the prisoners and with his own staff. He interpreted his juniors' 'correctness' as leniency. 'A British Orderly openly refuses obedience to Corporal Schädlich,' recorded Eggers in his diary. 'He reports to me. I to Lt. Col. Prawitt. He orders Schädlich and myself into his office. In a rage, Prawitt thumps his fist on the table and cries: "If a POW does not obey orders, repeat the order and push your rifle into his back. If he continues disobeying, shoot him on the spot." The orderly was punished by Prawitt with bread and water rations. Like Capt. Püpcke, I was resolute not to use arms for compelling obedience, but only in self-defence.'

Prawitt enjoyed parties and good wine, and he was openly opposed to Hitler – at least until the assassination attempt of July 1944. But his approach, which contrasted so sharply with the tactics adopted by Püpcke and Eggers, created a divide that would last until the end of the war. Prawitt's 'new broom' also made an impression upon the German guard force. 'Escaping was the prisoners' greatest ambition, because they wanted to show us that despite all the barbed wire and all our precautions we still couldn't stop them,' remembers Peter Hoffman, a young guard. 'But when Colonel Prawitt appeared, they found it much more difficult. Prawitt made the camp much more secure. On the days we weren't on watch, we all had to put on gloves and fit more barbed wire. The whole of the steep slope around the castle was covered in tripwire, and then criss-crossed with barbed wire – if you fell on it, you would tear badly, and it was impossible to run through it.'

Prawitt erected a new catwalk over the terrace gate, and placed a machinegun on the pagoda that stood on the north-west corner of the lower terrace. It was manned twenty-four hours a day. The improvements to camp security made up for the fact that there was now an acute shortage of manpower. General von Unruh had been deputed to find a further 800,000 men for the Eastern Front, and as a result the entire guard company had undergone a medical. Several of the more able-bodied soldiers left, but the only casualty among the officers was Priem, the alcoholic who had once been security officer. The medical declared that Priem – 'the only German with a sense of humour' – was so unhealthy that 'death may supervene at any moment', and he was retired early. The doctor's remarks were prescient: in August 1943 Priem was found dead in his bed. Now, with the exception of Prawitt and the adjutant, all the officers at Colditz were over fifty, and some of the guards under their command could not even fire a rifle. 'The weapons we had here were very old,' remembers Francis Kreutz, a young guard recruited to Colditz in 1943. 'They were old French carbines that were very long in the barrel, and heavy. We were quite ashamed of them, and the old sidearms which banged down to the knee. I couldn't have used it properly anyway, because I had smashed my left hand in a workshop accident. Even the machinegun on the pagoda hardly had any ammunition, as supplies were very scarce.'

Prawitt made the camp as secure as he could with his limited resources, but it was not just the extra barbed wire and machineguns which stemmed the flow of escapes during 1943. The prisoners themselves had ensured that Colditz was a much more difficult place to escape from. To date, there had been 135 attempts to break out, and with each foiled attempt another potential exit was closed; one by one, the doors were being shut.

What's more, some of the officers now arriving at Colditz did not share their predecessors' determination to escape. In the middle of February, a second Prominente arrived. Michael Alexander — a young lieutenant who had been captured in North Africa — was on a murder charge for killing an Italian officer he had encountered on a commando raid. He had evaded the death sentence because he claimed Field Marshal Alexander was his uncle — he was, in fact, a more distant relation, but the High Command recognised his potential as a hostage, and sent him to Colditz. 'I'd been sent on a mission which invited capture,' he recalled. 'And I'd seen quite a lot of action in the two years I was in North

Africa, so I reckoned I'd had the war – I didn't feel deprived, and I didn't want to escape because I didn't want to draw attention to myself at all, if I could help it. There was nothing for me to go back for. They weren't longing for my services again in the Army. They could get on without me quite well, I think.'

Michael Alexander might have found it difficult to escape, in any case: as a Prominente, his movements were watched, and he spent every night guarded under lock and key with Giles Romilly. But his attitude was by no means unique. Many officers who arrived at Colditz had already escaped from other camps – sometimes from several different camps; the fact that they had been sent to Colditz was proof of their courage, and finding themselves behind the high walls of the prisoners' courtyard, they were happy to accept their fate. As time went on, a 'curious atmosphere' developed in the camp: 'There were many people there who were captured in France in 1940 and '41, who'd been there for two or three years by the time I got there,' Alexander remembers. 'They must have felt not guilty exactly, but certainly that they were missing out on it. It wasn't their fault they got caught, but I think they were keener to escape, to show their professional devotion to the system. Because the system says "thou shalt escape if you possibly can" – if only to make trouble, because it ties up resources. This is one of the principles behind the escaping philosophy: it wasn't that you desperately had to get back to be used again – more that you had to get out and make a bit of aggro.'

Micky Burn was another officer who shared Mike Alexander's reluctance to escape. He was a commando who had been captured at St Nazaire, and he had found his way to Colditz by a very circuitous route. Burn had been a *Times* journalist before the war and, briefly, an admirer of the Nazi

Party. In 1936, he had met Hitler, who signed his copy of *Mein Kampf*. By the time war broke out, Burn's politics had swung across the political spectrum to the far left, but the Germans still believed they could use his skills as a journalist. He was sent to a 'propaganda camp', where Allied officers were recruited to write pro-German articles and leaflets to be dropped over England. Burn refused, whereupon he was threatened with a concentration camp, but was sent to Colditz instead.

'I wasn't interested in escaping,' he recalls. 'I admired the escapers enormously, and did what I could to help, but I felt someone had better consider why we there at all; why the war had started; why there should be any wars. Since I had some experience of journalism and I was considered an intellectual, I thought this is what I should do. And it was very fortunate because it gave me a sort of escape within myself without having to get out. So I studied, I took a degree at Oxford under the auspices of the Red Cross and the Swiss, who used to come around and examine the castle from time to time.'

Micky Burn came to regard Colditz as something of a haven, in which he could safely pursue his interests. He learned Russian, and gave a series of lectures on Marxism. 'About which I knew not very much, but something. Of course, in prison you have a captive audience who will listen to anything. A certain senior officer forbade his juniors from attending, and another said I should be tried for treason. But they didn't stop me.' Giles Romilly, the Prominente, had also been a journalist before the war, and he shared Burn's political views. The pair of them became known as 'the Colditz commies'. Other officers gave lectures on subjects ranging from wine-tasting to Worcester Cathedral, and for some these cultural interests became a full-time occupation.

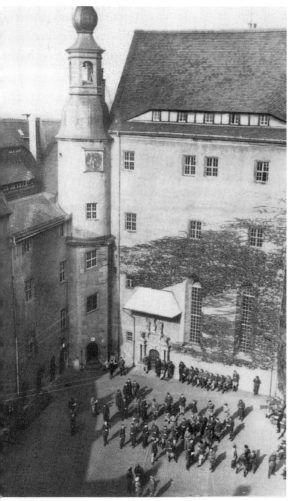

The French tunnel.
It began at the top of the clock tower adjacent to the chapel, descended 90 feet into the ground, and then continued a further 100 feet horizontally under the chapel and out of the castle.

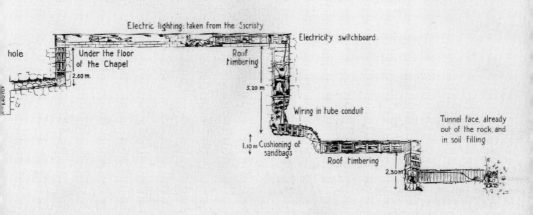

Electric lighting: taken from the Sacristy

Electricity switchboard

hole

Under the floor of the Chapel

2.60 m.

Roof timbering

5.20 m

Wiring in tube conduit

Tunnel face, already out of the rock, and in soil filling

1.10 m Cushioning of sandbags

Roof timbering

2.30 m

Left Churchill's nephew, Giles Romilly – the first Prominente

Below A group of Dutchmen – some wearing their 'Wehrmacht greatcoats

1942 – another
[fail]ed escape re-enacted:
[M]chiel Van den Heuvel
[(Va]ndy) emerges from the
[stov]e supported by Peter
[Do]rie-Pugh. An hour
[earl]ier the Englishman had
[pos]ed for the photograph
[bel]ow.

[(top row left)] Mike Sinclair,
[nex]t to Padre Platt; (top
[row right with pipe) Pete
[Tun]stall; (middle row left)
[Jim] Rogers, next to Lulu
[Law]ton; (seated left to right)
[Jim]my Yule, John Watton,
[Ha]rry Elliott, Dominic
[Br]uce, Gris Davies-
[Sc]ourfield, Dickie Heard,
[Ral]ph Holroyd, and
[Ken]neth Lee

The castle censors reading POW letters

A haul of opened Red Cross parcels in the parcel office

Clayton Hutton's compass concealed inside a walnut

A corner of the Kommandants' Escape Museum

In one minute a perfect fitting walking out suit can be made — which is also waterproofed.

Take out Buckram
Take off Badges
Tear off Pockets & Flaps
Take off Belt
Tear off Sleeve Piping
Buttons replaced by those from inside Trouser Tops
Tear off Stripes

MI9's toys: *(above)* Escape suit, *(middle left)* Reichsmarks inside a gramophone record and *(below left)* a concealed map of Danzig

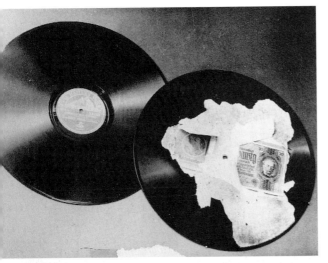

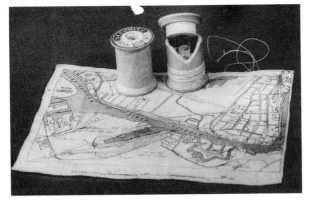

e king of the 'gaz d'arts' Frédo Guigues

Brian 'never a dull moment' Paddon

e British contingent Christmas 1942: *(seated centre)* Douglas Bader, *(between his legs)* his medical
erly Alec Ross

The Dutch lockmaster Damiaem van Doorninck Bill Fowler

German soldiers re-enact their escape

There was little resentment of these men on the part of the escaping fraternity – quite the opposite, in fact. 'We were only too thankful because the more people who wanted to escape the longer they would have to wait,' recalls Gris Davies-Scourfield. 'One of the difficulties of Colditz was that so many people wanted to escape from such a small space that you had to wait in line. The escape committee might tell you your lovely scheme was good enough, but not this year – "Wait till next year." "Next year?" you'd say. "Yes, next year. We don't want any activity in that part of the camp this year – we've got two escapes being planned there, and I'm afraid you must wait." So one didn't want too many people escaping.'

Within the close confines of the courtyard, national stereotypes were identified and boisterously mocked. The British contingent was particularly lively because of the variety of nationalities it contained: French Canadians, Canadians, Australians, New Zealanders and South Africans – not to mention Englishmen, Irishmen and Scotsmen – all served in British uniform. But there was one member of the British contingent who felt particularly isolated – Dr Biren Mazumdar, a member of the Royal Army Medical Corps, was the only Indian at Colditz. 'Jumbo', as he was known, was a man of high principle who firmly believed that once he had taken up his commission in the British Army, he was duty-bound to honour it. He was born a Brahmin, and had come to England in 1932 to learn his trade; though he was proud to be a British subject, he made no secret of his dislike of the British Raj, and the attitude of the British Indian Army officers towards their soldiers.

Throughout the war, German agents had studied the POWs under their control, in the hope of finding potential converts to their cause. Soon after his capture in 1940,

Mazumdar was approached by agents who attempted to persuade him to join the fight against the Allies. They thought he would be tempted by their offer to help throw the British out of India. But Mazumdar consistently refused and was sent to work as a doctor in POW camps across Germany. He worked in seventeen different camps before he fell foul of the authorities; his file was labelled *Deutschfeindlich* and he was sent to Colditz in October 1941. Unfortunately, there was no one there to vouch for him when he arrived: in the paranoid atmosphere of the camp, prisoners needed reassurance that newcomers were who they claimed to be. Micky Burn, who arrived from a 'propaganda camp', was treated with suspicion until several of his fellow commandos already imprisoned in the castle vouched for his integrity. Mazumdar was liked by many of the British officers, but he was regarded with mistrust by an equal number.

Knowing where his political sympathies lay, Prawitt arranged for Mazumdar to be be sent to Berlin to meet a man whom he held in high esteem. 'Jumbo was a great admirer of Subhas Chandra Bose,' recalls his messmate, Gris Davies-Scourfield. 'At that time, Bose was trying to raise a "national army" from among Indian prisoners of war to fight alongside the Japanese and help drive us out of India. Jumbo was therefore extremely excited when Chandra Bose arrived in Germany and was highly gratified when summoned to Berlin to meet him. "Goodbye, Jumbo," we all said, "have a good war in Burma . . . Don't be too hard on the poor old Fourteenth Army" – and similar valedictory chaffing. We never expected to see him again: yet in a few days he was back. "Good heavens," we exclaimed, "didn't he want you after all?" "Oh yes," said Jumbo, "he wanted me all right, and I would very much have liked to have accepted his offer to join him. He's such a wonderful man. But then of course

I couldn't, could I?" "Whyever not?" we asked. "Because I hold a British commission, and therefore I owe my loyalty to the King, whatever my political views and my private feelings may be."'

Mazumdar's high principles endeared him to his brother officers, and baffled the Germans; they recognised that he was isolated at Colditz, but they refused his applications to be sent to an Indian camp because of his anti-German attitudes. Three weeks after he returned from Berlin, Mazumdar was summoned before Prawitt again; this time there were two other Indians present who had switched their allegiances. The Kommandant gave him one last chance to join them, but Mazumdar refused.

Back in the courtyard, rumours began to circulate among the British contingent that he was a spy. Mazumdar was more acutely aware than ever that his race had set him apart, and he gravitated naturally towards the other prominent non-white member of the Colditz fraternity – Major E. Engles, the Senior Dutch Officer, who was half Indonesian. Both men realised that, as non-Europeans, their prospect of escaping from Germany was bleak. They would not get far once beyond the walls of the castle without being recognised, but Biren Mazumdar still believed he had the right to try his luck. The first Senior British Officer, Guy German, did not agree: he greeted his applications to escape with derision. But his attitude did not discourage Mazumdar – in fact, it only fuelled his desire to get out. If the Germans would not transfer him to an all-Indian camp, he would force them to act. On 7th February 1943, he decided to go on hunger strike. Dick Howe knew of his plan and gave him an 'arse-creeper' and some German money to help him on his way. Eggers was concerned: he noticed that Mazumdar's hunger strike coincided with Mahatma Gandhi's in India, and he did not want his death on his conscience. After three weeks of salt and water, Mazumdar had lost a great deal of weight and the Germans relented; they moved him to a camp for Indians soldiers in France, from where he escaped and linked up with the French Resistance, who conveyed him to the Swiss border in 1944. Mazumdar took great pleasure in writing to Guy German, informing him of his safe arrival. He had proved that an Indian could escape across occupied Europe.

There were others who believed they were in the wrong camp, and insisted on being transferred elsewhere. The Irish doctor Ion Ferguson was inspired by Mazumdar's example, and he too made use of his nationality to facilitate an escape. He wrote a letter to an old acquaintance, Dr Eamon De Valera – the son of Eire's Prime Minister – complaining of his ill-treatment at the hands of his captors and encouraging his father to bring Ireland into the war. As anticipated, the letter never got home, but two weeks later, Ferguson's request to continue working as a doctor was granted. He was transferred to Stalag 4D at Torgau, where he spent six months certifying lunatics for 'compassionate repatriation' before attempting to convince the authorities that he had gone insane himself. The scheme worked: he was repatriated in January 1945. In September 1942, Chief Petty Officers Wally Lister and Tubby Hammond arrived in Colditz with the Royal Navy contingent. They had been promoted to the rank of officer so that they might stay with their friends, but technically they were in the wrong camp, and after a month they applied to be transferred to the troop camp at Lamsdorf, where they joined work gangs in the local fields and factories; escaping was easy, and after a series of adventures, they crossed the Swiss frontier on 19 December.

In spring 1943, Colditz's mini-famine came to an end as

more Red Cross parcels arrived, and the well-fed officers began once again to think about escaping. But the fact that the escape attempts were often improvised suggested a degree of desperation – 'snap escapes' had worked well in 1941, as the French had proved, but under Prawitt's new regime, they were unlikely to succeed. On 7 March, Bag Dickinson was taken out for exercise during another spell of solitary in the town jail. Screened by a couple of other POWs, he managed to dive under the table in the dim hallway outside the cells. He slipped over a back wall, stole a bicycle and bicycled to Chemnitz, forty miles away. It was exactly the same route he had used in August, and once again he was caught at the train station. Operation Mousetrap used to send out alarms to every station within a twenty-five-mile radius of Colditz, but Prawitt had extended its range – his Operation Hare Drive now covered every station within fifty miles of the castle. The local police and the Hitler Youth were also automatically informed when a prisoner broke out; an escaper needed extraordinary luck to break through the ring.

On 2 April 1943 two Frenchmen – Edouard Desbats and Jean Caillaud – made a daring bid for freedom. When they originally conceived the scheme, they felt it would only work with a covering of fog to shroud their movements; they waited several weeks, but the weather remained clear, and in the end they decided to risk it anyway. That evening after *Appell*, they climbed out of the window in the French quarters and leaped six feet to a ledge on an adjoining roof. Their target was a lightning conductor that trailed into the moat from one of the Kommandantur buildings. The thin zinc rod began on a roof sixty feet above the German yard. To reach it, the two Frenchmen set about climbing a chimney that abutted the roof. Desbats went first, and he managed to get past the brick projection and the barbed wire. The chimney was braced with metal hoops, which he used as belaying points for the rope. He had reached a point sixty feet above the German yard, where he was in full view of the lights and the sentry, when he dislodged a piece of brick. It bounced down into the German yard, where Peter Hoffman was on guard duty. 'I saw them high up in the light of the searchlights,' he recalls. 'I shouted: "Halt or I'll shoot!" But they kept on climbing, so I fired off a warning shot. It ricocheted off the roof tiles beside them, which frightened them, I think; I heard them shout, "Don't shoot, don't shoot, we're coming back!" I pressed the alarm button and all the guards came running, and trained the searchlight on the rooftops. They crawled behind the chimney, so we fired off another round, which hit the chimney where they were sheltering. Then they called out again: "*Nicht schiessen! Nicht schiessen!*"' Püpcke, the most cool-headed of all the German officers, arrived and ordered a ceasefire. Another volley might well have found its mark. The escapers were dragged down and given two weeks in solitary.

An even more desperate attempt was made by the wiry Canadian pilot Don Thom. Thom had cared for his compatriot Don Middleton during the dark weeks when he had made several attempts at suicide, and since then his own behaviour had grown ever more eccentric. Eggers was unable to decide whether the pilot was genuinely unhinged or knowingly provocative: 'Lt Thom always plays the fool,' he wrote in his diary. 'He sends a telegram to Princess Elizabeth to tell her that she is his bride. He formally asked for an aeroplane to return him to England. He comes to roll call with a broom and then uses it like a rifle for saluting.' Thom's eccentricities also confused his fellow prisoners, who marvelled at his audacity. 'He came down to *Appell* one day wearing long johns, rugby socks and half a football on his head,' remembered Pete Tunstall. 'He marched straight up to the front of the parade and began to dance about. The guards ran after him, but he was too nimble for them – he leaped on to a wall and then jumped up to the bars of a window. He hung there and scratched under one of his arms like a monkey. We were all falling about laughing. Eventually, they got him down and dragged him off to the cells.' Don Thom told his fellow officers he had been a 'swimming coach and gigolo' before the war. But he had also been an Olympic gymnast, a skill he made use of when he tried to escape one afternoon; Eggers thought it was 'the maddest attempt' he had ever seen.

On 11 May, during a spell in solitary confinement, Thom was taken out with the other prisoners for exercise on the upper terrace on the west side of the castle. The terrace was surrounded by a balustrade, and there was a drop of thirty feet to the terrace below, where a sentry was stationed beside the machinegun pagoda. The parapet that surrounded the lower terrace was topped by a wire fence, beyond which a wooded slope descended steeply towards a stream. On the far side of the stream was the final obstacle – the castle wall, which was eight feet high. Prawitt had good reason to believe that the western aspect of the castle was the most heavily defended, and yet it was here that Don Thom chose to escape.

Three prisoners descended the spiral staircase to the terrace. Don Thom led the way, followed by Bag Dickinson and the guard. As soon as Thom opened the door, he jumped on to the balustrade. Bag Dickinson stepped into the doorway and braced himself against the frame, preventing the guard from getting past. It gave Thom a precious few seconds to leap off the balustrade, and drop to the lower terrace. Thanks to his gymnastic skills, he was able to break his fall – he clung on to the bars of two windows as he bounced thirty feet down the wall. The sentry was twenty yards away when he reached the ground and Thom ran past him before he had time to react. The machinegunner in the pagoda was caught unawares as well, and before he realised what was happening, Thom had vaulted over the parapet and landed in the woods below. Now the firing started. Somehow, Thom avoided being snagged on the wire that Prawitt's guards had strewn throughout the wood, and plunged into the stream at the bottom of the slope. By now, the alarm had sounded. Thom dragged himself out of the water, and ran up the steep slope on the other side as bullets flew past him. Officers were leaning out of the windows of the Kellerhaus and screaming at the guards in an attempt to distract their aim. Thom had almost made it. Breathless, he reached the wall and began to climb. But he got no farther: the park sentries caught up with him, and dragged him to the ground.

Don Thom's extraordinary gymnastic attempt was executed with unique skill, but there was no doubt that he was one of half a dozen British officers suffering from the effects of long-term confinement. Peter Storie-Pugh, who had been studying medicine at Cambridge before the war, acted as a paramedical worker in the sick bay. He treated POWs with many different ailments, and he estimated that 10 to 15 per cent of the British contingent were suffering from the psychological effects of imprisonment. The long hours of enforced idleness were beginning to take their toll, which is hardly surprising: many of the British were into their third year of captivity, and the fact that they had no idea how much longer it would last made their ordeal harder to bear. The prisoners invariably greeted newcomers to the castle with the same question: 'When is the war going to end?' Pat Reid had a term for the onset of the madness that

afflicted so many Colditz inmates: he called it 'locker pottering'. A prisoner who was 'locker pottering' would stand
for hours in front of his cupboard, obsessively arranging and
rearranging his 'little and all'; he would talk to his possessions and ask them questions.

Others were less restrained: 'One of the Army officers used
to go down into the courtyard with a prayer book in one
hand and a poker in the other,' says John 'Bosun' Chrisp,
who arrived with the Navy party in 1942. 'He used to rush
to the main gate and hammer it with the poker and yell,
"The lord of hosts be with you yet, they're burning their
dead in the outer courtyard!" Then he'd run upstairs and
hide.' One man was found with slashed wrists sitting over a
bucket; another took to living on top of a cupboard; another
supposedly tried to cut off his own penis, saying he had 'no
further use for it'. In a public incident, one man tried to
strangle another because he thought he had stolen his girl!
The Germans were naturally suspicious of such behaviour,
for they were aware it could be a ruse to get sent home; a
German admiral had already used insanity to initiate his own
'compassionate repatriation' from Britain.

'The Germans were very unsympathetic about mental
illness – but then so were we, albeit in a different way,'
remembers Jim Rogers. 'Most of the men who went down
the drain were young and we honestly thought they were
missing their mothers or sweethearts. They were missing the
protection of women – cuddling, if you like. And so we
thought we mustn't give them a replacement. If everybody
started mothering them, looking after them and tucking
them up in bed, more people would go. It was much better
to treat them, not exactly roughly, but not to cuddle them
– not to show them any respect. We felt that approach kept
others from going the same way.'

The majority of prisoners thought mental deterioration could be avoided; some even regarded it as a shameful weakness; and the British suffered from it more than their counterparts. 'We Poles thought that the British tended to get more upset, and go insane more often than anyone else because they were from good families and they were used to better things,' remembers Anthony Karpf, a Polish cadet officer, 'but it didn't bother us Poles as much. Lack of space was the worst thing.' The physical restrictions of the castle were particularly wearing; 'Lulu' Lawton, who had been in Colditz since 1941, remembers that it was impossible to walk more that thirty-five yards in any one direction – a figure that came to haunt him during his long years of confinement. Surrounded on all sides by ninety-foot-high buildings, the courtyard was a grey, shadowy place, and winters were long and bitterly cold. Though the prisoners were occasionally allowed to walk down to the park – the small wire enclosure below the castle – many shunned the opportunity: being herded about by nervous, aggressive guards made them feel like 'caged animals'.

Throughout the day, the yard was filled with the babble of voices and the clatter of boots and clogs on stone stair-cases. There was no privacy. Extraordinary tolerance was required for prisoners to live together. 'It was a mental battle to keep sane,' recalls Jimmy Yule. 'People did all sorts of things, sometimes questionable things; other people read a lot, others learned languages, and some just leaned against the fire and talked. A major in the Ulster Rifles always used to get hold of me. We started talking by the stove and he would get very close, so I would take a step back – and then he would take a step forward, and I would take a step back – in a kind of dance. I would go right across the mess-room and find myself against the back wall. It was ridiculous. But you had to learn to live with it and not let it get to you.'

One French artillery officer, Captain Busch, took extreme measures to be alone: he covered himself in rancid butter. But the easiest way to escape from the cramped, noisy world of the prisoners' quarters was to break the rules, and earn yourself a two-week spell in solitary. For some, solitary confinement was a welcome respite from Colditz life; but for other, more persistent offenders, it held few pleasures. The arch goon-baiter Pete Tunstall once spent thirteen weeks in the cooler: 'Every morning when I woke up in the cell, my first sensation was a drop, when I realised where I was. Then I got an uplift when I thought about the girl to whom I was engaged. I began to live a fantasy life, thinking about what it would be like when I came back, how we would meet, what we would do. In effect, I wasn't in the cell at all. Then after three and a half years I got a "Dear John" letter. So I woke up with a drop, and then another drop. And when the great love of your life tells you she's going to marry someone else, that becomes one of your motives for pushing it to the limit. Maybe I had a bit of a death wish, even; I just didn't care any more.'

Tunstall never revealed his thoughts to his brother officers, but others felt the same way. Some men found less socially acceptable outlets for their frustration. Padre Platt, one of several vicars in Colditz, was troubled by rumours about a 'small mutual masturbation group'. 'They hold what they hope are secret sessions,' he wrote in his diary on 6 December 1941. 'Occasionally they are absent at meal times or from a lecture that most other officers attend. Secret gatherings are quite impossible in these crowded conditions . . . Two of our number have sat up after all the others have gone to bed discussing Plato's acquiescence in the homosexuality of his disciples. At one of these late adolescent discussions, they foresaw themselves as the founders of a Platonic cult.'

Padre Platt concerned himself with such matters because he was responsible for the moral wellbeing of his flock. But the kindly old Yorkshireman, who rarely ventured out of his 'priest's hole', had already acquired a reputation as a 'gullible old crow', and it is likely he was being wound up by some of the more boisterous members of the camp. In the clatter and bustle of the prisoners' courtyard, there was little space for any private activity, though many officers remember risqué remarks directed at particularly good-looking officers, especially those in the Highland Division, who often wore their kilts. 'I think there was a general reprobation of anything of that sort,' recalls Micky Burn. 'Anyway, it would have been very difficult to find sufficient privacy to make it enjoyable, unless you had a guard on the door. The British behaved very correctly about sex, whereas the French had things organised in a way that was rather shocking. One of the first remarks one of the French officers made to our officers was "*Quels sont les garçons?*"; which are boys? There was no answer to that at all. I think they were very disappointed and rather surprised and thought, "The stupid English."'

The British never discovered whether there was any substance behind this remark; most of them had been brought up to believe that homosexuality was an evil. 'When I was at prep school there was a mysterious ritual,' recalls Gris Davies-Scourfield. 'The school leavers went to see the headmaster after supper. No one would tell us what he said, but when it was my turn to leave I found out. We all sat there, and he said, "God reserves his worst punishment for people who behave like that. That's madness!" I've always thought it was an extraordinary thing to say.'

The British contingent may have behaved 'correctly' as regards sex, but Peter Storie-Pugh believed there was a connection between the British officers who went 'round the bend' and unrequited emotional attachments. Occasionally, he held 'clinics' in the sick bay, and he noticed that repressed homosexual longings were a common cause of depression, which, without opportunities for reciprocation or physical sex, only deepened as the war went on. Storie-Pugh was alone in making this diagnosis; most believed madness was caused by the frustrations of captivity – and it was those who were keenest to escape who suffered most. After two years in Colditz, Pat Reid knew he would go mad if he could not escape. Others felt the same, and many hoped that, one way or another, 1943 would be their last year in captivity. Outside the castle, the tide of the war had turned; inside it, the British hatched a new plan that would require all the resources of the Colditz escape industry. It was a mass breakout – a scheme that involved more British prisoners than any to date.

CHAPTER ELEVEN

Frans Josef

Many escape attempts from Colditz involved deception as part of the plan. Prisoners had walked out as guards, women, orderlies, Hitler Youth – the Frenchman, Perodeau, had even imitated Willi Pöhnert, the camp electrician. In April 1943, Mike Sinclair and Monty Bissell approached the British Escape Officer, Dick Howe, with a plan more audacious than any impersonation attempted so far, which, if successful, would result in a mass British break-out. Their model was one of the camp's most conspicuous personalities, Stabsfeld-webel Rothenberger – known to the prisoners and guards as 'Frans Josef'. It was the old sergeant's bushy white moustache which drew comparisons with the late Emperor of Austria; it sat upon his upper lip 'like a contented cat'. His unique appearance invited disguise.

One of Rothenberger's tasks was to make a nightly

inspection of the sentries on the eastern terrace of the castle overlooking the park. These men were stationed at thirty-yard intervals around the floodlit walls of the Princes' House, and their tour of duty lasted four long hours – it was one of the least popular beats. 'The eastern terrace used to really strain your neck,' recalls Peter Hoffman, 'because the path was so narrow and we stood so close to the castle. You couldn't look up at the walls for more than five minutes at a time.' Halfway through the night Rothenberger made his rounds, checking than the sentries were awake and alert, then he left the terrace via the barbed-wire gate close to the Kommandantur. This gate was manned by two sentries, one patrolling the wire catwalk above, the other stationed beside the door to allow soldiers to pass through. Oberstleutnant Prawitt had taken care that the terrace gate was particularly well lit and well guarded; once through it, it was easy to slip down into the woods and away.

Mike Sinclair intended to imitate Rothenberger, and instead of waking the sentries up he would give them a bogus story about an escape attempt on the other side of the castle, and order them back to the guardroom. Having . dismissed them, he would then march up to the terrace gate and replace the two guards with two of his own – British officers in disguise – and then order the gate sentry to hand over his key. It would take this sentry approximately four and a half minutes to march back to the guardroom, and in these brief minutes twenty officers would swing down ropes from the windows above and Mike Sinclair would let them through the gate. If the Germans still hadn't discovered them, a further wave of ten would follow, scrambling down to the woods below. When the gate sentry reached the guardroom, he would be confronted by the real Rothenberger, where-upon 'all hell would break loose'. By this stage Sinclair and his two guards hoped to have set off 'in pursuit' of the escapers, and should any genuine Germans join them, Sinclair would order them back to the castle to bring up reinforcements. The slender head start would give the escapers an opportunity to climb over the park wall, split up into pairs and make for the open countryside.

The audacity of the plan immediately appealed to Howe; even if it failed 'it would make a damn good story', but the demands it placed on Sinclair were huge: the twenty-five-year-old officer would have to age thirty years, bark orders in a flawless Saxon accent, and, most challenging of all, wear a convincing white handlebar moustache. But the darkness would disguise his features, Mike Sinclair spoke impeccable German, and, like Stabsfeldwebel Rothenberger, he had red hair.

To the Germans Mike Sinclair was 'the Red Fox'. He made nine escape attempts in all, two of them before he even arrived at the castle. By the summer of 1943 he had already escaped from Colditz twice, reaching Cologne and the Dutch border, and on both occasions he slipped away from his captors before being recaught once more. Photographs of Sinclair in various disguises were circulated to police stations throughout the Reich, a testament to his own persistence and the desire of the authorities to catch him. The British regarded him as their greatest escaper, but even within the close confines of Colditz few could claim to know him; he was a remote, intelligent man, who did not seek out company. His almost reckless indifference to danger won him admiration, but few friends. 'For Mike Sinclair, there was God – then the Sixtieth, and that was it,' recalled Mike Edwards. 'His only aim in life was to get back to his regiment.' Even Gris Davies-Scourfield, his oldest and greatest companion, was struck by his addiction to the 'escaping game'. 'I would wake up in the middle of the night, as we were usually in the same room,' he recalls. 'Mike would be standing at the window just watching the sentries patrolling below, counting the number of seconds it took them to turn around and walk back on their beats. He was constantly looking for any information that might be useful to him.'

While on the run in Warsaw, Sinclair had found shelter with a Polish family, who helped him escape to Bulgaria when the Gestapo infiltrated the underground organisation. He was eventually recaught and sent to Colditz; they were sent to their deaths at Auschwitz. Their fate, as well as the ignominy of his own capture, was one of the many tangled motives that drove Mike Sinclair. 'The only times I ever spoke to him in the Colditz yard he just wanted to get out and kill as many Germans as possible,' recalls Pat Fergusson. 'He seemed to be on a personal crusade between himself and the whole of Hitler's occupied Europe.' If any officer had the audacity to impersonate Stabsfeldwebel Rothenberger, it would be Mike Sinclair.

The success of the scheme relied heavily on the well-drilled guards obeying their senior officer, without examining too closely what he looked like. The British recognised that this ingrained German attitude ran particularly deep in the garrison at Colditz, in which grandfathers and adolescents served together. 'We were proud of our Prussian traditions,' recalls Peter Hoffman. 'We all thought Rothenberger was a real German soldier. He had fought in the First War, he had an Iron Cross – and his moustache. Of course, if he ordered one of us young ones to do something we would certainly do it.' The British were not alone in recognising this weakness: Prawitt was well aware that, while unquestioning obedience was appropriate on the battlefield, it was less useful inside a POW camp, and ever since his arrival he had been at pains to foster a more suspicious culture among his men. 'Be suspicious, ask questions, don't assume anything.'

Preparations for the Frans Josef scheme were extensive, and harnessed the skills of up to fifty officers in the British escape industry. Hours of enforced idleness in the 'Escape Academy' had turned these young men into experts in their particular fields, using any items that came to hand to make what was required. They worked alone or in small cells, and as each object was finished it was handed on to the next department by 'the toasting committee', the escape committee's preferred monicker. The smooth running of this machine was the responsibility of the British Escape Officer, Dick Howe, who, by virtue of his position, was not allowed to join in the escape. Howe had promised himself that once he had overseen ten British home runs, he too would make his break for freedom; the success of the Frans Josef attempt might provide him with the excuse he needed to step down.

To begin with, three perfect uniforms were required, produced by the camp tailors, who dyed blankets the precise shade of field grey to make the sentries' greatcoats. The insignia were carved out of linoleum, cut from the floor and painted with watercolours bought in the canteen shop. Rothenberger's prominent Iron Cross was cast from zinc, which an enterprising thief had stolen from the roof; the metal was soft enough to melt in an open stove, and could be fashioned with a broken-off table knife. Similar close observation was required to make Frans Josef's hat, which the theatre props makers created from an old RAF cap – adding a peak and painting it green.

To obtain the exact dimensions of a guard's old French carbine, the officers surreptitiously measured the real thing in the yard while the sentry was distracted. 'We built a home-made lathe to turn the wooden barrels,' recalls Jack Best, who was given the task of making these props. 'Then we cut the triggers out of tin with a cutlery knife and sliced steel off our bedsteads to make the bolts.' Rothenberger's pistol presented a different challenge, because it was rarely seen. 'It turned out to be a nine-millimetre Walther P38,' recalls Hugh Bruce, another of the escapers. 'The only part of the pistol which can be seen when the holster is closed is the black base of the magazine at the bottom of the hand grip. So that was the only part of the pistol which had to be manufactured. The pistol holster was, however, a little more complicated. To emulate the dull red leather, this was made from heavy cardboard, given some false stitching and buffed with dark brown boot polish.' A piece of wood padded out the holster so that Sinclair would at least appear to be armed – even if he wasn't.

While the experts worked on the props, Mike Sinclair spent every day observing Rothenberger as he strode about the yard; and under the direction of Teddy Barton, Colditz's theatre impresario, he got into character. Barton was also responsible for making the famous white moustache out of shaving brushes; it took him fourteen attempts to achieve the exact shade and shape. Sinclair's guards would be played by John Hyde-Thomson and Lance Pope, both of whom spoke good German, and they too practised their 'goon drill'. Pope was a veteran of this method of escape; he had used his fluent German to impersonate guards and walk out of both his previous camps, and at Eichstätt he had even convinced the sentries to open the gate to a visiting 'general' and his party; the general was none other than Lieutenant-Colonel 'Tubby' Broomhall, the new Senior British Officer at Colditz.

The perfection demanded of the main party extended to the thirty 'civilian' escapers ready at the windows, each of whom required a convincing set of clothes and a full set of false papers, together with a pre-planned route taking them to the border. 'Civvies' were each individual's responsibility, but their papers were mass-produced by the forgery department. Their most important document was an *Ausweis*, a travel permit which permitted civilians to move around Germany. This forgery had to withstand close scrutiny, and at Colditz so many were required that they were produced by an assembly line.

'I suppose we worked union hours,' remembers Kenneth Lee, one of the chief forgers. 'Every day we sat at a table opposite each other painstakingly copying the German Gothic script on the paper forms. We started in pencil then carefully went over the top of everything in Indian ink. The raw materials came from the canteen shop and I suppose it never occurred to the Germans that we might be able to use this for escaping purposes, they thought we were all drawing still lives. There was always a stooge at the window to warn us if the Germans were coming. We had a special hide under the table to put our equipment in, and I think it took about ten seconds to cover everything up and do something else. I spent over three years in the forgery department and we were never rumbled.'

Lee's task was to make the 'blank' *Ausweis*, which was then passed on to the next department to be filled in. Tight security ensured that Lee was never told what happened to his documents or who would use them, and he magnanimously accepted this as part of his job. 'I didn't know anything,' he recalls, 'and that must have been a good thing.' The next stage of the elaborate forgery relied on two inventions made by 'Andy' Anderson, one of the principal prop makers to the escape industry. Anderson, who had been busy polishing up the dummy rifle barrels with pencil lead, had also made a home-made typewriter – constructed from wood and wire which he fitted with accurate letters on the type bars. This was used to type in the date and time of travel, whereupon the *Ausweis* was passed to the escaper to sign. A photograph was then required, preferably of the escaper in his home-made civvies, for which Anderson made an 'imitation box Brownie'. 'I used an old cigar box and a pair of broken spectacles as the lenses,' he recalls. 'A goon supplied the film and developer, and when London finally got us a real camera we didn't want to use it. My Brownie was bigger and better.' Every escaper was photographed, in character, by Ralph Holroyd, an Australian soldier who in peacetime had been a professional photographer. 'I remember putting on my home-made jacket which was too small and brushing black boot polish into my hair,' recalls Corran Purdon. 'Then I went up to one of the dormitories to the "studio" and tried to look as serious and "Belgian" as possible.'

Once each *Ausweis* had been forged, typed, signed and the photograph attached, the document had to be stamped. 'Someone gave me the design of an eagle stamp copied from a pass,' recalls George Drew, who acquired a reputation as a skilled woodcarver. 'I would carefully trace this on to a spare shoe heel that we used to get in our Red Cross parcels. I then cut away all the rubber with a razor blade, which took weeks, and was about as boring as watching paint dry. At the end of that I inked it up using an indelible pencil – kindly provided by the Germans – and spit. This produced the right shade of purple ink used for stamping. We'd then cover the *Ausweis* with five or six stamps, the more the better because the Germans loved stamps. And the end result should get you right across Germany, if not examined too closely.'

This assembly-line approach was urgently required to mass-produce maps. Only a few genuine maps survived the searches to make it into the camp, and these were provided by pilots or by MI9's magic handkerchief method. Copying them risked their exposure and proved a laborious business, which Kenneth Lockwood hoped to overcome using an old trick he remembered from his schooldays. 'When I was at prep school I used to print a newsletter for our form, and I used gelatine,' he recalls. 'I knew we had jellies inside our Red Cross parcels, so I thought jelly, gelatine, maybe we could try this out. I made a small wooden tray, melted a bit of jelly, poured it in and waited for it to set. It had to be a light colour – I found Chivers Lemon Jelly to be the best. Someone had traced off a map of Germany from the camp original, using an indelible pencil on greaseproof paper. I pressed this down on to the jelly, smoothed it out, and then carefully pulled it off, hoping the indelible pencil would have been picked up by the jelly. It had. I then put a piece of blank paper on to the jelly, pressed it down and, pulling it off, I had a copy of the map. The system was good for about thirty copies, working rather like a miniature printing press. And the jelly was never wasted at the end of it; we ate it.'

In June 1943, while preparations for the mass escape were well under way, the prisoners heard that sixty-five British officers had escaped from Eichstätt camp through a tunnel. Every civilian within two hundred miles was sent out to look for them, and not a single man got home. It was sobering news. 'We knew that it is always better to escape in small groups rather than larger ones,' recalls Jack Best. 'But the point of escaping is not necessarily to get back to one's unit and rejoin the war. What difference is one more man going to make? The point is to get out and give them a problem. The more people the bigger the problem – it ties them up, keeps them busy.'

Throughout the summer the preparations gathered momentum. As each *Ausweis*, German uniform, dummy rifle and civilian suit was made, it was handed over to the escape committee and secreted away in a hide. Wherever there was nefarious activity in any part of the camp, the elaborate system of 'stooges' kept a watchful eye open for the first sign of the German ferrets. Their rubber-soled boots afforded them the element of silent surprise, but during the summer of 1943 they often went away empty-handed; the Colditz escape industry had become a very efficient machine.

Each night Rothenberger made his rounds his movements were scrutinised and the guards were watched; officers singled out a particular 'ivory-headed goon' and planned the date of the escape around his tour of duty. While this took place one of the most delicate operations of the entire scheme was under way: cutting the window bars. Bar-cutting at Colditz was a stock-in-trade, but these bars presented a special problem: both were directly above the sentry on the terrace gate, and one was framed by a searchlight. 'The bar-cutter would draw his blade as slowly as possible across the face of each bar, trying to make as little noise as possible,' remembers Jack Best. 'Beside him lay his accomplice holding a mirror on a wire, who would warn him when the sentry was directly underneath. At the end of every night the cut would be camouflaged with boot polish. This work was nerve-racking and it might take a week until the window bars were hanging by threads. The final cuts were only made moments before we went.'

The last, and most important, piece of information Mike Sinclair required could also be obtained immediately before the escape. Every member of the German garrison was issued with a camp pass which changed in colour every few days. At each checkpoint the pass was presented, and the bearer was asked for a number from one to fifty — the security code of the day. Both of these were required to proceed through the terrace gate, and to obtain them the officers relied on Flight Lieutenant 'Checko' Chaloupka. 'Checko' was, unsurprisingly, a Czech; tall and charismatic, he had an unrivalled ability to extract anything he wanted out of the guards. 'Each morning he would be down in the yard with coffee and cigarettes passing the time of day with the goons,' recalls Gris Davies-Scourfield. 'He would begin with small gifts, chocolate for the *kinder*, stockings for the wife. Soon photographs would be exchanged and a great friendship would develop. Then he might ask for something, a pass, or a railway timetable. If the reaction was "no" then Checko would let the guard know that the Kommandant wouldn't be very pleased if he found out the guard had accepted gifts from a prisoner. The poor German was like putty in his hands.'

At nine o'clock in the morning an officer nonchalantly wandered around the courtyard clapping his hands; the number of claps indicated the security number of the day. The coloured camp pass was more difficult to get hold of, as the guards were required to present them wherever they went. Nevertheless Checko acquired one. 'He ran upstairs with this pass,' recalls Kenneth Lockwood. 'And an hour later the guard who had lent it was looking nervous. He was approaching the end of his shift and he had not been given the pass back. The forgers finished their work, and Checko ran down the stairs and gave it to him. We watched as the sentry presented the pass to the guard on the courtyard gate. It was checked, and then handed back: everything was in order, and he was let out of the courtyard. The guard was unaware that we still had his original pass. The forgers had copied it and attached his photograph to their forgery.'

With the very latest information in their pockets, the escapers were finally ready to go; 4 September was Rothenberger's next tour of duty, coinciding with the 'ivory-headed goon' manning the terrace gate. The windows bars were made ready so that the entire grid could be removed in a moment; equipment was checked, and each *Ausweis* was carefully stowed in a 'creeper'. It was a warm afternoon, and the hours passed slowly towards the evening *Appell*. 'What worried me most was the short start we would get,' recalls Hugh Bruce. 'Probably not more than four minutes at the most. We could expect that in the excitement the Germans would panic, and there might well be some shooting. But the countryside was still lush with vegetation and standing corn, and our plan was to hide up for a day or two until the initial heat came off.'

At 9 p.m. the *Appell* sounded and the officers were roused from their quarters. As they emerged into the floodlit yard the Germans counted their charges without incident, and all faded back to their bunks, and Sinclair, Hyde-Thomson and Pope wandered up to the quarters above the sick bay. Soon all was quiet. Rothenberger was reported to be safely in the guardhouse. Five minutes later a skeleton key turned in a locked door, and thirty British escapers were led silently up the stairs and into the old Polish quarters. They entered a small, dark room on the first floor, directly above the floodlit terrace gate. Below them the bored guard stood at his post; another paced the wire catwalk above. All along the eastern side of the castle lookouts took their places, peering through cracks in blackout blinds. Once everyone was in position the all-quiet signal was received, and the escape began. Sinclair – now Rothenberger – and his two guards were lowered down into the sick bay. The prepared window was removed and they slipped out on to the terrace.

From their windows, the lookouts heard the crunch of boots on the gravel below. Sinclair, followed by Hyde-Thomson and Pope, were marching to the eastern corner of the castle, where the first sentry stood. There was a brief exchange in German, then the sound of boots marching away. 'Mike came around into view and I knew he'd relieved the first sentry,' recalls Gris Davies-Scourfield, who was a lookout in a window above. 'He approached the second sentry, and I heard him tell the story about there being an escape on in the other part of the castle. After a moment the sentry clicked his heels, saluted – and he too marched away into the darkness. I reported back in a loud whisper "second sentry duly relieved".'

The tension rose in the small room. Each escaper strained to hear the sound of the footsteps as the three officers approached the third sentry. Sinclair took care to stand directly in front of him, silhouetted against the bright castle wall. In his best imitation of Rothenberger's thick Saxon accent he repeated the escape story and dismissed the guard. In the half-darkness, the sentry peered at the stooped frame, medals and moustache of the man he took to be Stabs-feldwebel Rothenberger standing before him. Then he too saluted and marched away to the guardroom. 'It's going to work,' whispered an escaper. 'It's really going to work!'

Now Sinclair and his party walked up to the main terrace gate. Up ahead the two guards stood at their stations, one on the catwalk, the other standing beside the barrier. Both turned to watch as the familiar figure of 'Rothenberger' approached, with his two relief guards behind him. Here in the arc of the searchlight it was brighter than at any other point on the terrace. Sinclair slowly climbed the catwalk and ordered the guard to return to the guardroom. His place was taken by Hyde-Thomson. Descending the ladder,

Sinclair closed on the final guard on the gate, the 'ivory-headed goon', the only German left on the eastern side of the castle. A salute was exchanged, and Sinclair ordered him to hand over the keys to the gate. The guard did not react. Sinclair repeated the order. 'I heard an argument start, and I could hear Mike raise his voice,' recalls Gris Davies-Scourfield. 'Mike spoke perfect German. And the guard kept saying "*Nein, Herr Stabsfeldwebel. Nein*".'

The argument spelt trouble for Mike Sinclair. Contrary to all expectations the ivory-headed goon refused to hand over his keys, and then he asked his senior officer a question; he asked to see his pass. Sinclair began shouting at the guard for his impertinence, but realising he would not be swayed, he handed it over. It was at this point that the guard did become suspicious; the passes must have changed *that* evening, because Sinclair's was the wrong colour. The guard pushed the alarm bell. Sinclair was now screaming with rage, a scream he had spent months practising, but it was too late. The escapers knew that, as the seconds ticked by, their chances were diminishing. Hyde-Thomson and Pope stood their ground, but moments later the relief party came running through the gate. What happened next is confused: the British tell one story, the Germans another.

'I was one of the guards who came from the guardroom, and Pilz – the relief officer – was in front of me,' remembers Peter Hoffman. 'Beside the gate there was a huge commotion. Sinclair was screaming at the guard and then Pilz began screaming at him. Pilz had his pistol out and was waving it at everyone, it was chaos. The two British sentries were ordered down next to Sinclair. They had their hands up. Sinclair would not put his hands up. I thought that Sinclair then went for his pistol, and Pilz shot him at point-blank range. He sank to his knees. A soldier standing

next to me said, "For God's sake, you've shot Rothenberger."
He really believed Sinclair was the sergeant. Then the windows above us erupted. "German murderers, you bloody
murderers!" It was only then that we began to understand
what was going on.'

Knowing that Sinclair's holster contained nothing more
than a piece of wood, the British were convinced they had
just witnessed an execution. The screams from the windows
continued, but Mike Sinclair was not dead – the bullet had
passed through his left lung, missing his heart by three inches.
Sinclair placed the blame squarely on the shoulders of the
panicking Pilz. 'His whole attitude was one to provoke and
increase the tension and excitement instead of taking charge,'
he wrote later. 'Pilz drew his pistol and brandished it in a
reckless and gleeful manner and obviously enjoying the
possibility of using it. He screamed at me, "Hands up." I put
my hands up. He screamed at me again, "Hands up," and
I shouted back at him, "My hands are up, they are high
enough." He then repeatedly shouted a word which sounded
like "*absehnalen*" to which I replied, "I do not understand."
Owing to the state of confusion I do not remember exactly
when I was shot, but I do remember being extremely
surprised that the shot should be fired, there being no reason
for it. The shot was fired into my chest from a yard in front
of me, and slightly to the left.'

Soon more Germans arrived, including old Rothenberger,
himself incredulous to see his doppelgänger lying on the
grass before him. Sinclair was eventually picked up and taken
to the solitary cells, where he lay 'as if the subject of some
circus freak show' while German soldiers came in to mock
him. In the snap *Appell* that followed feelings were running
high. 'We were bloody angry,' recalls David Hunter, an escaper
who had watched the drama from the window. 'I think it

was disappointment at so many months of planning gone to waste. We would have rioted, but there were fifty goons in the courtyard with bayonets fixed. They were in no mood for trouble. I had shouted "bloody murderers" from the window and I really lost it at the *Appell*.' Hunter was dragged off to the cooler, and the Senior British Officer put in a formal request to have Pilz, whom they knew as 'Big Bum', court-martialled for shooting an unarmed prisoner. Prawitt stood firm, but a month later the unfortunate Pilz was sent to the Russian front and never heard of again. Significantly, a year later the Kommandant also chose to burn Sinclair's bullet-holed uniform, thereby removing any incriminating evidence against him.

If nothing else, the Frans Josef attempt did succeed in 'making a damn good story' and completely bewildering the Germans. 'We laughed about it afterwards,' remembered Peter Hoffman, 'because everything about Sinclair was perfect, he had even copied Rothenberger's attitude with his soldiers. But our training had proved itself. The guard had asked a question of his senior officer.' Hauptmann Eggers had his own theories as to why the dimwitted guard excelled himself. When Rothenberger climbed up on to the catwalk it was his custom to pause and look out across the dark woods beyond the wire, a detail that Sinclair omitted. Also, examining the false moustache in the cold light of day, Eggers pronounced that it did not curl in quite the right manner.

The British were inevitably disappointed; but there was also considerable relief that Pilz's bullet had not resulted in a tragedy. Mike Sinclair was quick to recover, and within four months he would escape again, this time with a daring bordering upon madness.

CHAPTER TWELVE

A Very British Camp

During the course of 1943 a very significant change had taken place at Colditz; its effects would last for the remainder of the war. At the end of May, Wehrmacht High Command, the OKW, decided that from now on Oflag 4C should house only British and American officers. The Dutch departed in June, followed in turn by the Poles and the main contingent of French and Belgians. Each nation carried their escaping traditions before them, and from time to time news of their exploits filtered back into the prisoners' courtyard. Some of their efforts were to end in tragedy, but many were successful. It was the sixty-eight Dutch officers who proved themselves to be the most troublesome. 'They made a veritable hornets' nest out of Stanislau,' wrote Reinhold Eggers, who felt some sympathy for their new Kommandant. 'Many more of them got away from there than would have done from Colditz. It was another of the OKW's big mistakes in that it mixed hardened escapists with comparatively harmless prisoners. The old lags got away from an easier clink – the innocents became infected with the same idea.' By the end of the war thirteen of the original sixty-eight Dutch officers had made home runs; two more had reached Russia and died there, and a further twenty-seven had tried to escape. Their place at the top of the escapers' league table was assured.

The final group of French officers were moved to Lübeck camp on 12 July. The upheaval of a large number of men proved too good an opportunity to miss, and their ranks were infiltrated by three British officers, leaving three Frenchmen behind. When this folly was uncovered, the three British men were returned to Colditz, and on arrival it was discovered that one of them was French. So he was sent back to Lübeck – and Lübeck was taken apart to find the missing British officer. These shenanigans provided the bored prisoners with endless amusement as they revelled in their aim to create 'merry hell' and use up hard-pressed Wehrmacht resources. The piles of French kit-bags, musical instruments and packing cases were stacked up on the platform of Colditz station awaiting their transport to Lübeck. A lone sentry watched over them. His task was not to find escapers but to prevent civilians from pilfering the bags. As he stood there he noticed one of the boxes begin to wobble; moments later a purple-faced Giles Romilly emerged, complete with a packet of biscuits and a saw – he had been left standing on his head. Ten guards escorted 'Emil' back to the castle, and the entire garrison felt Prawitt's fury; had his most prized prisoner escaped, the Kommandant would have been executed. As it was, Hauptmann Lange – his Chief Security Officer – was given three days' bread and water, then sent off to another camp.

The departure of the other nationalities made room for new arrivals, the majority of whom were sent from Eichstätt. Sixty-five British officers had been captured after the mass escape from the tunnel and eleven more followed having attempted a 'walk-out' disguised as a group of high-ranking officers on a visit. By the end of July 1943 there were 228 British officers inside the castle and a handful of Free French. Colditz became a very different place, and many of the old inhabitants noted with regret the passing of an era. Tensions had existed between the nations, but these were outweighed by the natural curiosity and friendly rivalry that the international camp had provided. There was a Polish choir, a Dutch Hawaiian guitar band, a French orchestra, the 'Colditz Olympics'. Although the atmosphere in the prisoners' yard could never be described as studious, many British officers embarked on one-to-one language courses with friends from other nations: they learned German, Dutch, French and Russian as well as more obscure languages such as Croatian, Flemish and Swahili. But the most obscure language of all was one which Cyril Lewthwaite gave lessons in. Lewthwaite, who was a keen practical joker, said he would teach a Polish officer Mandarin – a language he could not speak. Lewthwaite invented his own language instead, and pretended it was Mandarin, but the Pole made such rapid progress in his made-up gobbledygook that Lewthwaite found he could not keep up, and was forced to abandon the game.

As well as these cultural pursuits, the different nations had also attempted to outdo each other in finding ever more ingenious ways of relieving the tedium. 'One summer we had a plague of wasps infesting the creeper which grew on the wall of the castle,' recalls Jim Rogers. 'Bill Fowler, an Australian airman, caught a wasp, tied a thin thread to its waist and attached it to a rolled-up cigarette paper. Bill's idea was that, since leaflets were being dropped by the RAF all over Germany, it was up to us to play our part. Hundreds of wasps were caught and to each was attached a cigarette paper with the message *Deutschland Kaput*. The French, never to be outdone, caught a large number of wasps, tied a little square of paper to each, put them in matchboxes and released them together on parade. It was like a reversed snowstorm with the wasps flying upwards in furious mood. Pande-monium raged with all of us warding off the angry wasps, or pretending to.'

Wasps were not the only animals the French proved adept with. Charles Elwell was a regular visitor to the French quarters, and one afternoon he saw a toy tank moving across the floor. 'It was made out of milk tins – and even the gun turrets swivelled. I looked closer and saw two little mice inside on a home-made treadmill. When the tank hit an object the wheel stopped and the mice turned around and starting running in the other direction. So the mouse-powered tank went into reverse. It was absolutely ingen-ious.' The French quarters also proved popular among those searching for a more interesting meal, and several British officers had the novel experience of eating meat stew. Inside Colditz meat was an unheard-of luxury, and on one occa-sion this 'meat' created an international incident. 'I was invited to dinner with my French mate Georges, and for the first time in three years I got some meat with a bone in it,' remembers John Chrisp. 'It was wonderful. And the next day someone asked me how I'd got on. And I told him about the wonderful meat with a bone in it. Then he said, Haven't you heard? What? The English cat's missing. The English cat's missing? Then I shut up. I saw Georges the next day and I said, Now what about this meat, the English cat's missing. Oh, he said, *ça ne fait rien*, it doesn't matter, we always eat cat in the North. And that's where the English cat went, which I ate. And it was nice.' To the Germans, cat-eating was a disgusting habit worthy of admission to Colditz, as one Belgian officer, Major Flébus, discovered. He arrived on the charge that he had 'captured a cat, not belonging to him, and did share in the unnatural consumption of the same'. By the end of the war several British officers had also put aside their squeamishness in pursuit of a cat stew.

The arrival of the seventy-six Eichstätt officers replaced the international flavour of the camp with something more familiar. They were welcomed into Colditz with what had become a standard ritual for new British prisoners. 'We arrived like new boys at a school, and were pretty green about the sort of regime in the camp,' recalls Pat Fergusson, then a young lieutenant in the Royal Tank Regiment. 'We were taken one by one down to the medical room, where we were interviewed by a German doctor in a white coat. We were told to do all the usual things – drop your trousers, cough. Then a bucket of purple paint appeared, which was duly slapped on in the appropriate places, and we were told to get the hell out of there. All the time the German doctor was shouting loudly and rudely at us; and of course, he wasn't a German. We all fell for it and felt quite silly, but the advantage was with the home side.'

The hysterical doctor was played by Howard Gee, a fluent German-speaker; the purple paint was administered by 'medium-sized man' Dominic Bruce. Once the games were over the new arrivals settled into the old French and Polish quarters and took the measure of their new surroundings. They were as cosmopolitan as the 'old guard', comprising English, Scots, Canadians and Australians, and many of them had been prisoners since 1940. But from the outset there were tensions between the rival groups: the 'Eichstätt mob' lived on the other side of the courtyard, their senior officer immediately took over as the new Senior British Officer, and according to Padre Platt their arrival 'marked the end of the British family life', replacing it with 'the atmosphere of a larger camp . . . small friendship circles, complete in themselves and almost exclusive'. The new arrivals were equally critical of their new companions. 'We thought they were all mad; they'd been locked up in the same place far too long and were terrible show-offs,' recalls Mike Edwards. 'Their intentions were always to provoke the Germans to the limit, and they succeeded because it often appeared the Germans were more than careful not to start a riot. It was almost anarchy. We, apparently, didn't know the form, because we would try and get along with our nefarious activities without drawing too much attention to ourselves. And it created a great rift between us.'

Goon-baiting by the 'men of spirit' was not the only aspect of Colditz life the new boys felt uncomfortable with. Previously the escapers at Colditz had kept their activities very much to themselves, as a security against the inevitable gossip that flew around the prisoners' courtyard. Now that the camp was almost entirely made up of one nationality, the new arrivals felt that this 'need to know' attitude was a device to keep them outside the escaping fraternity. There was a feeling that if you wanted to escape 'you first had to escape from the escape committee' – it had become an exclusive occupation. 'I had no dealings with the escape committee at Colditz, but going on the behaviour of escape committees in other camps they were a very lofty set-up. I mean they barely spoke to lesser mortals,' recalls George Drew, a new arrival who carved the stamps for false passes. 'You really had to get down on your hands and knees and bow deeply before you could talk to the escape committee. I don't think I even knew who was on it.'

Part of the new arrivals' frustrations inevitably arose from the predicament they now found themselves in. Sixty-five of them had escaped through a tunnel, and tunnels by their nature relied on a lot of 'coolie labour', for which each humble digger was awarded a place on the scheme. Under Prawitt's regime Colditz was now extremely secure, and it seemed the only escapes taking place were inspired individual efforts in which there were few places available for foot-soldiers. 'That was tried in 1941, this was tried in 1942,' recalls Pat Fergusson. 'It was obvious that these guys were pretty good and quite humbling to think of the amount they'd attempted which had failed.' By mid-July 1943, 210 officers had tried to escape in 111 attempts, and 123 of them had been caught inside the castle. These figures were enough to make a number of the new arrivals realise they would never escape from Colditz, however much they might want to: Colditz would be where they would spend the rest of the war. The rest did have one advantage; as newcomers they saw the idiosyncrasies of the castle's ancient structure with fresh eyes and, unlike the guards, they were on duty twenty-four hours a day.

One of the most talented new arrivals was a young sapper called Jock Hamilton-Baillie. Captured with the Highland Division at St Valery in 1940, 'HB' was an extremely experienced escaper who had already put his formidable practical skills to good use in his previous camps. He made his first solo effort from Tittmoning, where he set off for the Swiss frontier with only a general map to guide him. Following the River Inn, he 'boy-scouted' for nine days, sleeping rough in the woods and avoiding all contact with Germans. On the tenth day he broke cover and crossed the river, wandering into a meadow which he now believed to be in Switzerland. The border guard watched as this ragged figure approached; and unshouldered his rifle. Though this meadow lay on the Swiss side of the river it was still German soil, a crucial anomaly not shown on HB's large-scale map. The luckless Englishman was recaptured only yards from freedom; even his captor felt sorry for him.

He was returned to Warburg, a camp holding three thousand Allied officers. This hutted camp was built on a sandy plain surrounded by wire fences, and by the time Hamilton-Baillie arrived many tunnelling schemes were under way, 'so many that they were doomed to failure' he recalls; nevertheless he became involved in one that soon extended well beyond the perimeter fence. While working on the tunnel he also put his talents to use in another direction, and came up with the brilliant solution for a mass escape over the wire. Known as the 'Warburg Wire Job', this was one of the most audacious mass escape attempts of the war in which fifty men would travel over two eight-foot perimeter fences in under a minute and a half. 'I designed two-part ladders held together with ropes,' he recalls. 'The first man would run at the wire with the ladder and lean it against the fence. He then climbed the ladder, pushing the second part of it up in front of him. This pivoted and tipped down to form a bridge across the two wire fences. The escapers then ran across this bridge and swung down to the ground from a trapeze bar I had made at the end. There was bound to be shooting, so this all had to happen in the shortest possible time.'

Four ingenious hinged ladders were made from cross-beams in the prisoners' huts. To pass German inspections they became racks for sheet music, and while the camp orchestra was in full swing the ladders were erected inside the huts and the escapers relentlessly practised their drill. Their secret training meant that each man could cross the wire in eight seconds: in eighty seconds the operation would be complete.

On the night, at the prearranged time, the prisoners fused the lights and staged a decoy escape on the other side of the camp. In the ensuing chaos the teams rushed their ladders across to the fences and hoisted them into position. Three ladders worked with the hoped-for precision, but the fourth, wielded by the RAF, came to grief: they erected it upside down. Once out into the darkness of the plain, the escapers ran straight through the line of outer sentries, who were too surprised to react. Not one escaper was shot; and of the forty-three men who crossed the wire, three officers reached Holland, where a priest put them in touch with an escape route to England. They all made home runs.

Jock Hamilton-Baillie and his fellow tunnellers had planned to break out of their 140ft tunnel the same night as the wire job, but a tragedy had forced its discovery. A young officer in the Seaforth Highlanders, John de Pree, was crawling up to the face to begin his shift when a section of the roof fell on top of him carrying the electricity supply. Dressed only in shorts he received an electric shock and was knocked unconscious. The prisoners made frantic efforts to pull him out, but the tunnel was too narrow, and by the time the Germans had dug down to him, de Pree was dead. His death did not deter Hamilton-Baillie and his companions; shortly afterwards the entire British Contingent was transferred to Eichstätt, another hutted camp, and here 'HB' provided detailed construction diagrams for a tunnel that ran out of the camp, up a hill and under a road. The tunnel break came on the night of 3 June 1943: sixty-five officers escaped – a record at the time – but the German response was also unprecedented; the next day the whole of the surrounding countryside was put on alert, and 250,000 Hitler Youth, boy scouts and civilians were asked to hunt the escaped prisoners down. Every means of transport was searched and every field was combed, and within a week every escaper had been rounded up.

This heavy-handed response was a sign of the increasing wariness of the German authorities towards the millions of prisoners of war now interned in their country. The majority of these men were Russians and Poles, to the Nazis *untermensch* – subhumans – who, together with two million Frenchmen, now made up almost half the German work-force. The cheap labour they provided as farm labourers, miners and skilled metalworkers played an increasingly vital role in the economy, and the Nazis came to fear a bloody uprising, instigated by Allied spies or underground movements, and believed that sinister hands were at work behind every mass escape. Their concerns were, in fact, groundless, but large escapes advertised themselves and risked provoking a reaction that would have potentially tragic consequences.

'We'd all been told at Eichstätt that we would be shot if we got out on a mass escape, and this news was greeted with prolonged applause,' recalls Mike Edwards, who was recaught in a field one moonlit night by a gang of nervous farmers. 'When they'd got all of us we were all locked up in an SS barracks at Willibaldsburg and I think there was a row going on between the Wehrmacht and the police as to whether we should be exterminated. There happened to be a few lords and honourables among us, and I think because of that we were too conspicuous and not that easy to disguise if we all went missing. I think we were too indigestible for them.'

And so the 'Eichstätt mob' were sent to Colditz. Now that the camp was an all-British affair, cliques began to appear that reproduced, in miniature, the world of pre-war Britain. 'The class structure in Colditz was like the class structure at the time,' recalls Micky Burn, the communist commando. 'There was a working class, who were the soldiers, the orderlies who had to work for the Germans. And then there was a middle class, officers from minor and major public schools, and then there was an upper class, with the Prominente and several lords of the realm. And it was natural that people from similar backgrounds would mix together. Curiously enough, when I arrived at Colditz I was asked to join this very smart mess nicknamed the Bullingdon, named after an exclusive club at Oxford. It was made up of the sons of landed gentry, and a few lords, but none of them knew that I had been blackballed from the real Bullingdon when I was at Oxford before the war.'

Alongside the Bullingdon was the 'junior Bullingdon,' made up of people who would undoubtedly become members of the Bullingdon after the war, 'the House of Lords', 'the kindergarten', and many others. Some were very exclusive. 'There was a poker school which I joined almost as soon as I arrived,' remembers Michael Alexander, the second Prominente at Colditz. 'The sort of people who were used to a bit of gambling, White's Club types. I used to go there, and we played for hours every day. And I amassed quite a lot of money; of course, it would be paid after the war. After about a year and a half of serious play, I was about fifteen hundred pounds up, which I was spending in my mind, buying a motor car or something. And then David Stirling, of desert fame, suddenly arrived. He was a real blood, he'd gambled with the best of them. David introduced chemin de fer, which we'd never played. And almost the very first game I took on the bank and I did a thing called *suive*, in other words you follow your losses really, and you think, God, it's going to turn up next card, I'm going to win. Well, in fact I didn't, and after about six *suives*, I'd lost all my money that I'd gained, and another thousand besides. That dampened my ardour, I didn't play any more of that game. But it was a very good time-passer. We were rather cliquey up there, if the truth was known. Probably not all that popular.'

It was understood that gambling debts were to be honoured at the end of the war, and by and large they were; but the amount of promised money changing hands at the card tables began to concern the Senior British Officer, who at one stage made a fatherly intervention in an attempt to prevent the rich young men gambling their inheritances away.

The all-British Colditz had become more fragmented; and the atmosphere had changed, too. Committees and cliques replaced the old league of nations; it was now closer to a British military institution, alive with jealousies, self-awareness and suspicion of individuality. For some, this was a much less interesting proposition; the gossiping Padre Platt complained that Colditz had become a 'psychological mud flat' where the attractions of the 'other' had been replaced by 'British Bulldogs in various stages of plethoric and phlegmatic prison weariness'. And undoubtedly class did matter to those who cared about such things, but most felt that Colditz's unique entrance exam eliminated snobbery. 'Colditz was so much orientated to escape, escape, escape, that those things didn't matter at all,' recalls Frank Flinn, a sergeant pilot who had come up through the ranks. 'We came from different places but we were tied together by our desire to get out. Uniforms weren't worn much by the British, people didn't throw their ranks about. If they were good at anything, they were respected, it was a very healthy attitude.'

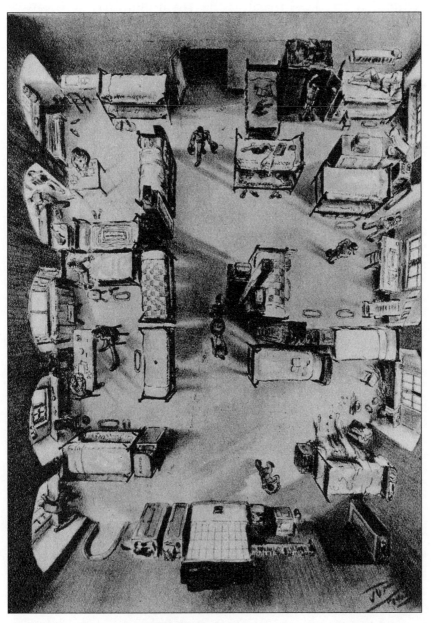

Aerial View Inside Prisoners' Quarters

Among the British this sense of national solidarity extended to the orderlies, the small number of ordinary soldiers employed by the Germans to work in the castle. Some of these men had also proved themselves in some way *Deutschfeindlich*, but most were not, and given that they could have been down a salt mine or working in a factory, they regarded the menial work at Colditz as 'a cushy number'. Some tidied the rooms of the senior officers, polished their boots and made their beds, others ran the German kitchens or performed chores in the Kommandantur. Occasionally they did complain, notably during the hot summer of 1941 when they refused to work in the heat, and then the Senior British Officer was embarrassed to discover that he had no power over them – they would only take orders from their employer, the Kommandant. Work apart, the orderly's life at Colditz was identical to the officers'; they were given their own quarters in the Saalhaus, they ate the same food and wore the same clothes. They were strictly forbidden to help their officer friends, and Prawitt in particular regarded any collaboration with escaping activities as a serious breach of trust. But it was impossible for them not to assist their countrymen. 'Occasionally we used to collect German uniforms from a storeroom,' remembers the medical orderly Alec Ross. 'We were guarded of course, but we used to try and pinch a couple of epaulets or insignia to give to the officers. Dick Howe gave us a large lump of chewing gum, and when we got in the door we put our chewing gum against the keyhole, took it out and walked away. I suppose they used it as a mould to make a duplicate.'

Orderlies were not told of escape plans – for the same reason that no one else was told, except those directly involved. Officially, as Allied soldiers, they too were expected to attempt to escape, but Reinhold Eggers knew these men were not committed to the cause, and he was keen to exploit any wavering allegiances. He had some success; in March 1942 a Ukrainian orderly betrayed a Polish tunnel in the sick bay, and to Eggers' disgust the culprit was then soundly beaten up. Then Julien Kerignard, a French NCO, betrayed the existence of 'Arthur 1', one of Guigues' contraband radios that had been bricked in behind a map of Tunis in the French quarters. The knobs were towns on the map. Kerignard won his freedom in return, and this time Eggers was careful not to reveal his source. His attempts to exploit the British orderlies had no success, justifying the confidence the officers had in them; but there was a feeling that involving orderlies in escapes would somehow compromise their status. The Geneva Convention made no distinction between officer and other ranks if they were caught escaping; twenty-eight days' solitary confinement was the maximum punishment. However, as employees of the Wehrmacht who had 'abused the trust placed in them', extra-punitive measures were threatened which might result in a court-martial and a spell in a military prison.

'When I first got to Colditz, I thought this is going to be a bloody good place,' remembers medical orderly Alec Ross. 'Everybody seemed to be friendly, and there were no ranks being pulled. Everyone was called by their name. But my job was looking after Douglas Bader. I used to have to go up at eight o' clock in the morning, take him his tea and he'd have his breakfast in bed. Then he'd take his legs off, jump on my back and I'd carry him down two flights of stairs for a bath. I sat outside the bathroom till he'd knock on the wall, and then I'd go in, he'd climb on my back and I'd carry him up two flights of stairs again. He was no light-weight. And I did that every day of the week.'

As a medical orderly Ross had no desire to escape; he

was due for repatriation in 1943. 'Hauptmann Püpcke came into the courtyard and he called me down. "Good news, Ross," he says. "You're going home." Douglas Bader happened to be there, and he said, "No he's bloody not. He came here as my lackey and he'll stay as my lackey." Püpcke looked at me and shrugged his shoulders. And so I had to stay another two bloody years when I could have gone home with the rest of my mates.'

Wing Commander Bader's treatment of his 'lackey' was the exception rather than the rule, and he alone is remembered as the one officer prone to throwing his rank around. In particular he often attempted to muscle in on escape schemes over roofs and through tunnels that were patently impossible for a tin-legged man. After the Senior British Office, 'Tubby' Broomhall, refused him a place on yet another scheme, the incensed Bader replied: 'Do you realise that the government at home would rather have me back than all the rest of you put together?' And he meant it.

As the British gradually found ways of living together, beyond their claustrophobic world the fortunes of war were changing. In August 1943 air raids became a regular event, and at the beginning of September the prisoners received news of the first Allied landings in Italy. Later in the month two thousand Red Cross parcels arrived, the largest consignment ever. Evidently Geneva anticipated a winter of disorganisation and shortages in Germany. Not long afterwards the prisoners received more indications of the hardening mood towards escapers. On 19/20 September forty-seven Polish officers broke out of a tunnel at Dossel, seven of whom had been at Colditz. Nine men escaped to safety; but thirty-eight were rounded up, removed by the Gestapo and taken to Buchenwald concentration camp, where they were hung from butchers' hooks. The Eichstätt mob had been lucky. That autumn the German propaganda minister, Goebbels, privately proposed to Hitler that all captured pilots, including those already in camps, should be shot as a deterrent to the bombing of Germany, which was reaching new levels of destruction. At the end of July, in an air raid codenamed 'Gomorrah', Allied bombers hit Hamburg, Germany's second-largest city, creating a firestorm of over 1,000 degrees Centigrade and 150-mile-an-hour winds; 40,000 civilians were incinerated. Cologne, Berlin and the Ruhr valley were also repeatedly targeted, as Bomber Harris stepped up his campaign to bring an early end to the war. Hitler did not favour retribution against POWs for these acts; he was aware of the thousands of Luftwaffe men now interned in Canada. But he took no official action against the bloodthirsty civilian lynch mobs who hunted downed aircrew after the raids, and the fate of the Dossel men provided an official warning of the Nazis' growing impatience with the escaping game.

The Wehrmacht was also becoming tougher. David Hunter, the naval lieutenant whose shouts of 'murderers' at the *Appell* after the Frans Josef escape fell foul of Eggers, was to be court-martialled for his bad behaviour. Unlike Pete Tunstall, who had already been court-martialled three times, Hunter was not exonerated; he was sentenced to three months at Graudenz, a military prison for Germans and POWs alike. His experiences there underlined what an island of safety Colditz had become.

'Graudenz was a professional prison, and they made it damned clear to you from day one that you marched double speed everywhere you went, you put your hands on top of your head to make sure that you weren't carrying anything, and you stayed in your cell for twenty-three hours out of the twenty-four. You had no one to talk to and nothing to read. Every time somebody came and looked through the peephole, you had to spring to attention and say who you were and what your number was. The incident that really brought it home to me how different life was involved this little guy, a lieutenant in the Italian military, who was sent to Graudenz for some act of disobedience, and then he had an attack of appendicitis. The Germans diagnosed it and two guards came in with a stretcher, carried him out, put him in the back of the ambulance, but they failed to shut the door properly. They then drove off at the standard sixty miles an hour, whereupon he shot out at the back – still on his stretcher – and they jumped out after him and shouted, "He's trying to escape!" So they bayoneted him in front of my eyes and that poor little sod took about four hours to die. They just wiped their bayonets on his tunic and drove off, leaving him on the stretcher lying in the middle of the parade ground.'

At Colditz the Germans' high regard for the rules of capture prevented this kind of retribution. By now the officers were well aware that beyond the walls of the castle there were any number of vengeful sergeants and sadistic policemen operating beyond the Geneva Convention, whose wrath was fuelled by Allied bombs and insolence. The persistent escapers at Colditz remained undeterred; in fact, the new boys had only made the escapers' queue longer. One man, who had been patiently waiting in line, was about to get his opportunity.

CHAPTER THIRTEEN

Ghosts

The failure of the Frans Josef attempt in September 1943 provided conclusive proof – if any more were needed – that the camp was now extremely difficult to get out of. The culture of suspicion Oberstleutnant Prawitt was so eager to foster now appeared to have taken root; the two-hundred-strong guard company under his command were well drilled, and replaced every six months to prevent them from becoming 'too friendly' with the prisoners. Each new batch that arrived was part of the National Protection Battalion 395 – they had trained together at Dresden and knew each other by sight. 'I knew practically everyone in the guard company,' recalls Peter Schneider, a young Gefreiter who arrived in 1943. 'I remember standing in the garrison court-yard talking to a sub-lieutenant, and somebody walked past in the distance and saluted in a very military fashion. At the time we had a lot of sappers here wiring the slopes around the castle, all wearing work clothes and fatigue jackets, as things here had become very informal. This man walked past smartly dressed and he saluted very correctly. It was unusual. I told the corporal that I thought an escaper had just gone past. He jumped up and immediately ran downstairs to tell the sergeant. "There he goes, there he goes, jump to it!" he shouted. The escaper managed to get as far as the guard on the gate, and there they caught him. The prisoners knew the sappers were here and they had taken advantage of it. But his uniform gave him away; it was too good."

Trying to escape across the Kommandantur courtyard was the plan of Lieutenant Gris Davies-Scourfield. A moustach-ioed young officer in the King's Royal Rifles, he had been left for dead in the street battle for Calais in 1940, and awoke to find himself lying on a road, at night, with his tin helmet still on his head. It was a dish of blood − his own. Looking up, he saw a scavenging German soldier looting the bodies around him. He approached Gris brandishing a bayonet. '*Verwundet?*' wounded? Gris nodded in reply. '*Hilfe kommt.*' The soldier spared his life, and when Gris recovered he was sent to Laufen and then on to Posen POW camp. From here he escaped with Ronnie Littledale and his friend Mike Sinclair, and found shelter with the ubiquitous Mrs M of the Warsaw underground. She harboured him for eleven months before he attempted to escape again, but he was caught heading south, and sent to Colditz. Eggers regarded Davies-Scourfield − somewhat charitably − as 'one of our most dangerous escapers'. 'I think I was more of an enthusiastic amateur,' he recalls. 'I was no locksmith and I didn't partic-ularly like tunnels, but I was an escaper, and escapers must always escape. Wherever an escaper was, if he was locked up in a room the first thing he would do would be to look at

the windows, try the door, see what the walls were made of
– it was a natural instinct. He wasn't going to be locked up
without a jolly good try to get out of it. I think that most
of the successful escapers weren't going to ever stop trying
to escape – I like to think I was like that too.'

Davies-Scourfield's previous escape from Posen had been
in a box of rubbish, and this was to be his chosen method
for escaping from Colditz. 'The idea was put into my head
one hot sunny afternoon when I was sitting on a step in
the courtyard,' he recalls. 'One or two of the orderlies came
up to me and said, "Look, we know you're keen on escaping,
we've got an idea that you might like to think about." On
certain days of the week they had to clear all the straw and
cardboard from the parcels office, put it in a handcart and
take it into the German part of the camp escorted by a
German corporal. Once there they emptied it into a cellar.
They said we can cover you in rubbish and get you into
that cellar, and when it is all quiet you can just walk away.'

The simplicity of the idea was attractive. The orderlies told
Gris that Corporal Schädlich – 'Dixon Hawke' – had only
checked the rubbish with his bayonet once, so if he was lucky
he would not be stabbed to death before he left the prisoners'
courtyard. They were also confident that Hawke could be
distracted while Gris was emptied out of the handcart and
concealed under the rubbish in the cellar. The idea was
approved by the escape committee in the spring of 1943,
well before the Frans Josef attempt was conceived, but in due
course the size and complications of that escape shunted
Davies-Scourfield's scheme back down the queue.

With time on his hands, Gris channelled his frustrations
into working out the many details of this 'simple escape'.
As an enthusiastic amateur, he relied upon all the machinery
of the escape industry which served the Frans Josef attempt

so well to help him in his solo effort. After four months of false starts and guidance from the experts he possessed a civilian suit, a Gefreiter's uniform, passes, maps, money and two very valuable keys. The first, coincidentally a key already in the escape committee's possession, would allow him to unlock the door of the cellar. Obtaining the second proved more of a challenge. Davies-Scourfield had decided the best way out of the camp was through a small wicket gate the prisoners passed on their way down to the park. At this point their procession was always heavily guarded, and no officer had yet tried to unlock this gate. 'The Dutch agreed to help me,' Gris remembers. 'On the way back from the park they staged a riot, and two people made a very foolish attempt to escape. Of course, all the guards unslung their rifles and ran after them. While this was going on a Dutchman sidled up to the lock, inserted his home-made lock-measuring device and took his measurements. A few days later he gave me the key. "I can't guarantee it will work", he said, "but it might. Good luck."'

Gris hid his equipment deep under the floorboards of the British quarters. At the last minute he slipped in a small box of raisins, a fragment of mirror and a comb to straighten his appearance before leaving the cellar. On 29 September 1943, he shaved off his trademark moustache and had his hair cropped in the German style. He was ready.

'My plan was to go immediately after the first roll-call of the morning,' he recalls. 'Once the guard was drawn away from the door of the parcel office, I was whisked fairly quickly across the courtyard by Dick Howe and Lulu Lawton dressed up in all my disguises. I had on my civilian suit, the German uniform over the top, some dungarees over everything and probably a cloak as well. Into the parcel office, and I was packed into this tiny cart. It was jolly small and

I felt rather like an oven-ready chicken with my legs up by my ears. I was covered over with straw and paper, then the two orderlies carried me out, and I hoped – because it wasn't very comfortable – that they'd take me straight through the main gate. Not a bit of it. Dixon Hawke decided that he had some business to do in the camp and he told the two orderlies to put me down in the courtyard and wait till he returned. I could see through a crack in the box some of my friends walking past, and I thought, I wonder if he knows I'm lying in this beastly box. Eventually the Hawke returned and fortunately he didn't stick his bayonet into me, so down we went, through the massive wooden door – it was a jolly bumpy ride as these two Scottish soldiers staggered over the cobbles. They were a marvellous couple, and after all, this was their idea. Halfway down the cobbled passage to the cellar I heard one of them say under his breath, "I can't hold him," and the other said, "We're nearly there, man, just hang on, keep it up, you'll do it all right." They opened the cellar door and dumped me down in this great pile of sawdust and cardboard. At this point one of them took the Hawke outside and began talking to him, while I was buried in the rubbish. Then the door shut and all I had to do was wait. I didn't move for ten minutes. I then emerged, took off the dungarees and buried them so I was now dressed as a German corporal. I got out my little mirror and comb, and smartened myself up as best I could, made sure my hat was straight on my head, then I waited till I was sure there were plenty of German soldiers walking about. I unlocked the door and stepped outside, hoping it was not obvious that I was a British officer dressed as a German corporal.'

All Davies-Scourfield had to do was to walk across the busy German courtyard. He was not aware that all the guards knew each other well, and had made no provision for pretending to be a stranger. 'I'd watched how the average German soldier walked – did he march or did he shuffle along? It was something in between, and so I tried to imitate what I'd seen, and somehow I reached the archway at the other side of the courtyard. I resisted the very strong temptation to look back over my shoulder. I came out into the light and was already clutching this important key in my hand, it was like a big church key the Dutchman had made for me. This was the great decisive moment of the escape – was this key going to work? I heard the lock turn, and then "click", and the gate fell open. I was through. It was a great moment, to smell the autumn countryside and be walking in among all these leaves. I walked up to the top of the hill and I was gone.'

Davies-Scourfield shed his German uniform for his home-made suit, skirted around Colditz town and headed west into the forest. He aimed for Bad Lausich, a small spa town ten miles away, from where he intended to travel by train north to the Dutch border. Holland was now the preferred choice of Colditz escapers; though the castle was closer to Switzerland, ever since the Germans and Italians entered Vichy France in November 1942 returning to England from its borders had become a dangerous business. Bill Fowler and Ronnie Littledale were the first successful Colditz escapers to attempt the trip: they travelled in disguise across Vichy France to the Pyrenees, where a guide led them over the mountains and deposited them in Spain. There, as they had hoped, they were arrested by the border guards and taken to Figueras jail, where the British consul was informed of their presence. But they then faced a delay of three weeks while the paperwork was completed, during which time they were put in a filthy cell with fourteen others; they were all inoculated with the same needle, and conditions were so bad that by the time the escapers were released two of their cell mates had died.

Davies-Scourfield knew that on reaching Holland, which was still under German occupation, he could contact one of the escape lines that smuggled prisoners directly back to England. 'I spoke a bit of German, and was confident my papers were in order, so I bought a ticket to Leipzig. I had no intention of going to Leipzig because I knew that the security, if they had discovered my escape, would have put an extra guard there. And my "ghost" was standing in my place, so I had a fair chance of getting away.'

'Ghosts' were not unique to Colditz, but Colditz had more need for them than other camps because so many officers were frequently 'missing'. The idea of having two officers in the camp who were 'there but not present', covering for escapers while they were out, originally arose out of a British tunnel scheme under the chapel. 'Since the French had made a large hole in the floor the building was alarmed and invariably locked,' recalls Jack Best. 'So to get in we went under some stairs and through a series of five trapdoors, each of which was camouflaged. This in itself was very laborious, and by the time we reached the chapel tunnel, there was yet another *Appell* and we had to come out again.' Jack Best, an RAF officer, and Mike Harvey, a naval lieutenant, volunteered to work on the tunnel permanently, and to disappear they first had to 'escape', in a carefully constructed event.

On 5 April 150 prisoners turned out for the park walk. Eggers, ever suspicious, prepared for mischief as the officers milled about and deliberately confused the count. Once under way the large column snaked down into the Kommandantur, and halfway across the yard a Dutchman leaned out of a window and ordered all the Dutch officers to return to their quarters for a lecture. The Dutch turned on their

heels and obeyed, causing chaos as the guards tried to contain
the ranks of men marching in opposite directions. In the
middle of this confusion two German officers appeared down
at the park gate with permits to visit the grounds of the
castle. By chance the German post sergeant, 'Beau Max', was
passing, and recognised these two as Captain Dufour and
Flight Lieutenant van Rood attempting to escape. This was
too much of a coincidence, and all 150 officers were ordered
back to the prisoners' courtyard for a head count. The *Appell*
that followed began at 5 p.m. and lasted four hours as the
Germans counted and recounted every officer in the camp.
By 9 p.m. they finally realised that Best and Harvey were
missing, and presumed they had escaped in the confusion
in the German yard.

'The first three days we spent underground in a specially
prepared hidey-hole under the pulpit in the chapel,' remembers Jack Best. 'In the evening we were let out for an hour
and there was a meal waiting for us and some hot water to
have a good scrub down. Then we went back again. We'd
taken bottles with us for the necessities of life in the hole;
so it wasn't too bad. For the next three weeks we came up
every night and someone went down in our place. We slept
in their bed, because very occasionally the Germans did a
knob count in the dormitories; they didn't identify people,
they just counted who was there. Then after a couple of
months we were up and about all day. Whichever room we
were in there was always someone on the door to tell us if
the Germans were coming up. If they did come we would
hide in a cupboard and prayed they wouldn't inspect it. They
never did. We always hid on parades, unless we had to take
the place of someone who was escaping, and then we would
stand in the middle rank so we would not be counted
directly. Both of us had assumed identities – mine was Bob

Barnes, which passed a couple of thorough searches. We both became professional liars, and the Germans were quite gullible. Once all the Eichstätt officers arrived we even used to go down into the courtyard disguised in army uniform and walk around with them; they didn't know who we were, and the Germans certainly didn't.'

The ghosts' greatest sacrifice was their inability to contact the outside world. 'The Navy were very good and told Mike Harvey's next of kin,' recalls Jack Best. 'His parents knew exactly what was happening. But the RAF wouldn't tell anybody anything. My wife even went to the Air Ministry, who just talked a lot of waffle about what a good job I was doing, and they pretended they didn't know anything. So this led to some very embarrassing questions coming from the Red Cross to the Kommandant asking where the hell I was. He assumed I had escaped.' In return for their noblesse, Best and Harvey did enjoy one perk: they went straight to the front of the escape queue. Until now escapes had generally been organised on a first come, first served basis: the officer who dreamed up the scheme and pitched it to the escape committee was allotted the first place; then, if there were any spare berths for travelling companions, these were awarded to men who would be most useful to the war effort. During the first two years of the war pilots and submariners received this preferential treatment because they had been trained to perform specific tasks. The call-up could be unexpected: David Wheeler, a young submariner, was alarmed to find himself suddenly escaping on Christmas Eve. 'Pat Reid asked me if I wanted to escape, to which the reply was a confident affirmative,' he remembers. 'So he then took me out to the courtyard, pointed what seemed to be five hundred feet into the air and said "See that roof?" and I said, "Yes, I saw the roof all right." "Well," he said, "it's a piece of cake really, you just climb out through that window on to the gutter of the roof, and slide along for about twenty yards, then you can get in the German quarters. After that it's simple. Are you still keen?" I was much too afraid to say that I was afraid, so I said "yes", thinking of my Christmas dinner which I was really looking forward to, it being the highlight of our culinary year. I gathered my various passes and clothes ready, then Reid came to me and said that unfortunately the French were unable to get into the attic and so the escape was off. I was not unpleased.'

By 1943 this system had been replaced by a meritocracy where the ghosts had a pre-booked ticket, which in its turn created some frustrations among those farther down the line. But it was fair, and such was the authority of Dick Howe, the Escape Officer, that these decisions were never challenged.

Mike Harvey, alias 'Lieutenant Bartlett', had now appeared from the fabric of the castle and was patiently making up the numbers for Gris Davies-Scourfield at every *Appell* for which he was absent. Nothing had been heard of the escaper for two days, and during that time he had made steady progress north-west. Every train carried him ever closer to the Dutch border, and he was enjoying an unusual degree of escaper's luck. 'I boarded a packed train which stopped at Halberstadt,' he recalls. 'And a team of Gestapo came on, checking everyone's papers in great detail. I was standing right at the end of the carriage, and directly in front of me stood an old woman. When they got to her, she gave them her permit and something was wrong, I couldn't quite work it out. The German policemen started shouting at her, whereupon she shouted back, and this good old barney started. It went on so long that the train began to move off. The two policemen immediately stopped what they were doing, barged past me and jumped off. They never asked to see my papers.'

A British Officer 'Touring' in Germany

Davies-Scourfield reached Hildesheim at midday, three days after leaving Colditz. Now less than ninety miles from the Dutch border, he had a five-hour wait before his connecting train to Osnabrück. It was a small local station and, not wanting to court suspicion, he decided to wander into the town and spend a few hours in the cinema, a favoured hiding-place of escapers. However, as he left the platform the ticket collector appeared so interested in him that Davies-Scourfield decided to change his plans. Looking at his timetable, he realised that the train also stopped at Elze, ten miles farther up the road.

He decided to walk. 'I don't know whether it was a good or a bad decision, but it seemed sensible at the time,' he recalls. 'After all, the escaper, alone in a world of enemies, cold, hungry and tired, can only do what his instincts tell him is best. The road stretched endlessly before me. I looked carefully around: I could see no one in the fields. I soon found myself approaching a small village, a mile or two from Elze, which I could see in the distance. I considered for a moment whether I should avoid the village and take to the field, but thought it would be more natural to keep to the road. I walked straight on. As I entered the village I suddenly saw in front of me two policemen sitting on motorcycles chatting together. They looked fairly harmless, but they turned to look at me as I approached. I was obviously under scrutiny, but I felt fairly happy and natural in my role as a Belgian worker. "Good day, lovely weather," I said. They nodded amiably enough, and on I went. I had covered a good hundred yards or more when I heard both motor-cycles start up, and down they swooped on me from behind. They pulled up either side of me. And one said, "*Ausweis Bitte.*"

'So I got it out, and showed them my papers that had been made in the camp. They studied them very carefully, then one of them waved the paper in my face.

'"This paper," he said with great emphasis in that loud, slightly hysterical voice so beloved of German officialdom, "IS FALSE."

'And he was right. There was a small mistake on one of the papers.

'So I said, "Don't be ridiculous, how can it be false, it's got a stamp on it, look."

'"IST FALSCH! IST FALSCH!"

'And so I was arrested.'

Once at the local police station Davies-Scourfield main-tained his Belgian worker identity for as long as he dared. The police grew ever more aggressive and threatening, and it was clear they did not believe him, so he revealed his nationality. '"English?" they said, and their voices betrayed that curious respect which Germans seemed so often to show us.' The pacified policeman handed him a greasy cup of coffee and a cigarette, and locked him in the cells for the night. Gris knew his 'ghost' would stand in for him for ten days, and then return into hiding. Having been out for only three days, he needed to assume another identity to protect him, so Gris told his captors that he was Private Brown, who had escaped from Lamsdorf, a large other-ranks POW camp. The Germans accepted this and put him in the local Russian POW camp while the paperwork was prepared. On the eleventh day Gris revealed that he was, in fact, an officer who had escaped from Colditz, but this news fell upon deaf ears. If he said he was Private Brown, then Private Brown he must be, and soon a 'genial-looking Fritz' appeared to escort him back to Lamsdorf. Initially offended to be thought so harmless as to merit only one old guard, Gris soon took every opportunity to give him the slip, including the oldest trick in the book. '"May I go to the lavatory?" I asked. "Yes, down that way," said Fritz, and to my utter astonishment I was allowed to wander off down the corridor on my own, pushing past sleeping, sprawling soldiers, until I was almost at the end of the train. Once in the WC I locked the door, opened the window and waited for the train to slow down. But it hurtled on at sixty miles an hour, much too fast for me to contemplate a jump. Finally people started knocking on the door, and I waited and waited but the train wouldn't slow down. Eventually they broke the door down and the old guard said, "How can you do this to me when I am so kind to you, this is the second time you have tried to escape." He woke up then and they cleared out a compartment and I was surrounded by six German soldiers, including one who sat opposite me with pistol drawn. So I couldn't get away again, but I arrived at Lamsdorf feeling like a proper escaper.' Eventually he was returned to Colditz, and Eggers was amazed; he was not even aware than Davies-Scourfield had left. Eventually he worked out that the escapers' rubbish route had been followed a week later by Alan Orr-Ewing, who was recaptured in Colditz town; but the mystery of the ghosts continued to haunt him for another five months.

By the time Davies-Scourfield returned from his obligatory spell in the cells, his old friend Mike Sinclair was planning another escape. Having barely recovered from being shot at point-blank range in the Frans Josef attempt, Sinclair now spent his evenings gazing out of the windows of the Kellerhaus overlooking the town. The ghost Jack Best kept him company during these vigils. 'Mike reasoned that nobody had ever escaped from this corner of the castle,' he recalls. 'Therefore the Germans hadn't increased their defences here and therefore it must be the easiest place to get out. This was as good a theory as any and a very sensible one.'

The western side of the castle was hardly unprotected. Directly below the windows of the British quarters ran an upper terrace, approached by a door in the guardhouse. It was lit and at night patrolled by a sentry. Thirty feet below this was a garden, laid out on the western rampart. At the north-west corner stood the machinegun pagoda. The rampart was ringed by an eight-foot wire perimeter fence, beyond which the hillside fell away precipitously towards the town. Only Don Thom, the disturbed Canadian gymnast, had leaped thirty feet from the upper to the lower terrace and then vaulted the wire down into the park below. This extraordinary feat could not be repeated, but Sinclair's patient hours of observation suggested a brief moment of opportunity no other officer had noticed. Just before dusk the sentries changed from their day to night positions, so their vision of the terraces would not be impaired once the castle searchlights were switched on. The pagoda was vacated, and the guard climbed up to a machinegun mounted in a small tower on the north-west corner of the castle. At the same time the sentry on the upper terrace was replaced by the sentry in the garden below. It took a minute for this changeover to occur, and during this time there were no guards out on the western terrace.

Sinclair intended to use this precise moment to stage a dramatic exit. He would leap out of the second-storey window and down the two terraces on a ninety-foot rope. Then he would cut a hole in the perimeter wire and drop a further hundred feet into the town. With a mere sixty seconds in which to attempt this, Sinclair asked Dick Howe, the Escape Officer, to direct operations. Even John Watton, the camp artist, was enrolled to record in his sketchbook the best ways of exiting through a barred window at speed. To save precious seconds they decided to launch Sinclair out of the window off a polished table following a strict drill. One other place on the scheme was available, and it went to six-foot-two Jack Best as a reward for his days as a ghost.

'I had no experience of rope-climbing before,' remembers Best, a pilot shot down in Greece. 'But we practised. We built a little trapdoor the size of the gap between the bars, and set it up at the top of a spiral staircase. That gave us a drop of about fifteen feet. We practised going through wearing all our clothes so that there would be no hesitation. Mike would lead, exiting feet first and hanging on to the rope. Just before he hit the terrace two strong fellows would break his fall and then I would follow, head first on my back.' The plan was to stay attached to the rope and descend the next thirty-five-foot drop to the garden using the same technique. On touchdown the rope would be hastily hauled back up into the barred window. It was audacious and physical, and to be successful both men needed complete confidence in the ninety-foot bed rope designed to carry them at high speed. 'Because I was in the Navy and used to do all the rigging of the boats, the laying of buoys and so on, I took on the job,' remembers John 'Bosun' Chrisp, the official Colditz rope-maker. 'I had a team of eight, and the escape committee provided me with needles and thread. Dick Howe brought me the sheets and said, "We want a ninety-foot rope out of that," so I got on with it. We rolled them up tight and stitched them together in six-foot sections so there were no ragged edges. It was a wonderful rope, thick enough to get hold of and perfect for sliding down, so the getting away was as efficient as a gun drill.'

The attempt was set for dusk on 19 January 1944. There were eight men in the room: on the polished table angled in front of the window lay Mike Sinclair with the coiled rope next to him. Jack Best waited beside the table, and two strong officers stood either side of the window to bend back the iron bars. Dick Howe, his face blackened against the searchlights, watched the terrace below. Lurking in the background sat John Watton, the artist; he had recorded the positions of the men as they swung out of the practice window in the stairwell — now he would sketch the real thing. All eyes were focused on the darkening sky to the west; the atmosphere was one of almost unendurable excitement. 'I cannot describe the tension in the room the actual night of the launch,' recalls Davies-Scourfield, who watched the preparations with silent regret; Sinclair had originally asked him to go, but Jack Best the ghost had been awarded the place. 'I remember standing in the darkness by the doorway, seeing my friend Mike Sinclair lying face downwards on the table. He gripped the rope under his elbow, and round his waist he had the second part of the rope for the descent from the upper terrace. He was dressed head to foot in black, wearing a Balaclava and socks over his shoes. He had a large pair of wire cutters strapped to the inside of one leg, then all the paraphernalia he needed for crossing Germany – a compass, maps, money some train timetables and everything else. One could almost feel the intensity of his fierce and single-minded concentration, remembering all the things he would have to do the moment he was projected through the window.'

At the adjacent windows stooges stood reporting the movements of the sentries just as they were about to change into their night positions. Gris relayed these whispered instructions into the room.

'Sentry A. Moving right.

'Sentry C. Now at point 3.

'Sentry B. No movement.

'Sentry A. Now at point 1.

'Sentry B. OK.

'Sentry C. OK.

'Guardroom no movement.

'Sentry A. OK.

'All OK now . . . I felt so excited I could hardly say the great word. All ready, all is ready. At which point Dick Howe said, "GO!"'

Two strong men wrenched the bars back and Mike Sinclair shot feet first out into the blackness, the rope fizzing out behind him. At thirty feet two officers braced the rope and Sinclair landed silently on the first terrace. In seconds Jack Best had slid down next to him. Sinclair ran to the balustrade and threw over the end of the second rope, attached to which was a small briefcase on a rotten piece of string. This dropped down silently on to the lower terrace garden thirty feet below. Still braced by the men up at the window, Sinclair swung over the parapet and down to the lower level; Jack Best climbed on to the rope above him and started to slide down. As he began his descent he heard the sound of a key in a door – the guardhouse door opening on to the terrace.

'As soon as I heard the sound I knew something was wrong,' he recalls. 'Somehow, when Mike was throwing the rope down to the lower terrace or when I was leaning over, one of us must have pressed a warning bell without realising it. We didn't know we had done it. We crouched in the shadow of the wall; the rope was whisked back up into the window. The guard came out wearing spectacles, and stepping out into the darkness somehow he missed seeing the ninety-foot rope flying across the terrace and up the wall into the window. We got the signal to cross the garden on the lower terrace, and Mike crawled to the wire, preparing to cut the three strands. When you cut a wire it goes "ping" all down the line. It doesn't matter how you do it, whether quickly or slowly, you can't avoid it. So you cut one, wait thirty seconds, and then the next. He cut the first strand and stayed absolutely still. The guard immediately turned towards the sound and looked. No, no, he thought, it was his imagination – he turned away. Mike cut the next one, and then the last, his timing was perfect. He fastened the small rope to a post and dropped away down the precipice. I crawled over to the hole he'd made, wriggled through and lay on the parapet beside it. My job now was to patch it up with boot-laces so the wire looked as if it hadn't been cut and there might be a chance for someone to go the next night. But while I was lying on the parapet the goon on the terrace must have been staring at me. "Hullo?" he said.

'And I reckoned then that discretion was the better part

of valour. I dropped out of sight as quickly as I could. When Mike saw me coming he had a few rude remarks to make until I explained the situation. We then went absolutely flat out. It was a forty-five-degree slope of shale with eighteen inches of barbed wire all over it which ripped our clothes to shreds. We made such a racket that an old woman appeared at the window of the nearest house and gawped at us. Why the hell she didn't shout out the Lord alone knows. We then came to the final piece of wire at the bottom, and again we should have cut a little neat hole and patched it up. But we cut a hell of a hole and went straight through it, dropping into the back yard of a cottage. We took off our escape gear, climbed into our civvies, opened the doors on to the street and just walked away. After all, it was our street, we owned it.'

Best and Sinclair had broken out of the castle in under sixty seconds. Up in the dark room above the terrace, the men were silent; moments before they too had been escaping. Somewhere down in the town their two companions were walking as free men, while almost inexplicably they remained, prisoners within the castle walls. 'It was,' remembers Gris Davies-Scourfield, 'an extraordinary feeling.' The searchlights flashed on and the world beyond was thrown into darkness.

As soon as Best and Sinclair reached the safety of Colditz forest they set about mending their clothes. Best darned the rips in his coat by the light of Sinclair's cigarette, and together they set off for the Dutch border. A day later they arrived at Rheine, where they were forced to wander into the town at night, waiting for their train connection. Here their luck ran out – a Gestapo agent followed them and picked them up in the street. 'I think it was because of my face,' remembers Jack Best. 'Mike was all right, because he was red-faced, red-haired, and in the north of Germany they are very much that colouring. He was wearing a brown coat and a hat, whereas I was in black. Black was apparently a very unGerman colour. And I had a very white face because I was still a ghost, and I had hardly been outside for months. I just didn't look German enough.'

They succeeded in convincing the Gestapo they were not spies, and the two escapers were returned to Colditz, Jack Best still maintaining he was his alias 'Bob Barnes'. Eggers would not unravel the mystery of the ghosts until two months later, when he caught Mike Harvey attempting to escape with Bush Parker. Using an old photograph, he was able to identify him as Harvey and not 'Bartlett', his alias. Despite a convincing story, Harvey could only prolong the inevitable conclusion, and soon the riot squad were combing the prisoners' courtyard looking for Jack Best, the man who had 'escaped' with Mike Harvey in April 1943. It was beyond Eggers' comprehension that the two officers had been hiding inside the castle for almost a year, avoiding all searches, and even posing as other officers. His incredulity was shared by the OKW in Berlin; on receiving his report they dispatched their own detective to Colditz to investigate. How could two officers be absent from 1,326 *Appells*, and three Gestapo *Appells*? Berlin preferred their own theory: Jack Best and Mike Harvey had escaped in April 1943, but after several months at large in Germany they found life too difficult on the outside and together they broke back into the castle. The Kommandant was not amused. 'Is this place a damned hotel?' he asked. 'Where people come and go as they wish?' The Wehrmacht detective reluctantly confirmed Eggers' suspicions, and both men were sentenced to twenty-eight days' solitary for the trouble they had caused. There were no more ghosts in Colditz.

CHAPTER FOURTEEN

A Radio, a Madman and a Spy

The year 1943 ended, unusually, in a truce. The British decided that between Christmas Eve and 2 January there would be no escaping; and in return they asked for no midnight searches or snap *Appells*. 'We naturally agreed – with considerable relief,' wrote Eggers, well aware that his captives may have called a truce but their country certainly hadn't; the distant thunder on Christmas Eve was the sound of the first thousand-bomber raid on Leipzig, only twenty-four miles away. Inside Colditz Castle the prisoners' party carried on. The Red Cross supplied the food, meagre though it was, and the inmates supplied the alcohol, concocted in the growing number of illicit stills around the courtyard. The celebrations concealed the truth that by this time escaping from Colditz had slowed to a trickle. The figures spoke for themselves: in 1942 sixty-six escape attempts had been made, and thirteen resulted in home runs; 1943 saw the number drop to twenty-six, and only one Frenchman got home. Despite the elaborate efforts of the prisoners, the German star was now in the ascendant: their Sonderlager could at last justifiably claim to be escape-proof. As was his habit, Padre Platt recorded the mood of his flock in his final diary entry of the year: 'Young men have grown old from prison-weariness and hope deferred. Conversation has almost stagnated except for topics of war news, letters, and sex perversion. But the high moral behaviour of the majority is eloquent testimony to the character of fighting men who, after four years of abnormal activity and inhibition, are as clean of mind and thought as ever. Pat Reid married an American heiress in Switzerland two months ago!'

This last piece of news must have appeared from another world; but ever since July 1943 the world beyond the castle had seemed tangibly closer. Before the French contingent left the camp for Lübeck, the ingenious Frédo Guigues let Dick Howe into a well-kept secret: the French had a radio hide high up in the attic of the Kellerhaus. With the help of his wife, Guigues smuggled two radios into the camp; the first, nicknamed 'Arthur 1', had been betrayed, but 'Arthur 2' remained so well concealed that only a structural engineer might guess that its hiding place even existed.

Ever since 1940, the Germans had done everything possible to prevent the POWs entering the empty attics above the prisoners' courtyard. At the top of each spiral stair-case they installed steel doors which they bolted, padlocked and secured with cruciform locks – all to little effect. Frédo Guigues, the master locksmith, had found a way through, as had Damiaem van Doorninck, his Dutch counterpart. Now the French and Dutch had gone, the British came to rely on their own experts to let them in, and in particular an

ebullient young Australian fighter pilot named 'Bush' Parker.
Bush was an 'extraordinarily handsome man' whose sleights
of hand included pulling cigarettes from behind his friends'
ears, counting cards, and on one occasion surviving a German
search holding a handful of tools. As the ferrets inspected
his pockets and clothes, Bush disguised the tools in a handkerchief, and to his friends' amazement moved them from
hand to hand unnoticed. He also claimed to be able to open
any lock in the castle; and the British in particular were
keen to hold this cocky young Australian to his word. Don
Donaldson, his compatriot, was there to witness Bush's first
attempt to get into the attics. 'The scene was just like you
have seen time and again in the movies; three desperate men
up in a dusty old attic with very poor light, all concen-
trating on that door. A tube of toothpaste was the only
equipment Bush had. With his ear pressed against the door
he cautiously worked the lock dials. When a tumbler lifted
he injected the toothpaste to hold it in the open position.
Finally he manoeuvred all of the tumblers the right way,
and the door swung open. Within a week Bush could master
a lock in thirty seconds without using the toothpaste.'

Once the door was open the British officers entered a
vast dusty space above the Kellerhaus, two storeys high and
triangular in shape. To reach the radio hide, the officers
would have to walk the length of the attic, which appeared
easy enough – but for a few pieces of rubbish the floor
was empty. Frédo Guigues had warned them otherwise; on
his first reconnaissance trip he was surprised by some suspicious ferrets searching the attic, and with nowhere to hide
had leaped up into the roof beams. 'As soon as they had
closed the door behind them,' he recalls, 'I watched one of
the ferrets take a two-metre rule from his pocket and, aided
by his companion, measure the distance of a rag "left

behind" on the floor between the metal door and the adjacent wall. The two searchers then examined the attic floor
close to the metal door where people would be obliged to
walk, attempting to detect traces of footprints. Luckily we
had taken the precaution of sprinkling the floor with dust
after each visit.'

Guigues' warning did not go unheeded; the two pairs of
British officers chosen to operate the radio hide were accompanied by a 'putter-in' whose sole task was to disguise their
tracks across the attics. Wearing shoes without any tread, the
radio team followed a designated path to the far wall, where
two loose floorboards revealed a heavy section of joist the
French had brought up from the chapel. Lifting this aside,
the radio operator and the 'scribe' dropped down into a tiny
compartment, wedged between the pitched roof of the
Kellerhaus and the ceiling of the room below, whereupon
the putter-in replaced the joist above them. They now found
themselves in the most carefully guarded hide in Colditz. 'It
was an amazing place,' recalls Jim Rogers, who became one
of the two radio scribes. 'The French have a flair for comfort
and convenience. Dick Howe and I were seated side by side
at a small table. Opposite Dick was the radio and opposite
me a writing area with papers and pencils all ready. Our
seats were upholstered. There were charts and maps on the
wall to help us in following the course of the war. The walls
were lined with blankets to protect us from the cold, and
to avoid light penetrating. But ingenuity did not end there.
The French had scraped an area near our feet to the very
ceiling plaster of the room below. If the Germans were ever
to penetrate to the hide via our entrance, hopefully the
occupants would get clean away with the radio and other
precious contraband hidden there.'

Several times the Germans came close to discovering the

hide, and the two prisoners were condemned to sit in total darkness trying not to sneeze or cough; but its unusual position between the roofline and the ceiling guaranteed its safety. Each evening the two-man radio team would go up to catch the 7 p.m. BBC nightly news bulletin, which lasted about twenty minutes, and very occasionally they tuned into other programmes. Jimmy Yule, the piano-playing Royal Signaller, was another of the radio operators. 'The very first time I went up I was a bit early for the news so I searched around for something to listen to. I sat there and then I heard a curious sound . . . pock, pock, pick, pock . . . fifteen love. It was a tennis match at Wimbledon. This was the most unreal sound I've ever heard in my life, quite ridiculous to think of me sitting inside an attic in Colditz listening to Wimbledon.'

Once the news was over, the scribe and operator left the hide and retraced their steps back to the prisoners' quarters, where the representatives from each mess awaited them. While a stooge stood on the door, the radio scribe then dictated from his pages of shorthand the news of the day, and this was passed rapidly around the camp. The nightly news bulletin soon became a high point in the prisoners' monotonous existence, and confirmed what the bombing raids all around them indicated; the war was now running firmly in the Allies' favour. As the British and American forces advanced up through Italy during the autumn of 1943, bets were placed on which town would fall next, and when the war would end; and Jim Rogers, nicknamed 'The Old Horse', soon gained a reputation as a master storyteller as he drew out the process of revelation to his eager audience, who had money riding on his every word. Eventually these news bulletins – complete with Jim Rogers' 'spin' – replaced escaping as the greatest source of morale in the camp.

Eggers knew the British listened to the BBC bulletins; he could read it in their mood. But he never found the hide, and towards the end of the war the British realised that he too was listening to the BBC, an illegal act punishable by death. He never admitted as much, and neither did they.

January 1944 was a nervous month for the Kommandant: barely two weeks after the unofficial 'truce' was over, Jack Best and Mike Sinclair made their daredevil sixty-second escape out of the window, and this provoked the SS, led by the Criminal Commissioner from Dresden, to make their second official search of the camp. They uncovered a few altered uniforms and some home-made fat lamps, meagre fare considering the treasures that now lay well concealed within the castle. Three days later the Prominente were about to sit down to supper when a German officer walked in and ordered them to be locked up in their rooms. They refused, whereupon Hauptmann Püpcke appeared with the riot squad; the order was enforced at gunpoint. It was clear that, as the war turned against Germany, the potential value of these hostages grew; and the OKW even suspected the British secret service might attempt to parachute into Colditz and recapture these men. Since the middle of 1943 they had stationed a rapid response unit at Bad Lausich, equipped with lorries and tanks to deal with any potential threat. The Prominente were being carefully protected; for what, they could not tell.

A month later the unease increased when a young naval officer, Sub-Lieutenant E.W. Purdy, walked into the castle. 'In March 1944,' wrote Reinhold Eggers, 'a British Merchant Officer was sent to us by the OKW. He said he had been broadcasting propaganda on our behalf from the Concordia studios in Berlin, where he'd had a row and been sacked. He at once offered me his services as an informant.' This was too good an opportunity to miss. Eggers sent Purdy into the prisoners' courtyard, but warned him to be careful; the prisoners had a short way with stool pigeons, as the Polish officers had demonstrated when they had unmasked the traitor Bednarski two years earlier. Forewarned and fore-armed, Purdy stepped through the gate and, like any new arrival, immediately found himself the centre of curiosity. Where had he come from? Where was he captured? And inevitably, when was the war going to end? Purdy, a small 'miserable-looking man', was visibly nervous, more so when he recognised the camp dentist, Captain Julius Green. Green was the last man he expected to see here . . .

The information Purdy had given Eggers was true; he was a sailor by profession, and had been awarded his rank in the Royal Naval Reserve when his ship was taken over for war duties. His ship was sunk while assisting in the evacuation of Narvik, and by early 1941 he found himself at naval POW camp at Marlag, in northern Germany. After a few months Purdy came to the attention of Sonderführer Gussveld – the chief security officer – when he bought a book enti-tled *Twilight over England* by William Joyce, better known as 'Lord Haw-Haw', the fascist broadcaster. Gussveld had spent time in America before the war, and he was looking for English-speakers to broadcast German propaganda to Britain; he suggested to Purdy that he could send the book away to be signed by the author. The signed book spread rumours that eventually arrived at the surgery of the camp dentist, Julius Green. Ever since his capture in 1940, Green had been in contact with MI9 via coded letters, and he duly noted Walter Purdy's political leanings. Green's communication perhaps confirmed what MI9 already knew: Purdy had been a member of the British Union of Fascists before the war.

On 10 May Purdy left Marlag for Berlin and spent some

time at Stalag 111D at Genshagen, a recruitment camp for British prisoners who might be persuaded to work for the German propaganda machine, or join the ranks of the British Free Corps, a renegade group serving alongside the Wehrmacht on the Russian front. Many of the officers used Genshagen as merely a welcome holiday from the stress of the larger POW camps; Walter Purdy was not one of them. He accepted the Germans' offer, and went to live in the suburbs of Berlin as an anti-British broadcaster. On 2 August 1943 he made his first appearance on 'Radio National', a covert radio station that purported to be transmitting from somewhere in England. He took another name, was allowed to write his own scripts, and several of his broadcasts were bugged by the British monitoring service and used in evidence against him after the war. Around this time he came into contact with BQMS John Brown, a British sergeant employed by the Germans to administer to Stalag 111D. 'Busty' Brown had also been a fascist before the war, but unknown to Purdy or the Germans he was a double agent, actively communicating with MI9 in London, using the HK code that Julius Green had taught him.

Walter Purdy, now calling himself 'Bob', was given ration cards, and set up home with his new girlfriend, a pastry cook named Margaret Weitemeier. She became pregnant, but in March 1944 this domestic scene came to an abrupt end when Purdy tangled with the German authorities. Why he was sacked is not known, but Margaret Joyce, Lord Haw-Haw's wife, described him as 'dotty, without much brains and what he had was in a whirl'. Purdy was sent to Colditz in the role of an officer prisoner. It was his bad luck that Captain Julius Green had been transferred to Colditz from Marlag; Green recognised Purdy at once. 'From the first he seemed strange and jittery,' wrote Green. 'And he told me he had escaped from Genshagen and had lived in Berlin with a "bird". It sounded a bit thin to me and I asked him some questions about Genshagen and mentioned Busty Brown. This rather shook him . . .' Double agent Brown may have communicated Purdy's activities to London – Green was in no doubt where his sympathies lay. The stool pigeon now found himself in an embarrassing predicament: he was inside a camp where everyone already suspected him of being a spy. The following day he was interrogated by the camp security committee, and then later by Lieutenant-Colonel Cecil Merritt, VC, and Willie Tod, the new SBO. Purdy confessed that he had been 'a rat and a traitor', and said he only wanted to return to his woman in Berlin. He was placed under close arrest, and nine officers were detailed to prevent him witnessing anything he shouldn't and to serve as his protection. Colonel Tod went straight to the Kommandant and told him that unless Purdy was immediately removed he would not answer for his safety. On 11 March, three days after he had arrived, Walter Purdy was removed from the prisoners' courtyard and placed in a cell in the Kommandantur.

During those brief three days several 'coincidences' occurred that fuelled the paranoia and suspicion inside the courtyard. As Purdy and his posse of 'guards' went up a staircase an officer appeared from the entrance of 'Crown Deep', a well-concealed tunnel on the first floor. 'The Marlag boys are at it again!' he is reported to have said; the tunnel was discovered shortly afterwards. Eggers vehemently denied there was any connection, but a more significant discovery was to follow. 'There was a very big, well-concealed hide underneath the cupboard next to my bed,' remembers Jock Hamilton-Baillie. 'Someone was getting something out of it just as Purdy went through the room. Soon afterwards the

Germans came in and put up a show of saying there was a bottle of home-made hooch in there that had leaked. They broke open the bottom of the cupboard and found the hide. This was done with a lot of confidence; too much confidence, I think. Maybe he didn't see it, but I think it was Purdy who gave it away.'

The hide was a gold mine – literally, for it contained the prisoners' treasury, and Eggers had spent three years looking for it. Under the floorboards were 2,250 marks, 4,500 French francs, passes, tools, and Clayton Hutton's miniature radio, the first to be found in a German POW camp. Had Purdy betrayed it? Eggers was not prepared to say; after the war he admitted that Purdy had revealed to him that prisoners' letters passed out of the camp 'underground' via a German guard, but nothing more.

The most contentious story about Purdy's brief stay in the castle has only recently come to light, and it is only remembered in detail by one man. 'I was walking around the courtyard for a bit of exercise and Dick Howe accosted me,' recalls Gris Davies-Scourfield. '"What do you think of this fellow Purdy?" he said. I said not very much. "Well, some of us think that he is a traitor and should be hanged. I've got some volunteers assembling in one of the rooms in the attic and we're going to string him up. I thought perhaps you'd come along too, seeing the way you feel about him." So I agreed. Upstairs in this little room there were people sitting round and a rope was swung over a beam in position. And the wretched Purdy was being held between two stalwart officers. Dick Howe then addressed us. He said, "We are all here because we agree that it is our very painful duty to carry out the hanging of the traitor Purdy. He came here as a stool pigeon, and unless we put him away for good and all he'll be taken away by the Germans and sent to another camp, and discover more secrets. So it is quite clearly our duty to do it, is it not?" We were a bit silent on this, but we all mumbled in agreement. "Right," he said, "all we need is a couple of volunteers to do the deed." And there was a very long silence. And finally he said, "Well, we've all agreed, haven't we, we've go to do it, we've always believed in duty in this camp." Then one officer stood up and said, "Dick, you are the instigator of this, presumably you are going to be one of the people."

'"Well, no," said Dick, "because the Germans know I am up to all sorts of things and I would be one of the first to be suspected. It would be wiser if two others did it." It turned into a very British situation, because no one was prepared to kill in cold blood one of our compatriots, whatever he had done. On reflection I think we were entirely in the wrong, we should have done it, because he did undoubtedly go on to do more damage. We had failed in our duties.'

This story has sparked a hot debate among the veterans of Colditz; the lynching of a brother officer would have been illegal, and some feel this brings into disrepute those officers who were present, particularly Dick Howe, the protagonist. They cannot believe he would have carried out the act, and they claim there was no room in the crowded castle where a lynch mob could have secretly convened. Moreover, this was exactly the kind of scene the posse of nine officers assigned to watch over Purdy were there to prevent. But there were several officers who considered rough justice to be the only solution, Gris Davies-Scourfield was one, and he believes Mike Sinclair was another. As Escape Officer, Dick Howe had the authority to ask young men to do anything he wanted; but not on this occasion, and that is why this 'very British situation' has remained so vivid to Gris Davies-Scourfield over half a century after the event.

The debate is symptomatic of so much that happened at Colditz; if officers were not directly involved, then it was unlikely they would ever be told. The prisoners' courtyard was a warren of rooms, staircases and attics, and so much happened behind closed doors; the less people knew about a lynch mob, the better.

Walter Purdy escaped from Colditz with his life, and a month later he went back to broadcasting in Berlin. From his brief conversation with Julius Green about 'Busty' Brown, he was able to reveal to the German authorities what double agent Brown was up to, and thereafter compromised Brown's communications with London. When the war ended Purdy returned to Britain, where he was arrested for high treason: he was found guilty of broadcasting on behalf of the enemy and working for the German Secret Service; and he was sentenced to death in Wandsworth jail. Two days before the hanging the hand of execution was stayed on the grounds ill health; so Purdy – described in one government memo as 'the greatest rogue unhung' – spent the next eight years behind bars. On his release he changed his name and returned to the obscurity of civilian life in Dagenham. He died in 1982.

In the spring of 1944 the prisoners at Colditz received good news; the Swiss Red Cross Medical Commission would be visiting the camp to examine the sick and maimed POWs for possible repatriation. All prisoners were entitled to this examination under the Geneva Convention, but in four years the Commission had never been allowed inside the castle. Their visit was scheduled for 6 May, and a list of twenty-nine prisoners was duly presented; several were TB cases, alongside Dan Hallifax, a badly burned fighter pilot whose face urgently needed skin grafting, and Kit Silverwood-Cope, who had developed a thrombosis of the leg as a result of his mistreatment by the Gestapo at Pawiak jail in Warsaw. These men were genuine cases; and there were several others faking illnesses to 'work their ticket'. Harry Elliott was one; he was a member of the original Laufen Six who, with the assistance of several sympathetic Allied doctors, had created an appalling medical record and a 'stomach ulcer'. The artist John Watton regularly painted his face a sallow green and darkened his eyes to create a ghoulish impression; and he took care that any new arrivals saw him in his most debilitated state. When the Eichstätt mob appeared, Elliott sat at the end of a mess table dribbling while another officer fed him soup: no wonder they thought the old guard had all spent too long inside the castle. One man who looked ill even if he wasn't was Micky Wynn. Wynn had been severely wounded during the Commando raid on St Nazaire when his motor torpedo boat received a direct hit as he stopped to pick up some survivors in the water. He owed his life to his engine mechanic, who swam him over to a Carley float and lashed him to it. The following day the float was spotted out in the Atlantic by a German trawler, with only three of the original complement of thirty-six left alive. Wynn was missing a finger, he was peppered with shrapnel and his left eye was hanging from its socket. After several operations without anaesthetic, Wynn's eye was removed, and thereafter he proved himself such a troublemaker that 'Wicked Wynn' was sent to Colditz. 'I had an advantage because I had a glass eye and a steel finger,' he recalls. 'So I looked like a casualty, but in fact I was fine. I had to ask my commanding officer if it was all right to attempt repatriation. He said certainly, if you can pull it off. Nobody but him knew what I was up to. So I made out I had a terrible pain in my back. The Germans were suspicious but couldn't prove anything. They sent me to a hospital in Leipzig, and I was the only

Englishman there. I spent most of the time on crutches. The only place I could exercise was down in the cellars where the French soldiers were kept. I used to sneak down there and run up and down to keep fit.'

Micky Wynn's deception took six months to execute, and he would have to wait until January 1945 to be repatriated. Another man on the list was Frank 'Errol' Flinn, widely regarded as one of Colditz's 'madmen'. But was he as mad as he seemed? Flinn arrived at Colditz in 1941, having been caught in the cockpit of a Heinkel attempting to fly to safety. A burly man who was keen on boxing and, unusually for the time, yoga, Flinn continued trying to escape from Colditz, earning him 171 consecutive days in solitary confinement. During these lonely months he realised there was another way out. Without telling anyone, not even his Senior British Officer, he decided to go 'round the bend', but try somehow to stay sane. Most officers regarded this method of escape as far too dangerous; not only did German doctors regard 'madmen' with unqualified suspicion, there was also a good chance of becoming genuinely mad in the process. Occasionally, the camp was visited by an army doctor – a clinical psychologist – who would assess the worst cases; and only after a long period of unbalanced behaviour would he consider referring them to a civilian doctor in Leipzig – the first step on the road to repatriation.

Without the luxury of any visible injuries to further his case, Frank Flinn had to alert the Germans to his condition. He was inspired in part by *The Road to En-Dor*, a classic escape tale from the First World War, which many prisoners had read as schoolboys – there were even several dog-eared copies floating around the camp. In a graphic scene the author E. H. Jones describes how he and his fellow British officer fake a double suicide, hanging themselves from the roof of their cell while their Turkish captors drink tea outside. Both were cut down in time, and the act was instrumental in proving their insanity; Frank Flinn decided to follow suit. 'My first idea was to try and get sent out of the camp to another one, where I might have a better chance of escape,' he remembers. 'So I did it in the lavatory. I had this rope round my neck and I put it over the cistern, put one foot on the floor and one on the lavatory seat, so if I wanted to ease the pressure on my throat I could. I made sure I had a good red mark on my neck, and then I arranged for a Frenchman to run in and cut me down. The goons charged up the stairs and saw the red mark and thought I'd tried to kill myself. It went down on my record.'

The dangerous ploy worked; the Germans became concerned but they wanted more proof, so Frank Flinn was sent on to another camp. Unfortunately this was not the sort of place he had in mind. 'When I arrived at the new camp for some reason I was kept in solitary confinement. I couldn't really see what sort of place it was. Through my window I saw barbed wire and all these people looking starved walking about in striped uniforms. They had a glare in their eyes like animals trapped and ready to be killed. Some of them were dying. When the Germans were cleaning my cell I looked through to next door and there was a man in a straitjacket writhing around trying to eat potatoes off the floor. I was thinking, what is this place? Who are these people?' Flinn witnessed enough to realise that this camp, whatever its purpose, was far more dangerous than Colditz. He recovered rapidly – and returned to the castle, sane. When the escape committee questioned him about his adventure, Flinn explained how the guards had attempted to conceal the camp from him; but he did not reveal that he was 'working his ticket', and he would continue to do so.

'The walls have ears, and particularly in Colditz,' he recalls. 'Nobody knew of my intentions. In fact I wasn't sure of my intentions myself. I was trying to escape, and I was building up a medical record so I might as well keep up the act for as long as it took. When you're sitting at a table with people year in year out, you can only say so many things of interest, and they get said. You sit there and you know exactly what a man is going to say before he says it and what he's going to do. It's very boring and it's easy to get into a state where you don't care about very much. I walked around on my own, at mealtimes I used to drop my head and lose interest. I carried on with my yoga meditation, and that helped because at the time people didn't look upon yoga as anything but a sign of going round the bend. In Colditz it certainly wasn't accepted. The other officers thought I was a bit eccentric, probably, but not demonstrably so. By 1943 so many people were behaving in a ridiculous fashion, without being around the bend, many of them found it easier to do something silly than to do nothing. And the Germans were no fools – they kept a good eye on you at all times, so you had to keep it up.'

Frank Flinn spent a year in this state, working towards the day when the Commission would come around. In April 1944 he was sent to see a professor in Leipzig, another promising sign that he was being considered for repatriation. On the train there he attacked his travelling companion, Julius Green, who was also trying to work his ticket; the incident improved both of their chances. The Medical Commission were due to appear at Colditz on 6 May; but on the 5th at the midday *Appell* the Germans made a surprise announcement – the Gestapo had seen the list of twenty-nine names, and six had been struck off. These included Douglas Bader, on the grounds that he had lost his legs before the war, three of de Gaulle's Free French, and Kit Silverwood-Cope, the officer who had concealed his contacts with the Polish Underground and been ill treated by the Gestapo.

This news caused uproar, and the SBO, Colonel Willie Tod, decided upon a dangerous strategy. The following morning the Swiss Commission arrived and a special *Appell* was called. Eggers counted the 250-odd men, then he asked Tod to parade the walking cases for inspection by the Commission. Tod's reply was blunt: the German decision was dishonest and unjust, and if all twenty-nine officers were not examined then he would not hold himself responsible for the actions of his officers. He handed the *Appell* back to Eggers and then returned to the ranks; there was a silence, then Eggers tried to address the parade. As soon as he began to speak the shouting began, and his voice was drowned under a mass of stamping boots, catcalls and jeers. This was a mutiny, and moments later the riot squad doubled into the yard, bayonets fixed, pistols drawn. They attempted to snatch the twenty-three prisoners up for inspection out of the angry mass of khaki, but it was impossible. Over in the German courtyard the Swiss were getting impatient; they heard the riot getting louder, as catcalls and screams filtered across the rooftops. Oberstleutnant Prawitt was spotted outside the prisoners' gate giving orders; even he dare not enter. Eventually Colonel Tod was asked to come out of the yard and meet the Swiss.

Tod apologised to his protecting power and explained the predicament; six officers had been struck off the list – by order of the Oberkommando der Wehrmacht. The Swiss were amazed and demanded an explanation, so Prawitt was forced to telephone Berlin; and Berlin backed down. Most of the twenty-nine officers were passed for repatriation, but there were some notable omissions; Douglas Bader and the burned pilot Dan Hallifax – on the grounds that he was a 'security risk'. It took several more months of protests before Colonel Tod secured Hallifax's repatriation. Surprisingly Kit Silverwood-Cope and Julius Green were also passed, but the Gestapo made certain they would not enjoy their freedom; on 6 February 1945, ten months after the Medical Commission had visited the castle, Rudolf Denzler of the Swiss Red Cross entered the camp and was amazed to find the two men still there. 'The Kommandant informed me,' he wrote 'that he had orders to detain furthermore these prisoners. Captain Green is a "non-Aryan" and Lt Silverwood-Cope sustained considerable ill-treatment after recapture by the Gestapo'. Evidently they did not want Silverwood-Cope's stories of brutality towards Jews and POWs in Warsaw to get home; neither could they forgive Green – the Jewish dentist – for unmasking Purdy.

Once the dust had settled over the incident, the prisoners felt they had won a moral victory; at last some of them would be going home. Frank Flinn packed his bags – his long labours had not been in vain. 'I remember being taken down to the doors of the castle and I was left standing outside. And I thought, this is it, I'm going. It was an overwhelming feeling to see farther than the walls. And I could feel water trickling down from my eyes, both eyes, not crying – just water pouring down my face. That's a memory I have of freedom, that's what freedom can mean. It sounds a bit sentimental, I know, but there we are.'

CHAPTER FIFTEEN

Rattling the Cage

On 18 November 1943, Lieutenant-Colonel Willie Tod took over from 'Tubby' Broomhall as Senior British Officer at Colditz, and his accession to the role brought a change to the camp. Up until then bad behaviour and goon-baiting had been officially encouraged; they kept spirits high and the Germans on the back foot. Tod was less tolerant of 'the men of spirit' than his predecessors, and many goon-baiters now began to sense his disapproval, although he was slow to show it. A tall, serious Scot with a 'bashed nose' and an air of cool detachment, he possessed a sangfroid that on occasion even disarmed his brother officers. On 18 January 1944 he received the news that his only son had been killed in action; he told no one, and his fellow prisoners only discovered it, by accident, six weeks later. Dick Howe was among those who offered his condolences. 'It happens, to soldiers,' Tod replied, and changed the subject. The strength of his personality commanded the loyalty of those beneath him and the respect of the Germans who guarded him; his was to prove a steady hand in the storm that would eventually overwhelm Colditz as Germany collapsed.

One element of Colditz life that even Willie Tod was unable to do much about was home-made hooch. Alcohol had been brewed in the camp since the very early days, and it was the Polish officers who blazed the trail. 'I wandered into the Polish quarters through a blanketed door,' recalls Michael Alexander. 'They had very secretive quarters, the Poles, very dark and gloomy and smelling of garlic. And whenever I went there I was given a swig of some foul-tasting hooch. "Where d'you get this from, is it schnapps?" I said. "We make it," they replied, and they proceeded to show me how.'

The Polish distillers used a recipe of water, yeast and ersatz German jam to concoct their bitter brew, which convinced the British there was enough sugar in the jam for fermentation. Overnight a cottage industry was born producing 'Jam Alc'. 'Life as a prisoner was so boring that one way of escaping from it was getting stoned out of one's head,' recalls George Drew, who joined forces with Mike Edwards and Pat Fergusson to set up 'Glenbucket', one of several illicit stills secreted about the prisoners' quarters. Each new moon they laid a brew down, following the advice of a former professor of chemistry at Nottingham University whom Mike Edwards had met at Tittmoning. Into the German *Kübel* (soup container) went the measures of water, jam, sugar and yeast. The lid was sealed with plaster of Paris bribed from the sick bay and then the *Kübel* was hidden in a cupboard and its contents left to ferment for six weeks. After that, a stolen pipe was attached to the lid, and wrapped in a cool damp bandage as the whole contraption was heated up. Gradually a clear, rubbery-smelling liquid began to drip from the end of the pipe; this was Jam Alc, 120° proof. The taste was so vile prisoners would flavour it with anything they could get their hands on: plums, brown sugar, even Chanel No. 5 that an officer had been sent in a parcel.

As the hooch stills began to appear, so they were confiscated, but in time the Germans became more relaxed, knowing that the effort put into distilling provided another distraction from escaping. Having mastered Jam Alc, Mike Edwards then became more adventurous; he teamed up with Michael Farr, whose family ran Hawker's Gin, and, remembering the advice of the chemistry professor, attempted to make champagne. 'We put the jam, water and yeast in a lemonade bottle with a flip-top lid and waited till it had stopped fermenting,' he recalls. 'Then we added a little sugar, and started the whole process again. I then collected some snow from the windowsills into a saucepan and added a bit of salt. I stood the bottle upside down in the snow until the neck froze and then I took it out and held it upright again. Slowly the Alc began to melt, and suddenly there was an enormous explosion as all the sediment shot out of the top. I jammed the lid back on, and in that bottle we now had sparkling wine. We added a bit of sugar to taste, and called it Château Colditz.'

The hooch provided an excuse for parties, and the calendar was scoured for suitable events: Christmas, New Year, Valentine's Day and, because 1944 was a leap year, 29 February. 'The colonel didn't like it, and the doctor didn't like it, they thought it was a misuse of Red Cross sugar, but anyhow we made it,' recalls John 'Bosun' Chrisp. 'If you overdid it the first thing that happened was your fillings fell out. Then your tongue became so swollen that you couldn't talk, and of course you could never steer a steady course. So if you ever met a man with black teeth who couldn't talk or walk straight, you knew he was "jam-happy".' Jam Alc even caused temporary blindness in some revellers, but this was a minor consideration given the brief escape it offered.

Another pastime that sustained the British through their long hours of captivity was 'stoolball'. During the castle's days as an international camp, stoolball had been the only game the British had excelled at, and now Colditz had become an all-British affair interest in the game had, if anything, intensified. A descendant of various arcane public school games, stoolball was invented specifically for the cobbled courtyard; it was highly energetic and almost guaranteed injury – both added attractions for pent-up young men. 'There were two stools at either end of the courtyard and you could score a goal by knocking the bloke off the stool,' recalls 'Bosun' Chrisp. 'There were no rules other than not biting and kicking, so whenever you played you were in for a rough time. The RAF used to play the Army and the Army used to play the Navy, and the Scots played the English; it was ferocious. Because of his tin legs Bader used to play in goal, sitting on the stool, but if you got near him you wouldn't come out alive. When I was about ten feet away I'd throw the ball just over his head where he couldn't reach it. And as he tried to stand up I would whip the ball under his legs and score a goal. He created trouble about that – that wasn't cricket. But that was stoolball, and it was tough. It was nothing to see someone with their nose half broken or a black eye. If you wanted to thump someone then you'd play them in stoolball, where you could thump them as much as you like.'

'Stoolball'

On two occasions the officers were allowed to go down to the village football pitch to play rugby, but this was a short-lived privilege. To leave the castle the prisoners had to give their 'parole', in other words promise not to escape, and this was a promise most officers were not willing to make more than once – if at all. During the early months of 1944 officers 'on parole' were even allowed to go to the local cinema, though the choice of films was often bizarre. 'I remember going to a film about mentally deficient Germans in hospital,' recalls Kenneth Lee. 'They had this quirk, the Germans, they wanted to make one feel really down because we caused them all this trouble. It didn't make us feel bad, it just made us feel very sorry for these poor people.' Others recall watching films about the invention of diesel and the life-cycle of the rabbit, both of which provided a welcome interruption from their otherwise endless ordered life in capitivity.

As the weather became warmer the more traditional
distractions of the escaping season began. After four years of
probing the crazy geography of the castle it might appear
that every escape avenue had been fully exploited; but the
committed escapers from Eichstätt were determined to find
their own exits, and throughout the summer of 1944 they
brought a new enthusiasm to a game the Germans appeared
to have won. Their first efforts began directly under their
feet. Ever since 1941, the Polish officers had been steadily
at work on a tunnel which began in the middle of their
dormitory on the first floor. Running down the inside of
the courtyard wall, it burrowed under the cobbles of the
courtyard and linked up with the main sewer pipe. They
had kept the tunnel's construction a close secret; and the
only British officers to be invited down into it were Mike
Harvey and Jack Best, during their days as ghosts. 'When
the main sewer pipe became too narrow, the Poles had dug
a side tunnel parallel to it,' recalls Jack Best. 'It was tiny, and
where it rejoined the main tunnel it passed the place where
the silly fools of British had cold showers every morning.
You always got stuck in that dip, when you got hit by a
river of cold water right up your arse, so you had to go to
work soaking wet. It was so unpleasant that when Mike and
I were asked if we wanted to continue work on the tunnel
we both decided neither of us wanted to go down there
ever again.'

The Poles were proud of their dangerous tunnel – some
of them had fainted and almost drowned while digging it;
and sensing a British snub, they preferred to entrust their
scheme to the Eichstätt boys, whom they thought were
'untainted' by the old guard. It was not long before the
enthusiastic arrivals discovered for themselves the perils of
tunnelling through Colditz Castle. 'We persevered down the

sewage system until we came to an electric cable running right across the middle of the drain,' recalls Hugo Ironside. 'When you finished your shift, filthy and soaked you had to slide back under this large electric cable. It scared me to death.' Somehow the British scraped their way into the main water drain undetected; and the pipe they now found themselves in disappeared off in the direction of the Kommandantur. To explore its course the three smallest officers in the camp were chosen: Dick Lorraine, an Australian, Dominic Bruce, the 'medium-sized' flying officer, and John 'Bosun' Chrisp, the rope-maker. Dick Howe assisted their descent by making sure no taps were left running in the kitchen and a game of stoolball was in constant progress in the yard, to divert the guards away from the manhole covers.

'We were stripped of everything and put on long johns, gloves and a Balaclava,' recalls John Chrisp. 'Dick Lorraine led the way with a torch. We went down the inside of the wall to the drain and then underneath the courtyard. It was completely dark and about halfway along there was a slit and we could see people playing stoolball above us. This tiny slit was a godsend because it gave us a little bit of fresh air. The sewer was about three hundred years old and full of slime. We followed it along forty feet and then we came to solid rock. In one corner was a very small hole which the Poles had dug just big enough to get into, but once inside all you could do was wriggle forward. This tunnel had pools of slimy water in it that came up to your nose as you wriggled through them. At last we rejoined the main sewer and followed that on till we came to a deep well, half full of water. On the other side of the well about fifteen feet below us was the entrance to a pipe. It was obvious that when the water rose it left the castle via that pipe and we hoped it flushed directly down into the river below. It looked old enough. Above us was a manhole cover that we could see was in the German courtyard. So we returned back the way we had come, the doctor plastered us with iodine and we were sent down again. This time Dick Lorraine had a large spike and a hammer. Our plan was to lower him into the well by a rope, he would hammer the spike into the wall, and we could then hang the ladder off the spike and climb down into the pipe below. Very carefully he started hammering, but there was a goon up above who heard the noise. Pulling up the cover, he thrust his rifle inside and saw Dick down in the well. We bolted, but it was too late.

'They hauled us out, all covered in slime, and marched us into a guardhouse next to the park gate. Eggers came in and asked us where the entrance to the tunnel was. Little Dominic became our spokesman. "We are not going to tell you." "All right, I'll go away and come back again." So half an hour later, he came back. We were still only wearing our long johns and vests which were wet and slimy, so we were cold by now. He asked us again, and again little Dominic said, "No, no." We all felt like saying "Come on, Dominic, they'll find it." But we maintained stiff upper lips, so Eggers went out again. And another half an hour passed, and he came back for the third time. "For the last time, where did you get into the sewer?" And Dominic gave the same answer. "OK," said Eggers, "I'll take you out and have you all shot." "You can't do that, we're protected by the Geneva Convention," says Dominic. "If you don't tell me I'll shoot you,' he replied, and we then heard this guard of eight march up with rifles ready, and we were taken outside. There was a bare wall in front of us. "Right, over to that wall," he said. So the three of us, very cold and bedraggled, were pushed over and lined up. I thought, My God, he can't do this, can he? We turned around to face the firing squad. "All right," he said, and he called them off. "But you're going to pay for this, and you'll get punishment." It was an awful feeling, but I somehow knew that Eggers couldn't do it, he wasn't fierce enough; none of them were.'

John Chrisp was right about Eggers, who had recently taken over as the camp's Chief Security Officer, but his confidence in the rest of the German staff was misplaced. The use of force – though contrary to the Geneva Convention – had been hotly debated in the German mess for several years; Oberstleutnant Prawitt, the Kommandant, was in favour of using it on persistent offenders, and he was supported by the exotic Staff Paymaster Heinze, an old Saxon soldier who strutted about the Kommandantur bedecked in boots and spurs and armed with a sword. They found a new ally in the red-faced Major Amthor, an unbridled young Nazi who had joined the garrison as second-in-command in May 1943. Known to the prisoners as 'Turkeycock', he found himself in direct opposition to the two old moderates, Hauptmann Püpcke and Reinhold Eggers. 'Amthor also tried to compel Püpcke and myself to employ rough measures,' recorded Eggers in his diary. 'When we continued on our way he said to me, "Your whole work here is *Scheisse*! If I put a corporal in your place he at least would execute my orders!" I reported to the Adjutant and asked to be immediately removed to another camp.' As Eggers was the only German left on the staff who spoke English and French, his request was turned down. Young Amthor offered an apology, and thereafter an uneasy truce was maintained that would last until the final months of the war. It was clear who the prisoners respected; whenever Amthor or Prawitt entered the courtyard they were whistled and howled at, and after several attempts to curb this indiscipline failed, Prawitt gave up visiting the prisoners' yard altogether.

Another of the Eichstätt arrivals tried his luck in the early summer of 1944. Jock Hamilton-Baillie, the sapper who had designed the ladders for the 'Warburg wire job' and the tunnel at Eichstätt, now unleashed his talents upon Colditz. He made a surreptitious survey of the castle, adding new information to the original scale plan sent in by MI9, and created the most detailed map of the castle and its defences to date. This undertaking brought him to the same conclusion as so many prisoners before him – that the weakest line of defence was the dividing wall that separated the two courtyards. 'The old inhabitants told us that the Germans had fitted burglar alarm wires all the way along this wall,' he recalled. 'These were strung on the floor around the doors and on the ceilings to prevent anyone from moving across. Well, I thought we could do better than that, and decided to try and get over them.'

To find a way over the wires Hamilton-Baillie broke into the attic of the spiral staircase in the south-east corner of the courtyard. Pressing himself between the eaves and the plaster ceiling, he wriggled up to its apex, and sure enough, looking down, he saw the wires stretched out across the floor of the room below. He then tentatively took a few tiles off the roof and realised he was adjacent to the outside wall of the Kommandantur. Hidden from view by the spire on top of the spiral staircase, he climbed out on to the roof and began to burrow a hole through the Kommandantur wall. After a few days' work his hole was big enough to squeeze through, and he now found himself in the attics of the massive garrison building; from here he crept along its entire length, unlocking partition doors as he went until he met an apparent dead end. In front of him stood an iron fire door which his skeleton keys could unlock but not open. To find out what held the door, Hamilton-Baillie made an ingenious device; he cut a thin strip of mirror glass and fastened it to a coat hanger which he threaded through the keyhole. Articulating the mirror so that it sat up, he saw four hooks on the back of the door holding it in place. Returning with an accomplice and a long piece of wire, he fished the hooks off their fastenings, and crept down into the German storerooms beyond. These rooms were an escaper's paradise, for here were piles of German uniforms, hammers, files, keys, and something Hamilton-Baillie was particularly tempted by – a potato peeler. He resisted the urge to take anything, and retraced his route, planning a second visit when he could guarantee not to be disturbed.

Hamilton-Baillie chose the next bank-holiday, Whitsun, to make his return trip; and this time he was well prepared. His two accomplices carried sacks, intent on stealing as much of the equipment as they could. Even though Hamilton-Baillie had now found a safe route deep into the Kommandantur, escape was not his primary aim; he was prospecting for a room with a window from which he could jump down on to the terrace below. The last prisoners to have reached this far undetected were Pat Reid and his fellow escapers eighteen months earlier. 'The other two were upstairs in the storerooms filling their swag bags with loot,' he remembers. 'I was downstairs in the workshop of the castle locksmith looking for some keys and a file to help me to open a door. This old man was a one-legged veteran of the Boxer Rebellion who lived in a flat adjacent to the castle. It so happened that his wife's iron had broken and she forced him to go up to his workshop to mend it. Being a bank-holiday he didn't want to go but she forced him. So up he trudged, and just before he opened the door of his workshop I heard him. I was trapped. He entered, and found me – dressed in a filthy vest and long johns, playing with his keys. I must have looked a very strange sight. *"Posten! Posten!"* he shouted, and threatened me with the iron. The sentries all came running and they caused quite a commotion. Luckily my friends upstairs heard the noise and managed to get away, back through the iron door on to which they replaced the hooks. Eggers found my route in – but he could not understand how I'd managed to get through the iron door when it was locked on both sides. I did tell him – twenty years later.'

Hamilton-Baillie's extraordinary escape route was entirely original, an achievement in itself given the number of captive minds that had spent four years looking at the same problem; but one of the most successful Eichstätt arrivals used a variation on the oldest trick in the dossier of Colditz escapes. John Beaumont, a slightly built lieutenant in the Durham Light Infantry, intended to follow in the footsteps of Alain Le Ray, who three years earlier had recorded Colditz's first home run. For several seconds on the walk back up from the park, the procession of prisoners moved out of sight of the sentries as they turned up the hill, and in this brief moment John Beaumont would slip away.

Captured in May 1940, Beaumont had devoted his years in captivity to music and escaping, a combination that he found difficult to sustain. 'The Germans allowed us instruments because they felt that they might stop us escaping,' he recalls. 'Well, I was interested in music, but I still wanted to escape. In my first camp at Laufen I was sent a French horn courtesy of the Swedish YMCA. But when I escaped I had to leave it behind, because I couldn't go walking around Germany with a French horn under my arm. After I was recaptured I was sent to another camp, and the Germans sent the French horn on to me. And when I escaped again, and was recaptured again, the Germans did the same thing. So the horn followed me all the way to Colditz.'

All 'Hornblower' Beaumont's escapes were motivated by hunger, and this attempt was no exception. As the prisoners walked up the hill, his plan was to break ranks and, using his own unique method, metamorphose into a pile of leaves. It was a transformation that required hours of practice. 'He used to walk round and round the theatre with a blanket under his arm,' recalls George Drew. 'Suddenly he would fling himself to the floor, draping the blanket over the top of him. I asked him what he was doing and he told me he was "in training".'

Perfecting this deft movement would be crucial, as the sentry on the other side of the column was only five yards away. When he was not practising Beaumont absorbed himself in creating his camouflage. 'I found an old piece of canvas from somewhere around the castle and I had to sew a lot of things on to it; the rubbish you might find on the side of the road, leaves and branches. Then I was told that dogs don't like the smell of garlic, so I got hold of some and smothered my blanket with the stuff. The whole thing was very heavy and very smelly, and known to my friends as the syphilitic camel.' By the beginning of May the camel was complete, and there were still plenty of leaves underfoot; he was ready to go.

'On 5 May we all went down to the park to watch a game of netball,' he remembers. 'I was wearing my blanket and a greatcoat over the top which was incredibly hot and stank.' Once the game was over, the column formed up and began to walk back up the hill; John Beaumont marched on the outside surrounded by a phalanx of tall officers. As they came to the bend the column began to straggle. '*Schnell! Schnell!*' shouted the guards. 'What's the hurry?' came the reply. The man behind took his overcoat, and in one sweeping move Beaumont sank down beside the path, obscured by his blanket. His hours of practice had paid off; the guards passed on up the hill. Tentatively he stuck his head out, only to see the last German with an Alsatian coming up the path towards him. 'I darted back under my blanket thinking this is it, the dog will find me. But my luck held, the garlic worked and they walked straight past. After a while I got up and climbed the bank and slipped over a fence. Then to my horror I saw a German patrol about a hundred yards down the road. I had no alternative but to walk straight past them. They were far too busy having a chat to bother with me, so I just walked straight out into the countryside. If I had found a bicycle I would have taken it, because my plan was to go to Czechoslovakia, only seventy miles away. But I couldn't find one, so I set out to walk. After a mile or so I met a German patrol on bicycles who were obviously out looking for me, because my mates hadn't been able to fox the count on the return from the park walk. So I said I was a Belgian worker on parole and produced my home-made *Ausweis*. They seemed to believe me and let me go. Then a mile later another bicycle patrol stopped me and I told them the same story. "Aha," they said, "you must be from Colditz," and they thought it was a terrific joke. So, back I went.'

John Beaumont was the last man to break out beyond the confines of Colditz Castle: the war would continue on for another year, but no prisoner would even make it to the park wall. And his ingenious escape attempt would have an ironic twist, for the two jovial Colditz guards who recaptured him may well have inadvertently saved his life. Beaumont's escape route would have taken him to Czechoslovakia, the 'Protectorate' as it was now known, and once there he intended to look up an address in Prague given to him by

Lieutenant Bill Millar, a Canadian survivor of the Dieppe raid. 'Dopey' Millar was another new arrival from Eichstätt, who, four months earlier, had been idly looking out of the windows of the Saalhaus into the German yard, when he saw an opportunity for a snap escape; coincidentally it was an idea that had also occurred to an English submariner, Tommy Catlow. 'A lorry had been backed up to the barred windows of the kitchen on the ground floor,' remembers Catlow. 'And it suddenly struck me that if I could get under the lorry, which would certainly move the next morning, I would get a ride out of the castle. So I went as fast as possible to our Escape Officer – Dick Howe – and told him all. He stopped me short and said Bill Millar had just seen the same thing and beaten me to it by a short head. I was very disappointed, but agreed that it was a job for one man only. I asked Dopey where he was going and he told me to the "Protectorate" – Czechoslovakia.'

Bill Millar had broken out of the kitchen and hidden under the lorry, and the next morning it had gone. The weeks passed without news, and the prisoners assumed, hopefully, that he had made a home run; if not, then he was still at large somewhere in Germany. Among his Canadian peers Bill Millar was the 'Escape King' – he spoke good German, and was perfectly capable of looking after himself; but as the year wore on his continuing silence grew ominous. Tommy Catlow had his own theory as to what had happened, which he received from an unlikely source. 'A major in the SS periodically arrived with his bunch of thugs to search the camp – not trusting the army personnel to do the job properly. The SS major had been a POW in England in the First World War and liked to air his English to us. We in our turn used to twit him. On one occasion we asked him for a good place to escape to. Surprisingly he said, "If you've any sense you'll keep out of the Protectorate or you'll get shot."'

Bill Millar was never heard of again. Even in 1946 his fellow Canadians hoped he was still at large in Germany, but many more suspected that Millar had fallen foul of the vengeful Nazi mood outside the castle. He may well have reached the safe house in Prague, little over a hundred miles away, where he was then picked up by the Gestapo. There is another theory that he was recaptured near Lamsdorf after months at large, and executed on Saturday 15 July 1944 in the extermination camp at Mauthausen, Austria, where thousands of other escaped Allied POWs shared a similar fate. His death and those of many like him would soon have a profound effect on the prisoners of Colditz.

CHAPTER SIXTEEN

The Weather Changes

There was one prisoner at Colditz whom the German authorities could count on not running away. Douglas Bader, the tin-legged fighter pilot, enjoyed special privileges; twice a week under guard he was allowed out for a walk in the countryside, to exercise the muscles that propelled his aluminium legs. His limbs were regularly serviced by the local Colditz blacksmith, and Bader used these walks as an opportunity to trade openly with local farmers, swapping cigarettes and Red Cross chocolate for eggs and millet, which he concealed within his bespoke trousers. Hanging from his belt were long sausage-shaped pouches made for him by the Polish tailors, and once they were fully loaded he staggered back up the hill to the castle, much to his friends' amusement and his own. Douglas Bader's forays out into the countryside became more important as the year dragged on and the supply of Red Cross parcels dwindled, but his trousers were not the only source of local produce in the camp: there were other officers whose contact with the outside world was more illicit but just as effective.

Flight Lieutenant Ceněk Chaloupka, 'Checko', had been running the black market in Colditz ever since he arrived in January 1943. A large, saturnine man who spoke fluent German, Checko used his considerable charm and presence to extract from his 'soft goons' railway timetables, hacksaws, flashlights, dyes, yeast, radio parts and anything else the prisoners required. Prawitt considered trading with the prisoners to be a very serious offence, and warned his soldiers against it as soon as they entered the castle. 'When we arrived we had to stand to attention and be told the story of a guard who traded tools with the Polish prisoners,' recalls Peter Hoffman, then a new recruit. 'He was caught and sentenced to death by the War Court, and he wasn't pardoned, on instructions from Hitler himself. The sergeant said: take this as a warning and don't do anything as silly yourselves.'

These threats appeared to have had little effect on Checko's operations. In his diary he describes a typical day in his life at Colditz during 1944. 'After a night of "hard work" I got up lazily and after my modest breakfast I washed and shaved,' he wrote, having obviously been engaged in some nefarious nocturnal activity. 'This was one of my shaving mornings – one cannot afford to shave more than twice a week. I then looked forward to my morning brew at 11.15 which is the best drink of the day. Jack Zafouk, my cook, has it ready punctually every day. Soon after this I went to the second floor which has a good view of the town: my visit today was not in vain – I saw my favourite popsy in her panties as she was dressing at the window. Fortified by this I did my rounds of the goon snoops, finding out the latest news, flashes and rumours. Well armed with these, I was ready to stand the bombardment of questions from my fellow officers, and live up to the reputation of having the latest and most sensational gen. 12.40 was lunchtime. This German product consisted of water with a few cubes of chopped swede lying at the bottom. At one o'clock I had a second appointment with a goon: got ten eggs. At two o'clock on up to the second floor again to see my popsy. She arrived late today. Not like her, she ought to be more punctual. Between tea and supper I played "Tarochs" which is a Czech game with some of my friends. I earned my day's pay, and left them to meet a goon at 6.30 p.m. Got two loaves and some onions. Small fry, however better than nothing. After an excellent supper we discussed the war situation in my room till 9.30 p.m., when the lights went out, and I went to bed – only to be woken up again at 11.30 p.m. by a goon. I got 30 eggs and some more onions from him, and then went back to my bed.'

Checko's 'favourite popsy' may well have been Irmgard Wernicker, the town dentist's assistant. According to him, they had met in a train carriage while he was in transit, and she was so taken with the dashing young officer that she pleaded with him to be sent to the dentist. Checko smashed a tooth for the purpose, and turned his dental appointment into a romantic encounter, at the end of which he deliberately decided to leave his muffler behind. As he walked back through the wire gates of the castle Imgard came panting up the hill after him, waving his muffler; Checko gracefully accepted it, and the smitten girl received a lingering kiss for her trouble. From then on Checko kept in contact with her through his soft goons, and became the envy of his brother officers as the only man to have a girlfriend at Colditz. He was not alone in furtively watching the windows of the town for any signs of female flesh or sexual activity; there were several home-made telescopes around the camp, constructed for this purpose out of old spectacle lenses and cardboard; and these 'lecherscopes' were much in demand throughout the hot summer of 1944. The Australian officer Jack Champ stood in a queue for half an hour to wait his turn. '"You get five minutes," said the lieutenant. "At the moment we're on to two nurses from the local hospital who are sunbathing in a small clearing about half a mile away. Not much to look at but it's interesting to think we can see them quite clearly when they think they are completely hidden." I took up position and looked through the tele-scope. Sure enough there were two nude female figures sunbathing in the clearing. They were lying on their tummies. The telescope owner was right; they were no stars as regards physical beauty. Soon one of them stood up and rubbed herself free of perspiration with a towel. It really was an amazing sight.'

Snatched glimpses of female flesh weren't the only mem-orable sights on view from their barred prison windows; throughout the summer massed patterns of Allied bombers drifted by as the daylight air raids gathered momentum. Corran Purdon, the young Commando, watched them pass. 'We looked up out of the courtyard and watched formation after formation of Flying Fortresses coming over, silver against the blue sky. And the tiny German aircraft going in among them. They just glided by in enormous streams dropping little silver strips to neutralise the radar. The whole sky seemed to ripple.' It was an extraordinary sight, and one that provided yet another reminder to the prisoners of their impotence. 'I remember thinking I'm damn glad you're pounding these people,' recalls Purdon. 'But how I envy you going back to your girlfriends tonight and having a drink in an English pub.'

The sixth of June brought the greatest news the prisoners had heard so far: D-day. The German papers initially reported that 'A small raiding party landed in Normandy, they were all shot and their bodies thrown back into the sea', but the BBC radio bulletin that evening confirmed that this was the long-awaited invasion. 'It was wildly exciting,' recalls Micky Burn, who took down the news that day. 'At last there seemed some justification to the phrase that the war would be over by Christmas.' Checko was so convinced of it that he swore he would run twice around the courtyard naked, if he was still at Colditz on Christmas Eve. That night the Jam Alc flowed, and the following morning arch goon-baiter Pete Tunstall was feeling the effects of the party. 'I was late on parade,' he recalls. 'When the Germans came in to take the *Appell* they put guards across the doors, and if you came down late you received ten days in the cooler. It did not matter what you said. So I was marched up to Püpcke, and I was feeling pretty bloody-minded. Through an interpreter I was asked the usual daft question, "Why are you late for parade?" I knew it made no difference what I said so in a loud voice I replied, "I was so pleased at the news of the invasion that I didn't care if I was late for you bloody bastard Germans for the rest of my life!" A great cheer went up as I was marched away.'

Colonel Willie Tod had never had much patience with goon-baiting, and now Tunstall had overstepped the mark. Once the *Appell* was over he turned on his junior officers and using language 'borrowed for the occasion' harangued them for their drunken 'guttersnipe behaviour'. Many who heard this tirade silently agreed with him – they were tired of the antics of 'the men of spirit'; but afterwards Tod received a deputation from the old guard. They pointed out that ever since the earliest days goon-baiting had been a symbol of defiance that kept morale high and the Germans busy: if officers could not escape, then their duty was to create 'merry hell' and Flight Lieutenant Pete Tunstall had dedicated his life to that end, receiving four court-martials and hundreds of hours in solitary as a punishment. They wanted Willie Tod to recognise this. There was an awkward silence; and for the first time, Tod realised that his authority was being questioned. Diplomatically he defused the situation; but he would never forgive Pete Tunstall.

By now the years of goon-baiting and escaping had turned Colditz into a camp apart. Throughout the course of the war the strength of the German garrison had rarely dipped beneath two hundred, and whenever it was threatened with depletion Oberstleutnant Prawitt reminded the OKW in Berlin how difficult it was to keep control of his unruly prisoners: he needed every grandfather and teenager under his command, and through the POWs' continuing efforts he was allowed to keep them. Eggers realised how unique Colditz had become when he was sent to examine the security arrangements at Stalag Luft 3 at Sagan. On 24 March 1944, 76 airmen had escaped from a tunnel in the 'Great Escape', and Eggers was shocked to find only 250 soldiers guarding 7,000 British and American airmen; the ratio of guards to prisoners at Colditz was almost a guard per man. He also noticed, rather sourly, that 'discipline on parade was perfect'. Despite Tod's admonishments, Pete Tunstall and the other men of spirit had no intention of stopping their activities now.

'One afternoon in August,' Tunstall remembers, 'there was an *Appell*, and because we were all swapping identities with some Free French orderlies, it turned into an identity check. At one end of the yard they installed a goon behind a desk with a box of cards, and we all grouped down the other end waiting to be called forward in turn. This seemed to go on for ever. Eventually someone was called. He walked down, swinging his leg as if it was in plaster – this cracked everyone up. Alan Hacohen, the tall, bearded Palestinian officer, was next. He strode majestically down to the table, and bent right over the little German behind it. "My name is Ha-cohen," he bellowed. "I am a Jew, and what is more I was born in Russia!" Everyone cheered. Lastly came Scourgie Price, who could do a dance where he appeared to be running on the spot. By now there was such a racket that the windows above were crowded with other officers watching the proceedings. To howls of applause Scourgie did his dance, running towards the desk but not getting any closer. This was too much for the German officer, and he ordered the nearest guard, who happened to be a little old guy with glasses, to boot Scourgie up the arse. So the guard ran up behind him, took a swing, and unfortunately lost his footing and fell flat on the cobbles. This nearly caused a riot and Scourgie was hauled off to the cells.'

Beyond the high walls of the prisoners' courtyard another act of defiance had taken place that was to reverberate throughout Germany. On the evening of 20 July Eggers was playing skat in the German mess when the radio cut in to announce there had been a bomb attempt on Hitler's life; the Führer had survived. The conspirators, lead by Claus von Stauffenberg, all came from within the ranks of the Wehrmacht. At last the Nazis had their chance to cow the Army's officer corps which they had always despised: five thousand officers were arrested and many were brutally executed by slow hanging on piano wire. The assassination even had an effect inside Colditz; from now on captors and captives would exchange the Nazi salute, provoking a new wave of ridicule that the Germans were powerless to prevent.

More seriously, Heinrich Himmler was handed control of the Home Army, adding to the powerful position he held as Chief of the State Security Service, and the SS, and it was not long before the Nazis' suspicion of mass escapes manifested itself once more. The officers received more news of the Great Escape from Stalag Luft 3, confirming the rumours they had heard: three of the seventy-six men who left the tunnel made it back to England; the remainder had been recaptured, and fifty were selected at random and shot. Their remains were sent back to Sagan, along with their clothes, which bore no signs of bullet holes or blood. This was a premeditated massacre, undertaken by the SS and on the personal orders of Adolf Hitler; and it had the desired effect. 'When you were told of a highly successful escape that finishes up with fifty people being shot in the back of the head, it's more than shattering,' remembers George Drew. 'And to say you were upset is putting it mildly. It's one thing knowing you are going to be shot at while running away – well, we all knew that; that had always been the case. It is quite another to know that you are going to be murdered once you are recaptured; because the odds of making a home run are a thousand to one, and you're laying your life on those odds. I never gave up the thought of escape, I just realised I was not going to and I was going to have to sweat it out. It altered my thinking and most other people's as well.'

Many of the executed airmen had friends at Colditz, and some had even worked on the tunnel while at the Stalag Luft. The pilots John Wilson and Cenĕk Chaloupka felt themselves particularly fortunate; they would have been among the first men out. 'Checko and I were awarded numbers three and four in the tunnel,' remembers Wilson. 'This was an extremely good position, but had we stayed we would both have definitely been shot. The Germans shot every British and American officer who teamed up with either a Pole or a Czech. It was pure luck that we were caught on our next escape and were sent to Colditz.' The British officers had always assumed that the respect in which the Germans held them would prevent such a tragedy occurring; now they realised there were no exceptions to the rule. Impotent and angry, Tod ordered all communications with the Germans to cease.

The powerlessness of the now discredited Wehrmacht against Himmler's new regime manifested itself within the prisoners' courtyard in August, when the two Czecho-slovakian pilots came to the attention of the Gestapo. As serving members of the Royal Air Force and citizens of a country now under German control, 'Checko' Chaloupka and Jack Zafouk were technically 'Germans' who had taken up arms against the Reich. Paragraph 91A of German Military Law states, 'A German who serves in the forces of an enemy power during wartime against the German Reich or its allies will be punished with death or penal servitude for life.' This was the charge the Gestapo hoped to pin on them, and without warning both officers were sent to Prague on 14 August and thrown in jail. Tod formally requested to know why they were going and, receiving no answer, he immediately informed the Swiss authorities of their plight. Over the next two weeks both men were extensively interrogated, and Jack Zafouk was charged with treason and awarded a suspended death sentence; then mysteriously both were returned to Colditz. Perhaps Willie Tod's adroit response had made it more difficult for the two Czechs to 'disappear'. Later they would be joined by a further seventeen Czech officers, all fliers in the RAF and all under a death sentence. One of them, Ivo Tonder, had already miraculously survived the Great Escape massacre. 'I arrived at Reichenberg prison with five other Czechs from the tunnel,' recalls Tonder. 'And they were all shot but me. The Gestapo had put my family in prison the moment they discovered I had escaped, and for some reason they thought I could tell them something. So I was sent over to Pankraz prison for more questioning by the Prague Gestapo. This turned out to be one of those pieces of good luck within bad luck, because I was interrogated, and spent the next nine months in solitary. By the time I came back the Germans had forgotten where I came from. I was still expecting to be shot ten months later, when I arrived at Colditz.' Happily the war ended before Tonder and the rest of his compatriots could be tried for 'treason'.

Throughout 1944 Colditz received a steady trickle of men who had narrowly avoided the death sentence. In January six British officers arrived from the notorious Fresnes jail in Paris; all were SOE (Special Operations Executive) agents who had been parachuted into France and were variously engaged in sabotage and working with the Resistance. Jacques Huart was one, a well-known professional forger; Claude Redding, a wireless operator, was another, whose resolve in the face of his inevitable fate made a great impression on young John Beaumont. 'The Gestapo got him and he was sentenced to death,' recalls Beaumont. 'But he had to wait a couple of months before the sentence was carried out. Sitting in his stinking cell he thought, this is absolutely filthy, so he began to clean it up. In among the rubbish he found two halves of a walnut shell. He discovered that if he rubbed the shell for many hours on the floorboards it exuded an oil which polished the floor. He then rubbed the floorboards with his underpants and after many weeks he had a good-looking floor. One day, months later, he was deciding

he RAF: *(standing far left)* Jack Best, *(standing fourth left)* 'Errol' Flinn, *(standing fourth from right)* on Thom, *(standing extreme right)* Bill Goldfinch; *(seated third from left)* 'Bush' Parker, next to ouglas Bader; *(seated extreme right)* Dominic Bruce

he Navy: *(standing far left)* Hugh Bruce, *(standing fourth from left)* 'ghost' Mike Harvey; *(seated nd from right)* John 'Bosun' Chrisp

The Kommandantur yard: Pat Reid and accomplices entered
via windows on the second floor, while the sentry paced below

Pat Reid shortly after safe arr
in Switzerland October 1942

A week after Reid escaped, seven British Commandos arrived — escape aids were concealed in
their boots and belts — *(left)* Pte. Eric Curtis, *(centre)* Capt. Graeme Black, the Commandos' leade

Above Mike Sinclair
Right The man he impersonated –
Stabsfeldwebel Rothenberger 'Frans Josef'
Below Sinclair's false pass

Ausweis Nr. 301   Ausgestellt am 1.7.43.

Kommandantur
Oflag IV C Colditz

Dieser Ausweis berechtigt zum Betreten des deutschen
Teiles des Oflag IV C Colditz

Oberfeldwebel   Rothenberger
Dienstgrad   Eigenhändige Unterschrift des Inhabers

Rothenberger   A. B.
Name

Fritz
Vorname   Hauptmann und Adjutant

M/0161

Left Going down to the park walk

Above Corran Purdon's false Ausweis, his
photograph was taken with a home made
camera, but many were cut from German
photographs *(below)*: *(top right)* Biren Mazumo

e departure of the French, 1943.

ey were replaced by 76 British escapers, including Jock
milton-Baillie who designed the ingenious folding
ders for the 'Warburg Wire Job'

Prüf.-Nr. 150

OFLAG XVII 15878

BAILLIE   CLIFTON

Above The sanguine Scot with 'a bashed nose',
Col. Willie Tod, and *(right)* his jailer Col. Prawitt
Below Rubbish cart escaper, Gris Davies-Scourfield
Below right 'Ghost' Jack Best

OFLAG VII CH 530

OFLAG VII B 4131

rominente: *(above)* Michael Alexander and *right)* Charlie Hopetoun

elow Shortly after reaching the safety of merican lines, April 1945

16 April 1945. The morning after the battle, the Americans cross the Colditz bridge that the SS had unsuccessfully attempted to destroy

The sight that awaited them in the attic – the Colditz glider

how to decorate the walls when the cell door opened. This is it, I'm for it now, he thought. He was taken out, put in the back of a car and for some reason fetched up at Colditz. They had decided not to kill him. He proved to me that no situation is hopeless; even under the death sentence he was able to clear up the cell for the next poor blighter who went in there.'

On 23 August more counter-intelligence officers arrived and Colditz received its first Americans. Colonel Florimund Duke, Captain Guy Nunn and Alfred Suarez had been dropped into Hungary in an attempt to prevent it joining forces with Germany, and there they would have suffered the same fate as the seven British Commandos on Operation Muskatoon had it not been for the vigilance of the Swiss protecting power. Colonel Duke, who at forty-nine was the second-oldest American paratrooper of the war, immediately insisted on a separate representation to the camp Kommandant, adding weight to their presence, and this was accepted. The Americans were soon followed by another group of British troublemakers, including David Stirling, the founder of the SAS, and Major Jack Pringle; both men had shown themselves to be as effective behind bars as they had been in the field. Almost as an antidote to these 'personalities', on 14 October a quiet sheep farmer from New Zealand walked into the courtyard. He had arrived alone, and like every stranger he was immediately presumed to be a spy. There was one other New Zealander at Colditz who could vouch for him; and the spy turned out to be Captain Charles Upham, VC and bar, the only combat soldier ever to be awarded the decoration twice. Upham made light of his extraordinary bravery, and it was his quiet defiance and antipodean wit which endeared him to his fellow prisoners.

The arrival of all these superstars suggested that Colditz

had been marked out for some other purpose, and one group of prisoners now felt under special threat. The two Prominente, Giles Romilly, Churchill's nephew, and Michael Alexander, a distant relation of General Alexander, had lived a separate life ever since they arrived at the castle. They always suspected they were being held as hostages, and the arrival of the third Prominente, Charlie Hopetoun, from Eichstätt only confirmed their suspicions. Hopetoun, an ebullient raconteur with a flair for the theatre, had been captured at St Valery in 1940; and as the son of the Viceroy of India, Lord Linlithgow, he too suspected he had a price on his head, though this was never made clear. While at Eichstätt Hopetoun felt he was being 'watched' by the Gestapo, but when he took his fears to the Senior British Officer, they were dismissed as fantasy. Hopetoun then complained to the German Kommandant, whose answer was enigmatic. 'You are being protected. We do not wish to happen to you what happened to the Russian Royal Family in World War I. Do you remember Anastasia?' Hopetoun laughed and was given three days in solitary for insulting the Kommandant; by the time he came out he was convinced that he had been right.

In late 1944 the three Prominente were joined by four more, including a nephew of the Queen, all gathered in from camps across Germany. The War Office in London were aware of this development, and could only imagine what its purpose might be; but their role as potential hostages was one now shared by all 160,000 British POWs in Germany, as the country collapsed they might be used as human shields or even massacred. On 8 September the Foreign Office recommended a declaration to be sent to the German High Authorities warning that the responsibility for their safety lay with individual Kommandants and guards and, 'excuses or attempts to shift responsibility onto the SS or Gestapo would not be entertained'. They added, 'anyone believed to be guilty of maltreatment will be ruthlessly pursued and brought to punishment.' Now the Allies were winning the war this was no idle threat, but the War Office knew it would have little effect on Hitler or Nazi fanatics. The murder of the fifty airmen from Stalag Luft 3 underlined Hitler's flagrant disregard for the Geneva Convention, and two days after Himmler assumed command of the Home Army the Joint Intelligence Sub Committee submitted a report to the Chiefs of Staff in London. 'In isolated instances POW might be in danger if they fell into the hands of the SS or Gestapo' they wrote, and recommended, 'the issue of instructions to all POW to refrain from any action that might be pro-vocative, i.e. demonstrations over Allied victories, and *to remain in their camps until they received further instructions what to do and where to go*.' (my italics) Clearly there was concern that the continuing policy of encouraging officers to escape was only inviting them to take unnecessary risks. Not wishing a repeat of the Sagan tragedy, in August 1944 a memo was distributed to all Oflags and Stalags throughout Germany to release officers from their obligation to escape, though indi-viduals should not be prevented 'if they really wished it'. When this coded message arrived at Colditz remains a mystery: Willie Tod may well have received it in September 1944, but chose not to pass it on for fear that it would have the opposite effect to that intended. In any case, his tact was rendered obsolete on Saturday, 23 September, when the Germans posted up a notice of their own. It read: 'To all prisoners of war. Escaping is no longer a sport!' and went on to state that owing to commando activities and the contents of a pamphlet 'encouraging a non-military form of gangster war in spheres of operations including the enemy's

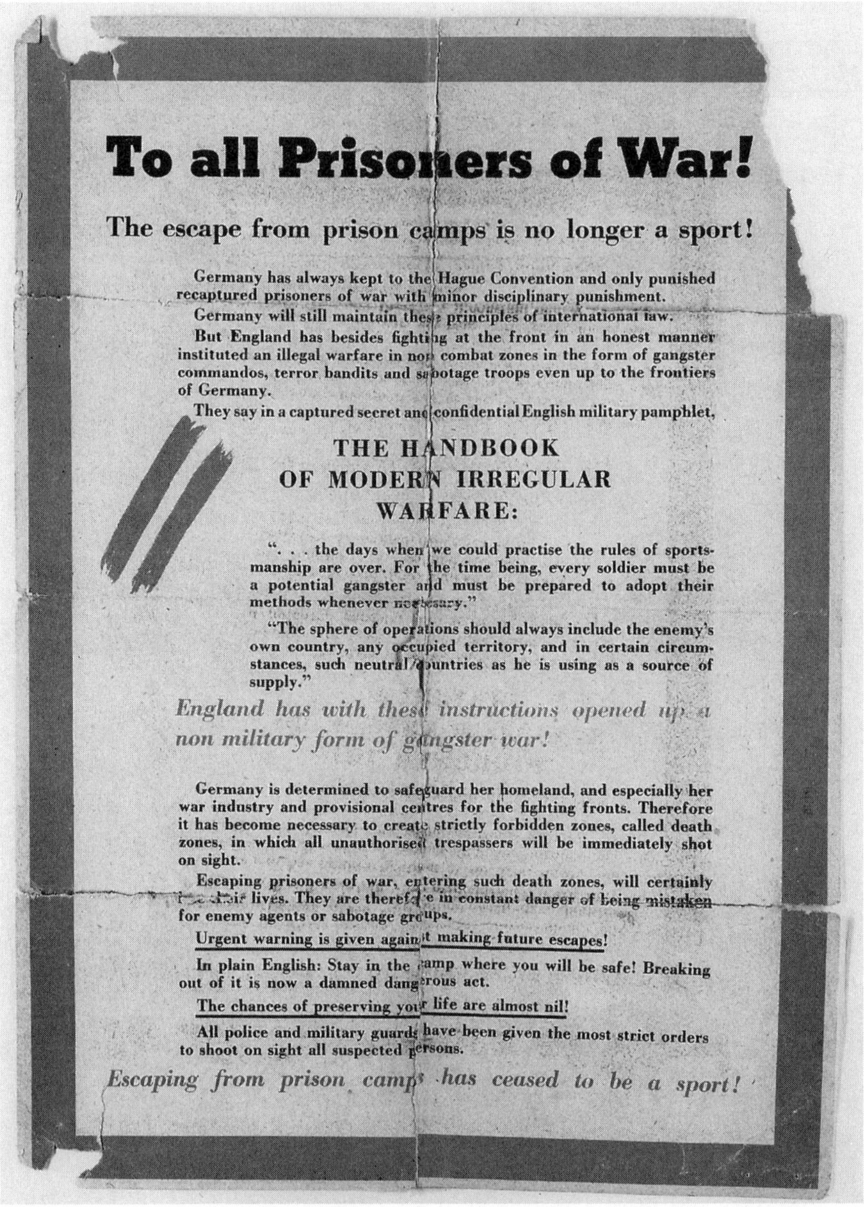

To all Prisoners of War!

The escape from prison camps is no longer a sport!

Germany has always kept to the Hague Convention and only punished recaptured prisoners of war with minor disciplinary punishment.

Germany will still maintain these principles of international law.

But England has besides fighting at the front in an honest manner instituted an illegal warfare in non combat zones in the form of gangster commandos, terror bandits and sabotage troops even up to the frontiers of Germany.

They say in a captured secret and confidential English military pamphlet,

THE HANDBOOK OF MODERN IRREGULAR WARFARE:

". . . the days when we could practise the rules of sportsmanship are over. For the time being, every soldier must be a potential gangster and must be prepared to adopt their methods whenever necessary."

"The sphere of operations should always include the enemy's own country, any occupied territory, and in certain circumstances, such neutral countries as he is using as a source of supply."

England has with these instructions opened up a non military form of gangster war!

Germany is determined to safeguard her homeland, and especially her war industry and provisional centres for the fighting fronts. Therefore it has become necessary to create strictly forbidden zones, called death zones, in which all unauthorised trespassers will be immediately shot on sight.

Escaping prisoners of war, entering such death zones, will certainly lose their lives. They are therefore in constant danger of being mistaken for enemy agents or sabotage groups.

Urgent warning is given against making future escapes!

In plain English: Stay in the camp where you will be safe! Breaking out of it is now a damned dangerous act.

The chances of preserving your life are almost nil!

All police and military guards have been given the most strict orders to shoot on sight all suspected persons.

Escaping from prison camps has ceased to be a sport!

Escaping is No Longer a Sport

own country', Germany would protect itself against such attacks. All over the country 'death zones' had been created, where trespassers would be shot on sight. The notice did not describe where these death zones were, but advised the officers to stay within the safety of their camp.

To one man, the threat of death zones and executions only increased the challenge. Mike Sinclair read the notice, and he still dreamed of escaping. To date his career in captivity had been virtually one escape attempt after another; he had been on the run in Poland, Slovakia, Hungary and Yugoslavia, where he was recaptured on the Bulgarian border. From Colditz he had reached Cologne, the Dutch border, the Swiss border, and been shot in the Frans Josef escape. He had made seven escape attempts since his capture at Calais, and for this feat alone he is remembered as one of the greatest British escapers of the Second World War; but 'The Red Fox' had never made a home run. As the summer of 1944 wore on, Mike Sinclair had withdrawn farther into himself. His mood had begun to worry his friend Gris Davies-Scourfield. 'Mike had been very strange, ever since he had learnt of his brother's death at Anzio in February,' he recalls. 'He wore an almost perpetual frown, looked well beyond his years, and I particularly recall the stems of his pipes were always quickly bitten through. I might have guessed that this threat to shoot escapers would merely act as an additional spur to his endeavour, an extra challenge which he would almost certainly accept, indeed one he would be unable to resist.'

On 4 September Mike Sinclair was caught wearing civilian clothes under his uniform on the walk down to the park; and he was sent to the solitary cells for fourteen days. In these cells three years earlier Pierre Mairesse Lebrun had conceived his spectacular vault out over the park wire, and

John Beaumont's blanket trick had proved that even in 1944 the park was still not secure: there were opportunities for the lone escaper. Few of his peers understood what relentlessly drove Mike Sinclair to escape, especially at this late stage in the war, but they understood better than anyone else the mental preparation required; for escaping was quite unlike any other activity. 'In war when you are attacking somewhere your blood is up and you have your soldiers around you,' recalls Corran Purdon, a veteran of the St Nazaire raid. 'Fighting is exciting and hot-blooded; whereas escaping is a cold-blooded act. One moment you are in a reasonably secure atmosphere, and you are inactive. You are surrounded by friends, there is food and it is reasonably warm, comfortable even. It takes tremendous courage to leave all that, and force yourself to do something in cold blood. You have had lots of time to think about it and plan it all out. You know you have only a short amount of time and you are likely to be shot at. To take that risk requires extraordinary courage.' By the time his spell in solitary confinement was up, Mike Sinclair had decided on his course of action; and he was about to test his courage to its limit.

A few days later Sinclair formed up with the other officers in the courtyard waiting to go down on the park walk. He was dressed in his big French khaki cloak, and his friend Gris Davies-Scourfield spotted him. He went over.

'"I see you're going on the walk. Would you like me to come with you?"

'"No, I'd rather be alone."

'"Oh, come on, Mike, I'll come with you. I don't mind."

'"I'd rather be alone, thank you." And he turned away. I thought, To hell with you, I've tried to be friendly and that's all I get. Go for a walk alone if that's what you want.'

Disconsolate at the growing distance between them, Gris wandered back to their room and began to write a letter. Only one man knew of Sinclair's intentions that afternoon – Kenneth Lockwood, the keeper of the escape money. 'I was walking around the courtyard, and Mike came up to join me. We walked around for a bit. Then he said, "I want some cash." So I looked at him. "Are you going to have a go?" And he said yes. I didn't say any more except, "Carry on walking around. I'll disappear and get it and then I'll join you again." So I slipped away and when I returned he said, "Kenneth, don't say a word of this to anyone, nobody knows." "Fine, Mike," and that was that. I didn't ask him about his preparations or anything else. I did a couple more rounds with him and left.'

Mike Sinclair knew that escaping was no longer a game; he knew about the fate of the airmen at Stalag Luft 3 and the 'death zones' in Germany; and he also knew that the war might end at any moment – all the more reason to escape before it was too late. Had he sought the approval of the escape committee, they might well not have accepted his plan; it was far too dangerous.

The column proceeded down the path as usual and emptied out into the wire pen. The guards carried on round the eight-foot perimeter fence and took up their positions, and inside the cage the prisoners started playing football. It was 25 September, and the leaves were starting to turn. Another unremarkable afternoon.

What happened next has never been accurately described; it is now a collection of images, half remembered, half seen. Sinclair was walking on his own up and down beside the fence. Casually he took a few steps away and turned, and suddenly his khaki cloak was off and he was wearing civilian clothes and a large pair of black gloves. He ran towards the wire. 'As we were going around talking of Christmas we heard shouts behind us,' recorded Charles Elwell, who was down in the park that day, in his diary. 'I looked around and saw Mike Sinclair sprawling on the top of the wire. He fell down on the other side. Shots rang out from all sides. He got up and ran, and I could see his face, red from exertion. I remember his eyes very clearly, they had an extraordinary fixed expression. They were staring hard. Lance Pope shouted out, "*Nicht schiessen! Nicht schiessen!*" Don't shoot! Don't shoot! More shots whizzed passed us and kicked up the dust at his feet. More shots . . . twenty in all. And then silence.'

Sinclair had disappeared from view behind some trees. Running fast and keeping low, he was a difficult moving target. He passed a shed beside the stream, and as soon as they saw him the guards from the other end of the park began to fire. Running a gauntlet of sentries, he reached the edge of the trees, then a bullet struck his elbow and ricocheted through his lungs and into his heart. He died instantly. But the prisoners knew none of this; the shocked guards had marshalled them all together and hurriedly marched them back to the courtyard. On the way up they passed the British camp doctor and two German NCOs running down to the park. Inside the courtyard another group of anxious prisoners waited beside the gate; they had heard the shouting and the fusillade from the windows, but no one knew what had happened. Immediately the bell sounded for an *Appell*. It was ten past four.

'Instead of saluting and thanking the SBO when the count was finished,' wrote Padre Platt, 'Hauptmann Püpcke spoke to the SBO and called off his guards, who went through the gate. Püpcke then saluted, and Tod called the parade to attention. His words were, "Par-a-de 'shun! Gentlemen, I am sorry to tell you that Mr Sinclair is dead. Fall out." For a second everybody stood immobile. It was a moment of extreme wretchedness.'

For many, Mike Sinclair's last desperate act was tantamount to suicide, especially at this late hour of the war. He had let his obsession consume him and his death, though heroic, was ultimately selfish; he became another unnecessary casualty, another son for his parents to mourn. Even if he had escaped the confines of Colditz Castle, what perils might have lain in store in Germany? There was no word from Bill Millar, the last man to make the dangerous trip to the border. But Mike Sinclair knew more than anyone the risk he was taking, and had taken the decision in cold blood. 'To him escape was a military operation and every factor had to be examined and thought through,' recalls Gris Davies-Scourfield. 'He knew it would take a good shot to bring him down, and it was bad luck that it ricocheted into his body. He was just a person, braver than the rest of us, who was prepared to take a greater risk. He was too brave; if one can be too brave.' Two days later Gris was packing up his friend's clothes to send them back to his parents. 'I came across this little note tucked into his shirt. It read, "I take full responsibility. Safe home to all you good chaps." It was tragic, but worthwhile as far as he was concerned. He would have had no regrets whatsoever.'

Mike Sinclair was twenty-six. Masses were said in the chapel, and three days later the funeral took place in the town cemetery. Ten British officers were allowed to attend, and the garrison provided a Union Jack. The Germans accepted full responsibility for their actions and they were not blamed for his death. The guards had acted according to their duty; tragically, Sinclair had acted likewise. A gloom settled over the courtyard. 'If there is indeed a Valhalla,' wrote Eggers, 'for the heroes of whatever nation, if the men who go there are men of courage and daring, if their determination springs from one true motive alone and that motive is love of their country — then in our own German tradition, Valhalla is the resting place of Lieutenant Mike Sinclair.'

The British Army felt similarly; after the war Sinclair was awarded the DSO, the only subaltern to posthumously receive the decoration for escaping during the Second World War. His grave is in Charlottenberg War Cemetery, Berlin, number 10.1.14.

CHAPTER SEVENTEEN

The Glider

A few days after Mike Sinclair's funeral, Lieutenant Colonel Willie Tod made an announcement at *Appell* reinforcing the German words on the notice-board. Escaping was indeed no longer a sport, and, as MI9 had advised him, the hostility shown towards Allied escapers by Himmler's units and civilians would only increase as the invasion of Germany began. Eggers recalls him saying 'It is no longer an adventure to get out of this camp', adding that as Germany was obviously losing the war 'he no longer approved of kicking a man when he's down'; a reference to goon-baiting, of which he had had more than his fill. Tod could not order his juniors not to escape, he could only 'tell' them not to; a slight yet significant difference.

The autumn of 1944 tested the nerves of even the most hardened prisoners: every radio bulletin brought fresh hope that their indefinite sentence would soon be over, only to be dashed a few days later. On 8 September the Germans began their V2 rocket campaign on London; 516 more attacks were to follow. Nine days later the Allied First Airborne Army dropped into Holland to secure the bridges of Eindhoven, Nijmegen and Arnhem, where they ran into heavy German counter-attacks. The Allies pressed on eastwards; on 13 October the US 1st Army finally entered Aachen, and a month later the US 3rd Army reached German soil; all the while their Russian allies advanced westwards towards them, crossing the Danube on 29 November. It seemed than the war would be over in three weeks, then Christmas, then next year; the prisoners could only sit by and wait. The sheer volume of Allied bombing raids over Germany inevitably meant that POW camps were not immune from their devastation; on 27 September an RAF Mosquito dropped its 'Cookie' bomb twenty miles south of its target, scoring a direct hit on Dossel POW camp. Ninety Polish officers were killed, nineteen of whom were ex-Colditz, and a further five hundred were wounded.

More unwelcome news was to follow: Ronnie Littledale, who had made a home run with Pat Reid in 1942, was killed when his Jeep ran over a landmine in Normandy. By a curious symmetry, he died within a week of his friend Mike Sinclair, with whom he had escaped from Poland to Bulgaria. In the middle of October Micky Burn, the radio scribe, heard on the news bulletin the voices of the repatriated Colditz officers who were now safely back in England. 'In the midst of such appalling horrors going on all around us this seemed to be something very civilised, and German prisoners were presumably repatriated to Germany,' he recalls. 'Unfortunately there was one man who didn't make it back. Lord John Arundell of Wardour was his name, the head of a very old English aristocratic family, who had contracted tuberculosis in Colditz. I listened to the people on the estate preparing the bonfires and speeches of welcome being made, but he never got home.' Lord Arundell was a gentle English eccentric, whose ascetic disposition made him the antithesis of his feisty young companions at Colditz; he had escaped from Eichstätt via the tunnel, but he was never awarded Prominente status, despite the fact that he held the oldest title of all. Arundell's habit of performing fifty press-ups a day, running around the courtyard in a vest then rubbing snow on his chest in midwinter was his undoing, weakening his resistance to a disease which the meagre Colditz rations could not counter. He died at a military hospital in Chester; having no male heirs, he was the sixteenth and last incumbent.

Winter came early to Colditz that year. In the grey world of the prisoners' courtyard, most of the 254 prisoners were about to spend their fourth winter in captivity, and retaining their sanity was now their prime concern. 'That last winter people did become quite strange,' recalls Pat Fergusson. 'They developed curious repetitive habits. Their behaviour would not have been accepted in normal society, but there it didn't seem too odd. Some became obsessed with doing laps of the yard. Round and round and round endlessly. Others became very lethargic and wouldn't get out of their bunks, they'd lie in bed all day because they couldn't see the point in getting up.'

The man most visibly affected by long-term confinement was the kitchen officer, Edmund Hannay. 'He is a quiet man by nature, but he is noisy now,' recorded Padre Platt in his diary. 'He is immaculately dressed, walks about with a wooden spoon and an iron poker in his hand, demands attention from anyone on whom his eye alights, and discourses unintelligibly on Egyptology, military technique, religion, or going north. Twice today he has set about finding Hamilton-Baillie whom he wishes to awake from the dead.' Hannay was then found inside a vat of potatoes trampling them 'to make the hooch'. The sight of this once sane man now half naked and delirious shocked his brother officers, and he was eventually sent to a mental institution and repatriated.

As the weather grew colder, the prisoners' thoughts turned once again to their almost constant hunger. The supply of Red Cross parcels had always provided Colditz with its own barometer; whenever it dried up, so the morale of the camp invariably drifted. Throughout the course of 1944 the prisoners had grown accustomed to consuming less and less, and at the onset of winter they were existing on a quarter of a parcel a week, assuming that every new delivery might be their last. German rations remained as meagre as ever: thin soups, ersatz coffee and slithers of black bread. One morning there was great excitement in the yard when the ration lorry pulled up with a horse's head on the back; it was promptly boiled up and eaten – there was little else. 'Feeling hungry dominated everything,' recalls George Drew. 'I had no other thought except for food, and the memories of food. Two chaps would be walking around the yard saying, "Do you remember that lovely steak we had at Simpson's?" "Oh, but it wasn't anything like the lobster thermidor I had at so and so." Drooling with saliva, without a hope of getting anything. Some people tried to catch pigeons with peas attached to fishhooks left on the windowsills. I don't think they had much luck. I think we all developed ways of sleeping to get over the worst pangs. The normal way was to sleep on one's face with a clenched fist in your stomach, so at least the walls of your stomach weren't flapping about endlessly.'

Hunger came to dominate all aspects of Colditz life. In the prisoners' library descriptions of banquets and parties were ripped out and burned; no one wanted to read about food, let alone imagine anyone else eating it. At mealtimes, each mess pooled their collective resources and divided their Red Cross parcels into eight, the usual number of men on a mess table. 'Angle-minded sappers' ensured that each portion was divided equally, but now the near-starvation conditions ushered in a new era of private enterprise. On Thursday, 7 December a 1938 Renault Coupé was bought for five pounds of Australian chocolate and £10; both the car and the money were in England. Five days later the last of the Red Cross parcels ran out; from now on the prisoners would have to rely entirely on the meagre German rations. Tea leaves were brewed up, then dried, repackaged, and sold on – often to unsuspecting guards, who complained that the English tea was not strong enough. Desperate smokers tried another ruse. 'When you smoked a cigarette you could nip it in the end,' recalls Pete Tunstall. 'And if you kept all the ends in a tin eventually you had another tin of tobacco. Cigarettes were sold as cigarettes, and "ends" were sold as "ends" – everyone was honest about this. But we craved fags so much we even used to keep the dog-butts of the "ends", and these were called "ends of ends" and had a very poor market value – even the guards wouldn't buy them, because they suspected they had already been smoked twice!'

Soon the yard became so busy with surreptitious deals between guards and prisoners that Eggers suggested to the Kommandant that they should set up a barter shop, where coffee and sugar could be exchanged for eggs and fresh vegetables. Prawitt was not amused. 'What do you suggest next – a brothel?' Inevitably, as the gap between the 'haves' and the 'have nots' widened, racketeering became the subject

of hot debate, fuelled by the discovery that some enterprising officers had tunnelled their way into the German
potato store and were plundering its contents for themselves.
'Our deprivations did change our political attitudes,' recalls
the Prominente Michael Alexander. 'Suddenly one saw the
advantages or the necessity of a more communistic, egalit-
arian approach towards life. In the trading world of the
prisoners' yard, someone had managed to get six eggs off a
guard, and we didn't feel it was fair he was going to eat the
eggs and we were going to be hungry. But of course it was
fair, because he had the incentive and the energy and the
entrepreneurism to get these damned eggs, and you can't
divide six eggs between two hundred people.' The argu-
ments went on, as the egg traders and the potato stealers
were reluctant to give up their spoils. Eventually Colonel
Tod put an end to private trading when he asked David
Stirling to take charge of the black market; from now on
only Checko and 'Dick Jones' – a British spy captured in
North Africa who spoke fluent Arabic, French and German
– and very little English – could barter with the guards,
who provided them with information in return. Whatever
they managed to acquire would be shared out among the
camp; unsurprisingly, this was an unpopular decision. Then
the potato stealers – who had all arrived from Eichstätt –
were asked to give up a portion of their plunder. 'I pointed
out that if we shared them equally it would have amounted
to one potato per man,' recalls Jock Hamilton-Baillie. 'But
we did eventually agree to give them a proportion, as long
as ours was the lion's share.' Once again Willie Tod saw that
fair play prevailed – but now even this quintessentially
'British' value was wearing thin.

In November 1944 one final escape project reached
fruition. It had involved almost a quarter of the British

officers in the camp, and the idea was so ambitious it had required enormous labour, secrecy and luck to keep going. In the attic above the chapel the prisoners had built a full-scale glider. The 'Colditz Cock' was the brainchild of Bill Goldfinch and Tony Rolt, two quite different men who independently recognised that, perched high on its rocky outcrop several hundred feet above the town, Colditz Castle was the perfect place from which to launch a glider. Tony Rolt was a tall, modest man who knew little of aircraft design; among his peers he was revered as a motor racing driver who had won the British Empire Trophy in 1939. But he was confident it could be done, and more importantly he had an idea about where to construct a glider in secret. Flight Lieutenant Bill Goldfinch, formerly a 'Bilge Rat' on a flying boat, had spent his life in captivity dreaming up various flying escapes. At Biberach, a large hutted camp twenty miles from the Swiss border, he had imagined constructing a large biplane kite, which with the aid of a strong wind and a rope would have floated an escaper over the wire and into the woods beyond. At Stalag Luft 3 he had adapted this concept into a gyroplane; but realising the practical difficulties it entailed, he decided to escape by 'moling' under the perimeter fence with Jack Best. They were caught, and it was only when Goldfinch arrived at Colditz that his flying ideas gained credibility.

'It was cold and the snow was falling,' he recalls. 'We were in a room with a window overlooking Colditz town, and the wind was blowing against the face of the castle. The snowflakes weren't coming down, they were actually drifting up and over the top. I watched the force of the wind at work on them, and what a smooth flow of air it was. And I thought this would be the perfect place to launch a glider. It would be like standing at the edge of a swimming pool, you could launch yourself into this rising air and float gently down. And that was it, that was Eureka. The French had dug tunnels under the chapel, others had gone through or over the wire. A few people had walked through the gate. Airey Neave had gone out of the theatre. All of these places had been sorted out and used. It seemed much simpler to me to just stand on the roof and jump off.'

From the castle windows Bill Goldfinch identified the perfect landing strip: a grassy field across the River Mulde five hundred yards away. In principle the idea was sound; Goldfinch would design the glider, Jack Best, ex-ghost and RAF pilot, would deal with the practicalities of making the tools, Geoff 'Stooge' Wardle would help in the construction, and Tony Rolt would manage the operation. Knowing the escape committee would take some convincing, Rolt enlisted the help of Captain David Walker to make the pitch. 'I think the audacity of it took their breath away,' he remembers. 'They thought it was great. Even though we hadn't quite worked out the most crucial aspect.' Building a home-made glider would be an achievement in itself, but launching it from the castle required a leap of the imagination. Once they had assembled the aircraft above the chapel, Tony Rolt's plan was to knock a hole in the exterior wall, wide enough to accommodate its wingspan, and then erect a platform perched on the ridge line of the roof below. This would serve as the runway, and the glider would then be fastened by a bed rope to a bath filled with concrete and earth; weighing one ton, this would be dropped from the third floor of the chapel block, catapulting the glider out in to the night.

Even to the optimists on the team, this was a fantastic idea. Jack Best had accompanied Mike Sinclair on the sixty-second rope escape, and he knew how closely the western side of the castle was guarded. 'It would be a hell of a gamble to get this platform built. Admittedly up on the roof we would be out of reach of the searchlights, but it would be dark, we might have dropped something or someone may even have fallen off. Personally I wanted the bath to go down the outside of the castle, so that when it hit the terrace it squashed one of the goons. But that was ruled not cricket, so we planned to drop it into the courtyard.' Bill Goldfinch was also unconvinced by the concrete bath. 'I thought ten people on a rope would be a much better idea. That would have been roughly the same weight as the bath, and we had no shortage of manpower. At the right moment they would just take hold of the rope and go down through the floor with it. That would have been eighteen hundred pounds of manpower. They'd be travelling fairly fast by the time they hit the bottom, but someone could have arranged some mattresses as a buffer.'

Despite the complexities of the launch, the scheme was approved and Willie Tod gave it his blessing. He shrewdly recognised that even if the glider never succeeded, the labour involved in building an aeroplane and concealing it from the Germans would keep many of his juniors sane; a worthwhile achievement in itself. Bill Goldfinch went straight to the prisoners' library and there he unexpectedly found a book that could help him. Entitled *Aircraft Design*, this two-volume work by C.H. Latimer-Needham laid out, in detail, the physics and engineering required to construct an aircraft. How this book arrived in the castle and why the Germans allowed it to remain is a mystery; perhaps the idea of building a glider appeared so far-fetched they assumed it would never enter the prisoners' heads.

'Gliders in those days looked like aeroplanes without engines,' Goldfinch recalls. 'So the shape was straightforward.

What I really needed to know was how long and wide to make the wings.' Latimer-Needham also included detailed diagrams of the Clark YH wing section, which gave Goldfinch the formula he needed to make this calculation. He decided to design a strutted, parasol-wing two-seater glider; one man would fly it and his crew would sit behind him inside the fuselage, facing the tail. The glider would have a wingspan of thirty-three feet, with its crew aboard would weigh 560lb, and if propelled off the roof at thirty-one miles an hour into a headwind, would – Goldfinch hoped – create enough lift to get airborne. It was a gamble that could not be tested until the night of the escape, and only then would the four originators of the scheme toss for the two places on board.

Once the designs for the glider were complete Tony Rolt began to prepare its secret workshop. His idea was to build a false wall in the attic above the chapel, shortening the space by seven feet. 'The Germans could only know how long the attic was supposed to be if they measured the length of the room below,' he recalls. 'And I don't think it ever occurred to them that we might make it shorter. The ferrets were far more interested in whether we had been up there or not.' Behind this partition the glider could be constructed undisturbed. One Sunday morning a working party assembled in the quarters adjacent to the chapel. As the camp orchestra began to practise, Mike Edwards picked the cruciform lock in the steel door at the head of the spiral staircase, and twelve men carrying various large sections of a wood-and-canvas 'wall' went up into the attic. Two hours later the false wall was in place, and then Jack Best arrived carrying a large bucket of mud. Best, who had spent his childhood in Africa, was familiar with mud hut construction, so he was given the task of creating the mud finish to replicate the original. Every day of the following week he returned to patch up the cracks in his handiwork, hoping that the ferrets had not paid the attic a visit: they hadn't. 'I was lucky – Allah was willing.'

Once the false wall was in place a camouflaged trapdoor was made in the ceiling below which served as the workshop's entrance. Entering this required a degree of agility; one man would sit on another's shoulders, remove the lid and pull down a short ladder to climb up into the space above. The trapdoor was well guarded and concealed; nevertheless its frequent use courted disaster. 'One of the German workmen came to me very excited one day,' recalls Jack Best. 'My knowledge of German is nil but it was perfectly obvious he'd discovered the trapdoor, but he hadn't seen the glider workshop. I got hold of Checko and said, "For God's sake fix it." Checko gave him seven hundred English cigarettes, and I was nervous, I never trusted a bribed man. Then quite by chance, the man died a fortnight later.' Allah was willing once again.

Construction began on 1 January 1944, and soon the glider workshop was a hive of activity. The four original members of the team were assisted by twelve 'apostles,' several of them RAF men, who helped with the complex manufacture, and a further forty acted as stooges. The space was only seven feet wide, so the wings and body of the glider had to be made separately, and to ensure that they would all fit together before take off, each element required a high degree of accuracy. Thirty-two ribs were made for the wings and the tailplane, each one steamed, pinned and glued together. Bill Goldfinch's working drawings were meticulous; the glider required over six thousand pieces of wood, each of a specific length and width, and many of them no bigger than a matchstick. Officers scoured the castle for

THE COLDITZ GLIDER

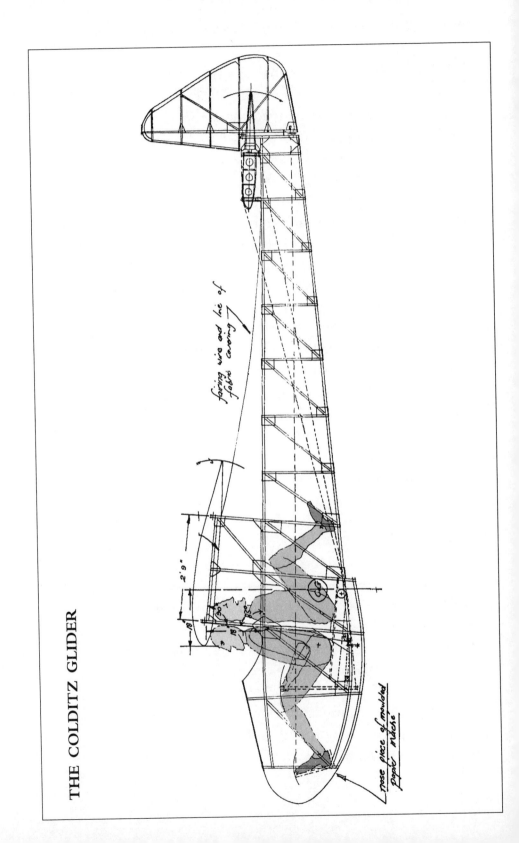

fairing wire and hic of fabric covering

nose piece of moulded papier mâché

2'9"

useful materials; the bolts for the wing and lift-strut attachments came from senior officers' beds, field telephone cable used to carry electricity around the prisoners' quarters was pilfered to serve as the control cables. Bed boards were given up, metal hinges were stolen from cupboard doors, and parties were sent out to discover flawless pieces of wood. 'Our greatest challenge was to find four "spars" with which to construct the wings,' recalls Jack Best. 'These needed to be sixteen feet long and preferably without a single knot in them. Eventually we found two perfect pieces in the Saalhaus right next to the German gateway. We couldn't just carry sixteen-foot pieces of wood across the yard, so we tacked them to a rather large table top, and then invented a reason to carry the table across the courtyard. When we got them into the workshop they were half an inch too thick, so we made a cut every inch of their length, and then just chipped away at them with the "pranger", a table knife, broken off near the handle. Then we had to plane them, and at that time we only had two home-made planes, the "big pisser" and the "little pisser". Why they were called that I have no idea, but they were very precise tools. The best saw I had was made out of the spring of an old gramophone. I cut teeth into it every sixteenth of an inch then tempered the blade in red-hot sardine oil on our stove. It was mounted on a frame stolen from a window bar.' On the other side of the courtyard, prisoners were gaily using the 'parole tools' lent by the Germans to construct their theatre sets. Having promised that they would not be used for escaping, the British were as good as their word, and these tools never entered the glider workshop.

Despite their ingenuity, the glider builders did face one limitation. 'We couldn't drill holes,' recalls Bill Goldfinch. 'So we would spend a lot of time wandering about looking for a piece of metal of a certain shape with the hole in the right place. We had a file and a hacksaw, so we could always make the hole bigger. The only other way to make a hole was to pinch the dentist's drill, and you didn't really want to go to the dentist after that.'

In the rafters above the workshop sat a stooge, peering through a crack in the roof tiles at a collection of coloured tins placed on a windowsill opposite. The arrangement indicated whether there were Germans in the yard; and the glider builders had such faith in this system that they believed the greatest risk posed to the glider was themselves. 'We left the wood shavings on the floor, and we all smoked like chimneys, and the only way the smoke could escape was through the hole in the roof that the stooges used,' recalls Jack Best. 'The only hazard was trying not to set fire to the damn thing. Only once the Germans did come into the attic and look around; we were all sitting on the other side trying not to breathe. One of them even banged the false wall and it sounded terrible, completely hollow and not made of solid masonry as you would expect. But they went away again.'

By the summer of 1944 the skeleton wings and fuselage had been assembled and the officers had stretched blue-and-white palliasse covers over the top; this material was painted with a 'dope' made from crushed millet and water that tensioned the fabric drum tight. Unfortunately both the dope and the glue that bonded the whole construction were not completely waterproof, adding another caveat to the already daunting requirements of the launch. The one and only flight would have to take place on a dry night, with a strong westerly wind, and preferably during an air raid when the searchlights would be extinguished.

At the end of November Willie Tod came up to the

workshop and was suitably impressed; the glider was in three pieces and the nose had yet to be made, but it was unmistakably an aircraft. Tod knew the glider could never be air-tested and its launch was fraught with complications; nevertheless its existence had assumed a greater significance. The arrival of the new Prominente suggested that Colditz would now play some part in the endgame of the war; in addition, Checko's girlfriend Irmgard Wernicker had informed him that there were squads of SS in the town who had orders to kill the prisoners when the time came. This was only a rumour, but came from a reliable source; Irmgard's father was the leader of the local Nazi Party. The prisoners were well aware of the gruesome fate of the Wehrmacht officers and their families implicated in the assassination attempt on Hitler's life; and there was no reason why the SS wouldn't exterminate their *Deutschfeindlich* captives in a similar manner. Plans were drawn up to defend the castle against the death squads; staircases would be sealed up with furniture, and in the attics a battering ram was prepared, to break through into the Kommandantur armoury. If Colditz Castle was to be the scene of a massacre, then the glider and its two-man crew provided a lifeline.

The new siege mentality encouraged officers to think about how they could remain self-sufficient. Major 'Skelly' Ginn recognised that one of their most important assets was the radio, which periodically broadcast messages specifically for prisoners of war. As the castle electricity was frequently cut off during air raids, he suggested making their own using the motor from the chapel organ. 'I knew that by removing the third brush it was an easy job to convert a motor into a dynamo, but the chapel was officially out of bounds for escaping, and there was a lot of debate about pinching this motor. Eventually Dick Howe decided communication with the outside world was more important than organ playing, so he took it. Up in the glider workshop we made a big wooden wheel about five feet in diameter out of bed boards and attached it to the motor with a sturdy rope. When two men spun the wheel fast enough the string belt drove the little electric motor, and we could listen to the radio in the blackouts; it was hard work, but we didn't miss a broadcast.'

As the end of the year approached the radio brought the disheartening news of the German counter-offensive in the Ardennes, dashing any hopes of an early conclusion to the war. This was particularly unfortunate for one Colditz prisoner; especially as on Christmas Eve the mercury had plummeted to -7°C. At 4 p.m. the courtyard was dark and deserted; wrapped up against the wind, an audience gathered at the windows to watch the unfortunate Checko fulfil the terms of his bet that if the war was not over by Christmas he would run twice around the yard – naked. To a chorus of muffled approval, Checko was as good as his word.

The freezing weather continued into the new year, which opened with a flurry of legal activity. On 5 January Pete Tunstall arrived in Leipzig for his fifth court-martial; his crime this time was shouting 'Bloody bastard Germans' the morning after D-day, thereby insulting the whole German nation. He had already spent thirteen weeks in solitary confinement awaiting this trial, which the court originally considered to be punishment enough; but some higher authority changed their mind, and Tunstall was tried again. As he stood in the corridor during a break in the proceedings, the German colonel came up to him. '"I have been told to give you three years. When I don't give you three years I'm in trouble with the Wehrmacht, when I do give you three years, I'm in trouble with the British. I'm going to give you nine months. Is that all right?" "Oh yes, very good, Colonel," I said. And that's what I got.' Tunstall was sent back to Colditz: by the end of the war he had completed 415 days in solitary, with several more months outstanding. William Schaefer – an American colonel – was not so lucky. He had arrived at Colditz on 6 December charged with preventing a German NCO from pinning up the 'Escaping is no longer a sport' notice at Schubin camp. This crime was considered far more serious than insulting the German nation, and on 29 December he returned from the Leipzig court having been awarded the death sentence. Schaefer remained stoical, but Padre Platt did notice a slight paleness and a difficulty in keeping his cigarette alight. The prisoners informed Geneva of his plight, and though they could not know it, the presence at Colditz of an American colonel awaiting execution would be significant in the events that would follow.

During the frozen month of January 1945 many officers went into hibernation, rarely stirring from their bunks, and if they did, they gathered around the few sources of heat in the castle. They had long realised that trying to keep fit on a starvation diet only made them feel worse, and now constant hunger had slowed the pace of life right down. Out in the yard, carts of old vegetables pulled up, heavily guarded, as prisoners risked beatings to try to steal them. One cart was drawn by healthy-looking chestnut draught horses, the other by a pair of thin, miserable-looking animals. Gris Davies-Scourfield asked the driver what had happened. '"Those," he replied, "are German horses: mine are Polish. Polish horses are not given as much to eat as German ones." I thought to myself as well as the "*Untermensch*" – sub-humans, the phrase the Germans used for Jews, Poles, gypsies and Slavs – they also have "*Unter-pferd*", sub-horses, as well!'

Inexorably the war inched closer to Colditz; the Russians

launched their Winter Offensive on 12 January, advancing from the east through Poland and into Prussia, and from the west the Allies reached the Siegfried Line by 1 February. Both armies were now gradually converging upon snow-bound central Germany. 'We watched, but with no pleasure, a few refugees going through Colditz to the west,' recalls Tommy Catlow. 'Day by day the numbers built up into a stream, and then they must have met up with refugees being pushed back by British and US forces in the west, because they started to come back. In spite of our own plight we felt desperately sorry for these old men, women and children with their pitiful possessions on prams and carts. There was precious little food for them, but worst of all no hope; one or other of the great forces would eventually roll them up. What could their future be?'

More VIPs arrived in the prisoners' courtyard with an equally uncertain fate. On 19 January 1945 four French generals were brought into the camp from Königstein, one short of the complement that had begun the journey. Hitler had ordered General Mesny to be executed *en route* in retaliation for the death of General von Brodowski, a German general shot while escaping from Besançon prison. The Germans claimed he was 'shot trying to escape' and the truth of this sordid little episode would only emerge fifteen years later, when the perpetrator was identified and sentenced to death. On 5 February General Bor Komorowski, head of the Polish Underground Army, arrived with his entourage. The general was a small, birdlike man whose terse authority over his staff, reduced to a simple '*Nyet! Tak!*' (No! Yes!), impressed even the weary British prisoners. They had all read of his exploits in the Warsaw Uprising, and now to a packed audience he gave his own account of the siege. Komorowski was only willing to talk if the two 'Colditz commies', Micky Burn and Giles Romilly, gave him their assurance that if the Russians liberated the camp first they would not reveal the general's identity. Both men assured him they were 'not that kind of communist'.

This lecture, interpreted into English by his aide-de-camp, gave a chilling account of the events in Warsaw. It was a tale of Polish courage and Russian duplicity; Bor described how the 42,000 Polish men and women 'rose out of the sewers' against the might of four German tank divisions. The Poles fought a bloody street battle, fully expecting that the Soviet Army, camped only a hundred miles away, would come to their aid. Instead Stalin stood by as the Germans counter-attacked with infantry and bombers, leaving the beleaguered Komorowski to fight to the bitter end. 'Destroy tens of thousands,' ordered Himmler; by 8 August more than 45,000 civilians had been executed. When Stalin sent his forces into Warsaw in October, he knew that any organised resistance to Soviet rule in Poland had been removed. The story thrilled the assembled audience, but it gave them little confidence in their own future: General Bor Komorowski had a price on his head, and if the SS did not avenge themselves on him then the advancing Russians surely would.

From the beginning of 1945 the War Office in London began to discuss how best to protect the Prominente. Churchill had received a letter from the King, who thought it 'rather sinister' that the Germans should have collected these young men inside Colditz; they now included his twenty-one-year-old nephew Viscount George Lascelles, and the Master of Elphinstone – John Elphinstone – the nephew of the Queen. In fact Churchill's nephew, the journalist Giles Romilly, was the hostage believed to be most at risk. He was not in the Army nor was he even an accredited war correspondent, and his civilian status gave the SS licence to remove him from the charge of the Wehrmacht and treat him as a spy. Memorandums flew between departments; the Army wanted to grant him an emergency commission, but Romilly's family objected. It was suggested that the plight of the Prominente should be trumpeted in the newspapers; but this would only advertise their concern. Even giving him the title official war correspondent was potentially hazardous; 'Do you think that if the Germans were informed officially of his change of status,' wrote the War Office to the Foreign Office, 'it would actually benefit Romilly, i.e. would they recognise it, or would their suspicions be aroused with unfortunate results?' It was a quandary to which there was no immediate answer, and until the British captured a few high-ranking Nazi prisoners of their own, they had little choice other than to wait and watch as events unfolded.

As for the rest of the POWs in Germany, the War Office had drawn up more concrete plans to assist their liberation. Small teams of SOE agents would parachute in ahead of the Allied forces, find their way into the camps and then make contact with the liberators via radio. The team destined for Colditz would be lead by Patrick Leigh Fermor, who happened to have served in Greece with Major Miles Reid, one of the recently repatriated prisoners. When the two men met and Reid was told of the scheme, he knew it was woefully inadequate; nine men and two radios stood little chance of entering Colditz Castle, let alone of springing anyone out of it, and he intended to take his concerns 'to Churchill if necessary'. In fact events unfolded too fast for this scenario to become a reality.

On 14 February prisoners inside Colditz witnessed the long and violent bombardment of Dresden, thirty miles south-east of the castle. They had seen heavy bombardments before, but this was the most intense; the eight-foot-thick walls of the castle 'shuddered like a tree' in time to the distant thunder of bombs, and 'it was impossible to play a gramophone record without the needle jumping'. The fire-storm in the night sky gave off so much light that officers were able to read books. The following day, Ash Wednesday, the Americans returned to drop 1,800 bombs and 136,800 firesticks on the largely wooden city, and most of the 55,000 dead perished in the flames that spread over eleven square miles. Several of the old guards lost their entire families in the raid, and for them the prisoners felt a small degree of sympathy, but little more – four years of reading the reports of the devastation wrought by the Luftwaffe on the cities of Holland and England had hardened their minds to the inevitable destruction of war. To them, the murmur of bombs and the unreal light across the night sky were a portent; they would soon be going home.

CHAPTER EIGHTEEN

The Flight of the Prominente

In March 1945, twelve hundred exhausted French officers arrived in Colditz Castle, and six hundred more were imprisoned in the village below. They had been marching for two weeks from a camp east of Dresden with little food and sleep, and their arrival turned the castle into a crowded refugee centre. 'Some of the French smell so strong that one almost vomits when one passes near them,' recorded Gris Davies-Scourfield in his diary. The corridors were full of men sleeping on straw, lavatories were blocked, and the *Appells* were chaotic. There was very little to eat. Now the Allied armies were advancing on Germany from all points of the compass; the Russians were approaching Berlin and Vienna, while the British Second Army was forging across the north of Germany, bound for the Baltic. Farther south, the American 3rd Army reached Frankfurt on 29 March –

the same day that the 7th Army reached Mannheim. By early April, the American 9th and 1st Armies were advancing towards Magdeburg, Leipzig and Bayreuth, in the East German industrial heartland, at the centre of which lay Colditz Castle.

As the Nazi empire crumbled, over three million Allied prisoners of war waited anxiously to know their fate. And no one could be less sure of their future than the Prominente held under lock and key inside Colditz Castle. They would be used as bargaining counters in the face of Germany's defeat, of that they felt sure; but would they be executed, or be led as shields to Hitler's last redoubt? Locked away in their quarters there were ample hours to discuss the issue. By March 1945 Giles Romilly, Michael Alexander and Charlie Hopetoun had been joined by four others, including Captain John Elphinstone, an impeccable but 'rather blank' officer who was a nephew of the Queen, Lieutenant Viscount George Lascelles, a sanguine twenty-one-year-old and the King's nephew, and Captain Dawyck Haig, a gaunt artist suffering from amoebic dysentery, who happened to be the son of Britain's World War I Field Marshal. General Bor Komorowski, his staff and the four French generals had recently swelled their ranks, and on 6 April Lieutenant John Winant Junior, the son of the American ambassador to Britain, arrived.

No one knew what would become of the Prominente once the Americans or the Russians came within striking distance of Colditz. On 10 April, shell-bursts were heard in the distance – the Americans had reached Leuna, only twenty-five miles away, and throughout the day German tanks, armoured cars and artillery streamed over the bridge back towards Chemnitz; they appeared to be an army in retreat. Later an SS division moved up into Colditz village, and undertook a feverish defence of the town. The bridge across the River Mulde was mined, and artillery rattled through the streets to take up position in the surrounding woods. The *Sturmgeschütze* − storm troopers − occupied houses and barricaded the main street; out in the fields, the Hitler Youth set about digging themselves into foxholes. Then, for two days, an eerie calm descended on Colditz.

On 12 April, Lieutenant Colonel Willie Tod was summoned by the Kommandant. Prawitt told Tod he had received a written order that the Prominente were to be moved out of Colditz immediately. The letter was from Reichsführer Heinrich Himmler, chief of the Home Army and the SS, personally, but it was left unsigned. Prawitt said two buses would be waiting for the Prominente outside the Kommandantur at midnight − where they would be taken, he was not at liberty to say, but the letter warned that Prawitt would pay with his life if any of them escaped.

While they remained in Colditz, the Prominente felt 'protected' by the fragile authority of the Wehrmacht, which gave them some comfort. Beyond the castle walls, the prisoners would be defenceless, and could easily disappear into the hands of those Nazis desperate to save their own skin. Tod urged Prawitt to disregard the order. Prawitt replied that, if he did, the SS would enter the castle, and see that it was carried out: 'There will be many deaths throughout the camp and still the Prominente will depart.' All that Tod could obtain was a guarantee that Eggers, the Chief Security Officer, would accompany the party and bring back word that they had arrived safely. At 1.30 a.m., the party of twenty-one men marched out across the floodlit courtyard, through a column of SS soldiers, and on to two waiting buses. It was a dramatic scene, witnessed by their fellow officers crowded at the windows, who shouted down words of encouragement. As they set off into the night, escorted by two motorbikes and an armoured car, Giles Romilly broke the silence: 'I thought you'd all like to know today is Friday the thirteenth.'

At dawn they passed through the charred remains of Dresden, 'bombed flat and smelling of death', and drove on towards Königstein castle, high above the River Elbe. The tension proved too much for Charlie Hopetoun. During the last six months of his captivity he had been increasingly 'reading too much philosophy and drinking too much hooch', and his ramblings regularly entertained and alarmed his fellow Prominente. 'On the bus my elastic snapped,' recalls the son of the Viceroy of India. 'I was round the bend. I could hear what they said to me but I could not answer.' Alternately screaming abuse and sobbing, Hopetoun had to be restrained from killing one of the guards; and as he staggered up the hill towards Königstein castle it was clear he was too traumatised to continue. That morning John Elphinstone, the senior British officer in the party, asked the Kommandant if Hopetoun could stay at the castle accompanied by Dawyck Haig, whose amoebic dysentery had been exacerbated by their upheaval. The request was granted, and there they were left with Corporal Mittai, one of two Maori orderlies who had volunteered to accompany the Prominente. The rest of the group then moved on, through Czechoslovakia, to Klattau, on the borders of Bavaria, where they spent the night. They drove on again the next day, and late in the evening on 15 April, the party came to a vast castle next to a bridge which bore a coat of arms. John Elphinstone recognised this place at once – it was Laufen, his first prison camp. The buses drew up outside, and Elphinstone read the sign. Laufen was no longer an Oflag but an 'Ilag', an internment camp for civilians. Elphinstone, who normally 'seemed to operate in a kind of deep freeze', turned white with rage, and refused to let anyone get off the bus, knowing that once inside the gate they were beyond Wehrmacht control. '*Wir sind englische Offiziere und müssen als englische Offiziere behandelt werden!*' he yelled. We are English officers and we must be treated as English officers! Giles Romilly, the civilian journalist, sank deeper into his seat. The scowling escort officer climbed back into the bus and slammed the door. The letter of the law was upheld, and they were driven to the medieval castle of Tittmoning, ten miles away.

When they arrived at Tittmoning, Giles Romilly found himself united with an old friend – Captain van den Heuvel, 'Vandy', the Dutch Escape Officer who had left Colditz in 1943. Vandy was well aware of the danger the Prominente were in, and his fears were confirmed on 19 April when he heard through his stooges among the German guards that Goebbels and Himmler had been seen driving through Tittmoning in a whirl of dust. They were headed for the Great Redoubt – the Nazis' last refuge in the mountains of Bavaria. On the same day, the Prominente were informed they were to be moved back to Laufen, where they feared Himmler's thugs would take control of their fate. A master of expediency, Vandy now proposed to the Prominente an escape plan.

The Dutch had dug a hole in one of the castle's eight-foot-thick walls which one entered by removing a stone. From the tiny entrance chamber, a low tunnel led to a vertical shaft three feet square and twelve feet high. Vandy suggested that five of the Prominente conceal themselves in the hide, while another broke out of the castle, making use of a further escape route he had already prepared. The Germans would believe that they had all escaped together, and the disappearance of no less than six men would throw them into a panic and facilitate the getaway of the real escaper. As the Prominente began to draw lots as to who should break out of the castle, Giles Romilly made a timely announcement; he had claustrophobia and could not stand to be secreted in the wall. So it was Romilly who would accompany two of Vandy's Dutch officers in their attempt to break out of the castle. The escape was planned for the evening of 20 April – Hitler's birthday. Five of the Prominente waited for their moment to enter the hide in the castle walls, while Giles Romilly joined the Dutch officers on their evening stroll on the castle ramparts. As dusk fell, and the guards shepherded the prisoners inside, Romilly and his Dutch companions hid in a ditch. When it was completely dark, Vandy secured a home-made rope to the timber frame of a watchtower adjacent to the parapet. While the sentry stood in the tower directly above him, van den Heuvel lowered the first of the Dutchmen over the parapet. Then it was Romilly's turn. Suddenly, he heard a voice call out above him. '*Halt!*' An elderly German guard ducked back into the cabin to grab his rifle. Romilly did not wait any longer: he reached the rope and swung out over the wall, burning his hands as he slid ninety feet to the ground. Moments later Vandy and the other escaper were surrounded, and the Germans congratulated themselves on a timely intervention. In the dark woods below, Giles Romilly and his Dutch companion, André Tielemann, crept away from the castle and struck out across the moonlit fields. They had a slender head start.

Earlier that evening Romilly's colleagues were escorted to the hide inside the castle walls. 'A stone slid out and revealed the entrance to the hide,' recalled Michael Alexander. 'A hole just large enough for us to wriggle through one by one. The five of us crawled inside, took up the only possible positions, and began to take stock of our appointed tomb. It was with misgivings that we listened to the sound of the stone being cemented back into place.' His fellow captives were George Lascelles, John Elphinstone, Max de Hamel and John Winant; General Bor Komorowski and his staff had decided that they would allow events to take their course. Two lay side by side in the low tunnel, one sat at the bottom of the shaft, another on a wooden perch above him, and the fifth on the lavatory bucket inside the entrance to the hide. They changed positions every two hours, and settled down to wait. 'It was,' recalled George Lascelles, 'something of a test of character.' They had been supplied with enough food and water to last seven days and nights.

The missing Prominente threw the camp into chaos: they had to be found. The first day, the Prominente could hear the castle being searched; the walls were tapped, but Vandy had made the hide echo-proof, and their presence was not detected. Another unsuccessful search was conducted on the morning of the third day, and the next morning efforts were resumed with renewed vigour. The crashes became louder and louder, until suddenly the wall caved in: 'A howling bloodhound leaped forward barking, and pistols and machineguns were poked into the hole, and we emerged shamefaced and embarrassed into the world,' recalled Michael Alexander. When the five men were hauled before the Kommandant, they discovered why the Germans had been so desperate to find them. When news of their escape had reached Berlin, the Kommandant and Security Officer had been sentenced to death. For the Prominente, it was sobering news: despite the fact that the country was descending into chaos, someone in Germany – someone with power over life and death, and with the will to exercise their power – was still interested in their fate. They also learned that three thousand men had been sent out to comb the countryside in search of Giles Romilly – he was yet to be found. The party left Tittmoning with an SS escort, and were returned to Laufen, where new measures were in place to prevent them escaping again. Barbed-wire barricades had been rigged up in the passages and halls, and a twenty-four-hour guard was mounted over them. They now found themselves in a prison within a prison.

The Allies were powerless to help them. The American 7th Army was advancing towards Munich, but the Germans still controlled the country around Fortress Tirol. A memo was sent from the War Office to Winston Churchill explaining the situation: 'As soon as it became known that the "special" prisoners had been moved, a telegram was dispatched to the Protecting Power and the International Red Cross Committee requesting that enquiries should be made as to their whereabouts.' On 23 April these enquiries received a reply; the German High Command had informed Dr Feldscher, head of the Swiss legation in Berne, that the 'special prisoners' were being held in Laufen. 'Now an Ilag, repeat Ilag'. This was a potentially dangerous development; the Swiss were well aware that technically the Prominente had now left the protection of the Wehrmacht. Two days later Feldscher left Berne in a cavalcade of six cars, equipped with supplies of petrol and food – items in desperately short supply near the front line. Meanwhile, from inside their cage, the Prominente had established contact with the outside world. They put a message in a matchbox, and threw it out of the window, hoping it would fall into friendly hands. They suggested that any reply should be left in another box under the single tree in the exercise yard. The following day they found a reply, left by a 'Felix Palmer', who had been captured while working for Military Intelligence in Norway. He reported that

exercise routines had been changed in order to accommodate them – a measure which suggested their stay would be
a lengthy one.

On 28 April, the German general commanding the
Munich area visited the Prominente, and summoned John
Elphinstone to a meeting with the camp Kommandant.
Elphinstone warned General Gusselmann that, if anything
happened to them, he would be held personally responsible
'*nach dem krieg*' – 'after the war'. Gusselmann gave his word
of honour that they would not be moved from Laufen. Later
in the day, the Prominente were visited by Dr Feldscher,
and an old friend who had come to visit them inside Colditz,
the erratic Rudolf Denzler. Drinking coffee in their rooms,
Dr Feldscher showed them a stern letter from the British
Foreign Office that warned 'whoever it might concern' of
the direct consequences that would follow if anything
happened to them contrary to the usages of war. He reas-
sured them that Rudolf Denzler, 'a funny, tall, untidy sort
of fellow' whom George Lascelles noticed had some 'spots
of blood on his collar where he had cut himself shaving',
would stay in the neighbourhood of the castle, and he was
under strict instructions to telephone Feldscher in his temporary headquarters in Bad Gastein the moment any attempt
was made to move them. Dr Feldscher suspected that General
Gusselmann might not have the last word about the
Prominente's fate.

Soon afterwards, alarming news reached the Prominente.
'Bus new to Laufen parked behind walls,' said the message
in their matchbox. 'They seem to be trying to keep it hidden.
Rumour you are to be moved.' The other inmates attempted
to sabotage the bus, but to no avail. On 1 May, an extra
report was delivered to the Prominente in a loaf of bread:
'Sabotage attempt unsuccessful. Double guards on gate.

Understand bus now filled with petrol. Trying to contact Swiss. Good luck.' At dawn the next day, they were woken by a guard. As they were dressing, the prison gates were thrown open, and two cars drove in – a black Mercedes and a smaller Opel. A tall figure stepped out of the Mercedes, dressed in a long leather coat: his lapels bore the insignia of a colonel, and on his cap he wore the death's-head emblem of the SS. From the other car emerged a round little Luftwaffe major with a close-cropped moustache and rimless glasses – at first glance it might have been Himmler himself. The other occupant was 'a hard-faced blonde' wearing trousers and smoking a cigarette through a long holder. Their sinister visitors said nothing, though the SS colonel tapped his holstered Luger meaningfully. To George Lascelles the scene was reminiscent of 'the last reel of a film'. Nervously the Prominente boarded their bus, aware that wherever their 'gangster-like' escort was taking them, this would be the last and most perilous stage of their journey. They could only hope that somehow Rudolf Denzler had been informed of their plight. As they were driven out of the village, they passed a tall man in a trilby trying to wrestle an umbrella into his tiny car. He stole a glance up at the cavalcade as it passed; it was Rudolf Denzler. He smiled; their departure had been noticed.

The convoy moved south, through the battered city of Salzburg, towards the Austrian mountains. Climbing the winding mountain roads, they passed a signpost inscribed in Gothic lettering: BERCHTESGADEN. Was Hitler's impregnable mountain-top headquarters, the Eagle's Nest, to be their final destination? Progress was slow, for the road was cluttered with traffic: Innsbruck, ninety miles to the west, had fallen, and its citizens were making their way towards Salzburg, only to meet Salzburgers fleeing in the opposite direction. Late in the afternoon, they entered a wide valley. Below them, they could see an encampment of huts, fenced in with barbed wire. A tall chimney rose up among the huts; it looked like an incinerator. They passed stilted sentry boxes and a notice-board which revealed its name: Markt Pongau. Their sinister escorts in the Opel and the Mercedes were nowhere to be seen. Markt Pongau turned out to be an international Stalag – a non-officers' camp. It was a squalid and dispiriting place, although the 'incinerator' was nothing more sinister than a water tank. The Prominente were led to a dismal hut segregated from the rest by rolls of barbed wire.

The next day, an enormous black Mercedes drew up in the courtyard. An awestruck German guard told them the identity of the portly figure propped up on cushions on the back seat of the car. It was Obergruppenführer Gottlob Berger – the SS general who had been in charge of all matters relating to prisoners of war since 1944. The Prominente now knew that it was Berger who held their fate in his hands. To their surprise, he seemed determined to ingratiate himself with them. He began by saying that they had no doubt heard that he had once been head of the SS during the war – this had been against his wishes, and after three months he had requested a fighting job from the Führer. He then began to speak of the difference between the Waffen SS, who were primarily soldiers fighting along-side the German Army, and the Gestapo SS – the SD, or Sicherheitsdienst, the security force on which the Nazi regime depended to retain its power. Berger said it was the Gestapo SS who were responsible for the concentration camps, and because he disapproved of their activities, he had asked to be transferred to the Waffen SS.

Having attempted to excuse his role in the war, Berger

then began to play the genial host. He offered the Prominente cigarettes and whisky. Finally, he broached the subject that was closest to the Prominente's hearts – the question of what was to become of them. The story he told was an extraordinary one. Germany was in chaos. Stalwart in its defence against the 'red virus' of communism, it had, nonetheless, been defeated, and even he could no longer guarantee that the rules of war would prevail. And he went on to explain why.

Berger had recently flown into Berlin for a meeting with Hitler in the war-torn city. His final orders had included a direct instruction from the Führer that the Prominente were to be shot. Berger decided to silently ignore the order for the time being: with Germany crumbling beneath the Allied assault, he hoped Hitler would have other things on his mind. But Goebbels – a dominant figure at the Führer's headquarters – was adamant that it should be carried out. 'When the whole German people is weeping, the English royal family should not be laughing,' he said, repeatedly. As soon as Berlin discovered that the execution had not been carried out, Hitler decided to enforce it by other means. On the night of 27 April, Berger intercepted a radio message from Martin Borman at Hitler's headquarters, to Gauleiter Giesler, the recently appointed Reich Defence Commissioner, in Munich. Firstly, Giesler was to punish Berger for his insubordination: he was, as the party jargon put it, to 'be made sure of for all time'. Then the Prominente were to be dealt with. The task was entrusted to SS Führer Ernst Kaltenbrunner, and a firing squad was assembled in the Ministry of the Interior in Munich.

Berger had confronted the fanatical Giesler in his office in Munich. They had argued: Berger had defied him to carry out his orders, and had stolen the list of the condemned men's names from his desk. Berger said it was he who had arranged the Prominente's 'abduction' from Laufen, but he could no longer guarantee their safety: Kaltenbrunner was notoriously ruthless, and he was known to be somewhere in the mountains, with his gang of thugs. The Prominente were a valuable prize: they could be used as bargaining counters — or Kaltenbrunner might decide to execute them himself, as a last senseless act of retribution. In order to thwart his plans, Berger was providing the Prominente with a special escort. They were to leave the next morning accompanied by a representative of the Swiss government, with his personal guarantee to ensure safe passage to the American lines. 'Gentlemen,' Berger declared, theatrically, 'these are probably the last orders I shall give as a high official of the Third German Reich.'

The Prominente did not know it at the time, but Berger's extraordinary performance owed much to the work of the Swiss legation. When Denzler informed Dr Feldscher that the prisoners had left Laufen, Feldscher sent his young deputy, Werner Buchmüller, off in a Buick to pursue the convoy. When Buchmüller arrived at Markt Pongau, he was told that the Prominente were being held there on the authority of General Berger, and that the Swiss should discuss the situation with him. Late on the evening of 3 May Feldscher drove up to meet Berger at his mobile command post at Kirchdorf, near St Johann, in the Tirol. In the ensuing confrontation, it became clear that Berger did not want to kill the Prominente, but nor was he willing to let them out of his hands. Feldscher pointed out that the Allies would soon overrun the Tirol: what better way to win their favour than by saving the lives of such important people? And what better way to save their lives than by handing them over to the protecting power immediately? But Berger had his own safety to consider. Hitler was now dead – he had committed suicide on 30 April – but his order to execute the Prominente had never been countermanded. Did Berger have more to fear from die-hard Nazis than he did from the Allies? The argument continued late into the night. When Berger arrived at Markt Pongau, his theatrical wooing of the Prominente proved that Feldscher had won him over.

The next morning, an American car with diplomatic plates and a Swiss registration number drew up outside the Prominente's hut. Werner Buchmüller stepped out of the car: he was to be their escort to the American lines. The party was ready to leave when it was discovered that their trucks had disappeared. There were no others. Finally, Buchmüller succeeded in commandeering two lorries from the town – a remarkable achievement, given that the entire district was mobilising to retreat – and he then produced two Swiss flags, which were draped over the bonnets of the lorries. Lascelles, Elphinstone and General Bor Komorowski rode ahead in Buchmüller's Buick. The others were in the lorries.

Darkness was descending on the valley as the convoy left Markt Pongau, escorted by a heavily armed SS guard, and an SS doctor. The Prominente were nervous; as the country slid into chaos, they knew that the die-hard remnants of the Nazi regime were seeking refuge in these mountains – they were entering the wolves' lair. Kaltenbrunner was on the loose here, and as the convoy crossed the high passes that connect the Salza and Inn valleys, they began to see him round every corner.

At midnight, the lorries suddenly halted. An SS officer stood in the headlights, waving a gun, and signalling to them to turn off to the right. They left the main road and climbed up into the mountains. Passing through a small hamlet, they turned up a dirt track, and entered the courtyard of what appeared to be a farm. Military vehicles were parked around its edges. There was no sign of life. Then a door opened, and an enormous man, dressed in SS uniform, ushered them into the house. They climbed the stairs, apprehensively, and entered a long hall, lit by lamps and candles. There was a feast spread out on a table in the foreground: cold meats, game, fish, crystallised fruit, and bottles of drink of all description. Beyond the table, on the floor, lay twenty SS men, 'sprawled like retainers on a Saxon hearth'. To Michael Alexander, it resembled a stage setting for the cave of a robber chief. Nervously, the captives stood about and waited.

A loud shout – 'Achtung!' – heralded the entrance of a familiar figure. It was General Berger, dressed in a white mess jacket. Berger welcomed each of the Prominente effusively, and made another speech. England and Germany, blood brothers of the same Aryan stock, should now settle their differences and unite in arms against the common enemy, the 'red virus'. They sat down to eat. Finally, Berger ceremoniously presented Lord Elphinstone with a pistol inlaid with ivory and decorated with golden oak leaves. The pistol bore the enamelled monogram of the SS, and it had been given to Berger by the Führer himself. He was giving it to the Prominente as proof of his good wishes for their safe arrival in Allied hands. It was a memorable performance.

At 5 a.m. the following morning the Prominente left Berger's stronghold. Roadblocks were being prepared on some of the road's steep curves, and engineers were laying charges beneath bridges. The Americans had now advanced beyond Innsbruck, and were forcing their way up the Inn valley; only one SS division – the last fighting troops in the western Alps – was holding them up.

Soon, the Prominente reached what was obviously a

forward area. Weary-looking soldiers were preparing gun positions by the roadside, and transports streamed past them, retreating before the American forces. Turning a bend, they saw ahead a river crossed by a stone bridge. Covering the bridge, and commanding a fine field of fire down the valley, was an 88-millimetre gun, waiting the approach of the first enemy tanks. This was the Germans' last line of defence, and the boys manning the gun – none seemed older than eighteen – let the convoy pass freely. Michael Alexander watched their faces as he passed. 'They were more like boy scouts, you know, just chaps defending the last line. It was very sad.'

In a meadow on the far side of the bridge was an old wooden barn. Creeping towards it were two American soldiers. The Prominente cheered. Round the next corner was a troop of three American tanks. Buchmüller flourished their papers, and the commander of the leading tank waved them on. The tanks were scouts for a squadron which they met in the next village. Here, beside a small white church, the convoy stopped, and they were presented with chocolate and bottles of wine. The Prominente were free. Later that day they reached the headquarters of the US 53rd Division, at Innsbruck, thirty miles away, and from there the party was broken up. Buchmüller returned to Switzerland, General Bor and his officers were sent to a concentration area at Murnau. The others travelled in open truck to the headquarters of the US 7th Army at Augsburg, and that night their American hosts were intrigued to watch John Elphinstone receive a personal call from his aunt, the Queen. Both Elphinstone and George Lascelles were flown home immediately. The rest of the party followed soon afterwards.

But what had become of the remaining members of the party who had left Colditz on 13 April? Evading the attention of the three thousand men who had been mobilised to

Map of the Prominente's Journey

search for him, the resourceful Giles Romilly had travelled by train and on foot to Munich. In a suburb of the city, he and the Dutch officer, André Tielemann, found lodgings with the wife of an SS sergeant who was fighting on one of the fronts in the far north. 'The fact that he was in the Waffen SS was a worry to her,' Romilly wrote. 'She knew, as every German did, that the war was about to end. She did not trust her neighbours. She was sure that one or other of them, as soon as Munich was taken, would report her connection with the SS to an Allied authority, in order to curry favour.' Romilly wondered whether her kindness to them was an attempt to ingratiate herself with the Allies, but the subject was never discussed. 'She never asked us who we were or what we were doing.' Romilly spent a week wandering through the streets, contemplating the ruins of a city he had known and loved as a journalist before the war. He found bombed houses and blank faces awaiting the inevitable in-vasion. After the Americans liberated Munich, Romilly became a regular visitor to the headquarters of the 45th Division of the 6th Army, and one afternoon, he was invited to accompany a famous war correspondent to Dachau. He was quite unprepared for the heaps of 'spillikin' thin bodies, which 'lay under a hush of horror'. Soon afterwards, he flew via Mannheim, to Paris, and returned to England on 2 May.

Dawyck Haig and Charlie Hopetoun, who were left behind at the fortress of Königstein, had fared less well. Haig's dysentery had so weakened him that his painfully thin appearance scared Hopetoun – the man Haig had been deputed to care for. Slowly both recovered, and as their health improved they were befriended by the Kommandant, Colonel Hesselmann, and his wife and children. Hesselmann, like Obergruppenführer Berger, ignored telegrams from Berlin instructing him to send his two sick captives south towards an uncertain fate; he too regarded them as future allies against the advancing Russians. Just before they stormed the castle, Hesselmann revealed that he had the Saxon crown jewels hidden in twelve suitcases in a dungeon. He asked Haig and Hopetoun to take them back home as a present to the British royal family, which they agreed to do. When the Russians arrived, looking to Charlie Hopetoun 'like a French revolution mob marauding across an aristocrat's garden', suddenly the two young men found themselves surrounded by terrified women seeking protection from their conquerors. The castle descended into chaos; there was widespread looting as the Russians ran around like naughty children, smashing everything they could find. In the midst of this a German officer who had hidden in the attics committed suicide, and even Mittai, their Maori orderly, became drunk and violent, attempting to strangle Haig before disappearing with the mob down into the town. They never saw him again. Soon the two young men managed to make contact with the American troops established in nearby Chemnitz, and they were driven back through the Russian lines to an airbase. Here Charlie Hopetoun wandered into a hut, where he was confronted by a British corporal. '"And who may you be?" "Hopetoun and Haig," I replied. He looked up. "Ah. We've been looking for you all over Germany."' The following day they flew back to England; the twelve suitcases were left behind. They were the last of the Prominente to be rescued, and three days later Germany surrendered. Their friends back in Colditz would not have to wait that long.

CHAPTER NINETEEN

Liberation

On 14 April 1945, the morning after the Prominente left Colditz, the prisoners awoke to find the town ready for a battle. German soldiers had dug in around the bridge, and the SS had set up a defensive position in a building just below the castle. Over to the east a battery of 88 millimetres were well concealed in the woods. From their vantage point the prisoners had a grandstand view of what would follow, and now they were very well informed about their own fate. Ever since David Stirling had taken control of black market operations he had recognised that Checko's illicit correspondence with his girlfriend Irmgard Wernicker was a vital link with the outside world; and he used it to discover the identities of the leading Nazis in the area and where they lived, believing that if the town descended into chaos and the prisoners found themselves in charge, this would be useful information. Also, with Irmgard's help and the assistance of a tame goon, a young boy named Heinz, the prisoners established an early warning system with the town. 'A Colditz man took up station everyday at 9 a.m., noon and 4 p.m. at a lamppost which was visible from the castle,' recalls Jack Pringle, who, together with David Stirling, devised the code. 'His movements could be interpreted by us and there were four alternative messages he could give. The first was "Nothing to report", the second "You are to be moved"; the third "German troops are pulling out" and the fourth "Break out at all costs". Leaning on the lamppost meant one thing, crossing the road another, lighting a cigarette another; and entering the shop behind him gave the danger signal to break out. Until 14 April the signal every day was "Nothing to report". And then on that day we got the signal "You are to be moved".'

The message was immediately relayed to Lieutenant-Colonel Willie Tod. He was well aware of the proximity of the Americans – now less than fifteen miles away – and the warning gave him a few hours to decide his strategy. Later that day Prawitt sent for him; the Kommandant had just received the orders 'ZR' – *Zerstörüng-Räumung*, 'Destroy-Evacuate'; the castle must be abandoned, all the papers burned and the food distributed, and the prisoners must immediately prepare to move off 'to the east' escorted by the garrison. Willie Tod expected as much, and he refused. What was more, if Prawitt tried to move the officers towards an uncertain future at gunpoint the inevitable casualties would not be Tod's responsibility. The two men understood each other well enough by now, and this was no bluff: General Daine, the Senior French Officer, and Colonel Duke, representing the Americans, were in complete agreement; the prisoners would not move. Prawitt considered his options; his garrison was two hundred strong, but the majority were over fifty-five years old. They were armed with a few machineguns and a collection of old French and German rifles. To force a thousand mutinous prisoners outside the castle and control them on the road would prove extremely difficult. There would be casualties. He rang the Generalkommando at Glauchau, and in an increasingly heated exchange he discovered that they did not want blood on their hands either: after all, any deaths might indict them as war criminals once the war was over. A few hours later Tod was summoned once more, and again he remained obstinate; he would not take responsibility for the casualties. As the day wore on the sounds of gunfire drew ever closer, and a few American shells dropped on the town. By mid-afternoon Prawitt knew it was too late to evacuate the prisoners; and if no one would shoulder the blame he had no option but to capitulate. Willie Tod demanded Prawitt hand over the keys of the castle, and then prepare a document of surrender, which was signed by all parties. Once this had taken place all the officers in the solitary cells were released, and the prisoners were given control of the armoury; but Willie Tod was anxious that the camp should retain an air of normality until the Americans arrived, disguising the surrender from the SS units below the castle. If they discovered that the Wehrmacht garrison had already capitulated, the consequences for all might be catastrophic. The sentries were ordered to remain at their posts, but their rifles were empty.

The Americans advancing on Colditz from the south-west were the 3rd Battalion of the 273rd Infantry in the 60th Infantry Division. They had left Southampton only a month before, and in three brief weeks these young soldiers, most of whom were barely out of their teens, had become hardened professionals. On arrival in France they were sent straight to the Ardennes, from where they had fought their way south, crossing the Rhine at Remagen and pushing down through Germany, taking thousands of prisoners and liberating the death camp of Stalag Tekla that lay in their path. On arrival on the outskirts of Leipzig they were immediately dispatched to Colditz, twenty-four miles to the southeast; someone, higher up the chain of command, knew there were important prisoners in the town, and special reference was made to an American colonel under a death sentence: W.H. Schaefer. This infantry unit, supported by half a dozen tanks and heavy machineguns commanded by Colonel Leo Shaughnessy, was now the eastern extremity of the US 1st Army; the Russians were less than sixty miles away. South of Leipzig they liberated Naumburg slave camp, and from there they followed the course of the Mulde across the plains of central Saxony, encountering only pockets of resistance. Beyond the small village of Hohnbach they reached a bend in the river, and from here they caught their first sight of Colditz Castle, standing on a spur of rock high above the town. It was a natural redoubt, and the obvious target for the advancing American guns.

'We were very afraid of friendly fire from our American allies,' recalls Jock Hamilton-Baillie. 'And we were right to be afraid, because at Eichstätt camp the Germans had marched the prisoners away just ahead of the American advance. The tail of the column was still inside the camp gates when a US fighter flew over and waggled its wings. The POWs thought it was an acknowledgment – but instead another fighter joined the first and they returned to machinegun the column. Several of my friends were killed and others quite badly injured, the day before they were going to be released. After five years in captivity this was a bit hard; so to protect ourselves we thought we would fly flags. Up in the theatre we all started making them, Polish, French and British. We made the Union Jack for a very utilitarian purpose and didn't expect to feel emotional about it, but we did. We became very emotional. It was just to see a Union Jack again after so many years of a Swastika flying over our heads.'

With their flags ready, the prisoners could only wait. Sunday morning, 15 April, broke fine and warm. Throughout the night sporadic shells had landed in the town and now an air of expectation filled the castle. 'I was standing at the window looking out across the town to the west,' remembers Hugo Ironside, who was preparing a meagre lunch for his mess. 'It was a view I had looked at for the last eighteen months so I knew every bush. I suddenly noticed to the left of a line of trees on the horizon a blob or two that hadn't been there before. So I yelled for Checko to come and have a look with his lecherscope. He appeared, panting, and he looked and said, "Aha – it's a line of tanks." He let out a great whoop of joy. I felt exaltation, relief. We might finally be free.'

There was an ominous lull, and the upper floors of the Kellerhaus filled with eager spectators. They did not have to wait long. Shortly after midday shells began landing in the town, and then several rounds came crashing into the walls of the castle. Douglas Bader, who in the excitement of the moment had forgotten to strap his legs on, was knocked down by the blast. The prisoners hurriedly strung their flags out of the windows, and Willie Tod considered it wise to evacuate to the cellars. No more shells arrived, and during the afternoon the more foolhardy prisoners climbed back up to the windows to watch the fighting. 'We had such a good view it seemed that the Germans and the Americans had laid it on for our benefit,' recalls Jack Best. 'During the battle I used a lecherscope to focus in on a machine-gunner about two miles away. This particular instrument was so powerful that when he pressed the trigger I could see his body vibrating and I automatically ducked.'

While the American tanks, heavy machineguns and mortars took up positions on the outskirts of Colditz, two of the three rifle platoons went down into the town. Entering from the west, they ran down a hillside towards the allotments beside the river, and halfway down the slope two concealed machineguns suddenly opened up, killing several soldiers and wounding many more. Only the prescience of the platoon sergeant, Gallagher, saved the second wave from a similar fate. Shaken, the GIs tried again, and this time, using suppressing fire, twenty-two riflemen found a way around the machineguns and into the allotments. They could see Hitler Youth and SS soldiers scurrying away before them. 'Through my telescope I watched the Americans moving very gingerly into the town, checking every house for hidden arms or soldiers,' recalls Ota Cerney, a Czech pilot. 'They were like cats in their rubber-heeled boots, silent and cautious with their guns ready. It was very professional and amazing to watch.'

In fact, the riflemen had not advanced very far before they found themselves in trouble. The SS headquarters was heavily defended, and in every street snipers at the windows kept them pinned down. Hiding behind lampposts and parked cars, the GIs rapidly realised they were outnumbered; at one point six GIs were charged by fifty screaming German soldiers down a narrow street. Bob Pierce, a battle-hardened nineteen-year-old from Michigan, recalls the scene. 'Sam Bourne fired our last bazooka round at them at point-blank range. My heart stopped — because it fell straight out the end and hit the cobblestones. I braced myself for the explosion, it didn't go off, it bounced up about four feet, it went some more and it hit again, skipping like a stone on the water, till that sucker went right into the group of Germans and it exploded. I didn't even look what had happened to them, but they didn't try it again.' Hiding in the shadow of a low wall, the GIs came under intense fire from all directions, and watched helplessly as the SS and Hitler Youth worked round them to cut off their exit. Suddenly a *Panzerfaust* exploded into the building ahead of them, throwing up 'gorgeous splinters of red and orange and yellow', remembers Pierce 'Old McCutcheon, my gosh, he's got blood all over his face, all over the front of his jacket. I said, "Mac, you're hit, you're hit" . . . he said, "Where, where, where," and he's looking down to see . . . I said, "No, no, your face." "My face?" He had a piece of shrapnel right alongside the bridge of his nose and I squeezed it and I pulled it out, then he had another piece of shrapnel from that *Panzerfaust* stuck under the skin of his Adam's apple and I couldn't get it out. I said, "Mac, you're going to have to go to the medic or get someone to take it out because I can't get it." He says, "Oh," – he'd never felt it, he got hit twice in the face and never felt it in the excitement of battle.'

The situation was desperate; Platoon Sergeant Gallagher attempted to contact his commander, but the field radio was smashed, and the NCOs made a collective decision to retreat before they were all killed or captured. At that moment twenty-three-year-old Lieutenant Ryan arrived – the only officer present. 'He was shaking, he said we're not leaving here, we're not going to surrender,' recalls Bob Pierce. 'We're going to win this, whatever. So he ran up the stairs and stuck his head out of a second-storey window. He's screaming, "Assemble in the houses, assemble in the houses, we're not leaving!" He no more than said it when he fell back from the window, then he comes staggering down the stairs an absolute mess, his left eye was shot out and he was hit in the shoulder, he was just covered in blood. Then Sergeant Coulter said, "You're the reason we are here, if we die here it's your fault," and he pulled out his forty-five and held it to Ryan's head. He pulled back the hammer and said, "I'm going to kill you." Ryan dropped to his knees slobbering and blubbering and prayed, "Don't kill me, please don't kill me." Ryan was a really pitiful sight. Platoon Sergeant Gallagher said in a really low voice, "Don't you kill him. Don't you kill him. You pick him up and you take him back." He was so pitiful Coulter put his pistol away.' Together the platoon fought their way out of the town carrying Ryan to safety. Sergeant Gallagher brought up the rear, and he was one of several who never returned. Fully expecting a German counter-attack, the soldiers dug in and spent a nervous night shooting at shadows, one of whom turned out to be their own sentry. Tank shells and tracer fire lit up the night sky as the SS company slowly withdrew north-east of the castle. Before they left they liquidated a small concentration camp inside the Cina pottery works containing four hundred Hungarian Jews, whose existence, Eggers claims, no German member of staff ever knew about. Just before dawn the firing stopped. 'I woke up the next morning, there was absolute silence,' recalls David Wheeler. 'I seemed to be the only person alive at the time, and I couldn't restrain my inquisitiveness. I walked up the steps to one of the turrets above the courtyard, and looking down I saw that the town was covered with white flags. The Americans had won.'

It was 16 April, a cold spring morning. By 10 a.m. the GIs were advancing warily up the hill towards the castle. They passed the looted bloody bodies of their comrades who had fallen, and a fifteen-year-old Hitler Youth, his face 'palish green', lying sprawled on the bridge. 'The white sheets were hanging out the windows, everybody was happy,' recalls Bob Pierce. 'The Hitler Youth had taken their helmets and their rifles and thrown them away. It was all "Hooray! Welcome! Welcome, GI, welcome, Americans!" I said, "Yeah, sure, you son of a gun, where was you yesterday!"'

It was not long before the first American patrol arrived at the castle gates. Colonel Shaughnessy, the US battalion commander, had seen the POW flags flying, but he did not know that the garrison had already surrendered. Captain David Walker, together with the American Florimund Duke, went down to the guardhouse to await their arrival. Nervously the first GI began to cross the bridge over the dry moat and was relieved to hear 'Good morning!' bellowing out of the guardroom. Duke and Walker revealed themselves, and there were handshakes all round. 'Say, you a goddam officer?' Walker was asked. 'Once upon a time I used to once was be,' he replied.

The American patrol continued on into the castle. In the first courtyard, the Kommandantur, they found the German garrison standing on parade, their weapons lying at their feet. Eggers came forward and presented a complete list of prisoners to the liberators. While the surrender was being dealt with, young Private Murphy, the advance point of the patrol, wandered deeper into the castle. He passed through the dark archway that led out of the German courtyard and up the alley to the guardhouse. So many escapers had walked down this path – Airey Neave and Tony Luteyn disguised as German guards, Mike Sinclair on his last walk down to the park; but Murphy knew nothing of that. It was a bright morning, the spring sunlight raking across the cobbles. Up ahead of him stood a sentry still manning the massive wooden door to the inner courtyard. On seeing Murphy approach, he too laid down his weapon. The young GI then ordered him to open the gate, and looking in he saw a grey cobbled courtyard surrounded on all sides by high buildings. A collection of thin, pale men were milling about dressed in various shades of khaki.

'Quite suddenly the door opened and in came the first American GI most of us had ever seen,' recalls Gris Davies-Scourfield. 'He was filthy from battle, steel-helmeted and armed to the teeth. And slowly we turned around and saw him. And we all cheered – and suddenly he stopped. He was frightened. He'd been through battle and he was under stress, and suddenly there were all these mad people waving their arms and shouting at him. Quickly he took down his rifle which had been on his shoulder and menaced us. "Stay back, stay back," he said. "We're friends, friends," we replied. And after a short while he saw that we were.' It was a sweet moment. Murphy was followed in by Private Robert Miller. 'The guys were screaming, it was like thunder, I mean it hurt your ears.' He too was mobbed and kissed and hugged. The GIs were taken up to the prisoners' quarters and given breakfast, the officers confidently ripping into their carefully hoarded stock of Red Cross parcels. Then the prisoners felt their first taste of freedom; foraging parties were assembled to go down into the town to find food, and bicycles, cars and motorbikes were commandeered for the purpose. Though the castle had been liberated, the fighting was not far away, and Tod instructed his officers not to breach the American cordon around the town. To enforce the measure, he took the rather drastic step of placing British sentries on the yard gate; only those with permission were allowed to pass through. This brought a flood of indignation from the French, who regarded it as a restriction upon their natural exuberance, but the following day Tod's caution was vindicated; four Frenchman unwisely ventured beyond the American perimeter, and they were swiftly recaptured by the SS and taken back behind the German lines. The townsfolk were bemused by this invasion of polite young Englishmen. 'I called at the door of a respectable German house,' recalls Charles Elwell. 'The owner came to the door and was obviously rather nervous at seeing two ill-kempt characters fresh out of the castle. To get rid of us he gave us a couple of goose's eggs and a bottle of crème de menthe. When I offered to pay he looked rather puzzled, and shut the door. So that was the first good breakfast of our captivity.'

Others came back with sides of bacon, slabs of butter and cheese, and soon an impromptu banquet began. A French officer returned, claiming to have just made love to a Polish maid working in the Colditz hotel. The atmosphere was jovial and exuberant. As US Private Bob Pierce stood sunning himself against the castle gate, he heard shouting down below. 'Suddenly this tall woman in khaki uniform came marching up towards me,' he recalls. 'She was just furious. There must have been about five cameramen with her and the officers of the regiment and Colonel Shaughnessy, and she was absolutely screaming at them. She was supposed to be there at the initial surrender and capture of Colditz and she was to have the exclusive story. The colonel was red-faced and embarrassed. And she was upset about the Hitler Youth kid lying dead on the road: boy, was she going to have an investigation into that – shooting children was murder!' Lee Carson, war correspondent and 'Rhine maiden', marched straight into the castle, whereupon Douglas Bader, famous tin-legged fighter ace, immediately presented himself for an interview. Relieved to find that she did have a story after all, she left the camp with Bader an hour later. He flew home the next day, three days ahead of his fellow prisoners; it was 'typical Bader'.

Later in the morning more GIs arrived in the castle, and the prisoners listened eagerly to their young liberators' story. 'They invited me to have tea with them,' recalls Justin Bloom. 'And I was embarrassed because my field uniform was very dirty, and I was absolutely filthy. I hadn't had any bath, I don't think I'd shaved – or even washed my face for two weeks.' These soldiers had taken tens of thousands of soldiers prisoner in their dash across Germany and they had been surprised at the ferocity of the Colditz resistance. 'I was certainly dumbfounded to see young boys, maybe thirteen or fourteen years old, trying to be soldiers,' recalls Bloom. 'I was only twenty-one myself, but these kids had obviously been instructed by the SS to fight to the death.'

Soon other stories emerged. As a tank turned into a street two boys threw a *Panzerfaust* at it, disabling both tracks. The commander was so incensed that he jumped out, chased the boys around the tank and knifed them. In another incident an American trooper saw a woman gesticulating wildly on a road; he approached her cautiously to find a twelve-year-old boy lying in the ditch aiming a Mauser at him. The boy was disarmed. Between fifteen and twenty GIs had been killed in the battle, 'far more than was necessary', and many more wounded. The Americans were particularly angry at the death of their platoon sergeant, Gallagher, and two others, respected soldiers who had fought with them all the way from Belgium. On reaching the castle the Americans were not in a conciliatory mood. The officers looked on, fascinated, as the GIs herded and kicked the garrison into columns; even Prawitt had his epaulets torn off. For years they had been unable even to touch a German soldier for fear of being court-martialled, and now they felt a curious mixture of relief and compassion as they watched their captors being marched away. One old guard helpfully turned up with his possessions strapped on to his bicycle, which was swiftly thrown into the moat; he was pushed off with the rest, to become a prisoner of war. 'My first taste of freedom wasn't at all what I expected,' recalls Micky Burn, the radio scribe. 'I was shocked by how rude the Americans were to the Germans. It was a ridiculous feeling. I suddenly realised how isolated we had been. Inside Colditz the Germans had not shouted at us very much, but these young American soldiers had seen things in Germany we never had. They had just liberated several concentration camps. We didn't really know what was going on at all.'

The GIs then offered to 'take care of anyone who had been bad to them'. No names were volunteered; in fact the British went out of their way to protect their favourite German officer, Hans Püpcke. Unlike the oily and ingratiating Reinhold Eggers, Püpcke was a straight man, and respected for it. He had been fair with them, and they wanted to return the compliment, and if possible save him from the Russians.

The lack of malice borne by the prisoners towards their guards was not shared by the former prisoner Micky Wynn. Wynn, who had lost an eye at St Nazaire, successfully 'worked his ticket' out of Colditz and was repatriated on medical grounds at the end of 1944. On his arrival back in England he immediately volunteered his services once again, only to be told it would not be safe for him to return to Germany, because if captured he was liable to be shot as an escaper. Undeterred, Wynn set off for Marlag, his old naval camp; he wanted to be the first man to liberate his friends there, and he had an old score to settle. 'Every prisoner's dream is to find the guards who hadn't been very kind to them,' he recalls. 'I was looking for the chief security officer Gussveld, a man who had been a nuisance to us and made our lives very difficult, shall we say. He'd managed to get back into the cage where all the German soldiers had been put. He'd got out of his officer's uniform because he knew people would be looking for him, and after a while we picked him out, dressed as a private soldier. We gave him a taste of his own medicine, made sure that he wouldn't be a nuisance any more. I didn't know what happened to him after that. That was that, as far as I was concerned.'

The true fate of Sonderführer Gussveld, the man who recruited Walter Purdy the spy, has never been recorded. Though no officer at Colditz took the opportunity for revenge, the young Commando Corran Purdon recognised that this was his last opportunity to lay to rest the ignominy of his POW status. Along with his mate Dick Morgan, he went to Colonel Tod and asked him if they could fight with the Americans. Tod gave them his blessing. '"Can we join you?" And they said, "Sure, join this section here." The guy who was commanding us was a Mexican. They were all hard, aggressive and, as I remember, unshaven. There was quite a lot of resistance on the outskirts of the town, particularly from the Hitler Youth. One unfortunate German officer refused to surrender, he just started shooting with this little pop pistol. He was dealt with. Then we went into the small concentration camp in the ceramics factory that had just been liberated. There were only four people left alive, the SS had killed the rest, and I remember these four emaciated faces staring at us, their eyes burning. This filled me with rage. But I felt better having joined the Americans, if only for a couple of days. I didn't want to be returned home like a Red Cross parcel.'

The Americans commandeered the sick bay in the castle,

converting it into a field hospital for their wounded, and it was not long before the four survivors of the concentration camp were brought up. Soon the grim fate of their comrades was revealed; as the GIs advanced north-east of Colditz they came across a roadside ditch full of bodies. Four hundred men had been executed in batches of five, and it was here, miraculously, that the four survivors had hidden under the piles of dead until nightfall, then crawled away. Kenneth Lockwood was one of the first men to see them. 'The American doctor, a man named Rose, was looking after them, and he told me they were Hungarian Jews, all intelligentsia,' he recalls. 'He gave me a mug of water and said, "Get them to sip this." They were literally skin and bones and nothing else. Their skin was a parchment yellow covered in bruises. Rose said, "It is important that they only sip very slowly, they mustn't swallow it." We both went round giving them the water, and after a time we ran out. Rose had a couple of German soldiers in there who hadn't left the castle, and he told one of them to go and fetch some more water. The German guard refused; he wasn't going to fetch any water for any Jews. And I thought, this is going to be tricky. Rose ordered the guard for the second time to get the water – and he refused again. So Dr Rose asked the man to come outside into the road. They went out and Rose produced his revolver and shot him – there beside the Kommandantur. The other German soldier went immediately to fetch the water. I shall never forget the state these Jews were in, it was appalling.'

Meanwhile, another, happier sight was emerging out of the attics. On the morning of liberation, Jack Best and Bill Goldfinch knocked a hole in the ceiling of the glider workshop and brought the three separate parts down into the British quarters. The wings, body and controls had never been assembled until now, and with the exception of one bolt, each part fitted together perfectly, and the glider was put on display. Even by Colditz's high standards of ingenuity and invention, the Colditz Cock was an impressive sight. 'They said, "We'd like to show you something," so fine, Murphy and I went with them,' remembers Robert Miller, the second GI into the castle. 'We went upstairs and, my God, it was incredible. I was thinking, How could they do that, where did they get it from?' The sleek aircraft was nineteen feet long with a thirty-three-foot wingspan, resplendent in its tight blue-and-white chequered fuselage. The controls wiggled the rudders, and it looked every inch a glider, more than capable of drifting down from the castle roof into the fields below. During those few brief days after liberation someone, possibly an American GI, took its photograph, and this has become the only visual record of the original Colditz Cock.

Two days after Private Murphy walked into the prisoners' courtyard, the British inmates of Colditz were on their way home. Each man stuffed his 'little and all' into a kit-bag; those that still had hides intact retrieved what escape equipment they could. Large objects, including the glider and Douglas Bader's spare legs, had to be left behind. Soon the ramshackle column of 250 officers and soldiers snaked out of the courtyard for the last time, underneath the coat of arms of Frederick the Strong and out across the bridge to the gatehouse. They passed the sentry box – now empty – and cheered when they saw the smiling black American drivers and their six open lorries. Few had any desire to look back. They were to be transferred forty-five miles to the west, as the immediate area around Colditz town was still considered a forward position. Bands of SS and Hitler Youth were at large in these forests, so several of the officers were given rifles, and Hauptmann Püpcke was placed in one of the forward trucks to navigate. The irony was not lost on him. 'You are my guards now,' he said wryly. '*Nein, nein,*' replied Pete Tunstall, the arch goon-baiter, and patted him on the back. 'I didn't want him to become what I had been for the last five years.' The sight of Flight Lieutenant Pete Tunstall with a rifle was too much for Willie Tod. 'Ah, Tunstall. Playing at soldiers now?' Evidently some events at Colditz would never be forgotten.

The convoy drove hard for Koelleda airfield near Erfurt, a heavily bombed former Luftwaffe base, and as the trucks swung through the gates a curious sight greeted them, as Mike Edwards remembers. 'I looked out of the side of the truck as we drove towards the barrack huts, and I noticed that everyone was wearing top hats. Troops were playing baseball on the grass wearing top hats, the sentry by the gate was wearing a top hat. Püpcke turned to me and asked, "What is going on?" I said, "I think you will find they have just liberated a top hat factory." And that is exactly what had happened. Poor old Püpcke could not believe it, that the German Army had been beaten by this rabble.'

That night they slept in American billets, enjoyed excellent American K rations, and experienced the intense, almost unreal feeling that they were now free. Early the following morning they arrived at the runway, but the Dakotas were not expected till later that afternoon. They wandered about, gazing hopefully up at the sky and at the curious debris of Luftwaffe paraphernalia littered all around them. It was strange to be in so much space. Colditz Castle had been a small world full of certainties – the grey walls, the endless *Appells*, the clatter of wooden clogs on cobblestones; now they were about to re-enter another half-forgotten place, which many had last seen in the spring of 1940. Some officers were convinced that their years in captivity had effectively made them redundant; after all, they had missed out on so much. Before leaving the castle, David Stirling had been around the yard recruiting for a new SAS unit he was hoping to form to fight behind enemy lines in Japan, and many had signed up to go with him, seeing little other use for their talents. As it turned out, the atomic bomb would be unleashed before they were. But first there was a home-coming; meeting families, girlfriends and wives, seeing children they had never known. So much would have changed. How different had they become?

The Dakotas touched down at Westacott near Aylesbury later that evening, Wednesday, 18 April 1945. A parade of pretty WVS girls was there to meet them, exotic creatures who spoke with 'strange squeaky voices'; their faces turned green and their lipstick black under the yellow hangar lights. The officers were showered with cigarettes and disinfectant, before settling down to an English tea and the newspapers, all carrying stories of Douglas Bader's triumphant return. The night was spent in a holding camp near Amersham, but for several of them this was one camp too many. Shinning down drainpipes, jumping out of windows, they escaped to the train station, and began their long journeys home.

In Germany, the war carried on. Püpcke, Eggers and Prawitt were held as hostages by the Americans for a further three weeks until it was proved that the Prominente were all safely delivered into Swiss hands. In June 1945 they were released and returned to eastern Germany. The Russian Army had reached Colditz in May, and following the Yalta agreement the town was ceded to them. Now in the Russian zone of East Germany, Colditz Castle was much less accessible than it had been. After several weeks of freedom Jack Best and

Bill Goldfinch's minds turned to a certain object they had left behind. 'As soon as we came back we "kriegies" only had three thoughts in our mind,' remembers Best. 'One was wine, the next was women, and then there was song. We didn't want to know anything except getting back to a normal life and enjoying it, and trying not to get run over by a bus. But after a time we asked if we could borrow a lorry and drive over to get the glider. The answer came that there were far more important things to get out of the Russian zone than that. So that was it. We never heard what happened to it.'

Two stories circulate in Colditz town regarding the fate of the glider – both with a similar ending. During the bitter winter of 1946, locals remember seeing parts of its distinctive blue-and-white fuselage scattered in the woods below the castle; the Russian soldiers stationed there had chopped it up for firewood. Others believe the glider's destruction was more considered; as schoolchildren they remember coming up to the castle to look at it and the museum of escape equipment in the old Kommandantur, but the glider's growing fame provoked the wrath of the East German authorities, and it was disposed of. In either case, all that remains of the original glider are Bill Goldfinch's plans, which he carried out of the castle under his arm on 18 April 1945, and a single photograph.

From 1946 to 1950 Colditz Castle reverted to its use as a punishment camp, employed by the Russians to hold 'undesirables', local bourgeoisie and non-communists. According to Colditzers thousands starved to death inside its grey courtyards, creating a sinister local reputation which the castle retains to this day. Since then various parts of the castle have been used as a mental institution, and the interior layout of both courtyards has changed. Over the years these alterations have revealed many unexpected treasures: undiscovered tunnel schemes, untouched hides, and the glider workshop.

In 1965 a group of French veterans led by Frédo Guigues returned to the Kellerhaus attic to unearth the radio hide; it had not been opened for twenty years, but inside they found Jim Rogers' pencils and notes still on the table, and the radio intact. Guigues removed his radio and resealed it, and once again the hide merged into the fabric of the building until it was rediscovered by Dick Howe ten years later, but even he never revealed its exact location; the Germans finally exposed it in 1992, during repairs to the roof. As recently as 1998 a kit-bag containing a map of France and a half-tailored German uniform, complete with a set of MI9 dyes, was found buried deep beneath the floorboards of the Kellerhaus: Colditz Castle has yet to give up all its secrets.

Since the end of the Cold War many of the British contingent have returned to Colditz, retracing escape routes, opening doors with their coveted skeleton keys, and collecting tools they left behind. And in the years since the war the British officers have kept in contact with their guards – in some cases brought them back into the fold. Hans Püpcke – the officers' favourite – was imprisoned in Halle by the Russians from 1946 to 1948. His family were then smuggled to Hanover, and with the intervention of the Foreign Office he too was released and moved to West Germany, where he managed a laundry business until his death in 1971. Reinhold Eggers returned to the life of a schoolmaster, but in September 1946 he was arrested and sentenced under Russian law to ten years' hard labour on the charge of supporting a fascist regime. He was released in 1956, and then with some ceremony he was flown over to England by the inveterate goon-baiter Douglas Bader, who surprised both his friends and Eggers by becoming his former gaoler's greatest champion. Eggers even arrived as a special guest for Pat Reid's *This Is Your Life* in 1974.

The last German to benefit from British magnanimity was the extraordinary Obergruppenführer Gottlob Berger. Berger came before a US military tribunal on 14 April 1949 and was found guilty of all four counts against him. He had committed war crimes and atrocities against civilian populations, as well as murdered and ill-treated belligerents and POWs. He was sentenced to twenty-five years' imprisonment, but after only two years this was commuted to ten. It appears that his kindness towards the Prominente had not been forgotten, proving that in the end the hostages had served their purpose, after all.

Appendix 1: List of Escape Attempts

NAME	NATIONALITY	DATE	METHOD OF ESCAPE	RESULT
Lts B. Cazaumayou, J.Paillie	French	18/3/41	Tunnel – NW tower – origins of French tunnel	Detected
Flt Lts W. Gassowski, W. Gorecki	Polish	2nd half March '41	Bar-cutting in canteen	Detected
Lts A. Boucheron, J. Charvet	French	End March '41	Out of canteen window	Detected
Lts J. Just R. Bednarski	Polish	5/4/41	Konigswartha Hospital. Escape from train	Recaptured Krakow, Poland
Lt A. Le Ray	French	11/4/41	Park walk. Hidden inside Terrace House	HOME RUN 1
Lts K. Dokurno, P. Zielinski, S. Bartoszewicz	Polish	25/4/41	Ceiling above canteen	Detected
Lt P. Allan	British	8/5/41	Escape inside palliasse from POW yard	Recaptured Vienna
Lts M. Chmiel, M. Surmanowicz	Polish	9/5/41	Out of a room into German quarters	Detected

NAME	NATIONALITY	DATE	METHOD OF ESCAPE	RESULT
Lt J. Hyde-Thomson	British	8/5/41	In palliasse in POW yard	Detected
Capt P. Reid, Flt Lt H. Wardle and others	British	early May '41	Locked room near 'Seam' tunnel started Jan. '41	Detected
Lts M. Chmiel, M. Surmanowicz	Polish	11/12 May '41	Out of solitary cells, along Kellerhaus ledge to guardhouse roof. Inside attic down guardhouse wall	Detected
Lts C. Moura, R. Boutellier	French	17/5/41	Over roof of Kitchen House	Detected
Two unidentified officers, Polish and French	Polish/French	Early May '41	Park walk – shelter	Detected
Lt J. Just	Polish	13/5/41	Solitary confinement cell – down west face of castle	Recaptured in Rhine nr Basle
Lt Col G. German, Capts P. Reid, K. Lockwood, H. Elliott, R. Barry, R. Howe, J. Lados, Flt Lts N. Forbes, H. Wardle, Lts P. Storie Pugh, G. Wardle, Z. Mikusinski (Capt C. Lewthwaite to close up tunnel)	British/ Polish	Started 29/1/41 29/30 May '41	Canteen tunnel	Detected
Lt J. Just	Polish	20/5/41	Escape from Villingen Hospital	Recaptured Wurtemburg
Lt R. Collin	French	31/5/41	Hides in rafters of pavilion in park	HOME RUN 2
Lt P. Mairesse Lebrun	French	9/6/41	Park – rafters of pavilion	Recaptured Grossbothen
Lt P. Odry	French	18/6/41	Park – rafters of pavilion	Recaptured Gross Sermuth
Lt E. Boulé	French	25/6/41	Park walk – disguised as woman	Detected
Lt P. Mairesse Lebrun	French	2/7/41	Park – vaulted over wire	HOME RUN 3
Two unidentified Polish officers	Polish	2/7/41	Hole in chapel	Detected
Two unidentified officers	French	Mid-July '41	Two-metre tunnel in French quarters	Detected

NAME	NATIONALITY	DATE	METHOD OF ESCAPE	RESULT
Lt J. Stepniak	Polish	16/7/41	Escape from hospital	Recaptured Krakow
Cadets J. Hageman, F. Geerligs	Dutch	Late July '41	Disguised as German workmen	Detected
Lt Tatistcheff	French/ Russian	18/7/41	Through wire from Schützenhaus camp	HOME RUN 4
Capts H. Elliott, J. Lados	British/ Polish	20/7/41	Park walk – Terrace House	Detected
Capt J. Lados	Polish	23/7/41 or 2/8/41 (Eggers)	From solitary cells down west side of castle	Recaptured on Swiss border
Lts A. Thibaud, R. Perrin	French	28/7/41	Through air shaft into Kommandantur yard, then as civilian workers through gate	Recaptured Leisnig
Lts Allan, Flinn, T. Elliott, Cheetham, Middleton, Hyde-Thomson, Barton, Arcq, Verkest, Cadet Officer Karpf	British/ Polish/ Belgian	31/7/41	Hole in toilet from British Long Room into Kommandantur	Detected
Flt Lt D. Thom, Lt J. Boustead	British	4/8/41	Park walk, disguised as two Hitler Youth	Detected
Capt A. Dufour, Lt J. Smit	Dutch	13/8/41	Park – hidden inside well	Recaptured Singen
Capt W. Lawton	British	14/8/41	Park walk for orderlies	Recaptured Zschirla?
Lt G. Dames	Dutch	15/8/41	Through hole in park wire	Detected
Lt F. Larive, F. Steinmetz	Dutch	15/8/41	Park – hidden inside well	HOME RUNS 5 & 6
Lt Kroner	Polish	20/8/41	From window in Konigswartha Hospital	HOME RUN 7
Lt P. Durant	French	21/8/41	Park walk for orderlies	Recaptured nearby
Capt P. Reid	British	Mid-Aug. '41	Window of solitary confinement cell in town jail	Detected
Capts M. van den Heuvel, N. Hogerland	Dutch	23/8/41	Cutting bars in canteen window	Detected
Lt A. Neave	British	28/8/41	Disguised as German lance-corporal via POW gate	Detected
Lt R. Mascret	French	29/8/41	From Schneckwitz Hospital	Recaptured Mainz

NAME	NATIONALITY	DATE	METHOD OF ESCAPE	RESULT
Lt-Col G. German, Sqd Leader B. Paddon, Maj A. Anderson	British	1/9/41	Tunnel through kitchen basement	Detected
Maj C. Giebel, Lt O. Drijber	Dutch	19/9/41	Hidden in park well	HOME RUNS 8 & 9
Lt A. Boucheron	French	25/9/41 3/10/41	Zeitz Hospital. Recaptured. Then from Dusseldorf prison	HOME RUN 10
Lts Proutchenko, Jurowski, Wbcholzew	White Russians	28/9/41	Through wire from Schützenhaus (small camp in town)	Recaptured Schaffhausen – imprisoned in castle
Lt P. Storie-Pugh & Dutch officer	British/ Dutch	6/10/41	Over roofs	Detected
Lt H. Desjobert	French	7/10/41	Attempt to climb park fence	Detected
British officers	British	7/10/41	1. British toilet wash-house 2. Subaltern's dormitory	Detected
French officers	French	Mid-Oct. '41	Tunnel from quarters	Detected
Lts P. Odry, Navelet	French	14/15 Oct. '41	From window in Elsterhorst Hospital	HOME RUNS 11, 12
Lts J. Charvet, P. Levy	French	15/10/41	From window in Elsterhorst Hospital	Recaptured Aachen, Dutch border
Lt G. Diedler	French	22/10/41	From window in Elsterhorst Hospital	Recaptured nearby
Lts M. Leroy, M. Lejeune, Verlaye	Belgian/ French	8/11/41	Cut wire of park fence	Recaptured park wall
Lts G. Wardle, Wojchieckowski	British/ Polish	22/11/41	Hidden in park well	Detected (end of that escape route)
Flt Lts D. Donaldson, D. Thom	British	23/11/41	Over roof of Kellerhaus	Detected
Capts J. Rogers, C. Lewthwaite, Lts G. Wardle, A. Neave	British	23/11/41	Polish orderlies' quarters	Detected
?	British	25/11/41	Tunnel in end room of British quarters	Detected
Lt M. Girot	French	25/11/41	Through main gate dressed as orderly carrying false message	Recaptured on train to Frankfurt
G. Romilly	British	28/11/41	Escaping as orderly loading cart	Detected

NAME	NATIONALITY	DATE	METHOD OF ESCAPE	RESULT
Lt F. Kruimink, Capt. van der Krap	Dutch	12/12/41	Park, under leaf blanket	Detected (discovery of 'Moritz')
Lt J. van Lynden, Capt. E. Steenhouwer	Dutch	15/12/41	Dressed as German officers through gate to Kommandantur	Detected
Lts J. Durand-Hornus, J. Prot, G. de Frondeville	French	17/12/41	Into foggy streets on visit to town dentist	HOME RUNS 13, 14,15 (Prot killed in action 29/1/44)
Lts A. Neave, A. Luteyn	British/ Dutch	4/5 Jan. '42	Under theatre out of guardhouse as German officers	HOME RUNS 16, 17
Lts H. Donkers, J. Hyde-Thomson	Dutch/ British	6/1/42	Under theatre out of guardhouse as German officers	Recaptured Ulm station
Lt de Bykowitz	French	9/1/42	On train to Riesa	Detected
Flt Lt F. Flinn	British	14/1/42	British tunnel above canteen	Detected
Lts R. Madin, J. Paille, B. Cazaumayou (originators)	French	16/1/42	The French tunnel. Clock tower under chapel, under terrace	Detected
Cadet Officer C. Linck	Dutch	20/1/42	Inside sack in parcel office	Detected
Padre Jean-Jean, Capt. Dr Le Guet	French	20/1/42	Ran away while walking in woods 'on parole' (religious/medical personnel)	Recaptured Frankfurt & Saarbrucken
Capt. P Reid, Lt A. Orr-Ewing, W. O'Hara, Mackinsie, J. Boustead, E. Harrison?	British	21/1/42	Snow tunnel across flat roof of canteen into Kommandantur	Detected
Flt Lt N. Forbes	British	27/1/42	Prospecting under stage	Detected
Capts G. Dames, J. Hageman	Dutch	27/2/42	Dutch buttress tunnel out under terrace	Detected
Flt Lt F. Flinn, Off. Cadt. C. Linck	British/ Dutch	2/3/42	Escape on way to Arrest House	Recaptured after 1 hour
Lts H. Desjobert, A. Thibaud	French	20/3/42	Hide in cartload of rubble, spoil from French tunnel	Detected in town by woman
Multinational		18/3/42 (started July '41)	Tunnel in sick bay	Detected
Flt Lt F. Flinn	British	3/4/42	Tunnel in British quarters	Detected

NAME	NATIONALITY	DATE	METHOD OF ESCAPE	RESULT
Lt J. van Lynden	Dutch	mid-April '42	Into German quarters via 'seam'	Detected
Lt P. Manheimer	French	24/4/42	Breaks at Colditz station	Recaptured
Lts W. Wychodzew, J. Niestrzeba	Polish	26/4/42	Military hospital, Gnaschwitz	Recaptured Singen & Stuttgart
Lt J. Just, Sqd. Ldr B. Paddon	Polish/ British			Recaptured Leipzig station
Capt L. Rémy	Belgian		Breaks at train station, takes boat to Algeciras	HOME RUN 18
Unidentified Dutch officer	Dutch	Late spring '42	Park – under leaves	Detected
Lt D. Gill, Polish officer	British/ Polish	10/5/42	Through POW kitchen	Detected
Lt M. Girot (murdered by Gestapo May '44)	French	28/5/42	Park (in place of French orderly on working party)	Recaptured on train at Frankfurt
Lt I. Price	British	28/5/42	Exchange with Lt Fleury (French)	Detected
Lt M. Sinclair	British	2/6/42	From Leipzig hospital	Recaptured outside Cologne
		8/6/42	From Stalag	Recaptured
Lts W. O'Hara, E. Harrison, I. Dickinson, V. Parker, Capts W. Lawton, R. Howe	British	9/6/42	In attic above British quarters	Detected
Sqd. Ldr B. Paddon	British	11/6/42	Sent for court-martial at Thorn. Escaped from work party	HOME RUN 19 (via Danzig)
Lt R. Bouillez	French	25/5/42	From hospital (sent for court-martial Stuttgart, jumps train, found unconscious beside track, returned to Colditz, sent to hospital)	HOME RUN 20
?	Dutch	6/7/42	Dutch buttress tunnel again	Detected
Lt J. Tucki	Polish	7/7/42	In Polish orderlies' working party	Detected
Flt Lt V. Parker	British	15/7/42	Exchange with Sgt Gollan	Detected
Lt M. Keillar	British	15/7/42	Exchange with Corporal Hendren – sent to Lamsdorf	Detected

NAME	NATIONALITY	DATE	METHOD OF ESCAPE	RESULT
Unidentified Pole and Belgian	Polish/ Belgian	19/7/42	Tunnel in Saalhaus	Detected
Lts Vinkinbosch, Verleye	Belgian		Seam tunnel (scullery)	
		26/7/42		Detected
Capt M. van den Heuvel, Lt F. Kruiminck, Lt P. Storie-Pugh	Dutch British		As above (witches' walk)	
?	British	26/7/42	tunnel in senior officers' quarters	Detected
Flt Lt J. Dickinson	British	18/8/42	Exercise yard of town jail. Jumps wall, steals bicycle	Recaptured Chemnitz station
Capts P. Reid, R. Barry	British	19/8/42	Delousing shed tunnel	Detected
Lt Delarne	French	20/8/42	Park walk – disguised as painter	Detected
Lt K. Lee, Flt Lt N. Forbes	British	25/8/42	In Leipzig for court-martial – break away in street	Recaptured
Flt Lt J. Dickinson	British	28/8/42	Hides under bread delivery van	Detected
Capt. R. Barry	British	29/8/42	Through solitary cell, cutting bars	Detected
Capt. P. Reid	British	29/8/42	Through solitary cell – digging	Detected
Lt W. Zelaźniewicz	Polish	1/9/42	Park walk	Recaptured Podelwitz
Lt-Cdr W. Stephens	British	2/9/42	Escape at Colditz station (arriving from Lamsdorf)	Recaptured
Flt Lt D. Bruce	British	7–8 Sept. '42	Tea chest into Kommandantur. Down wall via bed rope	Recaptured Danzig
Flt Lt J. Dickinson	British	8/9/42	On exercise in park from solitary confinement	Detected
Lts Donkers, G. Wardle	Dutch/ British	9/9/42	Into Gephard's office, hole into adjacent storeroom on N terrace. Out of storeroom as party of	Recaptured Commichau
Capts W. Lawton, E. Beets,			German soldiers and Polish orderlies	Recaptured Dobeln
Flt Lts W. Fowler, D. van Doorninck				HOME RUNS 21,22 (Fowler killed March '44)
?	British	4/10/42	Subaltern's tunnel	Detected
Maj. R. Littledale, Lt Cdr B. Stephens, Capt. P. Reid, Flt Lt H. Wardle	British	14–15 Oct. '42	From POW kitchens, into German yard, across yard into cellar in Kommandantur, out cellar down to dry moat through park	HOME RUNS 23 24,25,26 (Littledale killed August '44)

NAME	NATIONALITY	DATE	METHOD OF ESCAPE	RESULT
?	Dutch	23/10/42	Attempt at hole under theatre	Detected
Lts P. Storie-Pugh, F. Kruimink	British/ Dutch	End Oct. '42	Over roof of Kellerhaus. Discovered by dog on ground floor	Detected
Lts M. Sinclair, C. Klein	British/ French	26/11/42	Through light well out into German yard	Sinclair recaptured Tuttlingen 30/11/42, Klein at Plauen
Capt R. Barry, Lt Aulard	British/ French	27/11/42	Through light well out into German yard	Detected in German yard
Lt M. Bissell	British	End Nov. '42	Tunnel under altar steps in chapel	Detected
Lts Z. Kepa, T. Osiecki, A. Slipko	Polish	6/12/42	Over orderlies' roof	Detected
Lt M. Sinclair	British	14/12/42	From Weinsberg, after recapture (twice)	Recaptured
Lt van der Falk Bouman	Dutch	15/12/42	Disguised as German soldier	Recaptured Immendingen
ERAs W. Hammond, D. Lister	British	15/19 Dec. '42	Claim in wrong camp as not officers. Sent to Lamsdorf other-ranks POW camp. Escape from Breslau working party	Escaped to Switzerland
Lt A. Perodeau	French	28/12/42	Impersonates camp electrician Willi Pöhnert	Detected
Lt G. Davies-Scourfield & others	British	Early Jan. '43	Pulpit tunnel under chapel	Detected
Capt. B. Mazumdar, RAMC	British	7/3/43	On hunger strike in order to be moved to Indians-only camp. Leaves Colditz 3 weeks later	Escapes twice, reaches Switzerland 1944
Flt Lt J. Dickinson	British	7/3/43	Jumps over wall of exercise area of town jail	Recaptured Chemnitz
Capt. Dufour, Flt Lt van Rood	British/ Dutch	5/4/43	In park walk confusion – dressed as two German officers (Best/Harvey presumed to have escaped before them, they go into hiding as ghosts)	Detected

NAME	NATIONALITY	DATE	METHOD OF ESCAPE	RESULT
Capt. I. Ferguson RAMC	British	Early April '43 (leaves Colditz 28/4/43)	Writes letter to friend, son of Irish Prime Minister, asking Ireland to join war. Request to be moved to another camp granted	Works as doctor at Stalag 4D, certifying insane. Convinces Germans of own 'insanity'. Repatriated Jan '45
Capt. Pemberton-How	British	8/4/43	Schützenhaus. In manhole outside after search	Detected
Lts E. Desbats, J. Caillaud	French	8/4/43	Over roof of castle	Detected
?	British	End April '43	Hole under surgery chair of dentist	Detected
Flt Lts V. Parker, N. Forbes, Lt D. Wheeler	British	1/5/43	via 'Revier' tunnel	Detected
Lts M. Sinclair, G. Davies-Scourfield	British	May '43	Cutting hole in park wire	Detected
Flt Lt D. Thom	British	11/5/43	Vaults down terraces of Kellerhaus, over fence into park	Recaptured at park wall
Flt Lt J. Best, Lt M. Harvey, others	British	Summer '43	Attempt to reach French tunnel again	Detected
Lt J. van Lynden	Dutch	7/6/43	Dutch move to Stanislau	HOME RUN 27
Lt A. Perrin	French	11/6/43	Through witches' walk	Detected
Lt M. Fahy	French	8/7/43	Escapes from hospital at Hohnstein-Ernstthal	Recaptured Kaufungen
Lt A. Darthenay	French	12/7/43	Escapes from hospital at Hohnstein-Ernsttal	HOME RUN 28 (joins Resistance, killed by Gestapo 7/4/44)
Lt C. Klein, G. Romilly	Free French/ British	13/7/43	Hidden in French & Belgian belongings at Colditz station	Detected
Lts T. Barrott, D. Hamilton, C. Sandbach	British	13/7/43	Exchanged identities with French in move to Lübeck	Detected
Lts J. Best, M. Harvey & others	British	Mid-July '43	French tunnel in chapel reopened	Detected

NAME	NATIONALITY	DATE	METHOD OF ESCAPE	RESULT
Lts P. Allan, A. Campbell & others	British	10/8/43	'Whitechapel Deep' tunnel, under floor of clothing store	Detected
Lts M. Sinclair, J. Hyde-Thomson, Capt. L.Pope	British	3/9/43	Frans Josef attempt	Detected
Lt W. Miller	British	11/9/43	Exchange with Lt Stepninc (Polish)	Detected
Lt R. Boustead	British		Exchange with Lt Jablonowski (Polish)	
Lt A. Orr-Ewing	British	16/9/43	As French orderly on exercise	Detected
?	British	Autumn '43	'Mayfair Maggies' tunnel, in room next to dentist's surgery	Detected
Lt G. Davies-Scourfield	British	30/9/43	Out of yard in rubbish cart, across German yard dressed as Gefreiter, through park (place taken by ghost)	Recaptured Hildescheim
Lt A. Orr-Ewing	British	7/10/43	As above, to wastepaper dump	Detected
Cpls Green, Fleet	British	3/11/43	Orderlies who escape from work party at Colditz railway station yard	Recaptured Cottbus station
Lt J. Rawson	British	25/11/43	Exchange with Cpl Aitken to Muhlberg	Detected
Lts M. Sinclair, J. Best	British	19/1/44	'Sixty second' rope escape, down west terraces	Recaptured at Rheine
Lt W. Millar	British	28/1/44	Breaks into German courtyard and hides under German lorry	UNKNOWN Escaped to Czecho-slovakia? (possibly murdered by SS at Mauthausen 7/44)
Capt. C. Lewthwaite	British	31/1/44	Park walk – under rubbish	Detected
Lt A. Orr-Ewing	British	3/2/44	From orderlies' walk. Swims across Mulde river	Recaptured in Colditz town
British naval officers	British	17/3/44	'Crown Deep' tunnel, Ist floor Kellerhaus	Detected (Given away by W. Purdy, spy?)

NAME	NATIONALITY	DATE	METHOD OF ESCAPE	RESULT
Flt Lt V. Parker, Lt M. Harvey	British	26/3/44	From air-raid shelter cellar in cobbled alley (eventual detection of ghosts)	Detected
Two unidentified officers	British	Mid-April '44	Through 'Hexengang' corridor	Detected
Lt J. Hamilton-Baillie	British	April '44	Into prisoners' yard sewers from shower block	Detected
Flt Lt D. Bruce	British	19/4/44	Bars cut on north side of castle and reached wire	Detected
Lts D. Moir, M. Edwards, D. Wheeler, P. Fergusson	British	29/4/44?	Cut through seam in Kommandantur, with intention of being caught and sent to town cells and escaping	Detected (abandoned escape attempt from cells after news of D-day).
Lt J. Beaumont	British	2/5/44	Park walk. Hides under blanket disguised as pile of leaves	Recaptured three kilometres from Colditz
Lt G. Wardle	British	3/5/44	Escape through orderlies' quarters	Detected
Lt J. Hamilton-Baillie, Capt F. Weldon	British	Whitsun Monday 1944	Out of POW yard into Kommandantur attics, into storerooms on south side of German yard	Detected
Maj A. Anderson & 2 other officers	British	1/6/44	Tunnel under dentist's chair	Detected
Lts L. Pumphrey, M. Riviere	British	13/6/44	Through British kitchens	Detected
'Bosun' J. Chrisp, Flt Lt D. Bruce, Maj R. Lorraine	British	16/6/44	Tunnel through sewers into German yard	Detected
Flt Lt Thom	British	14/7/44	From hospital at Schmorkau	Recaptured
Capt. H. Elliott 1 Flt Lt F. Flinn 2 Lt J. Barnett 3 Lt M. Wynn 4	British	5/5/44	Repatriation board – faking illnesses 1 Stomach ulcer 2 Madness 3 High blood pressure 4 Back injury as result of wounds	HOME RUNS 29,30,31,32 repat. 6/9/44 repat. 10/1/45
Lt M. Sinclair	British	4/9/44	In park – wearing civilian clothes	Detected
Capt C. Lewthwaite	British	18/9/44	Park walk – under heap of leaves	Detected

NAME	NATIONALITY	DATE	METHOD OF ESCAPE	RESULT
Lt M. Sinclair	British	25/9/44	Park – jumps over wire, runs into park	SHOT
Flt Lt W. Goldfinch, Lt A. Rolt, Flt Lt J. Best, Lt G. Wardle and 12 others	British	From 1/1/44 – end of war	Building glider in chapel attic. Main construction completed by Oct. '44. By end of war, glider complete – runway yet to be constructed	Never detected or used. Glider destroyed postwar

316 OFFICERS INVOLVED IN 174 ATTEMPTS, 32 SUCCESSFUL*

* HOME RUNS

In the years since the war, home runs from Colditz have become a contentious issue. Previous publications have included many escapes from outside the walls of Colditz Castle, though still under Colditz jurisdiction; i.e. accompanied by Colditz guards. Officers often engineered a transfer in order to escape, or took advantage of a situation; they were prepared with the escape paraphernalia while inside the castle, so technically they have claimed Colditz home runs. This presents a more flattering picture than is actually the case. Escaping from the high-security Sonderlager, whether inside the castle or the park, was obviously much harder that escaping from a train, hospital or another less secure camp. Only 15 officers managed true Colditz home runs (Bill Millar is also often claimed as a home run, assuming he escaped to freedom before he was murdered by the Gestapo). Another grey area is the issue of repatriation: concocting a bogus medical record often required years of dedication and secrecy, and many fellow prisoners felt it demanded such a fundamental change that those who attempted to 'work their ticket' invariably became their creations. But these men can (and some do) claim to have escaped from Colditz. The following table shows how the list of 32 officers who escaped from Colditz to freedom breaks down.

HOME RUNS	FROM CASTLE	FROM PARK	FROM HOSPITALS, DENTISTS, OTHER CAMPS, MOVES	FAKE REPATRIATION	TOTAL
British	6*		1*	4*	11*
French		3	9		12
Dutch	2	4	1		7
Polish			1		1
Belgian			1		1

* Millar is also claimed a Home run	* Hammond, Lister and Mazumdar could claim Colditz home runs as aided by Colditz escape industry – though escaped from other camps not under Colditz jurisdiction	* Ferguson could also claim an escape, though he was repatriated from another camp	*(16)

Appendix 2: List of Interviewees

Michael Alexander	Commando, Prominente
Peter Allan	Laufen Six palliasse escape
Brig. W. F. 'Andy' Anderson	Prop-maker to escape industry
Rev. John Beaumont	Eichstätt arrival. Blanket escape
Col. Ted Beets	Dutch Officer. Clothing store escape
Jack Best	Ghost, tool-maker, glider-builder
Justin Bloom	US rifleman. Took part in liberation of Colditz
Mme Victoire Boutard	Wife of Pierre Boutard. Prepared and sent in contraband
Maj.-Gen. W.M. Broomhall	Senior British Officer June–December 1943
Maj. Hugh Bruce RM	Frans Josef escaper
Michael Burn	Radio scribe, commando, *Times* journalist, communist
Lord Alan 'Black' Campbell of Alloway	Prisoners' lawyer
Capt. Tommy Catlow RN	Submariner
Col. Bernard Cazaumayou	French tunneller. After moved from Colditz escaped as orderly, joined battalion of Glaziers in Berlin; escaped again, sent to Buchenwald then to a '*Bauzug*' repair train. At liberation weighed 35 kilos
Ota Cerney	Czech pilot
Col. Jean Chaudrut	French tunneller
Lt-Cdr. John Chrisp	Rope-maker, sewer escape
Col. Dominic Corcosteguy	French tunneller

John Davies	Chapel organist. One of earliest arrivals
Brig. Grismond Davies-Scourfield	Chief stooge. Rubbish cart escape
Rudolf Denzler	Member of Swiss legation watching over Prominente
Yves Desmarchelier	French electrician, friend of Guigues
Col. Georges Diedlier	French tunneller
George Drew	Eichstätt arrival. Stamp-carver. Hooch-brewer
Maj. Mike Edwards	Eichstätt arrival. Locksmith. Hooch-brewer
Charles Elwell	Actress, stoolball player
Capt. Michael Farr	Eichstätt arrival. Champagne maker
Patrick Fergusson	Eichstätt arrival. Glider-builder
Francis Flinn	'Madman' who successfully worked ticket
J. Giertych	First Polish officer sent to Colditz for escaping, October 1939
Major B.D.S. 'Skelly' Ginn	Electrician. Glider-builder
Lt. Col. Sir Martin Gilliat	Adjutant to SBO
L.J.E. 'Bill' Goldfinch	Glider designer, builder
Capt. Julius Green	Dentist. Coded-letter-writer. Revealed Purdy, the spy.
Dawyk, Earl Haig of Bemersyde	Prominente. Artist
Brig. 'Jock' Hamilton-Baillie	Surveyor. Leading lady, burglary escape
Maj. Edgar Hargreaves	SAS, SOE agent, sent to Colditz from Buchenwald concentration camp
Lt-Cdr Roger Heap	Escape committee member
Josef Hlebowicz	Polish officer witness to Bednarski's Trail
Prof. Peter Hoffman	Guard, 1943. Witness to Frans Josef escape
Charles Hopetoun (Marquess of Linlithgow)	Eichstätt arrival. Prominente, theatre impresario
Jacques Huart	SOE agent, Professional forger
Lt. Col. David Hunter RM	Goon-baiter. Sent to Graudenz for insubordination
Brig. Hugo Ironside	Eichstätt arrival. Set-builder. Tunneller
Anthony Karpf	Jewish Polish officer. British Long Room escape
Frau Erna Kraeschmer	Worked in canteen, 1942
Francis Kreuz	Guard, 1943
W. T. 'Lulu' Lawton	Assistant Escape officer 1942-5. Clothing store escape
Gen. Alain Le Ray	Achieves first successful home run from Colditz
Pierre Mairesse Lebrun	Third successful home run. Vaults wire, then bicycles to Switzerland
Maj. Kenneth Lee	Principal forger of documents
Kenneth Lockwood	Laufen Six. Clothing store officer. Escape treasurer
Col. A. 'Tony' Luteyn	Successful home run through guardroom with Airey Neave
Didier Manheimer	French Jewish officer. Youngest Frenchman in Colditz
Jean Louis Martin	French tunneller. Escaped successfully to Luxembourg after moved from Colditz
Robert Miller	US rifleman. Second man into Colditz Castle on liberation. Saw the glider
Lt. Col. Dougie Moir	Eichstätt arrival. Tunneller
Maj. Peter Parker	Eichstätt arrival. Stooge
Robert Pierce	US rifleman. Played active role in battle for Colditz town

Michel Proutchenko	White Russian serving in French Army. Escaped five times after leaving Colditz
Sir Laurence Pumphrey	Eichstätt arrival. Tunneller
Maj.-Gen. Corran Purdon	Commando. Youngest British officer in Colditz. Stooge. Glider builder
Maj. Pat Reid	British Escape Officer. Successful home run through Kommandantur
Jim Rogers	'The Old Horse'. Radio scribe. Mining engineer
Maj. Tony Rolt	Racing driver. Glider initiator, constructor
Alec Ross	Douglas Bader's medical orderly
Cdr Francis Steinmetz	Dutch manhole escape. Successful home run
Peter Storie-Pugh	Worked in sickbay. Numerous escape attempts
Jean-Claude Tiné	Member of Free French contingent. Held by Gestapo prior to Colditz
Ivo Tonder	Czech pilot. Survivor of the 'Great Escape' from Sagan.
Josef Tucki	Polish tunneller. Coded-letter-writer
Sqn Ldr Peter Tunstall	Arch goon-baiter. MI9 communicator
Lt-Cdr D. van Doorninck	Dutch locksmith. Successful home run
John Watton	Artist
Cdr. David Wheeler RN	Submariner. Coded-letter-writer
John Wilkens	NCO supervising orderlies
J.C. Wilson	Pilot on escape committee
Michael Wittet	Eichstätt arrival
Micky Wynn (Lord Newborough)	Exploited wounds to be successfully repatriated
Lt-Col. Jimmy Yule	Pianist. Radio operator

Additional Audio Sources

Several of the above-mentioned are also recorded in the Imperial War Museum Sound Archive. Other interviews in that archive that I found helpful are listed as follows, with their reference numbers:

George Abbott	4843/5	SOE agent. Held at Fresnes jail before Colditz.
Howard Gee	4432/10	Captured in Finland. One of the two civilians in Colditz. Fluent German-speaker – interpreted German newspapers before arrival of radio.
John Hoggard	16910/4	Naval officer.
Biren Mazumdar	4945/2	Only Indian at Colditz. Removed from camp on hunger strike. Escaped to Switzerland 1944.
Jack Pringle	17585/3	SAS operator with David Stirling in N. Africa and Italy.
Jerzy Stein	16974/3	Polish officer, Survivor of Dossel bomb 9/43.
Lorne Welch	10643/3	Pilot. Flew gliders before the war; assisted Bill Goldfinch in glider design and construction.
Micky Wynn (Lord Newborough)	9721/3	

Bibliography

Camera in Colditz, Ron Baybutt, Hodder and Stoughton, 1982

Mr Woo, J. Beaumont (privately published)

The Secret Conferences of Dr Goebbels 1939–43, ed. Willi Boelcke, Weidenfeld and Nicolson, 1970

Reach for the Sky, Paul Brickhill, William Collins, 1954

Les Indomitables, General Le Brigant, Editions Berger–Levrault, 1948

In Durance Vile, J. Brown, Robert Hale, 1981

Frederick the Great, Thomas Carlyle

A Sailor's Survival, T. N. Catlow, The Book Guild Ltd, 1997

L'Evasion Direct: Le Tunnel de Colditz, B. Cazaumayou and F. Guigues, Éditions France – Empire, 1982

The Diggers of Colditz, Jack Champ and Colin Burgess, Orbis, 1985

The Tunnellers of Sandborstel, J. Chrisp, Robert Hale, 1959

Official Secret, Clayton Hutton, Max Parrish, 1960

In the Presence of my Foes, Grismond Davies-Scourfield, privately published, 1991

Offizieren Achter Prikkeldraad 1940–45, L. De Hartog, Hollandia B.V. Baarn, Holland, 1983

Padre in Colditz, ed. Margaret Duggan, Hodder and Stoughton, 1978

Colditz: the German Story, Reinhold Eggers, Robert Hale, 1961

Colditz Recaptured, Reinhold Eggers, Robert Hale, 1973

The Escaping Club, A. J. Evans, Bodley Head, 1921

MI9 Escape and Evasion 1939–1945, M.R.D. Foot and J.M. Langley, Bodley Head, 1979

Doctor at War, Ion Ferguson, Christopher Johnson, 1955

The Second World War, Martin Gilbert, Weidenfeld and Nicolson, 1989

From Colditz in Code, J.M. Green, Robert Hale, 1971

Colditz 1941–43, F. Guigues, privately published, 1971

My Father's Son, The Earl Haig, Leo Cooper, 2000

The Tongs and the Bones, Lord Harewood, Weidenfeld and Nicolson, 1981

A Prisoner's Progress, D. James, William Blackwood and Sons, 1947

The Road to Endor, E. H. Jones, Bodley Head, 1919

The Second World War, John Keegan, Hutchinson, 1989

Hitler 1936–45 Nemesis, Ian Kershaw, Allan Lane, Penguin Press, 2000

Nazi Germany at War, Martin Kitchen, Longman Group, 1995

The Man Who Came in from Colditz, E.H. Larive, Robert Hale, 1975

They Have Their Exits, A. Neave, Hodder and Stoughton, 1953

Colditz Last Stop, Jack Pringle, William Kimber, 1988

Escape to Freedom, T.C.F. Prittie and W. Earle Edwards, Hutchinson, 1953

List the Bugle, Corran Purdon, Greystone Books, 1993

Première à Colditz, A. Le Ray, Editions Arthoud, 1980

The Colditz Story, P.R. Reid, Hodder and Stoughton, 1952

Colditz the Latter Days, P.R. Reid, Hodder and Stoughton, 1952

Colditz the Full Story, P.R. Reid, Macmillan, 1984

Tunnelling into Colditz, Jim Rogers, Robert Hale, 1985

The Privileged Nightmare, Giles Romilly and Michael Alexander, Weidenfeld and Nicolson, 1954

Colditzer Schlossgeschichten, Thomas Schädlich, 1992

Lean, Wind Lean, David Walker, Collins, 1984

Detour, ed. J.E.R. Wood, Falcon Press, 1946

Other Written Sources

The First Escape of the War (article), Rupert Barry

The Strange Story of Walter Purdy, (unpublished), Joe West

The Frans Josef Attempt (unpublished), Hugh G. Bruce

A Gentleman of Colditz (unpublished), David Ray

MI9 report on Colditz, 1945, PRO WO 208/3288

MI9 debriefings of many Colditz prisoners on return to England, 1945, PRO W0208/3333 to 3340

The Lone GI Robert Muckel

Great Escapes – Exceptionally Dangerous (article about and including interview with Miki Surmanowicz) Rafal Brzeski

Diary of Reinhold Eggers (translated), owned by Sir Rupert Barry

Diary of W. Ellison Platt (unedited), owned by K. Lockwood

Diary of Gris Davies-Scourfield

Diary of Charles Elwell

Diary of Ralph Holroyd

Diary of Stafsfeldwebel Gephart

Diary of Corporal Schädlich

Diary of 6349613 Private Curtis (Commando, murdered 21/10/42)

Colditz songbook of Jimmy Yule

Notes

Prologue

p.2   'Wars are not won by evacuations,' quoted in John Keegan, *The Second World War*, p.81.

p.3   'Field guns . . . collapsible boats' as recalled by Jim Rogers and Kenneth Lockwood.

p.4   'grow vegetables, even keep rabbits'. At Spangenberg Castle this was the case, and these privileges existed – for short periods – at Colditz.

Chapter 1

p.9   'Strange thoughts passed through my mind . . . so soon' Keith Milne in *Detour*, ed. J. Wood, p.52.

p.10   '"Escape-proof" camp during the First World War . . .' This was a piece of propaganda. Between 1914 and 1918 the castle was filled with psychiatric and tuberculosis patients, 912 of whom died of malnutrition.

p.10   'Saxon man of sin', Thomas Carlyle, *Frederick the Great*, Bk 6, p.80

p.11   'It probably was . . . be chosen', R. Eggers, *Colditz: the German Story*, p. 19. Even The War Office Records in London acknowledged the fact; 22/7/43: 'The Castle is an unsuitable place for an officers' camp.'

p.18   'Only German with a sense of humour . . .' Hugo Ironside interview.

p.19   'We do not recognise . . . generosity of the Führer'. John Watton interview, 4/11/86.

p.21   'London burns . . . Docklands on fire' as remembered by Terence Prittie in *Escape to Freedom*, p.67.

p.21   'He attempted to film fights . . .' *The Secret Conferences of Dr Goebbels 1939–43*, ed. Boelcke, p.37.

p.21   'Pornographic experiences in Paris.' Ibid, p.45.

p.21   'A small but growing number of Luftwaffe airmen.' Note Churchill memo to Secretary of State for Air, 'Let me have . . . on not more than two sheets of paper an analysis of the German aviators taken prisoner since July 1st showing the numbers, ages, amounts of training etc. Any other information about them would be welcome.'

p.24   'One could almost feel . . . run'. Rupert Barry article, *The First Escape of the War*.

p.24   'The villagers . . . experience.' Ibid.

p.25   'I could light a cigarette only with the greatest difficulty.' Ibid.

p.26   'A real four-letter man . . . in turn.' Ibid.

Chapter 2

p.31   'For days . . . seemed to me outrageous', A. Neave, *They Have Their Exits*, p.77. Verified by Didier Manheimer, a Jewish French officer, interview 31/10/86.

p.32   Mers-el-Kebir figures from, M. Gilbert, *The Second World War*, p.107.

p.35   Geneva Convention states 'Fresh air must be available'. Eggers, p.40.

p.35   'The march . . . and all the same again on the way back.' Ibid, p.41.

p.39   'Germans tentatively concluded'. Ibid p.31.

p.39   'Great game of escaping . . . Nothing was too difficult'.
           Recorded conversation, Pat Reid, 10/11/1986.

p.41   'A weedy-looking daredevil.' Full description in P.R. Reid,
           The Colditz Story p.148.

p.42   'I forced the end of the home-made lever . . . breathing
           the night air,' From article by Rafal Brzeski, 'Great escapes
           – exceptionally dangerous'. Includes interview with
           Surmanowicz (translation from Polish).

p.42   'Baffled Reinhold Eggers'. Eggers never discovered how
           this was done, referring later to the escape of the
           'disappearing Poles'.

p.44   'By April 1941 there were 873,000 Poles.' From
           M. Kitchen, *Nazi Germany at War*, p.159.

p.44   'The tension . . . make trouble'. Eggers, p.36.

p.45   'Suddenly came a movement . . . *Heraus!*' Ibid, p.37.

p.47–8   Description of Peter Allan's experience at US consulate also
           included in his article for *Detour*, ed. J. Wood, p.44.

p.49   'I claim some honour . . . masterpieces to beat us'. Eggers,
           p.24.

Chapter 3

p.52   'A French cavalry officer'. Platt's original diary, Monday,
           9 June 1941.

p.58   'Only 68 would not sign'. Figures from *After the Battle*,
           No. 63, Colditz, p.19.

p.59   'As far as I am concerned . . . just for the Germans'
           benefit.' As recalled by Gris Davies-Scourfield.

p.59   'Oh, but the French and the British . . . like urchins'.
           Eggers, p.28.

p.60   '*Arbeitsdienst*'. This and the similarities between Wehrmacht
           and Dutch greatcoats recalled by Damiaem Van Doorninck
           interview, 7/5/87.

p.62   'Let them tunnel . . . happy'. Priem's words, as recorded by
           Eggers, p.50.

p.64   'Dirty business of escaping'. Gephard's diary.

p.64   'A fairly tall big-chested man . . . very rare occasions'.
           P.R. Reid, *The Colditz Story*, p.158.

p.66   'The big brute glowered . . . learned a lot'. Hans Larive,
            The Man Who Came in from Colditz, pp.76–7.

pp.69–70 Description of Gerrit Dames' decoy action in C.D. van der
            Krap, *Against the Swastika*.

p.74   Description of unmasking of 'Max', Eggers, p.59.

Chapter 4

p.76   'Handed him a bunch of flowers'. As remembered by John
            Wilkens, NCO, interview, 12/9/86.

p.77   Orders concerning Romilly as recorded by Eggers, p.57.

p.77   Nicknamed 'Emil' as recalled by Francis Kreuz, a German
            guard who used to accompany Giles Romilly on walks out
            of the castle.

p.78   'Very much of the parlour variety'. David Walker *Lean,
            Wind Lean*, p.53.

p.78   'High-ranking . . . contempt'. Goebbels and Himmler's
            loathing of the British aristocracy is well documented.
            Note Goebbels diary entry 9th December 1943, 'A serious
            epidemic of influenza has broken out in England. The
            King, too, is ill. How wonderful if the epidemic were to
            prove fatal . . . that would exactly suit us.'

p.79   'Gefreiter Neave is to be sent to the Russian front' as
            recalled by Eggers, p.48.

p.79   For Neave's own description of his capture and the scorn
            he received from the Kommandant, see *They Have Their
            Exits*, pp.85ff.

p.83   Giles Romilly article reprinted in *Colditz Recaptured*, p.101.

p.85   'Ballet Nonsense' lyrics from Jimmy Yule's book of Colditz
            songs written in captivity.

pp.85–6 'It was primarily . . . thoroughly alive'. Platt's original diary,
            Tuesday, 18 Nov. 1941.

p.87   Eggers' league table tabulated from his book, p.63.

p.87   'Camp Orchestra played Beethoven's 1st Symphony'. Tony
            Luteyn was the principal double bass player in the camp,
            and his successful escape was a significant loss to both the
            orchestra and Jimmy Yule's jazz band.

p.89   For a full description of Neave and Luteyn's near-capture and evasion to cross the border, see *They Have Their Exits*, Chapter 8.

Chapter 5

p.92 'It has taken . . . hydrogen-inflated balloon'. Platt's original diary, Wednesday, 28 January 1942.

p.98 Description of Polish choir singing in *L'Evasion Direct; Le Tunnel de Colditz*, p.187.

p.100 'We had known . . . dirty grin on the POWs' faces'. Gephard's diary, p.13.

p.100 'I can still see . . . Absolutely genuine, of course'. *L'Evasion Direct; Le Tunnel de Colditz*, p.188.

p.103 'Nearly 8 to 10 . . . like a waterfall'. Gephard's diary, p.13.

p.103 'From the staircases . . . securely locked'. Ibid, p.12.

p.104 Embarrassment and desperation at not finding the tunnel described by Eggers, p.56.

p.105 Description of discovery of the first efforts of the Société Anonyme du Tunnel in A. Le Ray, *Première à Colditz*, p.59.

p.105 'I dropped . . . There are prisoners here!' Gephard's diary, p.14.

p.107 'This is . . . unsuccessfully'. Eggers, p.73.

p.108 'Tartuffe' interview with Louis Martin, 24/10/86.

p.108 'French ingenuity . . . two countries'. Eggers, p.124.

Chapter 6

p.110 'It was shaped like an arch . . . interior ice wall'. Reid, *The Colditz Story*, p.191.

p.110 Description of Reid's fall into the frozen yard remembered by K. Lockwood.

p.112 'Comfort before country'. Phrase recalled by many Colditz POWs, especially among senior officers at other camps. Lt-Col German returned to Colditz from Spangenberg Castle, Oflag 9A, on 17 June 1943, reporting 'vigorous knitting and tatting circles' in this 'deadbeats' camp'.

p.112 'Are you intending . . . disobey it'. As recalled in interview with Lord Campbell of Alloway, QC, 12/8/86.

p.112   'Annoying the Germans was seen as a good thing'.
Interview with Jimmy Yule, 2/10/99.

p.114   '*Où sont les Allemands?*' remembered by many admiring
British POWs, cf Jim Rogers, *Tunnelling into Colditz*, p.100.

p.115   'Never show . . . be photographed with a German' recalled
by Anthony Karpf, interview, 14/7/87.

p.116   'There is no longer a Poland . . .' as recalled in interview
with Jim Rogers, 12/12/86.

p.116   Many Polish officers received bad treatment prior to
Colditz. The Poles knew of the situation in Warsaw
through coded-letter-writers – Josef Tucki was one of
them.

p.118   'Status similar to that of the Red Baron'. Gephard refers
to Bader in his diary as 'The English Richthofen', p.18.

p.118   There are many stories of Bader's baiting of the Germans.
Jack Pringle remembers another: 'If they wanted to see
him, for whatever reasons, he always asked them to come
to our room. There he would greet them propped up in
his bunk, a truncated body, with his aluminium legs on the
bed beside him. He found that this kind of reception
embarrassed the Germans and made it impossible for them
effectively to discipline him or get him to agree to
anything. He would wave one of his legs at the Germans
much as a schoolteacher would wave a pencil at a pupil,
and address them in a language that would put anyone else
in solitary for a month.' *Colditz Last Stop*, p.141.

p.118   'I know . . . fuck-all.' Recalled by Charlie Hopetoun
(Marquis of Linlithgow) interview, 22/9/86.

p.123   'Tierarzt, go to Moscow'. Episode described by Gris
Davies-Scourfield.

p.124   'Loss of freedom sufficient' recorded by Eggers, p.80.

p.124   'I knew that . . . control myself'. Ibid, p.27.

p.126   '*Dienst ist Deinst* . . .' As recalled by Peter Tunstall.

p.128   '*Befehl ist Befehl*' as recalled by Martin Gilliatt, interview,
11/9/86.

Chapter 7

p.130   'German families often complained'. Source: M.R.D. Foot.

p.131   My wife's immediate reaction . . . Go to the War Office'
from Rupert Barry, 'The Prisoners' Kitchen', article reproduced in *Colditz Recaptured*, p.40.

p.132   'HK code'. This was employed by MI9 and POWs
successfully throughout the war, and the Germans never
discovered it. Only once was it almost compromised at
Colditz, as Gris Davies-Scourfield, a coded-letter-writer,
remembers: 'An RAF officer had just been sent to Leipzig
to the doctor, and he had come back with a mass of
information about the bombing, all of which was to be
sent back to London via coded letter. "Scruffy" Orr-Ewing
and I sat at the table opposite each other with our bits of
paper out in front of us. I was halfway through my letter
when suddenly without a word of warning the door burst
open and in strolled a couple of German ferrets. Now this
was a desperate situation. There was no way we could let
the Germans get hold of this, even if it meant attacking
them. We both instinctively leant forward and covered our
pieces of paper – about the size of A4 – which had the
grid and figures and letters arranged on them. We just
carried on talking. Whereupon one of them came up to
me and said, "Come on, hand it over". And in desperation
I said, "Look, this is an entirely private matter and it has
nothing whatever to do with escaping." "It doesn't?" he
said. And by now everyone in the room, seeing the trouble
we were in, had come and stood behind the ferret. And
this German, even though he had a pistol in his belt,
realised he was in a menacing situation and we were being
tough. I said, "I give you my word of honour that this has
nothing to do with escaping, it is a private matter." Which
it didn't and it was. And he decided he'd better not press
the point, and retreated.'

p.133   'Dear Mum . . . two days out and escorted home'. Julius
Green, *From Colditz in Code*, pp.195ff.

p.137   'Don't be a bloody fool, man . . . Dunkirk'. Story related
in Ian Dear, *Escape and Evasion*, p.16.

p.138   'We are looking for a showman . . . the bill'. Clayton Hutton, *Official Secret*, p.7. Descriptions of all Clayton Hutton's inventions and how he had them made are contained in this book.

p.138   This officer . . . department'. Ibid, frontpaper.

p.139   '1,642 "naughty" parcels', from Foot & Langley, *MI9 Escape and Evasion*, p.110.

p.141   'A while ago . . . to their POWs'. T. Schädlich, *Colditzer Schlossgeschichten*, p.56.

p.142   Illustrations of the blankets that became civilian suits and many other inventions, as well as the objects themselves, are to be seen at the RAF Museum, Hendon.

p.144   Description of Guigues and the line 'He was our God', Yves Desmarchellier interview, 5/11/86.

p.144   Guigues' method for measuring the cruciform lock in his article in *Colditz Recaptured*, p.48.

p.146   'After a parcel . . . never discovered'. F. Guigues, *Notes Personelles* (privately published).

Chapter 8

p.151   Hagemann description of digging the Dutch tunnel and his subsequent discovery in it, *Colditz Recaptured*, p.135.

p.155   'Gephard was already trading with the prisoners'. Recorded by Eggers in his diary, 3/12/43. 'Big search of Colditz with the help of Dresden Criminal Police. Little result.
Explanation: I know now that Oberstabsfeldwelbel Gephard was bribed. He has in his private room money, documents etc. of the POWs!'

p.157   'Returning escapers . . . dragged on', Reid, *The Colditz Story*, p.209.

p.158   Middleton's receiving a 'Dear John' letter, recalled by John Watton, 4/11/86.

p.158   'Lord . . . diversion'. Platt's original diary, Monday, 15 June 1942.

p.159   'Higher! Higher!' As remembered by Pete Tunstall.

p.159   'Remember Holzminden' story recalled by John Wilkens, NCO, interview, 12/9/86.

p.160   'Only three? . . . Where is the fourth?' recalled by Jerzy Stein, interview, IWM. 16974/3

p.163   'To the factory'. Just's own euphemism for concentration camp, as recalled by Anthony Karpf.

p.163   'He who travels best travels alone'. Eggers, p.85.

p.164   'In future . . . towards them'. Paddon's story was recorded in detail by Kenneth Lockwood in 1948; many of the details included here are based on that account.

Chapter 9

p.170   'The Black Bitch' as recalled by John Watton, interview, 4/11/86.

p.179   Dominic Bruce and 'Rex' Harrison's aborted 'little and large' escape was witnessed by John Chrisp.

p.181   '*Die Luft* . . . Farewell!' Eggers, p.95.

p.185   'I had one . . . unlocked'. Reid, *The Colditz Story*, p.254.

p.186   'This time . . . out of a tube', Ibid, pp.256–7. This feat was successfully repeated by two men of Reid and Wardle's size and build in December 1999. They managed it, wearing some thin clothing, in five minutes.

p.187   'We are . . . Dick'. Letter to Rupert Barry.

p.188   The full story of Pat Reid's escape once outside the castle walls can be found in *The Colditz Story*, pp.260ff.

Chapter 10

p.190   'The Germans . . . with our permission'. Interview with Charlie Hopetoun (Marquis of Linlithgow), 22/9/86.

p.191   'The seven Commandos . . . inside a book'. Schädlich, *Colditzer Schlossgeschichten*, p.58ff. Twelve commandos took part in Operation Muskatoon; five evaded capture and returned home via Spain.

p.192   'We discovered . . . the camp'. Ibid, p.59.

p.193   'What a sensation . . . holiday'. Ibid, p.57.

p.193   'Sachsenhausen . . . medical block'. Here the Commandos came under the supervision of the Chief Medical Officer, Baumkoetter, who regularly performed 'experiments' on his prisoners. He was instrumental in introducing Zyklon-B gas chambers to the camp, and he supervised the commandos' execution on the measuring stick. After the war Baumkoetter was sentenced to be hanged.

p.195   'Breathing fire . . . enemies' from obituary of Miss Jane Walker written by Gris Davies-Scourfield in *The Times*, 1963.

p.196   'By Day . . . incessant'. Statement written by 'Kit' Silverwood-Cope in Padre Platt's original diary.

p.196   'In the baths . . . the wall'. Ibid.

p.196   'The man . . . twenty minutes'. Ibid.

p.196   'I was unguarded . . . by train'. Statement written by Kenneth Sutherland in Platt's original diary.

pp.197–8 'It is useless . . . forced to shoot you'. Ibid.

p.200   'We faced . . . let in'. Platt's original diary, Sunday, 27 December 1942.

p.202   'A typical Prussian martinet'. Description by Maj.-Gen. W. Broomhall, 23/7/86.

pp.202–3 'A British Orderly . . . self-defence'. Eggers' diary entry, 7/9/43.

p.203   'Death may supervene at any moment'. Eggers, p.109.

p.206   'Propaganda camp'. Probably Stalag 111D in Berlin, where the officers' section was known as Special Detachment 999, situated in a villa on Kaunstrasse in Zehlendorf. There were several such recruitment camps, usually for prisoners who had already been singled out by Nazi agents as suitable candidates to join either the 'British Free Corps', a unit fighting alongside the Wehrmacht against the Allies, or to broadcast anti-British propaganda.

p.207   Biren Mazumdar's full story is told in the interview he gave to the Imperial War museum. IWM 4945/2.

p.210   Ion Ferguson's letter is reproduced in *Doctor at War*, p.150.

p.210   Hammond and Lister's burlesque escape story is recounted in P.R. Reid, *The Latter Days*, Chapter 13

p.212   'Lt Thom . . . saluting'. Eggers' diary entry 11/5/43.

p.215   'Locker pottering'. Pat Reid interview, 1987.

p.218   'Occasionally . . . Platonic cult'. Platt's original diary, 6 December 1941.

Chapter 11

p.221   'Like a contented cat'. Jack Best interview.

p.223   'It would make a damn good story' recalled by Kenneth Lockwood.

p.223   'the Sixtieth'. Sinclair was in the King's Royal Rifles along-side Gris Davies-Scourfield and Ronnie Littledale. All three had been captured at Calais. Sinclair was one of four broth-ers from a military family, and he had first met Davies-Scourfield at Winchester. He then went to Oxford, and it is also thought that he spent some time at Heidelberg universi-ty before the war, accounting for his fluent German.

p.225   'Be suspicious . . . anything'. Prof. Peter Hoffman interview.

p.225   'Howe had promised himself . . .' Kenneth Lockwood recalls this private bet.

p.226   'It turned out . . . boot polish'. Hugh Bruce's account, *The Frans Josef Attempt*.

p.232   'What worried me . . . came off'. Ibid.

p.235   'His whole attitude . . . slightly to the left'. Sinclair's account of the escape, handed over to the Senior British Officer, was written with the intention of being used as evidence in the court-martial of Pilz.

p.236   'Burn Sinclair's bullet-holed uniform'. Revealed by Reinhold Eggers to David Ray in the 1970s.

Chapter 12

p.237   'They made . . . same idea', Eggers, p.122.

p.239   'Lewthwaite invented his own language . . .' recalled by Charles Elwell.

p.239   'One summer . . . pretending to'. J. Rogers, *Tunnelling into Colditz*, p.116.

p.241   'Captured a cat . . . the same'. German document reproduced in P.R. Reid, *Colditz the Full Story*, p.52.

p.242   'Marked the end . . . exclusive'. Platt's original diary, New Year's Eve, 1943.

p.242   'You first had to escape from the escape committee'. Interview, Michael Alexander.

p.243 'Coolie labour' as Laurence Pumphrey, a tunneller from Eichstätt, described himself.

pp.244–6 The Warburg tunnel and de Pree's death in it described in T.C.F. Prittie & W. Earle Edwards, *Escape to Freedom*, pp.249-50. note: de Pree had made an early escape attempt with Charlie Hopetoun immediately after capture at St Valery 1940. Picked up at Le Treport, after 2 days on the run.

p.246 '250,000'. This figure is reported by many of the escapers; 50,000 is also mentioned Foot & Langley, *MI9 Escape and Evasion*, p.246.

p.248 'British Bulldogs . . . weariness'. Platt's original diary, New Year's Eve, 1943.

p.251 Julien Kerignard. Eggers kept secret the identity of this man until he died, stating that his name should only be revealed in 2000. In fact the French priests had always known Kerignard was the traitor, but they chose not to reveal it. His name appears here courtesy of Yves Desmarchelier, in an interview in 1987.

p.251 'British Orderlies . . . no success'. Eggers does not record how he went about persuading the orderlies at Colditz to change their allegiances; at Laufen, British orderlies were subjected to a German propaganda campaign: 'They were told, "The British officer-class wanted this war, and made this war on Germany. The British people are natural friends of the German people; the British officers are the real enemies of both peoples" . . . it says much for the British soldier that in very few cases did he succumb to what must have been a strong temptation.' T. Prittie, *Escape to Freedom*, p.57.

p.252 'Do you realise . . . together?' remembered by Maj-Gen. W. M. Broomhall, interview, 12/7/86.

p.252 'Forty-seven Polish officers' . . . One of whom was Mietek Chmiel, who escaped with Surmanowicz in 1941.

p.253 'Goebbels privately proposed' from *The Secret Conferences of Doctor Goebbels 1939–43*. Goebbels had a great fear of Allied air-raids. On 17th March 1945 (after the bombing of Dresden) he publicly advocated 'cutting loose from the Geneva Convention' and executing enemy pilots in captivity on the charge that they could kill '100,000 non combatants in two hours.' Hitler agreed in principle, but the idea was leaked to a foreign journalist and internationally denounced before it could take effect. See Rudolf Semmler, *Goebbels – the Man Next to Hitler*, p183.

p.253   'Gomorrah'. Figures and details from M. Kitchen, *Nazi Germany at War*, p.91.

p.253   'Graudenz'. In this military prison the Wehrmacht also punished their own men. David Hunter recalls the tale of his 'batman' and his compatriot in the next cell. 'I was given a batman who came in the morning to make my bed. He had been a colonel in the German Air Force, but was found guilty of "aviational unchastity". He used to fly an ME-109 under bridges on the autobahn, and then he was issued with a new aeroplane, the ME-110. This had a twenty-foot wider wingspan, so when he flew under the bridge he left ten feet off each end. At that time they were short of aircraft and they didn't need him, and so he was stripped of his rank and sentenced to four years in the slammer, and told he could clean my boots, which perhaps taught him a thing or two. In the cell next to me there was a man who had foolishly attempted to escape, a British RAF flight lieutenant named Thompson. He had got away and was recaptured in the cockpit of an aeroplane on a local airfield. He hadn't a chance of getting the engine to start but it had really brought one of the older German NCOs into disrepute. So when they brought him back to Graudenz the German NCO, who was a real hard-nosed joker, took his revenge. He shot him five times in the gut and quite deliberately didn't kill him, then he threatened me with the last one if I pressed the bell or called for help. Thompson lay there all night screaming and groaning until he died the next day.'

Chapter 13

p.256   '*Verwundet?*' The dramatic account of Gris Davies-
         Scourfield's involvement in the battle for Calais is described
         in his book *In Presence of my Foes*, pp.20–56.

p.256   'One of our most dangerous escapers'. *Colditz Recaptured*,
         p.73.

p.271   'Sentry A . . . GO'! *In Presence of my Foes*, p.213.

p.273   'I think it was because of my face'. Best's account of his
         capture and return to Colditz appears in *Colditz Recaptured*,
         p.85.

p.274   'Is this place . . . wish!' recorded in Eggers, p.133.

Chapter 14

p.275   'We naturally agreed . . . relief'. Eggers, p.134.

p.276   'Young men . . . two months ago'. Platt's original diary,
         New Year's Eve, 1943.

p.277   'The scene . . . toothpaste' recalled by Don Donaldson in
         The Diggers of Colditz, p.163.

p.277   'As soon as . . . after each visit', Guigues, *Notes Personelles*.

p.278   'It was an amazing place . . . contraband hidden there',
         J. Rogers, *Tunnelling into Colditz*, p.174.

p.279   'Greatest source of morale in the camp'. As described in
         M. Reid, *Into Colditz*.

p.280   'He too was listening to the BBC'. Jack Best was one of
         several officers who realised as much by interpreting what
         Eggers said.

p.280   'Rapid response unit' described in Eggers' diary.

p.280   'In March 1944 . . . an informant'. Eggers, p.141.

p.281   'Miserable-looking man'. Gris Davies-Scourfield, whose
         mess felt so sorry for him they cooked him lunch to cheer
         him up.

p.281   Purdy. I am indebted to the extensive research of Jo West
         into Walter Purdy, his activities in Germany, and his life
         after the war.

p.282   '"Busty" Brown had also been a fascist before the war'. See
         J.M. Green, *From Colditz in Code*, Postscript, pp.221–9, for

further evidence of Brown's double-agent status. Brown defends himself in his own book, *In Durance Vile*

p.282   'From the first . . . shook him'. *From Colditz in Code*, p.160.

p.283   'The Marlag boys are at it again!' Platt's original diary, Friday, 17 March 1944.

pp.284–5 Near-lynching of Purdy also recounted by Davies-Scourfield, *In Presence of my Foes*, p.217.

p.287   'Watton regularly painted his face a sallow green'. John Watton also remembers feeding him for the benefit of the new arrivals.

p.287   'I had an advantage . . . to keep fit'. Interview with Micky Wynn (Lord Newborough), IWM 9721/3.

p.288   *The Road to En-Dor*, Chapter 24.

p.290   'He attacked his travelling companion'. Described in *From Colditz in Code*, p.145.

p.292   'The Kommandant . . . the Gestapo.' Denzler's report in PRO FO 916 1151

Chapter 15

pp.293–4 'It happens, to soldiers' recorded in Platt's original diary.

p.297   'Invention of diesel and the life-cycle of the rabbit' as recalled by John Chrisp.

p.298   '"Untainted" by the old guard' as remembered by Laurence Pumphrey, one of the new arrivals.

p.301   'Amthor also tried . . . another camp'. Eggers' diary entry, 10/43.

p.305   '*Schnell! schnell!* . . . hurry'. Scene described by Jack Champ, an Australian officer who aided Beaumont's escape in *The Diggers of Colditz*, p.15.

p.306   'A lorry . . . only seventy miles away.' As described in T.N. Catlow, *A Sailor's Survival*, p.64.

p.307   'A major . . . you'll get shot.' Ibid, p.65.

p.308   Research into the fate of Bill Millar has been conducted by David Ray. Originally Millar's name was on the Canadian War Memorial at Bayeux, suggesting he had rejoined a fighting unit and was killed in action. But Canadian records now state he was recaptured in civilian clothes near

Lamsdorf and moved to an unknown destination. That destination is suggested to be Mauthausen in a Dutch book by Leo de Hartog, another Colditz veteran, *Officieren achter Prikkeldraad 1940–5*. It seems as likely, however, that Millar did reach the safe house in Prague and met his end in that city at the hands of the Gestapo, who ruthlessly executed many POWs. His name can now be found at the Commonwealth Cemetery, Brockwood, Panel 23, Col.2.

Chapter 16
pp.310–11

'After a night of "hard work" . . . back in the bed'. Included in Platt's original diary some time in 1944.

p.311   'Lingering kiss for her trouble' as witnessed by Hugh Bruce.

p.312   '"You get five minutes" . . . amazing sight'. Jack Champ in *The Diggers of Colditz*, p.191.

p.313   'A small raiding party . . . into the sea'. As reported in the local Leipzig newspaper to David Wheeler in the town jail.

p.313   'Borrowed for the occasion' recorded in Platt's original diary, 7 June 1944.

p.314   'They wanted Willie Tod to recognise this'. As recounted to Peter Tunstall after the event.

p.314   'Discipline on parade was perfect,' Eggers, p.156.

p.316   'No signs of bullet holes or blood'. As described in Foot & Langley, *MI9 Escape and Evasion*, p.258.

p.317   'Paragraph 91a of German Military Law states . . .' quoted in letter from Lt Col. W. Tod to The First Secretary of the Swiss Legation, Acting Protecting Power, 10/9/44.

p.317   Zafouk and Chaloupka described their ordeal in Prague in an attachment to the above letter, as well as the state of the various Gestapo jails they were sent to while in Prague.

p.319   'Presumed to be a spy'. As recalled by Martin Gilliatt; he was deputed to follow Upham.

p.320   'You are being protected . . . Anastasia?' interview with Charlie Hopetoun (Lord Linlithgow), 22/9/86.

pp.320–1 Excuses . . . entertained.' PRO CAB 7978

p.321   'The issue of instructions . . . where to go.' Ibid.

p.321   'A memo was distributed . . .' There is no official record of this in the MI9 files at the PRO, though several POW remember hearing of it. Tony Rolt, who was in charge of the Glider scheme, recalls being told to stop work on the project as a result, and Martin Gilliatt, Col. Tod's Adjutant also remembers it becoming policy.

p.321   'Escaping is no longer a sport'. Exact wording from original poster in possession of Dr Bill Watson.

pp.326–7 'Instead of . . . wretchedness'. Platt's original diary, Monday, 25 September 1944.

p.327   'If there is indeed . . . Mike Sinclair'. Eggers, p.161.

Chapter 17

p.329   'It is no longer . . . kicking a man when he's down.' Eggers, p.162.

p.331   'rubbing snow on his chest . . .' mentioned in 'A gentleman of Colditz', article by David Ray.

p.331   'He is a quiet man . . . from the dead'. Platt's original diary, Thursday 13 July 1944.

p.333   'A 1938 Renault Coupé . . .' Platt's original diary, 7 December 1944.

p.333   'What do you suggest next – a brothel?' Retold to David Ray by Reinhold Eggers.

p.335   'Moling'. Involved digging a tunnel 50ft long, then sealing the entrance, and by moving the earth from the front to the back moving the tunnel towards the perimeter fence. Air holes were made at 20ft intervals, and over the course of two days Best and Goldfinch travelled 100ft – 12ft beyond the wire, where they made their exit. They then stole a rowing boat but were recaptured on the River Oder the following day, making for Stettin and the Baltic.

p.343   'Plans were drawn up . . .' J. Rogers, *Tunnelling into Colditz*, p.183.

p.346   'We watched . . . future be?' T.N. Catlow, *A Sailor's Survival*, p.79.

p.346   '*Nyet! Tak!*', G. Romilly, *The Privileged Nightmare*, p.147.

p.347   'Destroy tens of thousands' and figures quoted in M.
         Gilbert, *The Second World War*, p.563.

p.347   'thought it "rather sinister"' contained in letter from
         A. Lascelles to John Martin, 4/1/45. PRO FO 916 1211

p.348   'Memorandums flew'. Miles Reid met Major-General Gepp
         on 7/2/45, and various options were discussed; this provoked
         the flurry of activity, resulting in no action being taken.

p.348   'To Churchill if necessary' related in Reid, *Colditz The Full
         Story*.

p.349   'Shuddered like a tree . . . it was impossible . . . jumping'.
         Interview, Charles Elwell.

p.349   'Read books' as remembered by Jim Rogers.

p.349   'Ash Wednesday . . .' Statistics quoted in M. Kitchen, *Nazi
         Germany at War*, p.97.

Chapter 18

p.353   'There will be many deaths . . . depart'. P. R. Reid, *The
         Latter Days*, p.263.

p.354   'I thought you'd like to know . . . Friday the thirteenth.'
         Interview Earl Haig, 13/7/87.

p.354   'Bombed flat and smelling of death . . . reading too much
         . . . hooch'. Interview Charlie Hopetoun (Marquis of
         Linlithgow), 22/9/86.

p.354   'Seemed to operate in a kind of deep freeze'. Interview,
         Michael Alexander.

p.355   '*Wir Sind* . . . English officers!' *The Privileged Nightmare*
         p.176.

p.356   'A hole . . . into place.' Ibid, p.214.

p.357   'A howling bloodhound . . . into the world'. Ibid, p.218.

p.358   'A memo'. PRO FO 916 1151

p.359   'A funny, tall . . . shaving', Lord Harewood, *The Tongs and
         the Bones*, p.66.

p.359   'Bus new . . . moved'. *The Privileged Nightmare*, p.223.

p.359   'Sabotage . . . Good luck'. Ibid, pp.233ff.

p.362   'When the German . . . laughing'. Interview, Michael
         Alexander.

p.363   'Gentlemen . . . Reich'. The story of the abduction from

Laufen and the journey into the mountains, including Berger's last performance, is described in the Master of Elphinstone's report published in *The Times*.

p.363   'Owed much to the work of the Swiss legation . . .' Interview with Rudolf Denzler, 3/11/86.

p.368   'The fact . . . doing'. *The Privileged Nightmare*, p.198.

p.368   'Ignored telegrams . . .' Both Haig and Hopetoun had a high opinion of Hesselmann and his family. On 13 February 1947 Hesselmann was arrested by the French authorities and charged with handing over General Mesny to be executed by the Gestapo, in retaliation for the death of General von Brodowski, a German general shot while escaping from Besançon prison. Hesselmann, who was already ill with a duodenal ulcer, died on 22 March. In April of that year, Haig asked a question in the House of Lords, and John Hope, Charlie Hopetoun's brother, asked a question in the House of Commons, both of which resulted in Hesselmann being cleared as a war criminal, thereby allowing his wife to receive a war pension.

p.369   Description of the Russian overthrow of Königstein castle: Earl Haig, *My Father's Son*, pp. 149ff.

p.369   'And who . . . Germany'. Interview, Charlie Hopetoun (Marquis of Linlithgow), 22/9/86.

Chapter 19

p.372   'A Colditz man . . . to be moved' Maj. J. Pringle, *Colditz Last Stop*, p.153.

p.372   'Destroy-Evacuate'. Eggers, p.179.

p.374   'Important prisoners in the town . . .' The Americans had been alerted to the precarious status of the Prominente and American prisoners inside Colditz Castle in a memo to SHAEF from the War Office, 6/4/45. It lists the British, American, French and Polish officers 'held by the Germans as valuable hostages' and concludes, 'We believe Germans will make every effort retain these POW and if any massacre is intended they will undoubtedly be in great danger.' PRO FO 916 1151 p.378   'Their own sentry'. According to Bob Pierce, this may have been his friend 'Pete'.

p.378   'Eggers claims, no German member of staff ever knew about'. Eggers ascertained that the only time a member of the SS came into contact with the staff of the castle was during the last months of the war, when the new paymaster whom he suspected to be a Nazi spy, arrived.

p.378   'Looted bloody bodies'. One of these had a lucky escape: 'His name was Donnelly,' recalls Bob Pierce. 'He was an Irish boy from a suburb of Pittsburg. His mother had left them when they were young kids, and him and his younger brother had been raised by his father, and his ambition in life all through was, "I'm going home and sit on the front porch and drink beer with the old man." So the next day we come there and here's Donnelly laying in the field, an absolute mess. He was shot seven times through the chest and the lungs and he's laying there and somebody says, "Oh my gosh, Donnelly's dead," and he opens his eyes and he said, "Donnelly isn't dead, Donnelly's going home and drink beer with the old man!" The Germans had rolled him over during the night to loot his body when they took their own wounded – they looted all the American bodies and took wallets and rings and watches and all that stuff – and when they rolled him over the medics believe that the blood, instead of running into the lungs and drowning him, was able to run out and because of the cold weather it coagulated and saved his life.'

p.379   'Say, you . . . used to be'. D. Walker *Lean, Wind Lean*, p.173.

p.381   'She was supposed to be there'. Bob Pierce noted that when their replacements arrived two days later from the 2nd Infantry Division they were wearing new battledress complete with their decoration ribbons; he assumed they were intended to be filmed liberating the castle.

p.382   'Typical Bader'. Interview with Jack Best, who was one of many junior RAF officers aggrieved at the hasty departure of their commanding officer.

p.383   'My first taste of freedom . . .' Burn asked and was given permission to drive off with the Americans in order to file a report to London concerning the whereabouts of the Prominente, which was still unknown. This was published in *The Times*, 19/4/45 and prompted the Foreign Office to press the Swiss Legation in Berne to pursue them.

p.387   'Ah, Tunstall . . . never be forgotten'. Recalled by Pete Tunstall. After the war Willie Tod was criticised for not preventing the removal of the Prominente. However, many of his juniors at Colditz have since sprung to his defence, and they believe that his obstinacy in refusing to leave the castle saved their lives.

p.391   Obergruppenführer Gottlob Berger. Judgement of trial. PRO.FO 646 Case II

Index

Figures in italics indicate illustrations and drawings; maps are indicated in bold.